D1590330

DISCOURSE THEORY AND CULTURAL ANALYSIS

Media, Arts and Literature

THE HAMPTON PRESS COMMUNICATION SERIES
Popular Culture
John A. Lent, series editor

Jewish Jesters: A Study in American Popular Comedy
Arthur Asa Berger

Discourse Theory and Cultural Analysis: Media, Arts and Literature
Nico Carpentier & Erik Spinoy (editors)

Dreaming The World: U2 Fans, Online Community
And Intercultural Communication
Arthur E. Lizie

Media in the Age of Marketization
Graham Murdock & Janet Wasko (editors)

Indian Popular Cinema: Industry, Ideology and Consciousness
Manjunath Pendakur

DISCOURSE THEORY AND CULTURAL ANALYSIS

Media, Arts and Literature

edited by

Nico Carpentier
Vrije Universiteit Brussel

Erik Spinoy
Université de Liège

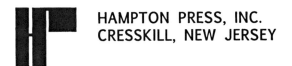

HAMPTON PRESS, INC.
CRESSKILL, NEW JERSEY

Copyright © 2008 by Hampton Press, Inc.

All rights reserved. No part of this publication may be reproduced, stored in a retrieval system, or transmitted in any form or by any means, electronic, mechanical, photocopying, microfilming, recording, or otherwise, without permission of the publisher.

Printed in the United States of America

Library of Congress Cataloging-in-Publication Data

Discourse theory and cultural analysis : media, arts, and literature / edited by Nico Carpentier, Erik Spinoy.
    p. cm. — (The Hampton Press communication series. Popular culture)
  Includes bibliographical references and indexes.
  ISBN 978-1-57273-809-6 (hardbound) — ISBN 978-1-57273-810-2 (paperbound)
  1. Discourse analysis—Social aspects. 2. Mass media and culture. I. Carpentier, Nico. II. Spinoy, Erik.
  P302.84.D5743 2008
  401'.41—dc22
                          2008017233

Hampton Press, Inc.
23 Broadway
Cresskill, NJ 07626

CONTENTS

ADS

ICT

LITERATURE

INTRODUCTION

From the Political to the Cultural

Nico Carpentier
Erik Spinoy

Although at first sight focused on reopening (and redirecting) the discussion on Marxist theory, *Hegemony and Socialist Strategy* (HSS - 1985[1]) also contains the earliest development of the discourse theory of Ernesto Laclau and Chantal Mouffe.[2] Next to Foucault's theoretical elaborations on discourse, especially in *L'Archéologie du Savoir* (1969), Laclau and Mouffe's theory remains one of the key approaches to discourse theory. Since it was first published, HSS has generated a considerable amount of secondary literature (e.g., Howarth, 2000; Smith, 1999; Torfing, 1999) and a number of political scientists have made good use of the discourse-theoretical toolbox, as is evidenced by the discourse-theoretical analyses (DTA) found in the readers *Discourse Theory and Political Analysis* (Howarth et al., 2000), *Laclau: A Critical Reader* (Critchley & Marchart, 2004) and *Discourse Theory in European Politics: Identity, Policy and Governance* (Howarth & Torfing, 2004).

Even when HSS can and should be conceived of as a major contribution to political philosophy in itself, its embeddedness in a larger body of thought cannot be denied. Laclau and Mouffe's early work already dealt with Marxist theory, as is illustrated by (the) early (English versions of) publications such as *Politics and Ideology in Marxist Theory: Capitalism, Fascism, Populism* (Laclau, 1977) and *Gramsci and Marxist Theory* (Mouffe, 1979). After the publication of HSS, their work has continued to develop on a highly dialogical basis. The discussion with Slavoj Žižek on the flaws in HSS' theory of the subject (and on the necessary distinction between subject and subjectivation) proved to be fruitful, whereas the dialogues with Richard Rorty and Jacques Derrida (published in Mouffe, 1996) and with Butler and again Žižek (published in Butler et al., 2000) represent important steps in the development of their theory. Partly on the basis of these dialogues, Laclau and Mouffe went on to elaborate their discourse theory and to add new dimensions to it, discussing, among others, the universal as the condition of (im)possibility of the particular (and vice versa), the rebellion of various particularisms, agonistic pluralism, third-way politics, the extreme right, and populism.

Nevertheless, their work has largely remained within the confines of political theory and research. In the past years the so-called Essex School (Townshend, 2004) has managed to address what Torfing (1999: 291) termed the caveat of the application of discourse theory in empirical studies. This application is far from self-evident because discourse theory is *"pitched at a highly abstract level"* (Torfing, 1999: 291). In the meantime, the Essex School *"extolled the virtues of 'discourse theory'..., and most members moved 'ontically' 'downstream' to apply Laclau and Mouffe's ontological concepts of 'logics' of 'difference' and 'equivalence,' 'dislocation' and the like to the analysis of specific political ideologies, although a few attempted 'upstream' minor theoretical refinements"* (Townshend, 2004: 283) But even readers such as *Discourse Theory and Political Analysis* (Howarth et al., 2000) and *Laclau: A Critical Reader* (Critchley & Marchart, 2004), which can be viewed as condensations of their research agenda, rarely included more culturally inspired analyses. This is, to say the least, somewhat odd.

To begin with, when culture is broadly defined as *"an assemblage of imaginings and meanings that may be consonant, disjunctive, overlapping, contentious, continuous or discontinuous"* (Lewis, 2002: 12), the close connection with discourse theory's focus on signification and identity construction is apparent. This broad definition of culture also clearly intersects with Laclau and Mouffe's broad definition of the political (which does not limit the political to institutionalized politics), thus creating a platform for potential interdisciplinary research. Second, Laclau and Mouffe themselves show a genuine and profound interest in the role and history of (high) culture, as is for instance illustrated by Laclau's discussion of Thomas Mann (Laclau, 1994) and by his quoting of the medieval German mystic author Meister Eckehart and the British poet Browning (Laclau, 2002).[3] Similarly, Mouffe (2001, 2007) has published and lectured on the relationship between politics and the arts. At the invitation of the Cork 2005 European Capital of Culture program, she held a lecture *"exploring what the current discussion about the 'public' in political theory could bring to the field of artistic practices.*"[4] Third, Laclau and Mouffe repeatedly claimed that discourse theory is to be considered as a toolbox that can be used in various domains.

Moreover, other (related) approaches (that have been key sources of inspiration for discourse theory), such as the deconstructionist/Derridean, the Foucauldian, and the Lacanian strands of poststructuralism, have of course been immensely influential in recent cultural analysis. Similarly, (critical) discourse analysis, too, managed to secure a strong foothold in cultural and political analysis, as is shown by the vast amount of monographs, readers and journals in this academic field (see Carpentier & De Cleen, 2007). With some exceptions (e.g., Phillips & Jørgensen, 2002), most academic work on (critical) discourse analysis does not enter into the domain of Laclau and Mouffe's discourse theory, although Foucault's discourse theory is considered a key source for discourse analysts as well.

Finally, the ideological structures of culture have been one of the most thoroughly researched areas within the fields of Literary Criticism and Cultural Studies. Both studies departing from the restrictive definition of culture as high arts[5] and studies embracing the more encompassing definition of culture as a *"structure of feeling"* (Williams, 1958) have given ample attention to the inseparability of culture, politics, and ideology. Said's (1978) *Orientalism* is one of the best-known examples of the first branch, focusing as it does on the ideology of imperialism and empire embedded in 19th-century literature. Cultural Studies has even more strongly emphasized the *"strongly coupled but not mutually exclusive concepts culture/ideology"* (Hall, 1981: 36). To name but two examples, *Policing the Crisis*, a key work by Stuart Hall et al. (1978), deals with the hegemonic understanding of the world found in (news)media representations and correlates these to the shifting patterns of state power, and Ian Ang's (1989) *Watching Dallas* analyzes the confrontation between the ideology of mass culture and the ideology of popular culture. Although some of discourse theory's vocabulary has been incorporated by Cultural Studies, as is illustrated by Hall's (1986) use of the concept of articulation, and some authors include discourse theory in their overviews of the field of Cultural Studies (e.g., Harris, 1992), Laclau and Mouffe's discourse theory remains surprisingly absent from the fields of Literary Criticism and Cultural Studies.

In short, Laclau and Mouffe's discourse theory so far has not managed to broaden its scope from (political) philosophy to the study of culture. DTAs of cultural phenomena have remained exceedingly rare, which can partially be explained by the institutional embeddedness of the Essex School in Political Studies, the processes related to the rise and fall of academic stars, and the antagonism Laclau and Mouffe's post-Marxist position provoked within its potential constituency.

The main objective of this book is to show that Laclau and Mouffe's discourse theory can be deployed (Howarth, 2000: 126) in the study of culture and signification, beyond the traditional disciplinary confines of political studies. The discourse-theoretical toolbox (or treasure chest) makes available a large number of analytical tools that can enrich contemporary cultural analysis. More specifically, DTAs in the study of media, literature, and other artistic disciplines allow for a dry-eyed, sobered-up continuation of earlier poststructuralist and deconstructionist research. They can, moreover, pave the way for innovative approaches to comparative and multimedia/ interartistic research.

Foucault's description of the potential use that can be made of his *"little tool boxes"* allows us to make an important final point with respect to our attempt to bring discourse theory into the cultural realm. In one of his interviews, Foucault (1996: 149) remarked:

> If people want to open them, use a particular sentence, idea, or analysis like a screwdriver or wrench in order to short-circuit, disqualify or break up the systems of power ... well, all the better.

Bringing these analytical tools into new areas will automatically involve their rearticulation, which implies that—to quote from Laclau and Mouffe's (1985: 105) own definition of articulation—*"their identity [will be] modified as a result of the articulatory practice."* Without abandoning the epistemology and ontology of Laclau and Mouffe's work, this volume inevitably contains a number of explicit and implicit interpretations and adaptations of it. Rigid intellectual and theoretical protectionism would have been detrimental to this endeavor. The interpretatory openness these texts bear to witness not only improves their analytical quality, but also cross-fertilizes discourse theory itself.

A SHORT OUTLINE OF LACLAU
AND MOUFFE'S DISCOURSE THEORY

However, it remains essential to present and discuss the key concepts of discourse theory as they can be found in Laclau and Mouffe's HSS and their later work. Highly valuable as it is, it is also a complex and sometimes hermetic work, which requires some introduction at least. HSS (and Laclau and Mouffe's discourse theory in general) can be read on three interrelated levels: as a social ontology, as a political identity theory, and as a radical pluralist democratic politics.

Laclau and Mouffe's Social Ontology

The first level—discourse theory in the strict sense—refers to Laclau and Mouffe's social ontology and to the position they negotiate between materialism and idealism, between structure and agency. Their theoretical starting point is the proposition that all social phenomena and objects obtain meaning(s) through discourse, which is defined as "*a structure in which meaning is constantly negotiated and constructed*" (Laclau, 1988: 254). In this (what they call) radical materialist position the discursive component of reality is emphasized without abolishing the distinction between discourse and reality. Laclau and Mouffe (1985: 105) also described discourse as a structured entity that is the result of articulation, which itself is defined as "*any practice establishing a relation among elements such that their identity is modified as a result of the articulatory practice.*"[6]

These definitions of discourse are clearly different from the more traditional definitions found for instance in discourse analysis, which has kept intact a clear connection with language. This results in what Philips and Jørgensen (2002: 62) called discourse-as-language. In contrast, Laclau and Mouffe's definition of discourse can be termed discourse-as-representation[7] or discourse-as-ideology (in the neutral meaning of ideology), as their approach is more macrotextual and macrocontextual (see Fig. 1). In congruence with Barthes (1975), they use a broad definition of texts, which are viewed as materializations of meaning and/or ideology. Their focus is *on* the meanings, representations, or ideologies embedded in the text, and not so much on the language *of* the text. And in contrast to for instance conversation analysis, where the context remains confined to specific social settings (such as a conversation), their macrocontextual approach refers to the social as the realm where the processes generating meaning are situated.

As Laclau and Mouffe's definitions of discourse indicate, the articulation of discursive elements plays a vital role in the construction of the identity of both objects and individual or collective agents. According to Sayyid and Zac (1998: 263) identity is to be defined in two related ways. First, identity is "*the unity of any object or subject.*" This definition is in line with Fuss' (1989: ix) definition of identity as "*the 'whatness' of a given entity.*" A second component of the definition of identity comes into play when the concept is applied to the way in which social agents are identified and/or identify themselves within a certain discourse. Examples Sayyid and Zac (1998: 263) gave in this context are "*workers, women, atheists, British.*" Laclau and Mouffe called this last component of identity a subject position (i.e., the result of the positioning of subjects within a discursive structure):

> Whenever we use the category of "subject" in this text, we will do so in the sense of "subject positions" within a discursive structure. Subjects

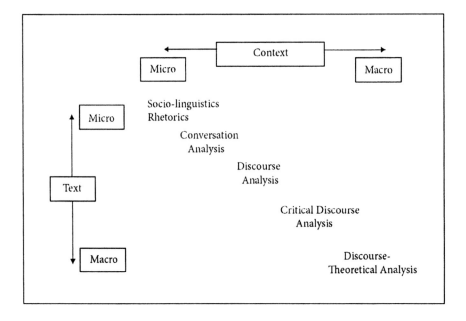

FIG. 1. Mapping the signifier discourse.

> cannot, therefore, be the origin of social relations—not even in the lim-
> ited sense of being endowed with powers that render an experience pos-
> sible—as all "experience" depends on precise discursive conditions of
> possibility. (Laclau & Mouffe, 1985: 115)

This definition implies neither a structuralist nor a voluntarist position.
Although Laclau and Mouffe endorse Althusser's critique of the
autonomous and self-transparent subject (a voluntarist position), they vehemently reject Althusser's economic determinism (a structuralist position),
because in their view this aspect of Althusser's theory leads to a "*new variant of essentialism*" (Laclau & Mouffe, 1985: 98). However, Laclau and
Mouffe's rejection of this aspect of Althusser's work does not keep them
from borrowing from him the originally Freudian concept of overdetermination, although not without altering its meaning:

> Society and social agents lack any essence, and their regularities merely
> consist of the relative and precarious forms of fixation which accompa-
> ny the establishment of a certain order. This [Althusser's] analysis
> seemed to open up the possibility of elaborating a new concept of artic-
> ulation, which would start from the overdetermined character of social
> relations. But this did not occur. (Laclau & Mouffe, 1985: 98)

Despite Laclau and Mouffe's careful positioning of the subject between structuralism and voluntarism, Žižek critiqued their reduction of the subject to its subject positions. In an essay published in Laclau's *New Reflections on the Revolution of our Time*, Žižek (1990: 250) explained this reduction as *"an effect of the fact that Laclau and Mouffe had progressed too quickly"* and did not manage to combine the *"radical breakthrough"* at the level of the concept of antagonism with an equally well elaborated theory of the subject. This criticism has led especially Laclau to acknowledge *"the importance of an understanding of subjectivity in terms of the subject-as-lack"* (Glynos & Stavrakakis, 2004: 202).

Although even in HSS identities were seen as a fusion of a multiplicity of identities, where the overdetermined presence of some identities in others prevents their closure, Laclau's later work more clearly distinguishes between subject and subjectivation, identity, and identification. The impossibility of the multiplicity of identities to fill the constitutive lack of the subject prevents their full and complete constitution because of the inevitable distance between the obtained identity and the subject, and because of the (always possible) subversion of that identity by other identities. In Laclau's (1990: 60) own words: *"the identification never reaches the point of full identity."* As Torfing (1999: 150) illustrated, there are many possible points of identification:

> A student who is expelled from the university might seek to restore the full identity she never had by becoming either a militant who rebels against the "system," the perfect mother for her two children, or an independent artist who cares nothing for formal education.

Precisely the contingency of identities and the failure to reach a fully constituted identity creates the space for subjectivity, agency, freedom, and the particularity of human behavior:

> The freedom thus won in relation to the structure is therefore a traumatic fact initially: I am *condemned* to be free, not because I have no structural identity as the existentialists assert, but because I have a *failed* structural identity. This means that the subject is partially self-determined. However, as this self-determination is not the expression of what the subject *already* is but the result of the lack of its being instead, self-determination can only proceed though processes of identification. (Laclau, 1990: 44)

In other words, and more generally, Laclau and Mouffe's discourse theory views discourses and identities not as stable and fixed: a discourse is never safe from elements alien to it. There is always a surplus (or a residue of elements)—the field of discursivity[8]—that prevents the full saturation of meaning (Laclau & Mouffe, 1985: 112). The overdetermination of discourses (and their impossibility to reach "*a final closure*" [Howarth, 1998: 273]) is made explicit in the concept of the floating signifier, which is defined as a signifier that is "*overflowed with meaning*" (Torfing, 1999: 301). Floating signifiers assume different meanings in different contexts/discourses, and are able to cross discursive frontiers. As Laclau (2005: 133) put it, the concept of the floating signifier[9] allows us to "*apprehend the logic of displacements of that frontier.*"

More structurally, in *New Reflections on the Revolution of our Time*,[10] Laclau introduced the concept of dislocation to further theorize the limits of discursive structures. He first discussed dislocation in a general way, claiming that "*every identity is dislocated insofar as it depends on an outside which denies that identity and provides its condition of possibility at the same time*" (Laclau 1990: 39). Identities and structures cannot be determined and be determining, as they are always faced with dislocations showing that other articulations are possible as well. In other words, dislocations show that the structure (before the dislocation) is only one of the possible articulatory ensembles (Laclau, 1990: 43). In this sense, dislocation is the "*very form of possibility*" (Laclau, 1990: 42). Second, Laclau also defined dislocations as more specific processes or events: "*dislocation refers to the emergence of an event, or a set of events, that cannot be represented, symbolized, or in other ways disrupted by the discursive structure—which is therefore disrupted*" (Torfing, 1999: 148). Laclau illustrated this more specific use of the dislocation concept by referring to the "*dislocatory effects of emerging capitalism on the lives of workers*":

> They are well known: the destruction of traditional communities, the brutal and exhausting discipline of the factory, low wages and insecurity of work. (Laclau, 1990: 39)

At the same time, dislocation does not imply that "*everything becomes possible or that all symbolic frameworks disappear, since no dislocation could take place in that psychotic universe: a structure must be there to be dislocated.*" (Laclau, 1990: 43). More generally, discourses have to be partially fixed, as the abundance of meaning would otherwise make any meaning impossible: "*a discourse incapable of generating any fixity of meaning is the discourse of the psychotic*" (Laclau & Mouffe, 1985: 112). The points that (partially) fix the discourse are called nodal points, by analogy with Lacan's *points de capiton* concept. These nodal points are privileged signifiers that fix the meaning of a chain of signifiers (or moments) (Laclau & Mouffe, 1985: 112), and have a certain degree of rigidity. Nodal points are constructed on the basis of articulation:

> The practice of articulation consists in the construction of nodal points
> which partially fix meaning; and the partial character of this fixation
> proceeds from the openness of the social, a result, in its turn, of the con-
> stant overflowing of every discourse by the infinitude of the field of dis-
> cursivity. (Laclau & Mouffe, 1985: 113)

Laclau and Mouffe's Political Identity Theory

A second—and strongly related—level of discourse theory is what Anna
Marie Smith (1999: 87) calls Laclau and Mouffe's political identity theory.
Key concepts at this level, which is tributary to conflict theory, are social
antagonism and hegemony. Here, (more) attention is given to how discourses, identities, and their nodal points are constructed and obtain fixity.

In order to refer to the situation that arises when nodal points (and the
discourses they belong to) (begin to) obtain social dominance, Laclau and
Mouffe used the concept of hegemony, which they borrowed from
Gramsci. Originally, Gramsci (1999: 261) defined this notion to refer to the
formation of consent rather than to the (exclusive) domination of the other,
without however excluding a certain form of pressure and repression: "*The
'normal' exercise of hegemony ... is characterized by the combination of
force and consent variously balancing one another, without force exceeding
consent too much.*" Howarth (1998: 279) described Laclau and Mouffe's
interpretation of the concept as follows: "*hegemonic practices are an exemplary form of political articulation which involves linking together different
identities into a common project.*" This does not imply that counter-hegemonic articulations are impossible and that hegemony is total (Sayyid &
Zac, 1998: 262):

> Every hegemonic order is susceptible of being challenged by counter-
> hegemonic practices, i.e., practices which will attempt to disarticulate
> the existing order so as to install other forms of hegemony. (Mouffe,
> 2005: 18)

Instrumental tools in the construction of hegemonies are myths, which are
defined by Laclau (1990: 61) as "*a principle of reading of a given situation.*"
Myths work on dislocations and try to suture them by creating new spaces
of representation and rearticulations that attribute meaning—"*a new objectivity*" as Laclau (1990: 61) put it—to the dislocatory events. The ultimate
objective of hegemonic projects is to construct and stabilize nodal points
that can form the basis of a social order, the aim being to transform myths
into a social imaginary, that is, a horizon that "*is not one among other
objects but an absolute limit which structures a field of intelligibility and is*

thus the condition of possibility of the emergence of any object" (Laclau, 1990: 64).

Hegemonic practices, and therefore articulation, require an open system. In a closed system there would be only repetition, and nothing would be left to hegemonize (Laclau & Mouffe, 1985: 134). It takes more than mere articulation, however, to speak of hegemony. According to Laclau and Mouffe (1985: 135-136), hegemony implies that antagonistic practices link elements in so-called chains of equivalence. They claim, *"in other words, that hegemony should emerge in a field criss-crossed by antagonisms and therefore suppose phenomena of equivalence and frontier effects. But, conversely, not every antagonism supposes hegemonic practices."* Antagonisms have (like the "binary oppositions" concept used by Derrida and Lévi-Strauss) both negative and positive aspects, as they attempt to destabilize the "other" identity but at the same time desperately need that "other" as a constitutive outside stabilizing their own identity. A good example of an antagonism is given by Howarth (2000: 106):

> Consider the emergence of the Black Consciousness Movement in South Africa during the late 1960s and early 1970s ... In its formative stages, leaders of this movement constructed a series of antagonistic relationships with different groups within South African society. These included white liberals, the National Party and its apartheid project, as well as other anti-apartheid organizations — the exiled African National Congress and its allies such as the Natal Indian Congress and the Inkatha Movement led by Mangosuthu Buthelezi. Their discourse emphasized that the main "blockage" to their identity was "white racism," which systematically denied and prevented the construction and assertion of a black identity. Their political project endeavored to link together all those who were opposed to apartheid and who identified themselves as black, rather than "non-white"' or "non-racial," by instituting a political frontier dividing the South African society into two antagonistic camps organized around the black/"anti-black" division.

Antagonisms are discursively constructed by means of the logic of equivalence and the creation of chains of equivalence, in which different identities are linked, made equivalent and opposed to another negative identity. To put this differently: The logic of equivalence brings together a number of identities in one discourse, without however totally eliminating their differences: They *"can weaken, but not domesticate differences"* (Laclau, 2005: 79). Howarth (2000: 107) illustrated this by using the letters a, b, and c for the equivalent identities (in which $a = b = c$) and the letter d for their common "negative" identity. The creation of two antagonistic poles through the logic of equivalence is then expressed in the formula: $d = - (a, b, c)$. Laclau (1988: 256) himself gave the following example of a possible chain of equivalence:

For instance, if I say that, from the point of view of the interests of the working class, liberals, conservatives, and radicals are all the same, I have transformed three elements that were different into substitutes within a chain of equivalence.

Next to the logic of equivalence Laclau and Mouffe also discern a logic of difference, which breaks existing chains of equivalence and incorporates the disarticulated elements in another discursive order (Howarth, 1998: 277). As opposed to the logic of equivalence, the logic of difference weakens existing antagonisms and relegates them to the margins of a society. In Laclau's (2005: 78) words, the creation of chains of difference leads to *"the assertion of a particularity ... whose only links to other particularities are of a differential nature (... no positive terms, only differences)."* In contrast to the logic of equivalence, the logic of difference does not presuppose the drawing of an antagonistic frontier.

Laclau and Mouffe's Radical Democratic Politics

Laclau and Mouffe's post-Marxist slant becomes even more apparent at the third level, where their plea for a radical democratic politics situates them in the field of democratic theory. HSS states explicitly that the contemporary liberal-democratic ideology should not be renounced (Laclau & Mouffe, 1985: 176) but rather reworked in the direction of a radical and plural democracy. This project is called radical because, as Mouffe explained in an interview: *"[it] means the radicalization of the democratic revolution by its extension to more and more areas of social life"* (Knowledge Network, 1999). Democratic struggles are to be waged in the whole of civil society and the state. With a view to this, the concept of citizenship is to be extended beyond the political society to include the civil society, and beyond the public to include the private (Laclau & Mouffe, 1985: 185). Second, their project is considered to be radically pluralist because of its embeddedness in a social ontology that leads them to emphasize that *"subject positions cannot be led back to a positive and unitary founding principle"* (Laclau & Mouffe, 1985: 167). Learning this from Carl Schmitt,[11] Mouffe (1990: 58-59) also warned us against the *"dangerous dream of a perfect consensus, of a harmonious collective will."* Each identity in a pluralist society is to benefit from a *"maximum autonomization"* (Laclau & Mouffe, 1985: 167), that is, it is to find acceptance for its own validity and not on the basis of a transcendent grounding creating a hierarchy of meaning. Laclau and Mouffe's model thus echoes Lefort's (1981) argument that the site of power in democracy is an empty space. This also implies that the radical pluralist democracy advocated by Laclau and Mouffe is not radical in the sense that it can identify *the* true and pure democratic model: *"its radical character implies on the con-trary, that we can save democracy only by taking into account its radical impossibility"* (Žižek, 1989: 6). For this reason, Mouffe (1997: 8) referred to radical pluralist democracy as a democracy that will always be *"to come."*

Despite this, the pluralism advocated by Laclau and Mouffe aims to realize specific and clearly demarcated objectives. First, it aims for the *"gen-eralization of the equivalential-egalitarian logic"* (Laclau & Mouffe, 1985: 167). Laclau and Mouffe (1985: 190) continued to situate themselves within the *"classic ideal of socialism"* and plead for a *"polyphony of voices"* in which the different (radically) democratic political struggles—such as antiracism, antisexism and anticapitalism—are all allotted an equally important role (Mouffe, 1997: 18). In this sense, Laclau and Mouffe can be seen to have helped construct the theoretical backbone of the alter-globalization move-ment. It comes as no surprise, then, that Mouffe (1995: 502) urged us to take the *"demands of groups exposed to the dislocating effects of globalization"* seriously. Because of this perspective radical pluralist democracy is of course sympathetic to left-wing ideology.[12] As Laclau and Mouffe (1985: 176) are looking to (re)create a *"hegemonic strategy for the Left,"* their explicit objec-tive is to establish a *"new hegemony articulated through new egalitarian social relations, practices and institutions"* (Mouffe, 1997: 86).

Second, radical pluralist democracy is delineated by the need to *"agree on the liberal-democratic rules of the game,"* although this is not taken to mean that *"the precise interpretation of the rules of the game"* would be given once and for all (Mouffe, 1995: 502; Torfing, 1999: 261). This condi-tion—which reminds us of the German proverb: Keine Demokratie für die Feinde der Demokratie—appears from the discussion of the extreme or rad-ical right:

> I don't think there is a possibility of an adversarial relation with the extreme right. Those are enemies, while the adversarial relation can only take place between left and democratic right. (Knowledge Network, 1999)

As this quotation already indicates, Mouffe (and Laclau) have in recent years been propagating an *agonistic* model of democracy, as contrasted to a *delib-erative* model (Mouffe, 2000). Explicitly based on the *"older"* model of radi-cal pluralism (Mouffe, 2000: 99)—which has been critiqued for not being very robust (Townshend, 2004: 285)—the agonistic model of democracy contains a more sophisticated elaboration of Laclau and Mouffe's normative demo-cratic-political thought. Echoing Connolly (1991, 1993), the agonistic model of democracy is built on a distinction between antagonism (between enemies) and agonism (between adversaries). While the existence of an adversary is considered legitimate and his right to defend his ideas is not questioned, an enemy is (to be) excluded from the political community (Mouffe 1997: 4). The aim of democratic politics then becomes *"to transform an 'antagonism' into 'agonism'"* (Mouffe, 1999a: 755), to *"tame"* or *"sublimate"* (Mouffe, 2005: 20-21) antagonisms, without eliminating passion from the political realm or relegating it to the outskirts of the private. Seen in this way, *"far from jeopardizing democracy, agonistic confrontation is in fact its very condition of existence"* (Mouffe, 1999a: 756). Although the concept of agonistic struggle is criticized by Žižek (2004) for being unable to challenge the present-day liberal status quo, Mouffe believes that it can and should *"bring about new meanings and fields of application for the idea of democracy to be radicalized"* (Mouffe, 2005: 33).

CRITIQUES OF LACLAU AND MOUFFE'S DISCOURSE THEORY

As can be expected, Laclau and Mouffe's discourse theory has not been spared criticism, coming both from authors sympathetic to their project and from authors (extremely) hostile toward their thought. In the eyes of many, developing a theory based on a combination of poststructuralist and post-Marxist sources of inspiration is sufficient reason for being discredited. This is often done by (mis)using "postmodernism" as a strategically rewarding umbrella term, connoting the traditional modernist accusations of nihilism, relativism, or eclecticism. This criticism is—ironically—summarized by Butler (1997: 249): *"discourse is all there is, as if discourse were some kind of monistic stuff out of which all things are composed; the subject is dead, I can never say 'I' again; there is no reality, only representation."* Geras (1990: 99) exemplified the same critical stance when he said that Laclau and Mouffe's discourse theory lacks any foundation and therefore inevitably *"slides into a bottomless, relativist gloom, in which opposed discourses or paradigms are left with no common reference point, usually trading blows."* One way to refute this critique consists in pointing out the importance Laclau (1996: 57) attaches to universal principles, which *"have to be formulated as limitless principles, expressing a universality transcending them: but they all, for essential reasons, sooner or later become entangled in their own contextual particularism and are incapable of fulfilling their universal function."* Another—and more weighty—argument is that Laclau and Mouffe stress that total contingency is just as impossible (and undesirable) as total fixity of meaning. They consider meaning to be partially fixed, and introduce the concept of nodal points to further theorize these partial fixations. Similarly, the notion of hegemony theorizes the attempts of social actors to stabilize and fix the contingencies of the social. At the same time, Laclau and Mouffe emphasize the situatedness and contextuality of their discourse theory, and in doing so reject "*the rigid separation of facts and values*" as an objective that cannot possibly be achieved because "*the discourse theorist and analyst is always located in a particular historical and political context with no neutral Archimedean point from which to describe, argue and evaluate*" (Howarth & Stavrakakis, 2000: 7).

Also from traditional Marxist positions, objections were formulated, especially concerning the decentering of the class concept and the rejection of economic determinism. Gledhill (1994: 183), for example, called Laclau "*a disillusioned Althusserian Marxist of the 1968 new left vintage who now declares himself a post-Marxist.*" Wood (1998: 7), in his turn, discards Laclau and Mouffe's statement that they see Marxism as one of their prime sources of inspiration as typical of "*the current [of NTS—New 'True' Socialism], in particular of its complicated, pretentious, and—it must be said—evasive theoretical contortions.*" This type of critique actually goes to the heart of Laclau and Mouffe's theoretical project, which aims to de-essentialize Althusser's and Gramsci's work (and thus indirectly also the work of Marx and Engels). From a less traditionally Marxist point of view, the decentralization of the class struggle allows incorporating other relevant societal struggles and identities (e.g., those related to ethnicity and gender) and, in doing so, correcting the earlier Marxist neglect of these areas (Torfing, 1999: 291).

In addition to the criticism leveled at discourse theory's poststructuralist and post-Marxist points of departure, four other points of critique have to be discussed here. A first point concerns the so-called idealist stance of discourse theory. Laclau and Mouffe (1985: 108) already anticipated this critique in HSS, as they rejected the realism–idealism dichotomy. However, their plea for a radical materialism as a "*tertium quid*" (Howarth, 1998: 289) does not alter their strong orientation toward the analysis of discursive components of reality, and more specifically toward the analysis of signifiers like democracy and socialism. Practically speaking, this means that their specific analyses pay considerably less attention to material components of reality (as e.g., bodies, objects, organizations or interactions) and to the complex interaction between discourse and materiality, which for instance Foucault (1975) has developed in *Surveiller et Punir*.

A second point has to do with the primacy of the political over the social that follows from the fact that Laclau and Mouffe interpret discourse and identity as political entities. This critique can be partly refuted by advancing that, although social relations are always formed by political struggle, their political nature tends to be forgotten as they become sedimented in social norms and values (which may be contested again at a later point in history) (Torfing, 1999: 70). A more convincing argument is the Schmittian distinction introduced (mainly) by Mouffe (2000: 101; see also Mouffe, 2005: 8) between the political and politics:[13]

> By "the political," I refer to the dimension of antagonism that is inherent in human relations, antagonism that can take many forms and emerge in different types of social relations. "Politics" on the other side, indicates the ensemble of practices, discourses and institutions which seek to establish a certain order and organize human coexistence in conditions that are always potentially conflictual because they are affected by the dimension of "the political."

In other words "the political"

> cannot be restricted to a certain type of institution, or envisaged as constituting a specific sphere or level of society. It must be conceived as a dimension that is inherent to every human society and that determines our very ontological condition. (Mouffe, 1997: 3)

A third point concerns the fact that, while Laclau and Mouffe spent a great deal of energy on defining the concept of discourse, some of their other core concepts such as identity, ideology, and power[14] remain undertheorized. As a consequence, these concepts are in danger of becoming vague umbrella terms or "black boxes,"[15] whose status spoils the theoretical elegance with which other key terms are developed. A more extensive theoretical elaboration of the tensions between individual and collective identities and their institutional and organizational sedimentations,[16] and of the tensions between idealist and materialist approaches—focusing on how discourses can be condensed into material structures—would also considerably strengthen the discourse-theoretical framework.

Finally, also methodological critiques are leveled at Laclau and Mouffe's theory. Howarth (1998: 291), for example, believes the following:

> Laclau and Mouffe need to lay down, however minimally, a set of methodological guidelines for practitioners, as well a set of questions and hypotheses (à la Lakatos) for clarification and development. Thus far, the only clear methodological rule consists in a "non-rule": rules can never be simply applied to cases, but have to be articulated in the research process ... The lack of adequate responses to the epistemological and methodological questions pose significant problems for researchers working within discourse theory.

In line with Derrida, who pleaded for the singularity of each deconstruction, and Foucault, who at all times wrote a specific *"history of the present"* (Kendall & Wickham, 1999: 4), Laclau (and Mouffe) advocated the articulation of theoretical concepts adapted to each specific empiric research question (Laclau, 1990: 208-209). The rejection of essentialism pushes discourse theorists toward developing open-ended theoretical frameworks. However, this tends to be detrimental to methodological clarity and rigor and (again) to the empirical application of the framework (Howarth, 1998: 288). In order to meet these difficulties, Foucault's archeo-genealogical method and Derrida's deconstruction can be used as methodological points of departure, although also other methodologies, including (as illustrated in this volume) those that can be borrowed from the social sciences, can be put to good use.

BEYOND THE POLITICAL?

In the beginning of this introduction we already referred to the need for bringing Laclau and Mouffe's discourse theory (further) into the realm of the cultural, which is the main rationale of this book. The fact that discourse theory has so far remained largely confined to the study of politics and the political contributes to perpetuating an untenable distinction between the cultural, the ideological and the political, and to unnecessarily impoverishing cultural analysis. In the remainder of this introduction, we want to briefly discuss the exceptions that *have* used a discourse-theoretical perspective for the analysis of cultural phenomena. We also (again briefly) introduce the chapters that are included in this volume, and that are all motivated by this same ambition to (in sometimes very different ways) deploy discourse theory in the cultural domain.

Bringing Discourse Theory to the Realm of Media Studies

Despite the rather limited attention discourse theorists have given to the realm of the (mass) media, a few authors have used elements of Laclau and Mouffe's discourse theory for analyzing media and/or have discussed its potential use for such analysis. A preliminary version of a research agenda can be found in Torfing's (1999: 210-224) chapter on discourse theory and the media. Torfing distinguishes three domains where discourse theory can be put to work: (a) the study of discourses *about* the media and their place and function in society; (b) the study of discourses *of* mass media (i.e., of the form and content of the discourses produced by the media), (c) the study of media *as* discourse.

An early example of a discourse-theoretical analysis in the media domain is James Curran's (1997) attempt to articulate a radical democratic (normative) theory of the media, which he distinguished from the more traditional liberal, Marxist and communist theories. Although Curran did not explicitly refer to Laclau and Mouffe's work, a clear link with their radical democratic theory is present. Other examples are our own analyses of community media identities, audience identities, and media professional's identities (Carpentier, 2001, 2004; Carpentier et al., 2003, 2005), where on all occasions Laclau and Mouffe's political identity theory is used as a theoretical frame of reference to analyze media-related identities. Gies (2003) used a discourse-theoretical perspective to analyze media representations of the Belgian judicial system in relation to the dislocation brought about by the "Dutroux affair,"[17] Chouliaraki (2004) used discourse-theoretical concepts to investigate what she called the politics of truth in mediated debates, and a number of other publications have been oriented at "deconstructing" information society signifiers such as the Internet (Brodocz, 1998) and the digital divide (Carpentier, 2003).

From a discourse-theoretical viewpoint, media are seen as not just passively expressing or reflecting social phenomena, or as sites where discourses merely circulate, but as specific machineries that produce, reproduce and transform social phenomena. These discursive machineries can be considered to be what Foucault (1984: 37-38) called systems of dispersion of discourses, with their own specific rules of formation. Torfing (1999: 210-224) rightfully criticized the classical sender–receiver model from a discourse-theoretical point of view, injecting a discursive dimension into each level of the model and in doing so inquiring into the discursive nature of the meaning of the message, of the identity of real and would-be communicators and of the identity of receivers. The signifier "audience," for instance, cannot be understood in isolation from a number of discourses that attempt to construct the audience as consumers, citizens, or masses. When "ordinary people" are granted access to the media system and are allowed to feature in specific media products, these products depart from discursive representations of the audience. This resounds strongly with the position that brings Allor (1988: 228), in a discussion of the audience as a theoretical construct, to the radical conclusion: *"the audience exists nowhere; it inhabits no real space, only positions within analytic discourses."*

Most of the chapters in this volume deal with a variety of media, including television, newspapers, film, ads, press communiqués, online forums, and video games. Content-wise, these chapters are majoritarily discourse-theoretical analyses of a wide range of conflicts and their representations. Three chapters tackle war: Nico Carpentier analyzes televisional representations of the Iraq War and the antagonistic ideological model of war that structures these representations, and also looks at how specific journalistic practices strengthen this model. N.Y. Potamitis' chapter looks back on the Greek civil war. He shows how the filmic production during the right-wing hegemony constructed the Greek nation as a fantasy-object. Evangelos Intzidis and George Prevedourakis enter into the world of video games, as they analyze how World War II first-person shooters are not just built on an antagonism between the self and the enemy, but also link up with present-day conflicts in the "real" world.

Three other chapters look at media representations of more traditional political conflicts. The focal point of Henrieta Anişoara Şerban's chapter is the 2004 Romanian elections. She analyzes how a series of media organizations intervened in the public debate, and contributed to ending the old Social Democratic Party hegemony (and the establishment of a new one). Lut Lams' chapter discusses the representation of the Hong Kong handover in mainland Chinese and Taiwanese newspapers. Besides pointing to clear antagonisms and supporting myths, this chapter also shows the complexities of media representations and the "polyphony of voices" they invariably offer. Anabela Carvalho's chapter adopts a broader political perspective on urban planning as a hegemonic project. In her case study of the Portuguese city of Braga she also shows how the spatial and material on the one hand and the discursive on the other become interconnected.

Two chapters deal with more economic conflicts. David M. Boje and Yue Cai analyze how the signifier McJob was re-articulated by social activists and used as a discursive tool to criticize McDonald's labor policies. Benjamin de Cleen's chapter focuses on the record industry, and on the discursive strategies the International Federation of the Phonographic Industry uses to hegemonize its articulations of music property through the nodal points of piracy and copyright.

Finally, the two remaining media chapters have a less dominant focus on conflict. Their main emphasis is on identity and identity politics. Germán Martínez Martínez's chapter uses the Mexican film *Amores Perros* as a case to analyze the end of the dominance of revolutionary Mexican nationalist discourse and the increasing interconnectedness of the United States and Mexico. Yow-Jiun Wang looks at the complex identity constructions in gay forums and at the way in which—within a counter-hegemonic setting—new gay hegemonies develop.

Bringing Discourse Theory to the Realm of Literary and Art Studies

While the application of discourse theory within Media Studies is rare, it is virtually nonexistent within the realm of Literary and Art studies. One rare exception is Fletcher's (2003) analysis of the politics of community-based theater. Attempts at operationalizing discourse theory in the field of Literary Studies are currently underway at Belgian universities (Liège and Ghent). This research seems to harbor promise for a nonessentialist description of literary development, aiming as it does at accounting for the rise and decline of literary movements in terms of the articulation of discourses aspiring at hegemony. This approach offers the additional advantage of establishing continuities between poetics and literature on the one hand and so-called extra-literary discourses on the other. In doing so, it fits in with recent criticism of the construction of the literary text as an aesthetic object transcending ideology. Finally, it redefines the author's identity—traditionally viewed as a positive essence, the source and ultimate touchstone of coherent meaning—as the provisional result of a (never fully accomplished) identification with one or several discourses and therefore as fundamentally expropriated.

In this volume, one chapter focuses on the visual arts, analyzing a mural painted by the Chilean artist Mario Toral. Hernán Cuevas Valenzuela shows how one of the mural's panels (called *Los Conflictos*), which deals with a series of political conflicts, including the military coup of September 11, 1973 and the bombing of the La Moneda presidential palace, makes social antagonisms visible but also gives rise to different interpretations of the mural and of the traumatic historical events.

The four chapters on literature share Said's (1983) concern for the worldliness of the text. Through a case study of Bunyan, Stuart Sim develops an agonistic aesthetic seeking out texts that resisted the authoritarian order of their time, and/or deploying texts from literary history to challenge such an order now. Sascha Bru looks at the potential of indeterminacy in German modernism, and more specifically in the writings of Kafka and Mann. His focus on what he calls the society effect also takes him to the counter-hegemonic potential of literature and vanguard modes of representation. Although she does so in a very different way, Ine Van linthout, too, shows the potential of indeterminacy as a counter-hegemonic force. Her analysis of Nazi attempts to incorporate Flemish literature into their hegemonic project through the construction of a Flemish–German sameness perfectly illustrates that hegemonies can never be total, even in totalitarian regimes. Finally, Erik Spinoy discusses the case of Flemish new realist poetry and in doing so reflects on how literary history could be rewritten on a discourse-theoretical basis. This reflection leads him to conclude that discourse-theoretical analysis offers the appropriate tools to do justice to the political dimension of literary development.

CONCLUSION

When Torfing wrote in 1999 that the focus of discourse-theoretical analysis was geared toward *"the study of ethnic, national and subcultural identities,"* he rightfully remarked that this orientation seemed *"to carry with it the benign neglect"* of a series of other topics and research interests. At the same time, it is just as symptomatic that Torfing's list of neglected topics, which includes "*the study of state-economy relations, the institutional underpinnings of relatively enduring social and political identities, and the stable reproduction of capitalist societies*" (Torfing, 1999: 291), used a clear Political Studies focus. Although these issues are extremely relevant for cultural analyses, too, the underlying focus leads to the exclusion of topics that are less taken-for-granted by Political Studies scholars, but are at the core of Cultural, Literary, or Art studies. This volume is the first structural attempt to take discourse theory away from its home base in Political Studies, and put some of the instruments in the toolbox at work in the alien settings of cultural analysis. The diversity of the included articles and their analytical quality show that this transplantation of discourse theory can contribute to the development of a new and viable approach to cultural phenomena (i.e., to media, literature and the arts).

At the same time, the specificity of the chapters raises questions concerning the viscosity of the Political Studies approach. Although these chapters have a clear focus on the analysis of representations that circulate in and through the media and in literary and artistic spheres, an important part of them analyzes the representation of (more traditional) political processes and conflicts, such as war, elections, or national identity. This book's attempts to redress the balance between cultural and political spheres in the discourse-theoretical research agenda shows the difficulties in escaping from the vortex of the Political Studies research agenda. A number of chapters (especially those dealing with literature, but also those that engage with more economic conflicts) do structurally shift the balance toward the cultural sphere and open up new analytical spaces. This retrospective analysis does of course not imply the acceptance of the artificial distinction between the political and the cultural as societal domains, as this would eliminate the political from the cultural, which would in turn negate the fundamentally ideological nature of the cultural.

Finally, this volume (again) demonstrates the possibility to deploy discourse theory, refuting the critique that its high level of abstraction creates an impenetrable barrier for its analytical application. Each author contributing to this volume has been—to some degree—a "*methodological bricoleur*" (Torfing, 1999: 292), finding methodological, analytical and theoretical support wherever necessary and, in doing so, sometimes reverting to a multiperspectival approach (for instance by translating elements of critical discourse analysis into discourse theory). At the same time this research strategy does not imply an anything goes position. While postpositivist perspectives—but also the hermeneutics of recovery and suspicion (see Howarth, 2000: 128-129)—remain unacceptable for discourse-theoretical analysts, the "traditional" requirements of academic rigidity still hold. The practice of research implies that delimitations and temporal closures need to be constructed, without suppressing the constructed nature of these delimitations and closures:

> Treating the delimitation of discourses as an analytical exercise entails understanding discourses as objects that the researcher constructs rather than as objects that exist in a delimited form in reality, ready to be identified and mapped. But this does not mean that anything at all can be called a discourse. Researchers have to establish in their reports that the delimitation they have made is reasonable. (Phillips & Jørgensen, 2002: 144)

As Howarth (2000: 140) suggested, the broad range of qualitative methods can be incorporated within the discourse-theoretical framework to provide it with empirical support. In the same way, the theoretical-methodological principles of qualitative research, and the way in which this tradition deals with the dialectics of temporal closure and structural openness, have proven to be extremely helpful. For instance Blumer's (1954) notion of "sensitizing concept," which he defined in contrast to a "definitive concept" — "*whereas definitive concepts provide prescriptions of what to see, sensitizing concepts merely suggest directions along which to look*" (Blumer, 1954: 7) — is highly compatible with the discourse-theoretical epistemology. But also discourse theory itself, with its dialectics between fixity and non-fixity, provides us with concepts that are perfectly adapted to theorizing the analytical process. Researchers unavoidably fix the objects (or better: subjects) of their study, but these fixations are never stable, irrevocable or uncontestable. In the end, as Howarth (2000: 142) put it, it will be the community of discourse theorists and the wider community of academics working in the social sciences and humanities that form the "*ultimate tribunal of truth.*"

And this of course also applies for this book.

NOTES

1. In 2001 a second edition of HSS, with a new foreword, was published. In this book we refer to the first edition, unless indicated otherwise.
2. Wenman (2003) correctly remarked that the twin identity of the two authors hides important differences between them. We will, however, not embark on a detailed comparison in this introduction.
3. One could in this context also refer to the fact that in recent years Laclau has been a visiting professor at various comparative literature departments or centers (in Toronto, Buffalo, etc.).
4. See http://www.cork2005.ie/programme/default.asp?id=653&p=371.
5. Arnold's (1869: viii) definition of culture still remains a valuable reference point: "*Culture being a pursuit of our total perfection by means of getting to know, on all the matters which most concern us, the best which has been thought and said in the world....*"

6. Elements are differential positions that are not (yet) discursively articulated. Moments are differential positions, which are articulated within a discourse.
7. Representation is used here in its cultural and not in its political meaning (see Hall, 1997).
8. Differences in interpretation arise on the question whether the analyzed discourses are part of the field of discursivity or not. In this volume, the first interpretation is preferred (in contrast to Phillips & Jørgensen, 2002: 56), so the field of discursivity is defined here as the combination of actual and potential articulations.
9. Laclau distinguished between *floating* and *empty* signifiers: whereas floating signifiers signal the blurring of frontiers, empty signifiers take the presence of a stable frontier for granted. At the same time, Laclau (2005: 133) also relativized the distinction: "*in practice, however, the distance between the two is not that great.*"
10. Critchley and Marchart (2004: 5) called the introduction of the dislocation concept in *New Reflections on the Revolution of Our Time* the second major reformulation of discourse theory, the first being Laclau's elaboration of a Lacanian theory of the subject.
11. Although Schmitt (like Heidegger) converted to Nazism, his theoretical work remains of considerable importance. As Mouffe (1999b: 52) wrote: "*Schmitt is an adversary from whom we can learn, because we can draw on his insights. Turning them against him, we should use them to formulate a better understanding of liberal democracy.*"
12. The first sentence of HSS is illustrative for the focus of their project: "*Left-wing thought today stands at a crossroads*" (Laclau & Mouffe, 1985: 1).
13. The phrasing of this distinction confusingly diverges from a series of (structurally similar) projects that want to maintain the word politics while broadening its meaning (see, in this context, for instance Beck's 1997 concept of subpolitics and Giddens' 1991 concept of life politics). In *On the Political* Mouffe (2005: 8) acknowledged these problems and offered an in-depth analysis of the problems with both Beck's and Giddens' projects, criticizing them for "*eliminating from politics ... the notion of adversary*" (Mouffe, 2005: 48) and/or reducing the adversary to the enemy, the "*fundamentalist who is opposing the process of reflexive modernization*" (Mouffe, 2005: 55).
14. Dyrberg's (1997) *The Circular Structure of Power* provides a welcome addition in this field.
15. Latour (1987) uses this term, which is inspired by cybernetics, to describe situations in which complex components are present in an argumentation without their complexity being fully developed or represented (see also Kendall & Wickham, 1999: 73).
16. See Howarth (2000: 119-120), although later, for example, Mouffe (2005) did address the question of democratic institutions.
17. The Dutroux Affair refers to the dislocatory events of the kidnapping and/or murder of young children in the mid-1990s in Belgium. Marc Dutroux and his accessories were eventually brought before a Belgian court in 2004.

REFERENCES

Allor, M. (1988) 'Relocating the Site of the Audience,' *Critical Studies in Mass Communication* 5(3): 217-233.

Ang, I. (1989) *Watching Dallas: Soap Opera and the Melodramatic Imagination.* London, New York: Routledge.

Arnold, M. (1869) *Culture and Anarchy: An Essay in Political and Social Criticism.* London: Smith, Elder & Co.

Barthes, R. (1975) *The Pleasure of the Text.* New York: Farrar, Straus & Giroux.

Beck, U. (1997) *The Reinvention of Politics: Rethinking Modernity in the Global Social Order.* Cambridge: Polity Press.

Blumer, H. (1954) 'What is Wrong with Social Theory,' *American Sociological Review* (18): 3-10.

Brodocz, A. (1998) 'Internet'—ein leerer Signifikant der Weltgesellschaft. Diskurstheoretische Überlegungen im Anschluß an Laclau,' *Berliner Debatte INITIAL* 9(4): 85-91.

Butler, J. (1997) 'Contingent Foundations,' pp. 248-258 in S.E. Bronner (Ed) *Twentieth Century Political Theory.* New York: Routledge.

Butler, J., Laclau, E., Žižek, S. (2000) *Contingency, Hegemony and Universality: Contemporary Dialogues on the Left.* London/New York: Verso.

Carpentier, N. (2001) *De Discursieve Articulatie van Publieksparticipatie in Vier Televisie Talkshows: Een Onderzoek naar de Constructie van Publieksparticipatie in het Televisiesysteem aan de hand van de Discourstheorie van Ernesto Laclau en Chantal Mouffe.* PhD thesis. Antwerp: UIA.

Carpentier, N. (2003) 'Access and Participation in the Discourse of the Digital Divide: The European Perspective at/on the WSIS,' pp. 99-120 in J. Servaes (Ed) *The European Information Society: A Reality Check.* Bristol, UK; Portland, OR: Intellect.

Carpentier, N. (2004) 'The Identity of the Television Audience: Towards the Articulation of the Television Audience as a Discursive Field,' pp. 95-122 in N. Carpentier, C. Pauwels, and O. Van Oost (Eds) *The Ungraspable Audience/ Het On(be)grijpbare Publiek.* Brussel: VUBPress.

Carpentier, N. (2005) 'Identity, Contingency and Rigidity: The (counter-) Hegemonic Constructions of the Identity of the Media Professional,' *Journalism* 6(2): 199-219.

Carpentier, N., De Cleen, B. (2007) 'Bringing Discourse Theory into Media Studies,' *Journal of Language and Politics* 6(2): 267-295.

Carpentier, N., Lie, R., Servaes, J. (2003) 'Community Media: Muting the Democratic Media Discourse?,' *Continuum* 17(1): 51-68.

Chouliaraki, L. (2004) 'Media Discourse and the Public Sphere,' pp. 275-296 in D. Howarth and J. Torfing (Eds) *Discourse Theory in European Politics: Identity, Policy and Governance.* New York: Palgrave Macmillan.

Connolly, W.E. (1991) *Identity/Difference: Democratic Negotiations of Political Paradox.* Ithaca, NY, London: Cornell University Press.

Connolly, W.E. (1993) *The Augustinian Imperative: A Reflection on the Politics of Morality.* Newbury Park, CA, London: Sage.

Critchley, S., Marchart, O. (2004) 'Introduction,' pp. 1-13 in S. Critchley and O. Marchart (Eds) *Laclau: A Critical Reader*. London/New York: Routledge.

Critchley, S., Marchart, O. (Eds) (2004) *Laclau: A Critical Reader*. London/New York: Routledge.

Curran, J. (1997) 'Rethinking the Media as Public Sphere,' pp. 27-57 in P. Dahlgren and C. Sparks (Eds) *Communication and Citizenship*. London/New York: Routledge.

Dyrberg, T.B. (1997) *The Circular Structure of Power: Politics, Identity, Community*. New York: Verso.

Fletcher, J. (2003) 'Identity and Agonism: Tim Miller, Cornerstone, and the Politics of Community-Based Theatre,' *Theatre Topics* 13(2): 189-203.

Foucault, M. (1969) *L'Archéologie du Savoir*. Paris: Gallimard.

Foucault, M. (1975) *Surveiller et Punir*. Paris: Gallimard.

Foucault, M. (1984) *The Archaeology of Knowledge*. New York: Pantheon.

Foucault, M. (1996) 'From Torture to Cellblock,' pp. 146-149 in S. Lotringer (Ed) *Foucault Live: Collected Interviews, 1961-1984*. New York: Semiotext(e).

Fuss, D. (1989) *Essentially Speaking: Feminism, Nature, and Difference*. London: Routledge.

Geras, N. (1990) *Discourses of Extremity*. London: Verso.

Giddens, A. (1991) *Modernity and Self Identity*. Cambridge: Polity.

Gies, L. (2003) 'Up, Close and Personal: The Discursive Transformation of Judicial Politics in Post-Dutroux Belgium,' *International Journal for the Semiotics of Law* (16): 259-284.

Gledhill, J. (1994) *Power and its Disguises: Anthropological Perspectives on Politics*. London, Boulder, CO: Pluto Press.

Glynos, J., Stavrakakis, Y. (2004) 'Encounters of the Real Kind. Sussing out the Limits of Laclau's Embrace of Lacan,' pp. 201-216 in S. Critchley and O. Marchart (Eds) *Laclau: A Critical Reader*. London, New York: Routledge.

Gramsci, A. (1999) *The Antonio Gramsci Reader: Selected Writings 1916-1935*. London: Lawrence and Wishart.

Hall, S. (1981) 'Cultural Studies: Two Paradigms,' pp. 19-37 in T. Bennett et al. (Eds) *Culture, Ideology and Social Process*. London: Open University Press.

Hall, S. (1986) 'On Postmodernism and Articulation: An Interview with Stuart Hall,' L. Grossberg (Ed.) *Journal of Communication Inquiry* 10(2): 45-60.

Hall, S. (1997) 'The Work of Representation,' pp. 13-64 in S. Hall (Ed.) *Representation: Cultural Representations and Signifying Practices*. London, Thousand Oaks, New Delhi: Sage.

Hall, S., Critcher, C., Jefferson, T., Clarke, J., Roberts, B. (1978) *Policing the Crisis: 'Mugging' the State and Law and Order*. London: Macmillan.

Harris, D. (1992) *From Class Struggle to the Politics of Pleasure: The Effects of Gramscianism on Cultural Studies*. London: Routledge.

Howarth, D. (1998) 'Discourse Theory and Political Analysis,' pp. 268-293 in E. Scarbrough and E. Tanenbaum (Eds) *Research Strategies in the Social Sciences*. Oxford: Oxford University Press.

Howarth, D. (2000) *Discourse*. Buckingham, Philadelphia: Open University Press.

Howarth, D., Norval, A., Stavrakakis, Y. (Eds) (2000) *Discourse Theory and Political Analysis: Identities, Hegemonies and Social Change*. Manchester: Manchester University Press.

Howarth, D., Stavrakakis, Y. (2000) 'Introducing Discourse Theory and Political Analysis,' pp. 1-23 in D. Howarth, A. Norval and Y. Stavrakakis (Eds) *Discourse Theory and Political Analysis: Identities, Hegemonies and Social Change.* Manchester: Manchester University Press.

Howarth, D., Torfing, J. (Eds) (2004) *Discourse Theory in European Politics: Identity, Policy and Governance.* New York: Palgrave Macmillan.

Kendall, G., Wickham, G. (1999) *Using Foucault's Methods.* London: Sage.

Knowledge Network (1999) 'An Interview with Chantal Mouffe and Ernesto Laclau,' downloaded on September 1, 2005 from http://www.ianangus.ca/cp1.htm.

Laclau, E. (1977) *Politics and Ideology in Marxist Theory: Capitalism, Fascism, Populism.* London: New Left Books.

Laclau, E. (1988) 'Metaphor and Social Antagonisms,' pp. 249-257 in C. Nelson and L. Grossberg (Eds) *Marxism and the Interpretation of Culture.* Urbana: University of Illinois.

Laclau, E. (1990) *New Reflections on the Revolution of our Time.* London: Verso.

Laclau, E. (Ed.) (1994) *The Making of Political Identities.* London: Verso.

Laclau, E. (1996) *Emancipations.* London: Verso.

Laclau, E. (2002) 'Ethics, Politics and Radical Democracy — A Response to Simon Critchley,' *Culture Machine. The Journal* (4). Downloaded on September 1, 2005 from http://culturemachine.tees.ac.uk/Cmach/Backissues/j004/Articles/laclau.htm).

Laclau, E. (2005) *The Populist Reason.* London: Verso.

Laclau, E., Mouffe, C. (1985) *Hegemony and Socialist Strategy: Towards a Radical Democratic Politics.* London: Verso.

Latour, B. (1987) *Science in Action: How to Follow Scientists and Engineers through Society.* Cambridge: Harvard University Press.

Lefort, C. (1981) *L'Invention Démocratique.* Paris: Fayard.

Lewis, J. (2002) *Cultural Studies: The Basics.* London: Sage.

Mouffe, C. (1990) 'Radical Democracy or Liberal Democracy?,' *Socialist Review* (May): 57-66.

Mouffe, C. (1995) 'The End of Politics and the Rise of the Radical Right,' *Dissent* (Fall): 498-502.

Mouffe, C. (1997) *The Return of the Political.* London: Verso.

Mouffe, C. (1999a) 'Deliberative Democracy or Agonistic Pluralism?,' *Social Research* 66(3): 745-758.

Mouffe, C. (1999b) 'Carl Schmitt and the Paradox of Liberal Democracy,' pp. 38-53 in C. Mouffe (Ed) *The Challenge of Carl Schmitt.* London: Verso.

Mouffe, C. (2000) *The Democratic Paradox.* London, New York: Verso.

Mouffe, C. (2001) 'Every Form of Art has a Political Dimension: Chantal Mouffe interviewed by Rosalyn Deutsche, Branden W. Joseph and Thomas Keenan,' *Grey Room* 2 (Spring): 98-125.

Mouffe, C. (2005) *On the Political.* London: Routledge.

Mouffe, C. (2007) *The Concept of the Agonistic Approach towards Public Space.* Lecture at Transformations of Public Space, 15-16 February 2007, Stedelijk Museum CS Amsterdam, the Netherlands.

Mouffe, C. (Ed.) (1979) *Gramsci and Marxist Theory.* London, Boston, MA, Henly: Routledge and Kegan Paul.

Mouffe, C. (Ed.) (1996) *Deconstruction and Pragmatism*. London/New York: Routledge.

Phillips, L., Jørgensen, M.W. (2002) *Discourse Analysis as Theory and Method*. London: Sage.

Said, E. (1978) *Orientalism: Western Conceptions of the Orient*. New York: Pantheon.

Said, E. (1983) 'The World, the Text, and the Critic,' pp. 31-53 in E. Said (Ed) *The World, the Text, and the Critic*. Cambridge, MA: Harvard University Press.

Sayyid, B., Zac, L. (1998) 'Political Analysis in a World without Foundations,' pp. 249-267 in E. Scarbrough and E. Tanenbaum (Eds) *Research Strategies in the Social Sciences*. Oxford: Oxford University Press.

Smith, A.M. (1999) *Laclau and Mouffe: The Radical Democratic Imaginary*. London, New York: Routledge.

Stavrakakis, Y. (1999) *Lacan and the Political*. London, New York: Routledge.

Torfing, J. (1999) *New Theories of Discourse: Laclau, Mouffe and Žižek*. Oxford: Blackwell.

Townshend, J. (2004) 'Laclau and Mouffe's Hegemonic Project: The Story so far,' *Political Studies* (52): 269-288.

Wenman, M.A. (2003) 'Laclau or Mouffe? Splitting the difference,' *Philosophy and Social Criticism* 29(5): 581-606.

Williams, R. (1958) *Culture and Society 1780-1950*. Harmondsworth: Penguin.

Wood, E.M. (1998) *The Retreat from Class: A New True Socialism*. London: Verso.

Žižek, S. (1989) *The Sublime Object of Ideology*. London: Verso.

Žižek, S. (1990) 'Beyond Discourse-Analysis,' pp. 249-260 in E. Laclau (Ed) *New Reflections on the Revolution of our Time*. London: Verso.

Žižek, S., Daly, G. (2004) *Conversations with Žižek*. Cambridge: Polity.

Media

1

DICHOTOMIZED MEDIA DISCOURSES OF WAR

The Construction of the Self and the Enemy in the 2003 Iraq War

Nico Carpentier

WAR, ANTAGONISM AND HEGEMONY

When a nation or a people goes to war, powerful mechanisms come into play in order to turn an *adversary* into an *enemy*. While the existence of an adversary is considered to be legitimate and his or her right to defend his or her ideas is not questioned, an enemy is excluded from the political community and his or her destruction is seen as a legitimate goal (Mouffe, 1997: 4). The transformation of an adversary into an enemy is supported by a set of discourses articulating the identities of all parties involved. These discourses play a crucial role. As Keen put it:

> In the beginning we create the enemy. Before the weapon comes the image. We think others to death and then invent the battle-axe or the ballistic missiles with which to actually kill them. (Keen, 1986: 10)

At times of war, little room is left for internal differences, as illustrated by the famous words of the German Emperor Wilhelm, who during World War I claimed that *"he would no longer hear of different political parties, only of Germans"* (Torfing, 1999: 126). U.S. President George Bush (2001) used an updated version of this dictum during his address to the Joint Session of Congress and the American People on September 20, 2001, when he said: *"Either you are with us, or you are with the terrorists."* Antagonistic discourses on the enemy (and on the self) tend to become hegemonic very quickly, defining the horizon of our thought and excluding other discourses. As this last sentence already indicates, this chapter contends that the domain of war and propaganda is an area of choice for the application of Ernesto Laclau and Chantal Mouffe's theory of discourse.

First of all, during war the primacy of the political is likely to be accepted as perfectly legitimate, as war tends to completely absorb the social. Moreover, the ontological position of the discourses on the enemy provides ample space for the changing nature of war. Despite certain rigidities, they remain contingent, undecidable, and subject to practices of rearticulation, as suggested by Laclau and Mouffe's definition of discourse as a *"structure in which meaning is constantly negotiated and constructed"* (Laclau, 1988: 254). This field of tension between discursive fluidity and rigidity will prove to be highly instrumental in understanding the nature of the ideological model on which war discourses build.

Second, social antagonism is one of the ultimate concepts to describe war-related social (discursive) practices. The specific meaning Laclau and Mouffe attribute to this key concept, which is related to the concept of "binary oppositions" used by Derrida and Lévi-Strauss, allows a clear focus on the (antagonistic) identity construction of the parties at war and their mutual dependencies. All actors involved attempt to destabilize the identity of the "other," but at the same time desperately need that "other" as a constitutive outside stabilizing their own identity (Laclau, 1990: 17). When dealing with the mechanics of these identity constructions, Laclau and Mouffe underscore the important role of the logic of equivalence and the creation of chains of equivalence, in which different identities are linked to each other and opposed to another—negative—identity. In the case of war, the constitutive outside provides us with the analytical backbone, whereas the logic of equivalence allows us to introduce more levels of complexity in the analysis of the identity of the self and the enemy.[1]

A third key notion in the analysis of war is hegemony. Within the framework of Laclau and Mouffe's discourse theory, hegemony remains connected to its Gramscian origins, but also becomes repositioned as a concept describing the mechanisms related to discursive societal struggles. In the event of war, the articulation of hegemony becomes relevant as the warring parties not only try to physically destroy the enemy, but also attempt to hegemonize their "own" discourses on the enemy and on the self. In order to become hegemonic, these discourses need to present themselves as coherent, almost impenetrable discursive entities. On top of this, they have to contribute to the deactivation (or "suppression") of the discourses they are struggling against (Sayyid & Zac 1998: 262). In wartime, this means the deactivation of the discourses produced by the enemy, of pacifist discourses and of other critical or counter-hegemonic discourses. It should be kept in mind, however, that this deactivation of non- or anti-antagonistic discourses will never be complete, because the contingency of the social makes it impossible for a hegemonic project to reach discursive closure (Laclau & Mouffe, 1985: 112-113).

DISCOURSES ON THE ENEMY AND THE SELF

Following Galtung and his colleagues (Galtung, Jacobsen & Brand-Jacobsen, 2001; Galtung, 1998, 2000; Galtung & Vincent, 1992; McGoldrick & Lynch, 2000), this chapter contends that discourses on the self and the enemy are based on a series of elementary dichotomies: good–evil, just–unjust, innocent–guilty, rational–irrational, civilized–barbaric, organized–chaotic, superior to technology–part of technology, human–animal–machine,[2] united–fragmented, heroic–cowardly, and determined–insecure. A second layer of dichotomies structures the meanings attributed to the violent practices of both warring parties. These meanings are, among others, necessary-unnecessary, last resort–provocative, limited effects–major effects, focused–indiscriminate, purposeful–senseless, unavoidable–avoidable, legitimate–illegitimate, legal–criminal, sophisticated–brutal and professional–undisciplined. The dichotomies in question can be defined as floating signifiers (Laclau & Mouffe, 1985: 112-113; Žižek, 1989: 97), binary oppositions and/or central oppositions (Berger, 1997). Floating signifiers have no fixed meaning, but are (re)articulated before, during, and after the conflict and inserted into different chains of equivalence. At the same time, they play a key role as nodal points in hegemonic projects, which attempt to fix their meaning. Both sides claim to be rational and civilized and to fight a good and just war, laying responsibility for the conflict with the enemy. In other words, both present their violent practices as focused, well-considered, purposeful, unavoidable, and necessary. The construction of the enemy is accompanied by the construction of the identity of the self as clearly antagonistic to the enemy's identity. In this process, not only the radical otherness of the enemy is emphasized, the enemy is also presented as a threat to "our own" identity.

Although the discourses that construct the enemy are widespread, specific groups of actors tend to play a vital role in the hegemonization of these discourses. These groups can benefit from unequal power relations that increase the weight of their statements. A first such group is usually referred to as the state, and includes governments, parliaments, political parties, advisory bodies and, last but not least, the military. A state holds decision-making powers, has to assume responsibility for waging war, and is held accountable for the course of war. However, thanks to its function as a political organ—representing and governing "the people"—its statements (and actions) also play a vital role in establishing or supporting a hegemonic process. As war is considered to be a very specific condition, threatening the existence of numerous human beings and possibly even the survival of the state itself, it is not sufficient to legitimate the war as such. Next to military victory, the mobilization of the support of the "home front" (national unity) becomes a prime political objective, legitimating hegemonic policies.

Next to censorship, one of the instruments that is widely used for the purpose of hegemonization is, of course, propaganda. Characteristic of propaganda is the fact that it is planned by organized groups, which can range from a small number of special advisors to large bureaucratic organizations responsible for propaganda and counter-propaganda efforts (Jowett, 1997: 75; Taylor, 1995: 6). This also marks the difference between propaganda and hegemony, as the latter is the relatively rigid but ultimately unstable result of a negotiative societal process determining the horizon of our thought in a specific social and temporal setting. Although propaganda can be instrumental in establishing hegemony, the societal construction of the collective will to fight a war transcends all propaganda efforts.

When attempting to further define propaganda, the parallel with ideology—again a much broader notion—is helpful. The traditional (negative) Marxist definition of ideology as false consciousness runs parallel with the common sense view of propaganda as untruthful. Taithe and Thornton (1999: 1) described this view as follows: "*most readers will assume that [propaganda] is largely composed of lies and deceits and that propagandists are ultimately manipulators and corrupt.*" More neutral definitions of ideology as a set of ideas that dominate a social formation allow for an approach that defines propaganda as a persuasive act with a more complex relationship toward truthfulness (Ellul, 1973). Taylor (1995) thus defined propaganda as the use of communication "*to convey a message, an idea, an ideology ... that is designed primarily to serve the self-interests of the person or people doing the communicating.*"

One of the major targets of the state's propaganda efforts are the mainstream media, which—as Kellner (1992: 57) remarked—should not be defined as hypodermic needles, but as "*a crucial site of hegemony.*" A wide range of information-management techniques has been developed in order to influence the (news) media's output. However, this does not imply that the mainstream media are defenseless victims. Here, the media's specificity should be taken into account, both at the organizational level and at the level of media professionals' identities. The majority of the Western media can be seen as relatively independent organizations, with specific objectives and specific values. Even the most liberal normative media theories focus on the obligation of mainstream (news) media to independently inform their audiences and to use that independence to subject state practices to public scrutiny. Moreover, media professionals claim to have access to the description of factuality and to represent truth or authenticity, which potentially runs counter to (some of) the propaganda efforts of the states at war. As a consequence, substantiation of this claim becomes unavoidable. Journalistic ethics and ritualistic procedures (Tuchman, 1972) have been put in place to guarantee the integrity, reliability and status of journalists as truth speakers (by analogy with Foucault, 1978) or truth reporters:

> The journalist's profession ... might be described as that of "authorized truthteller" or "licensed relayer of facts." ... Journalistic ethics can be seen as a device to facilitate the social construction of legitimacy, to mobilize the trust of the audience in what they are reading, hearing or seeing. (McNair, 1998: 65)

THE 2003 IRAQ WAR—THE PERSIAN GULF WAR II (OR III)[3]

The destruction of the World Trade Center on September 11, 2001, initiated the war on terrorism. Shortly after the attacks, the United States launched its first pre-emptive strike against the Taliban regime in Afghanistan and subsequently turned its attention to the Iraqi regime and the possible threat of weapons of mass destruction (WMD). As the UN Monitoring, Verification and Inspection Commission's (OVIC) new inspections appeared to have too little result, the United States tried to convince the UN Security Council to vote a new resolution. With the exception of the United Kingdom, the other permanent members of the Security Council made it abundantly clear that they would not support the resolution and might even veto it (Blix, 2004: 8). The United States and the United Kingdom (with the support of a number of other European states[4]) then decided to put an ultimatum to Iraq on March 17, 2003. Two days later the 2003 Iraq War started with a bombardment on Iraq's capital Baghdad, despite large anti-war protest marches, fierce resistance by countries like Russia, China, France, Germany, and (not to forget) Belgium, and the refusal by the UN Security Council to approve of the war.

After an initial quick march through the south of Iraq, resistance increased and the American troops were held up. There was also heavy fighting between Iraqi and British forces around Basra in southern Iraq. Despite this resistance, on April 4, American forces attacked Baghdad, which in its turn became the scene of heavy fighting, leading to the loss of many lives. On April 9, the war symbolically came to an end with the Firdos Square ritual, in which a huge Saddam Hussein statue was pulled down from its socket. Coalition troops gained control over the city of Tikrit on April 14 and 15, and George W. Bush declared major combat operations ended on May 1, during his speech on the USS Abraham Lincoln. After which the *"postwar war"* (Seib, 2004: 1)—which goes beyond the focus of this discourse-theoretical analysis—started.

Constructions of the Enemy and the Self: The Ideological Model of War

The 2003 Iraq War attracted global media attention and led to the deployment of large-scale media management. The state apparatuses ideologically positioned themselves long before the actual war started, by categorizing Iraq as one of the rogue states, belonging to the *"axis of evil"* (Bush, 2002) that formed a threat to world peace. Building on the constructions of the enemy created during the 1991 Gulf War and the subsequent cat-and-mouse disarmament game,[5] Iraq was isolated from the relative safety of the group of rogue states. The events of the preceding decade were translated into an antagonistic positioning between the USA (and its allies), which was seen as representing the (military) struggle against terrorism, and Iraq, which supposedly represented terrorism and the threat to world peace.

This articulation of the enemy once again centered on the Iraqi leader Saddam Hussein, who was defined through the state-as-person metaphor as the (individualized) main threat to the (Western) world. His evil nature was constructed (this time even more so than in the 1991 Gulf War) by referring to his (alleged) possession of WMD and his readiness to effectively use them. Strategic support for this construction was found in Iraq's brutal (military) history, especially in the first Gulf War (when between 1980 and 1988 Iran and Iraq fought a very bloody war) and in Iraq's use of chemical weapons against the Iranian troops that occupied the Kurdish city of Halabjah,[6] which resulted in the death of more than 5,000 civilians. Also Iraq's violent oppression of the Shiites and of the Kurdish minority added weight to the representation of the regime as evil and of its military actions as brutal, indiscriminate, and criminal. Based on this historical evidence and on new (but, as it turned out, faulty) evidence that Iraq had Nuclear, Biological, and Chemical (NBC) programs, the country and its military system ware articulated as a major threat to world security.

As the pre-conflict phase developed, the ideological model (see Fig. 1.1) underwent a further evolution. The processes of demonization were strengthened by the discursive creation of a victim. In this case, the Iraqi people were represented as the victims of Saddam Hussein's brutal dictatorship. The chain of equivalence linked with the enemy also included the fragmented nature of Iraqi society. At the civil level, this fragmentation became intertwined with the process of victimization, as the Iraqi people (as a whole) were disarticulated from the regime, which was defined as a threat to its own people.

Through this rearticulation, the signifier "people" was situated in the realm of the Anglo-American self, which was represented as its protector. At the military level, the fragmentation of Iraq was constructed by distinguishing between the elite Republican Guard and the regular army. The elite forces supporting the regime were dehumanized and considered to be part of the military technology. The regular army was seen as less supportive of the regime and remained (at least in a first phase) part of the "people," longing to be freed from oppression. This means that all Iraqi resistance became intrinsically linked with the regime, excluding all other legitimations for resistance.

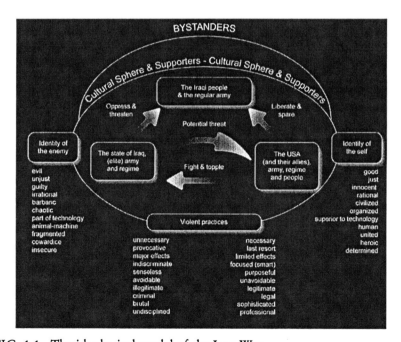

FIG. 1.1. The ideological model of the Iraq War.
Note: My special thanks to Sarah Maltby, editor of *Communicating War: Memory, Media and Military*, and her colleague Jarvis Cresdee, for improving the graphical quality of this model (published in Carpentier, 2007).

The so-called coalition, on the other hand, positioned itself as the heroic guarantor of world security. This positioning partially moved the process
of victimization to the level of the potential. The American (and other
Western) people were potential victims of Iraq's military force, directly
through Iraq's suspected possession and use of WMD and indirectly
through its supposed support for terrorist networks. The need to protect the
populations in the West legitimated the use of violence, which was presented as unavoidable and necessary. At the same time, the discourse on the self
was oriented toward the perceived need to liberate the main victim of the
pre-war situation, the Iraqi people. This articulation provided further support for the construction of a chain of equivalences that articulated the
Western states as good, just and determined.

This process of heroization was strengthened by the emphasis on the
coalition's mastery of superior technology, which it used rationally and with
care, and enabled it to execute surgical strikes with carefully circumscribed
and therefore limited effects, rendering human suffering almost invisible.
This virtualization of war excluded not only the destruction of human bodies on the enemy side from the discourses of war, but also embedded the
accidental loss of civilian life in the rhetoric of necessity. It furthermore
detached the good operator of military technology (the coalition soldier)
from the actual effects of that technology (death and destruction). These
processes of exclusion and detachment served but one purpose: to underscore the goodness of the professional coalition soldier, who only kills when
it is absolutely necessary. This goodness was linked to a homogenization of
the self. In contrast to the divided enemy, the coalition—its regimes, its military and its civilian population (the "home front")—was presented as united in its support for the just cause.

This ideological model of the war was supported by a huge propaganda effort, organized to manage the media output. Key elements in this were
the installation of an international press center at U.S. Central Command in
Qatar and the (renewed) use[7] of the embedding system. Although there
were unembedded journalists (unilaterals) at work in Iraq (with huge risks
involved—for an overview, see Gopsill, 2004), the images produced by the
embedded journalists, who drove along with the troops advancing through
southern Iraq, dominated much of the media coverage. *Chicago Tribune*
television critic Steve Johnson claimed these images painted "*a heroic picture of a rush to Baghdad*" (cited in Seib, 2004: 7). By means of their high-
tech videophones, embedded journalists produced low-tech-looking images
of tanks and armed troop carriers speeding through the desert.[8] Their comments were often as heroic as the images, as was exemplified by CNN
reporter Walter Rodgers (embedded with the U.S. Army Third Infantry
Division's seventh Cavalry Regiment), who spoke of "*a giant wave of steel
… ever pushing toward the Iraqi capital of Baghdad*" (Rodgers, 2003).

The Ideological Model Under Pressure

The ideological model described here cannot be considered as being stable or fixed during (or before and after) the war. From a Foucauldian perspective, it can be seen as the unstable overall discursive effect of a wide range of societal strategies aiming to define the enemy and the self. Although this ideological model was supported by a hegemonic project, different forms of resistance (outside as well as inside governments) attempted to rearticulate it. Furthermore, the stream of events generated by the war could in many cases—with the support of propaganda—become incorporated, but other events required the model to be rearticulated. In the more extreme cases, events even threatened the structural integrity of the ideological model. An earlier example of such an event was the Tet offensive during the Vietnam War, which severely crippled the Vietcong at the military level, but at the same time totally disrupted the American ideological framework. Within the discourse-theoretical frame, the term dislocation is used to refer to such a moment of social crisis. Torfing (1999: 301) defined dislocation as the destabilization of a discourse by events it is unable to integrate, domesticate, or symbolize. Dislocations disrupt discourses and identities, but at the same time form the breeding ground for the creation of new identities (Laclau, 1990: 39). Moreover, they bring to light the contingency of the social and in doing so become *"the very form of temporality, possibility and freedom"* (Laclau, 1990: 41-43, summarized by Torfing, 1999: 149).

In the case of the Iraq War, there were a number of events that put a major strain on the "original" ideological model. After the initial rush through the desert, the resistance of Iraqi forces increased, slowing down the advance. Illustrative of the surprise this caused was the repeated premature communication on the "fall" of Umm Qasr (and its harbor), showing how interpretations based on the original ideological model were contradicted by new events (in this case the continued resistance). Especially the resistance by (parts of) the regular army, which did not surrender *en masse*, required a first rearticulation of the ideological model, in which the regular army and the Iraqi people were seen as distinct from the regime. Further complications were the emergence of a new category of soldiers, the Fedayeen, and the first appearance of civil resistance, which was said to originate from members of the Ba'ath party. Second, the belief in the military and technological superiority of the coalition forces came under pressure following a number of "undesirable" killings, among others of Iraqi civilians, the relatively large number of American and British soldiers to die in accidents and under "friendly fire," and an American soldier's bizarre grenade attack on his "own" staff officers at Camp Pennsylvania on March 22, 2003. Especially disturbing, however, was the capturing by Iraqi forces of a number of American and British soldiers. During the Nassiriya incident, units of the

507th Maintenance Company (consisting of diesel and heavy equipment mechanics, a computer technician, supply clerks and sergeants, and cooks) ended up in the eastern suburbs of Nassiriya and were attacked. Nine 507th soldiers lost their lives. Two others and at least two Marines were killed during the rescue operation. Fourteen other Marines were killed in other actions in Nassiriya that same day (Rosenberg, 2003). Six were captured and soon appeared on different television channels. The United States chose to deal with this threat to the ideological model by reverting to propaganda of the act and on April 1 "airlifted" one captured and injured soldier (Jessica Lynch) from the Nassiriya hospital. Afterward, Lynch's capture was presented as a heroic event that strengthened the ideological model instead of threatening it. On April 3, 2003, the Fox News Channel Website brought the summary of this heroic story as it had been published by *The Washington Post*, on the basis of statements from *"unidentified U.S. officials"*:

> The Washington Post reported Thursday that the 19-year-old Army supply clerk shot several Iraqi soldiers during the March 23 ambush that resulted in her capture. She kept firing even after she had several gunshot wounds, finally running out of ammunition, the newspaper said, citing unidentified U.S. officials. (Fox News Channel, 2003)

From April 4 onward, the focus shifted to the battle for Baghdad, which posed no real threat to the ideological model. In this final phase, all disruptive events—such as the high number of Iraqi civilian casualties and the death of three journalists on April 9[9]—could be incorporated by referring to the fact that the victorious end of the war was at hand. In this short phase, the war could legitimate itself, because one of its main goals—the liberation of the Iraqi people—was close to its realization. When on April 9 the statue of Saddam Hussein at the Firdos square collapsed, the war (at least symbolically) came to an end and the *"postwar war"* (Seib, 2004: 1) commenced.

The second proclaimed goal of the armed intervention eventually lay at the basis of the ideological model's most fundamental disruption. The WMD were nowhere to be found. This fundamentally threatened the ideological model's structural integrity, because the goodness of the Anglo-American self proved to be founded on its prevention of the use of nonexisting WMD. Different strategies to cope with this near-dislocation were used in an effort to keep the model intact (at least during the war itself). A first and popular strategy was the blunt denial of the problem, by invoking arguments of time and space. More time was said to be required to discover the WMD that were surely there but were hidden somewhere in the immense country. A second strategy consisted in the repeated communication of important discoveries related to WMD. On March 27, for instance, the BBC reported that gas masks and protective suits had been discovered in an Iraqi command post, which according to the U.K. defense secretary was *"categorical proof"* of the fact that Iraq possessed chemical and biological weapons and was ready to use them (BBC, 2003). Third, war legitimizations increasingly stressed the dictatorial nature of the regime and the oppression of the Iraqi people, clearly steering away from the issue of WMD. In the meantime, little real evidence of WMD had been presented, which would lead to a number of political crises after the war. The above-described strategies were nevertheless successful in keeping the question of the possible existence of WMD unresolved until after the war.

Ideology and Structural Bias in the Media

Although media professionals and organizations like to believe that they are outside the operations of ideology (what Schlesinger, 1987, called the macromyth of independence), the ideological model proved difficult to escape. As the accompanying discourses on the enemy and the self were hegemonized and turned into common sense, they also became the interpretative frameworks of media professionals. Using Westerståhl and Johansson's (1994; see also Westerståhl, 1983) approach on objectivity[10] as a starting point, we can see how this ideological privileging of a specific interpretative framework strongly affected the construction of factuality and directly impacted on journalistic practices. In other words, what was to be defined as relevant and truthful and what would become represented in the media was contingent upon the ideological model.

The problems in the representation of war were aggravated by the application of the specific procedures and rituals (Tuchman, 1972) media professionals use to guarantee or legitimate their truth-speaking (and objectivity). On a number of levels, these procedures created so-called structural biases that were influenced by the operations of the ideological model of war. Daily journalistic practices and procedures are regulated by key concepts like balance, relevance, and truthfulness, which have an important impact on the representations journalists produce. As these fluid concepts have to be transformed into social practice, their content is rendered highly particular and specific. As we see here, this specificity in some cases favored the discourses of war. The specific articulation of these key concepts through the media professionals' daily practices thus found itself in a sometimes-strange alliance with this ideological model of war.

The specific articulations of relevance that are customary within the media system are strongly focused on elite sources or on what McNair (1998: 76-77) called *"establishment source[s]."* Bell (1991: 191) summarized this as follows: *"News is what an authoritative source tells a journalist. ... The more elite the source, the more newsworthy the story."* During periods of war, this often provides the political and military leadership with an almost unmediated access to the media, for instance through live and uninterrupted broadcasts of speeches to the nation and press conferences. Koch (1991) claimed that journalists tend to focus on journalistic events and ignore the actual occurrences (boundary events) that precede them, thus shifting the question of factuality from the fact-of-the-event to the fact-of-the-statement. Slightly overstating his case, Koch (1991) wrote that "*Reporters rarely question independently the legitimacy of the speaker's statements, and truth is reduced to the reasonably accurate reportage of what an official says in press conferences or a similarly public forum.*" These preferences allow the military and political representatives of states at war to communicate their ideological frameworks and discourses of the enemy and the self, thus maximizing the impact of their specific vocabularies and media management.

The impact of this specific articulation of relevance is further strengthened by the role of another key signifier: balance. Balance is often transformed into journalistic practice by guaranteeing access to "*legitimate elites on all major sides of a dispute*" (Entman, 1989: 37). In the case of war, this implies trying to complement statements made by the political and military representatives of the self with utterances coming from the political and military representatives of the enemy, although problems with access to the latter may skew the balance. Balance is often translated into a personalized balance, built on a comparison of (categories of) individuals. An argumentative balance, which creates a balance between arguments and/or discourses is rarely used. The result is that "*during warfare, objectivity in the sense of giving as much credibility to the enemy as to the spokespersons of one's own nation is close to impossible in the mainstream media*" (Tumber & Palmer, 2004: 165). The focus on members of the political and military establishment is further complemented by the contextualization given by military experts, (often retired) members of the military or academics who comment on the military strategies as they develop. Mainstream media attribute high relevance to the narration of war, which is supported by a continuous flow of images. Out of the complexity of military events, they try to extract a number of storylines allowing them to narrate the conflict on a daily basis. This narration is not only supported by the comments of military experts, but also by elements of the geography of war (maps and satellite pictures) and by images considered to be representative of "the day's events." These images often testify to the mainstream media's fascination for or, as Galtung and Vincent (1992: 211-212) have it, glorification of the technology of death and destruction, but tend to shy away from showing the effects of its use (human suffering). In other words, mainstream media dissociate themselves from the materiality of war (Carruthers, 2000: 276).

Media professionals also adopt specific articulations of truthfulness. Adding to the workings of the ideological frameworks discussed above is the fact that procedures and rituals meant to guarantee the factuality of mainstream media output (source diversity, check and double-check) often fail during periods of war due to spatial and temporal constraints. Moreover, information is often scarce and hard to obtain, while mainstream media are in constant need of new facts and events. As Jim Scotton remarked:

> we have a big, 24-hour machine that now demands to be fed, and if you don't have anything to feed it, make something up, or at least find something. The problem is that we have an operation that is ready to feed it, and that is the government. (cited in Seib, 2004: 65)

In many cases, this led to speculation and misinformation, based on assumptions provided by the ideological model. As mentioned previously, this was especially the case when mainstream media were dealing with the issue of WMD. Other examples are the counterattack of a column of ghost tanks from Baghdad, and the mythical popular uprising in Basra.

Finally, direct and indirect political and economic pressures (including censorship) had their impact on the mainstream media output as well, not just by limiting their access to Iraq (before, during, and after the war), but also by filtering the representations of war. An interesting example is the Pentagon's ban on images of dead soldiers' "homecomings" at Dover Air Force Base. This ban was eventually lifted following legal action undertaken by a Website called the Memory Hole.[11]

Media Resistance

Although the processes described here often characterize the mainstream media output, one should be careful not to homogenize the diversity of media organizations and practices. In a number of cases, mainstream media did manage to produce counter-hegemonic meanings. They provided spaces for critical debate, in-depth analysis and humor. They showed, on a number of occasions, the horror of war. They also attempted to counter some of the basic premises of the ideological model,[12] giving a face to the Iraqi victims and paying attention to the strong European and the less strong U.S. popular resistance against the war. Tumber and Palmer (2004: 164) summarized the situation in the United Kingdom as follows: "*Unlike the anti-Vietnam protests ... the anti-war protest over Gulf War II, consisting of a politically and socially diverse coalition, was given space and prominence in the media.*"

It should also be pointed out that a number of public spheres outside the mainstream media critiqued or complemented the hegemonic ideological model. As was the case during previous wars, (part of) the Internet served as a critical sphere, with Web sites like ZMag, Truthout and Oneworld and Web blogs like the Salim Pax blog.[13] Other spheres, like the streets, books, magazines, cartoons, and popular culture in general, can contain discourses that attempt to disrupt the hegemonic discourses of war. An almost visionary example of this can be found in George Michael's pop song and video clip *Shoot the dog* which contained a (rather amusing) critique of the British dependence on the United States, depicting Tony Blair as Bush's puppy and thus attempting to disarticulate the homogeneous Anglo-American self.

A CASE STUDY: A BROADCAST BY NORTH BELGIAN PUBLIC TELEVISION

To illustrate the presence of the ideological model in the mainstream media and the implications of their specific articulations of relevance, balance, and truthfulness, one North Belgian news broadcast (April 7, 2003, produced by the public broadcaster VRT[14]) is analyzed here. Given Belgium's specific status and policies during the Iraqi War and its still very present cultural proximity to the United States and the United Kingdom,[15] it is more than interesting to see how the discourses on the enemy and the "self" are still (partially) present, even when the state in which the broadcasting company is situated, is opposing the war.

Basic Binary Oppositions in the News Broadcast of April 7, 2003

In the news broadcast under consideration,[16] the discourses on the Anglo-American self and the enemy are present on a number of levels. Most of the representations in it focus on the military and their activities. First, the American and British troops are shown in Baghdad and in Basra, in full control of the situation. The individualized soldiers are portrayed as calm, professional, and masculine. In both cities, soldiers are seen to enter "Saddam's" palaces, an act symbolizing the defeat of the regime. On one occasion, a journalist adds the following comment: "*American soldiers walking around freely [in the palace], this must be hard to take for the Iraqi side.*" These palaces are indeed loaded with symbolism, not only because of their obvious connection with the Iraqi regime, but also because they played a crucial role in the history of the conflict at hand. Indeed, the refusal to grant the inspection teams permission to visit these sites contributed to the escalation of the conflict. Moreover, in both news items on the taking of the palaces images of the presidential bathrooms are shown, including shots of golden taps. These shots present the Iraqi regime as corrupt, irresponsible and wasteful and thus once again articulate the Anglo-American intervention as good and necessary. Furthermore, the emphasis is on the welcome given to Western soldiers, who are thus articulated as liberators. One British tank commander is quoted as saying: *"The reception is really positive, this is the best we've seen so far."* The item on the normalization, too, articulates the Western military invasion as a form of liberation because it emphasizes that the Shiites can now execute their rituals again and that Ahmad Chalabi, *"the leader of the official resistance,"* has returned to Iraq.

The Iraqi regime and its soldiers are portrayed in an entirely different way. The Iraqi soldiers are presently absent: Their presence legitimates and gives meaning to the entire military operation, but at the same time they are not represented. Their bodies are erased from the screens. In this specific broadcast, there are two exceptions to this interplay of presence and absence: In one shot, a number of Iraqi soldiers are seen from a distance fleeing, while in another members of the police force are shown in a rather fanatic dance of support for the Iraqi regime. These images articulate the enemy as defeated and cowardly on the one hand, and as mad and irrational on the other. The regime is formally represented by al-Sahaf, who is—as usual and without any (strategic) contextualization—quoted as saying that the Iraqi forces will *"slaughter them all,"* which only adds to the ridiculization of the regime. The attention bestowed on "Comical Ali"—the nickname is not used in this broadcast—is complemented with an item focusing on "Chemical Ali" (who is mentioned in this news broadcast by Captain Lockwood, the British military spokesperson in Qatar) or Ali Hassan al-Majid, who was reportedly killed in a rocket attack. This report is combined with the (horrific) images of civilians killed during the chemical attack on Halabjah and with footage of Ali Hassan al-Majid torturing prisoners.

Specific Articulations of Relevance, Balance, and Truth

As discussed earlier, a series of specific (local) journalistic practices strengthen the dichotomized articulations of the enemy and the self. The specificity of the key concepts of balance, relevance, and truth that structure journalistic behavior can be seen at work in this broadcast on a number of occasions.

Because balance is operationalized as balance between representatives of both political and military systems, elite sources dominate the broadcast (along with the media professionals' voices). Table 1.1 shows that out of 11 interviewees, 5 are formal (4) or informal (1) military spokespersons. Furthermore, one member of the British political elite (Defense Secretary Hoon) is quoted, and Kofi Annan is granted 23 seconds of speaking time.

Table 1.1. Statements Made During the April 7 Broadcast

JOURNALIST	SPEAKING TIME	INTERVIEWEE	TYPE*	SPEAKING TIME
J1 (anchor)	365	1	MS (I)	23
J2	121	2	MS (US)	22
J3	50	3	Victim 1 (I)	5
J4 (correspondent)	152	4	Victim 2 (I)	19
J5	105	5	MS (UK)	3
J6	24	6	CiV (I)	12
J7	58	7	MS (UK)	15
J8	62	8	P (UK)	9
J9 (correspondent)	151	9	MS (UK)	11
Headlines	4	10	ME (B)	129
		11	P (UN)	23
Total	1,092 seconds		Total	271 seconds

Note: P, politician; MS, military spokesperson; ME, military expert; CiV, civilian. The country code is added.

This also means that Western voices dominate the broadcast: Out of five military representatives, only one (al-Sahaf) represents the Iraqi enemy. Another opinion considered relevant is that of a North Belgian military expert, who in a relatively long interview analyzes the situation in Baghdad from a military perspective. All with the exception of Kofi Annan make use of the discourse of war in its many different forms.

Next to the discourses of war used by the enemy's and the Anglo-American selves' different spokespersons and political and military representatives, it is the narration of war that dominates the news broadcast. Especially the first item is intended to summarize the military events, as can be illustrated by the first voice-over in the broadcast:

> Day 19 of the war in Iraq. The center of Baghdad is the scene of heavy fighting between Americans and Iraqis. There is heavy fighting at the banks of the River Tigris . . .

This voice-over is preceded by an animation showing a little tank driving from the Baghdad periphery to the center of the city. The map then changes into a satellite picture of the site of one of the palaces. Also on other occasions, maps will illustrate the uninterrupted flow of (military) movement, which gratifies the media's need to narrate, but also entraps them in a militarized narrative. Finally, many illustrative subitems use footage showing coalition troops during their "professional activities," without showing the (lethal) end result of these activities.

Abstraction made from these specific articulations of relevance and balance, the problem of speculation and/or misinformation becomes very present when the Washington correspondent refers to the discovery of new "evidence" of the presence of WMD in Iraq. In a live interview during the news broadcast, the North Belgian correspondent claims that this *"evidence"* shows that *"there's something going on"* and that this *"discovery"* strengthens the case of the Americans. Again, the Iraqi enemy's supposed possession of WMD frames him as evil.

> Anchor: Now, for the first time, there are clues that illegal chemical weapons have been found, we've received brief reports on this, and I've mentioned this already. Do you know anything more about this?

> Correspondent: Well, in the past hours a few reports have become known. First: about 20 missiles, armed with chemical weapons, were found in a military camp south of Baghdad. Probably it was Sarin and mustard gas. ... And a number of barrels with chemicals were found in a chemical factory. ... There's something going on, and this is crucial for the Americans. They've been looking for what they call the smoking gun, the evidence for WMDs. This strengthens their case.

Critical Reporting

The Anglo-American intervention is legitimated by two major arguments, Iraq's potential use of WMD and the bloody oppression of the Iraqi people by "their" regime. Despite the aforementioned presence of the discourses on the enemy and the Anglo-American selves, a number of statements nuance these discourses of war. The threatening dislocation because of the absence of WMD in Iraq is already present in the broadcast. Before the correspondent announces the supposed discovery of the "smoking gun," the military expert already stressed that these types of discoveries are too insignificant to be defined as evidence (and to legitimate the war).

Second, the articulation of the Anglo-American self as good liberators is contradicted on two levels. On the first level, the horror and death caused by the war are explicitly shown and discussed. These narratives and images counterbalance the articulation of the Anglo-American forces as good and innocent and as fighting a clean war, because now they are seen to be responsible for the loss of innocent civilian lives. In the first item of the news broadcast, a man who has lost his family is given the opportunity to express his grief and fury, saying: *"Dead, they're all dead because of these sons of bitches."* Other men are seen (and heard) crying and comforting each other. The second item of the news broadcast focuses entirely on the human suffering in Baghdad, showing a number of injured people in the Al Kindi hospital. Again, one victim is allowed to express herself,[17] telling how her daughter was injured. Also the number of injured (176) and killed (4) people who were brought to this hospital, is explicitly mentioned. The news broadcast focuses not only on the deaths of ordinary citizens. It also mentions the two journalists and the four American and three British soldiers who were killed that day. However, with the exception of the announced death of an Iraqi regime leader (al-Majid), no mention is made of the number of Iraqi soldiers that were killed. Once again, they remain absent.

On a second level, the articulation of the Anglo-American self as liberators is contested by including an interview with an Iraqi car driver. In this *vox pop* interview, the man explains that he feels happy the regime has been removed, but that the Western military presence should only be temporary: *"the Americans and British can liberate Iraq, but they can't stay."* By allowing this (presumably) Iraqi citizen to express his position, the triumphant entry of the British troops in Basra is put into perspective, because a representative of the victimized Iraqi people is seen and heard to be not univocally satisfied with the liberation of his country.

Finally, the unity of the Western self is contested through a strong emphasis on the popular resistance against the war. These items disarticulate the Belgian identity from the Anglo-American selves, further shattering the desired discursive unity in the West and fundamentally criticizing the ideological model of war. A more general quantitative analysis of the war coverage in both the main commercial news broadcast (VTM) and the main public broadcaster's news broadcast (VRT) during the "entire" war[18] shows that a relatively large share of the war items actually focus on the civil protest against the war (see Fig. 1.2). Especially in the first week of the war, proportions as high as 15% and 20% are no exception.

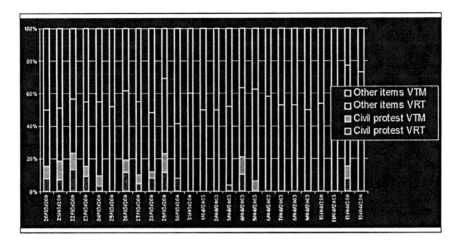

FIG. 1.2. Items on civil protest on VTM and VRT main news broadcasts (March 20–April 13).

CONCLUSION

The discursive-theoretical approach allows highlighting both the stability and the contingency (or the fixity and non-fixity) of the representation(s) of war. The complex series of events that make up a war appear to be highly elusive and impossible to adequately represent. Moreover, the processes of mediation involved in representing a war are highly politicized. Influencing them is an important goal for the hegemonic projects of the states at war. A variety of discursive strategies aiming to stabilize and fix meaning engulf the practices of war and propagate a dichotomized ideological model, built on such traditional binary oppositions as good–evil, just–unjust, innocent–guilty, rational–irrational, civilized–barbaric, organized–chaotic, superior to technology–being a part of technology, human–animal-machine, united–fragmented, heroic–cowardly, and determined–insecure.

Laclau and Mouffe's theoretical elaborations thus allow stressing the operations of hegemony and their impact on all societal levels. Hegemony (and the related notion of social antagonism) provides a crucial theoretical tool to better understand the interconnectedness of discourses emanating from the state and the media, the relative powerlessness of the media to escape the ideological model and the (direct or indirect) legitimation of what Knightley (1982) called "*the institution of war.*" Even in a North Belgian news broadcast, the difficulty to break loose from this ideological model becomes obvious.

This model is built on its taken-for-grantedness and indeed becomes a social horizon for the majority of social actors, including journalists. Within the media system, the workings of this ideological model are further enhanced by propaganda and censorship, and by structural, military, technological, and political pressures, resulting in media representations that can only be described as exclusionary towards a considerable number of other meanings, interpretations and discourses. The specific articulation of objectivity through journalistic practice leads to an overrepresentation of military and political representatives of the states at war, which is skewed towards U.S. and U.K. representatives, the contextualization of war by military experts and an emphasis on the episodic narration of (the course of) war. One of the main consequences of these specific articulations is the decontextualization of the conflict and, hence, the underrepresentation of its complex causes, of the motives and interests of all parties involved and of the future power structure. The human cost of the conflict and its long-term impact also receive only limited attention.

At the same time, this (discourse-theoretical analysis of the) war coverage provides us with some hope, given the way North Belgian editorial teams handled the identities of the American and British armies and regimes. The televisional presence of images showing the numerous victims of the war—horrible as they may be—combined with the ample attention for the civil and political resistance against the war forms the core of a critical media discourse that strongly nuances the Anglo-American ideological model of war. Media professionals in North Belgium have also shown a certain degree of openness to including footage produced by some of the Middle-East-based broadcasting companies (Al Jazeera can hardly go unmentioned here). This not only made the specificity of the ideological model even clearer, allowing for new and critical information sources to be included, but also showed the specificity and contingency of local media practices, routines and ideologies.

It should be added that the national consensus facilitated the North Belgian media professionals' work. Journalists working in the nations at war faced more difficulties when trying to deviate from the ideological model of war (Miller, 2004; Tumber & Palmer, 2004). In comparison to the British or U.S. media, the North Belgian media found themselves operating in a very different situation because the large majority of the population and of the political regime were opposed to the war. The presence of this inversed hegemony legitimated the inclusion of counter-hegemonic discourses. Even under these conditions, however, the dichotomized discourses of war, based on a Western perspective toward the enemy, managed to sneak into the war coverage.

In order to reduce this omnipresence of the discourse of war based on the good–evil and other dichotomies, a long list of needs can be drafted. Publications on the media–war relationship often end with the expression of some sort of hope—hope for more public debate, for organizational learning in the media or for the end of the pursuit of politics by other means. This text just ends with a needs list. These needs include the following:

- The need for more critical and structural information transcending the dichotomies embedded in the ideological model
- The need to rethink objectivity (neutrality, balance, relevance and truth)
  - v The need to explicitly protect the universal value of peace (and freedom and justice)
  - v The need to strive for an argumentative equilibrium
  - v The need to accept the relevance of civil society and their experts
  - v The need to avoid speculation
- The need to represent the horror of war
- The need to sketch the broader (past, present and future) context
- The need for a diversity of journalisms
- The need for more modesty
- The need for journalists to be given access
- The need for more safety for (unembedded) journalists
- The need for a critical dialogue between academics and media professionals

ACKNOWLEDGEMENT

Special thanks to Maite Ceusters for assisting in in the research project on North Belgian media representations of war, and to Sofie Van Bauwel for her valuable comments on an earlier version of this chapter.

NOTES

1. In this analysis, the point of departure is the construction of the Western (or more specific, the Anglo-American) self, which places Iraq in the position of the enemy. Naturally, this position (and this analysis) can be inversed.
2. See also Haraway's (1991) discussion of dichotomies, with its specific focus on the human–machine dichotomy.
3. The name of this conflict is in itself already problematic, as in most cases the count tends to exclude the "first" Persian Gulf War, namely the Iran–Iraq war (1980–1988). The absence of a clear Western involvement seems to justify this exclusion. In this chapter, the more neutral term "2003 Iraq war" is used. Media are of course confronted with similar problems, and their choices differ significantly, as Bodi (2004: 244–245) remarked: *"Al Jazeera's tag for the conflict was*

'War on Iraq,' in contrast to the BBC's neutral 'War in Iraq' and Fox News' jingoistic 'Operation Iraqi Freedom,' which merely parroted the Pentagon's name for the conflict."

4. On January 30, 2003, Spain, Italy, Portugal, Hungary, Poland, Denmark, and the Czech Republic joined the United Kingdom in signing a statement of solidarity with the U.S. position.

5. The northern no-fly zone was created by the United States, the United Kingdom, and France on April 7, 1991. On April 11, 1991, Iraq accepted Resolution 687, which imposed the dismantling of its long-distance missiles and nuclear, biological, and chemical weapons. This resolution also formed the legal basis of the inspections by the International Atomic Energy Agency, and the U.N. Special Commission, and approved the continuation of the sanctions imposed on Iraq after its occupation of Kuwait. The southern no-fly zone was installed on August 27, 1992. Both the inspections and the no-fly zones gave rise to a low-intensity conflict, resulting in the occasional bombing of Iraqi *"positions."* In order to alleviate the effects of the sanctions on the civil population, the Food for Oil program was put in place on April 15, 1995 (Resolution 986). France ended its collaboration to the protection of the northern and southern no-fly zones in 1996 and 1998 respectively. The weapons inspectors left Iraq in December 1998, only to return in November 2002, backed by Resolution 1441.

6. This was not the first time poison gas was used in this region. This doubtful honor belongs to Egypt, which used poison gas during its military campaign in Yemen (1962-1967) (Oren, 2003: 5).

7. For a brief history of embedded journalism, see Freedman (2004).

8. The videophones often malfunctioned. For an illustrative report see Kevin Sites' blog at http://www.kevinsites.net/2003_11_09_archive.html

9. Two of them (José Couso and Tara Protsyuk) were killed when a U.S. tank took a shot at the Palestine hotel. Al Jazeera journalist Tarek Ayyoub died when a missile hit the network's Baghdad bureau.

10. Westerståhl's model distinguishes between factuality and impartiality. Factuality has two components: relevance and truth(fulness). Impartiality, too, has two components: balance and neutrality.

11. http://www.thememoryhole.org, edited and published by Russ Kick.

12. A modest but interesting example of this is provided in the April 4, 2003 issue of the North Belgian newspaper *De Morgen*, which referred to the coalition as a *"mini-coalition."*

13. http://www.zmag.org/; http://www.truthout.org/; http://www.oneworld.net/; http://tv.oneworld.net/; http://dearraed.blogspot.com/. For a printed version of the blog, see Pax (2003).

14. Access to this broadcast was kindly provided by the Electronic News Archive.

15. This proximity legitimates the use of the Anglo-American self and the Iraqi enemy as an analytical construct. As mentioned before, this analysis could very well be inversed.

16. In this specific news broadcast, about half of the available time (22:51 of a total length of 44:42) is attributed to the Iraq War. In these 23 minutes, eight items can be distinguished, three of which are announced as headlines. These items are: (a) the events of day 19—the American forces are strangling Baghdad; (b) the situation in the Iraqi hospitals; (c) the current situation in Baghdad—a live talk with

the correspondent in Baghdad; (d) British troops are entering Basra; (e) a state of affairs with a military expert (Prof. Luc de Vos); (f) a return to normality in South-Iraq; (g) the post-war discussion: Blair/Bush & U.N.; and (h) a live talk with the Washington correspondent on future U.S. policies.

17. It is relatively rare for victims to be not merely portrayed, but also to be given the opportunity to express their views. This news broadcast contains two different items, in both of which a victim of the coalition bombardments is granted this opportunity.

18. The analysis included 1,185 news items, 569 of which were war items, broadcast from 20 March to April 13, 2003.

REFERENCES

BBC (2003) "Proof' of Biological Weapons Found, March 27, 2003.' Retrieved April 22, 2004, from http://news.bbc.co.uk/1/hi/world/middle_east/2892077.stm

Bell, A. (1991) *The Language of News Media*. Oxford: Blackwell.

Berger, A.A. (1997) *Narratives in Popular Culture, Media and Everyday Life*. London: Sage.

Blix, H. (2004) *Disarming Iraq: The Search for Weapons of Mass Destruction*. London: Bloomsbury.

Bodi, F. (2004) 'Al Jazeera's War,' pp. 243-250 in D. Miller (Ed) *Tell Me Lies: Propaganda and Distortion in the Attack on Iraq*. London: Pluto Press.

Bush, G.W. (2001) 'Address to a Joint Session of Congress and the American People, September 20, 2001.' Retrieved April 22, 2004, from http://www.whitehouse.gov/news/releases/2001/09/20010920-8.html

Bush, G.W. (2002) 'President Delivers State of the Union Address, January 29, 2002.' Retrived April 22, 2004, from http://www.whitehouse.gov/news/releases/2002/01/20020129-11.html

Carpentier, N. (2007) 'Fighting Discourses: Discourse Theory, War and Representations of the 2003 Iraqi War,' pp. 103-116 in S. Maltby and R. Keeble (Eds) *Communicating War: Memory, Media and Military*. Bury St Edmunds: Abramis.

Carruthers, S. (2000) *The Media at War: Communication and Conflict in the Twentieth Century*. London: Macmillan.

Ellul, J. (1973) *Propaganda: The Formation of Men's Attitudes*. New York: Vintage Books.

Entman, R.M. (1989) *Democracy Without Citizens: Media and the Decay of American Politics*. New York, Oxford: Oxford University Press.

Foucault, M. (1978) *History of Sexuality: Part 1: An Introduction*. New York: Pantheon.

Fox News Channel (2003) 'Report: Lynch Was Shot, Stabbed in Fierce Struggle with Iraqi Captors, April 03, 2003.' Retrieved March 15, 2004 from, http://www.foxnews.com/story/0,2933,82923,00.html

Freedman, D. (2004) 'Misreporting War Has a Long History,' pp. 63-69 in D. Miller
    (Ed) *Tell Me Lies. Propaganda and Distortion in the Attack on Iraq.* London:
    Pluto Press.
Galtung, J. (1998) *The Peace Journalism Option.* Taplow, Bucks: Conflict and Peace
    Forums.
Galtung, J. (2000) *Conflict Transformation by Peaceful Means: The TRANSCEND
    Method.* Geneva: UNDP.
Galtung, J., Jacobsen, C.G., Brand-Jacobsen, K.F. (2001) *Searching for Peace.*
    London: Pluto Press.
Galtung, J., Vincent, R.C. (1992) *Global Glasnost: Toward a New World Information
    and Communication Order?* Cresskill, NJ: Hampton Press.
Gopsill, T. (2004) 'Target the Media,' pp. 251-261 in D. Miller (Ed) *Tell Me Lies.
    Propaganda and Distortion in the Attack on Iraq.* London: Pluto Press.
Haraway, D. (1991) 'A Cyborg Manifesto: Science, Technology, and Socialist-femi-
    nism in the Late Twentieth Century,' pp. 149-181 in D. Haraway (Ed) *Simians,
    Cyborgs and Women: The Reinvention of Nature.* New York: Routledge.
Jowett, G. (1997) 'Toward a Propaganda Analysis of the Gulf War,' pp. 74-85 in B.
    Greenberg and W. Gantz (Eds) *Desert Storm and the Mass Media.* Cresskill, NJ:
    Hampton Press.
Keen, S. (1986) *Faces of the Enemy.* New York, Harper and Row.
Kellner, D. (1992) *The Persian Gulf TV War.* Boulder, San Francisco, Oxford:
    Westview Press.
Knightley, P. (1982) *The First Casualty of War.* London: Quartet.
Koch, T. (1991) *Journalism in the 21st Century: Online Information, Electronic
    Databases and the News.* Twickenham: Adamantine Press.
Laclau, E. (1988) 'Metaphor and Social Antagonisms,' pp. 249-257 in C. Nelson and
    L. Grossberg (Eds) *Marxism and the Interpretation of Culture.* Urbana:
    University of Illinois.
Laclau, E. (1990) *New Reflections on the Revolution of Our Time.* London: Verso.
Laclau, E., Mouffe, C. (1985) *Hegemony and Socialist Strategy: Towards a Radical
    Democratic Politics.* London: Verso.
McGoldrick, A., Lynch, J. (2000) *Peace Journalism: How to Do it?* Retrieved March
    15, 2004, from http://www.transcend.org/pjmanual.htm
McNair, B. (1998) *The Sociology of Journalism.* London, New York, Sydney,
    Auckland: Arnold.
Miller, D. (Ed.) (2004) *Tell Me Lies: Propaganda and Distortion in the Attack on
    Iraq.* London: Pluto Press.
Mouffe, C. (1997) *The Return of the Political.* London: Verso.
Oren, M.B. (2003) *Six Days of War: June 1967 and the Making of the Modern
    Middle East.* New York: Ballantine Books.
Pax, S. (2004) *The Baghdad Blog.* London: Atlantic Books.
Rodgers, W. (2003) 'Imagine a Giant Wave of Steel, March 21, 2003.' CNN.com.
    Retrieved March 15, 2004 from, http://www.cnn.com/2003/WORLD/
    meast/03/21/btsc.irq.rodgers/
Rosenberg, H.L. (2003) 'Bloody Sunday. The Real Story of What Happened to
    Jessica Lynch's Convoy, June 17, 2003.' ABCNews, Retrieved April 22, 2004,
    from   http://abcnews.go.com/sections/primetime/World/
    iraq_507convoy030617 _pt1.html

Sayyid, B., Zac, L. (1998) 'Political Analysis in a World without Foundations,' pp. 249-267 in E. Scarbrough and E. Tanenbaum (Eds) *Research Strategies in the Social Sciences*. Oxford: Oxford University Press.

Schlesinger, P. (1987) *Putting 'Reality' Together*. London, New York: Methuen.

Seib, P. (Ed) (2004) *Lessons from Iraq: The News Media and the Next War. The Lucius W. Nieman Symposium 2003*. Milwaukee: Marquette University.

Taithe, B., Thornton, T. (1999) 'Propaganda: A Misnomer of Rhetoric and Persuasion?,' pp. 1-24 in B. Taithe and T. Thornton (Eds) *Propaganda: Political Rhetoric and Identity 1300-2000*. Phoenix Mill: Sutton Publishing.

Taylor, P.M. (1995) *Munitions of the Mind: A History of Propaganda From the Ancient World to the Present Era*. Manchester: Manchester University Press.

Torfing, J. (1999) *New Theories of Discourse: Laclau, Mouffe and Žižek*. Oxford: Blackwell.

Tuchman, G. (1972) 'Objectivity as a Strategic Ritual: An Examination of Newsmen's Notions of Objectivity,' *American Journal of Sociology* 77: 660-679.

Tumber, H., Palmer, J. (2004) *Media at War: The Iraq Crisis*. London: Sage.

Westerståhl, J. (1983) 'Objective news reporting,' *Communication Research* (10): 403-424.

Westerståhl, J., Johansson, F. (1994) 'Foreign News: News Values and Ideologies,' *European Journal of Communication* 9(1): 71-89.

Žižek, S. (1989) *The Sublime Object of Ideology*. London: Verso.

2

READING THE NEW HORIZON

*The Role of Romanian Media Discourse
in the 2004 Election Power Shift*

Henrieta Anişoara Şerban

As all discourses, media discourses position objects and subjects within discursive structures. Following Laclau and Mouffe's (1985: 105) definition of articulation as *"any practice establishing a relation among elements such that their identity is modified as a result of the articulatory practice,"* we immediately need to stress the particularity of both these identities and media discourses. The starting point of this chapter is that media discourses (defined as discourses that circulate within the media sphere) are always the outcome of historically situated circumstances that are ever-changing and fluid. Moreover, media discourses are never safe from the intrusion of elements coming from the surplus of meaning generated by the field of discursivity. New events, actors, developments, or interpretations can change contemporary articulations and therefore also the shape of the discursive structure.

In this chapter, the focus is placed on the 2004 Romanian elections, which resulted in a major political and societal change in Romania, as the hegemonic discursive order was replaced by a counter-hegemonic order, which in turn established a new hegemony. Furthermore, this chapter investigates how a segment of Romanian media was instrumental in providing discursive support for this change by looking at the claims made by politicians in the media and especially at journalists commenting on politicians and on political events during the 2004 Romanian electoral campaign.

MEDIA AND DISCOURSE

Drawing on poststructuralist thought, Laclau and Mouffe showed that discourses (and therefore also media discourses) play a crucial role in the complex interaction between subjects and subject positions. Media discourses contribute to the structuring of social reality, a process resulting in a structure that never reaches full closure (Torfing, 1999: 19). Media discourses thus contribute to the present sociopolitical constellation without totally replacing the social and/or the political. They are essential, critical and necessary in picking, out of many possible alternatives and with some degree of legitimacy, the constellation that is to be "the present," our "present."

Media discourses lend themselves perfectly to the nuanced analysis Laclau (and Mouffe) offer when dealing with the relationship between the universal and the particular. The nuance resides in the rejection of a pure particularism (Torfing, 1999: 171) based on the view that the universal does exist, but only as an *"empty place which can be partially filled in a variety of ways"* (Laclau, 1996: 59). The universal does not simply adapt itself to a particular social constellation, it is in fact *produced* by it. The paradox is fundamental: the universal is irreconcilable with any particularity, and at the same time utterly meaningless without the particular (Laclau, 1996: 34). Arguing along these lines, I advance that media discourses create a space and a site for this dialectical play of the universal and the particular by providing the building blocks for the construction of solidarity through processes of universalization. This line of reasoning also provides support for the argument that media discourses are a vector of hegemonization.

Capitalizing on Antonio Gramsci's work, Laclau and Mouffe emphasized the usefulness of the notion of hegemony for theorizing attempts to achieve discursive fixity.[1] Media discourses cannot be seen in isolation from the hegemonic struggles that take place within society, which leads us to claim that the media contribute to the legitimation and hegemonization of a present. In other words, media can co-legitimize the intricate fabric of identities and subject positions, representing them as "stabilized" and "permanent" within a "present" social order.

Simultaneously, in their discussion of radical democracy Laclau and Mouffe (1985) stressed the importance of a radical pluralism allowing for a polyphony of voices, in which the different (radical) democratic political struggles—such as antiracism, anti-sexism and anti-capitalism—can play an important role without being muted by dominant ideologies and without one struggle being necessarily privileged over another (Mouffe, 1997: 18). Media organizations do not offer the ideal space for this polyphony of voices to unfold before a benevolent public. They do, however, constitute a discursive vista for the "noisiest" struggles, which may find their way to the newspaper columns and airwaves after all. The case study of the Romanian media shows that media organizations can actually take on this role. A number of Romanian media organizations even became part of the (radical) democratic struggle in their fight against corruption and for the democratization of Romanian society.

ROMANIAN MEDIA DISCOURSES ON THE NOVEMBER 2004 ELECTIONS

The Romanian media discourses during the November 2004 parliamentary and presidential elections articulated the identities of the political parties into two antagonistic groups. The Romanian political scene is characterized by a multiparty political system, but two main political forces were given the bulk of the public attention, both by citizens and by political analysts: the *Social Democrat Party* (SDP) and the *Liberal-Democratic Coalition Justice and Truth/Dreptate și Adevăr*.[2] The coalition consisted of the *Liberal Party* (LP) and the *Democratic Party* (DP), with Theodor Stolojan and Traian Băsescu as their respective political leaders. Adrian Năstase was the incumbent head of the SDP Executive. Before the elections, the SDP held most seats in Parliament.

Since 1989, when the SDP came to power, all non-SDP leaders had been more or less subtly persuaded to join the party. In Romanian, this phenomenon was called *pedserizare*, or *esdeperization*, which can be translated in English as being forced to become an SDP member. During the election period, SDP party members had to address this issue in order to prevent the identity of their party from becoming disarticulated from good governance, transparency, and democracy. For instance, after the second round of the presidential elections on November 17, 1996, Minister of Commerce Dan Ioan Popescu declared in a television talk show:

> For us as well, this is not a question of simply covering up our wounds, but of effectively cleaning whatever was wrong inside the party. You see, we have always been accused of *esdeperization*. In my opinion, this was not compulsory *esdeperization*, as it was generally seen. On many occasions, it had to do with a backward mentality. Some spineless people said

to themselves: "I will enroll into the party that is able to offer me protection." Which other party could have offered protection, except from the one that was in government? Thus, also bottom–up *esdeperization* existed. It did not only go the other way around. The political functions in the administration were available from a certain level only. It is very important to understand that, from the general director through the lower levels of the hierarchy, the accent is put on professionalism. If the political fluctuations that took place in these days and that will take place in the future, would lead to administrative convulsions, the effects would be huge. And I think the debates that have taken place here tonight are useful to clarify all problems of this sort. (Antena 1, 2004 — debate with [among others] Dan Ioan Popescu; author's translation)

As this party member explains, de-*esdeperization* is articulated as work-in-progress. The current level of *esdeperization* should be excused and understood given the fact that there was also bottom–up *esdeperization* (along with *esdeperization* imposed from above). In 2001, the vice-president of the *Christian Democratic National Peasants' Party* (CDNPP[3]), Vasile Lupu, stated that *esdeperization* meant that the peasants' property rights were ignored, as the structures of the state simply became SDP structures. He also maintained that justice became an SDP "family business," which was primarily concerned with intimidating journalists instead of bringing the "rule of law" to the country, and stated his intention to inform the European Popular Party about this situation. On June 9, 2001, the newspaper *Evenimentul zilei* published an article on this statement headlining: *A party with a vindication. The PNTCD tells the West about esdeperization* (Iacob, 2001).

At the time of the 2004 elections, the issue of *esdeperization* was far more openly addressed than before, when the SDP hegemony was stronger and journalists trying to address issues of local and national corruption were often sabotaged.[4] As Vasile Lupu pointed out as early as 2001, very few journalists were willing to put the phenomenon of *esdeperization* into the public spotlight. A coalition of critical media organizations proved necessary to break this spiral of silence. One of these media organizations was *Academia Caţavencu*, a political satirical magazine that now (with hindsight) can be seen as an archive of the history of *esdeperization*. The magazine dealt with *esdeperization* by means of puns and jokes containing different levels of signification that are hard to explain to non-native readers. *Academia Caţavencu* used the term *esdeperization* quite openly. In doing so, it was one of the few media organizations that brought this and other terms (such as the term local barons[5] of the SPD) to the attention of the public. Sometimes, even members of parliament would quote from *Academia Caţavencu*, as for instance when, in the March 23, 2004 Session of the Chamber of Deputies, Nicolae Enescu (2004)[6] quoted an article entitled *Esdeperization on four wheels,*[7] which stated that the professional association of cab drivers from the town of Sibiu had become annexed by the SDP.

Other media organizations, such as the newspaper *Evenimentul Zilei,* the radio station *Total,* and the *Antena 1* television station, launched similar critiques.[8] To give but one example: Ciprian Oprea (2004) from *Evenimentol Zilei* illustrated the pro-government bias of other Romanian media organizations in an article headlining *Radio Năstase Actualities.* The pun in the title pointedly summarizes the article, which criticizes the state-owned radio station *Radio Actualities* for allowing Adrian Năstase to talk freely about electoral matters when he, as the prime minister, was invited to talk about completely unrelated matters such as the passing away of Palestinian leader Yasser Arafat.

ANTAGONISMS WITHIN ROMANIAN MEDIA DISCOURSES

Traditionally, the term antagonism refers to a confrontation between two political and/or social agents with fully constituted identities. From this perspective, we can say that the SDP, with party president and Prime Minister Năstase and President Ion Iliescu, were confronted by a coalition headed by Traian Băsescu of the DP and Theodor Stolojan of the LP.

In this discursive (electoral) struggle, the fundamental antagonism was strengthened by a series of articulations of the self and the other. SDP spokespersons, and many political analysts, pointed to the fuzzy identity of the DP/LP coalition. One argument stressed that both leaders had at some point in time been members of the SDP's political ancestor, *The Front for National Salvation.*[9] Other arguments tried to disarticulate the chain of equivalence that the coalition had constructed by referring to the unnatural mixture of social democracy and liberalism. My argument, still within the confines of a more traditionally defined antagonism, is that the identity of the coalition parties was forged by their common critical attitude toward the key signifier *esdeperization* and the corruption it connoted. The SDP's strategy, to incorporate political personnel of other parties, thus became central to the counter-hegemonic attacks against the SDP by the coalition and their supporters.

These were not the only elements that were integrated into the articulatory chains of both parties. During the electoral campaign, the SDP constructed the liberals and democrats (and especially their leaders) as individuals unable to recognize the achievements of the SDP leadership and to value its political experience. They also argued that the DP/LP coalition wanted to seize power to further their obscure personal interests at the expense of the country's political stability. At the same time, through a logic of difference that tried to disarticulate (the fight against) corruption from the discourse of the opposition, the SDP campaign fell back on a sort of "good cop/bad cop" routine. Ion Iliescu played the role of the good cop willing to contribute to the creation of a "clean Romania" once he would be relieved of his function as president and had again become an "ordinary" member of his party. He pledged to eradicate corruption within the SDP, while the existing corruption was played down as consisting of only a small number of isolated "incidents." The "good cop," Iliescu, was contrasted to the "bad elements" within the party, but also to the "weak cop," Prime Minister Năstase, who was articulated as being too powerless to steer the party away from corruption. At the same time, the Prime Minister's identity was enhanced through his image as the great interlocutor with the European Union. Many SDP politicians tried to cash in on President Iliescu's image as the untarnished patriarch of Romanian politics. Unsurprisingly, the opposition (the DP/LP coalition) did not articulate corruption and *esdeperization* as consisting of isolated incidents, but as the general rule.[10]

Colors played an important symbolic role in these antagonistic articulations. The DP/LP coalition appropriated for itself the color orange, which became one of its visual symbols, in contrast to the SDP's traditional blue.[11] This strategy was partially based on the (correct) assessment that the media would be attracted to this play of colors. The coalition consistently and strategically portrayed itself as more daring and fashionable than the SDP. The choice of the color orange also allowed them to capitalize on the successful Ukrainian *orange revolution*. Thus, orange spoke *for* them and *through* them, as a symbol of the historical necessity of the coalition's victory over the old authoritarian political regime.

When we trade in the more traditional definition of antagonism for Laclau and Mouffe's position that antagonisms constitute identities and at the same time prevent them from being fully constituted, it becomes clear that the antagonisms described here were instrumental in the construction of political identities *and* in their destabilization. The political actors concerned did threaten each other's existence (in order to obtain political victory), but they also needed each other as their respective constitutive outsides. In this case, the articulation of one political party (the SDP) as corrupt allowed the other party to articulate itself as morally intact and reliable. In other words, the attempts made in the coalition's electoral discourse to show the evil character of the good SDP cops served also to define itself as radically new and clean-handed, whereas the SPD was presented as old-fashioned, outdated, and entangled in the history of authoritarianism.

The discussion of the Romanian media discourses during the 2004 election campaign allows us to highlight two phenomena. The first of these is the crucial role played by the signifier *esdeperization* in the socialist-democratic ideology. The other is the ability of the coalition to legitimate itself through a series of media discourses that contradicted the ideological line of the SDP and in doing so attempted to create a new (and more democratic) horizon.

A NEW HORIZON FOR ROMANIA

The antagonistic positioning defining the different political identities in Romania was strengthened through a diversity of media discourses. These discourses contributed to the stabilization of a series of nodal points, such as (the fight against) *esdeperization* and the establishment of a "liberated," more democratic European political and social order.

A heterogeneous group of media organizations, such as the radio station *Total*, the newspapers *Evenimentul Zilei* and *Ziua*, the magazines *Dilema* and *Academia Caţavencu*, and the television stations *Naţional TV* and (in a more ambivalent way) *Antena 1*[12] joined forces in framing SDP actions as corrupt and as forming part of (yet another) attempt to return to an undemocratic one-party political past. These media openly supported the coalition, and defended the democratic principle of elite rotation. The political interests of the opposition were portrayed as essential to the interests of the country and as morally superior, in opposition to the dubious and self-interested politics of the SDP, and the chances for progress, democracy and European integration were said to be served best by the coalition. Once labeled as "uncritical" and as mere "mouthpieces" of the established political forces, part of Romanian media now openly took position against the state powers and engaged themselves in the public debate.

In an article on the elections published by *Dilema* magazine, Patapievici (2004), for instance, talked about the debatable and biased actions of president Ion Iliescu:

> The most flagrant case is that of the president of the nation. According to the Constitution (art. 84, paragraph 1), the president of Romania cannot be a member of any political party. As a consequence, he cannot engage in party politics or take part in the disputes between parties. The evident consequence is that the president of the republic is not allowed to participate in the electoral battle. The reason for this is simple: since the Constitution obliges him to guarantee that the law is observed, the president cannot approach the law from a partisan perspective, but only from the point of view of the interests common to the entire society. ... Thus, whenever the president is expressing an opinion that is biased because it contains a political point of view, he is in fact breaking the fundamental law of the country. From this point of view, the current president of Romania, Ion Iliescu, is a recidivist. Remember his flagrant

interference in the affairs of justice, when—in the matter of the nation-alized houses—he asked the judges to stop pronouncing sentences in favor of the former owners [at Satu Mare, in 1995]. That by itself is enough to sustain what I am trying to say. I cannot make a full list of all the instances that have proven the current president to be a blind polit-ical supporter. I will remind you only of the most recent one: his involvement in the SDP electoral campaign—underhand, in the local campaign; and openly, in the legislative campaign. (author's translation)

This harshly critical position is in the first place remarkable because Ion Iliescu has always been a very popular figure within the media. Moreover, in criticizing the party's role as the guarantor of morality and political stabili-ty, this article attacks the very core of the SDP's identity. A similar instance can be found in a series of investigative journalism articles in the *Evenimentul Zilei*. The example presented here was headed *The Great Swipe of Năstase's Administration*.

The takeover of the post-privatization debts of Rafo Oneşti and Carom Oneşti[13]—for a total sum of 16,000 billion lei, the equivalent of over 400 million Euro—by the Authority for the Capitalization on State Assets (ACSA)[14] takes 100 American dollars out of every Romanian employ-ee's pocket. The unique beneficiary of this debt transfer—ordered by an emergency decision of Năstase's cabinet—is the British company Balkan Petroleum Ltd., the majority stockholder of both Romanian refineries. What is more, ACSA will convert these debts into stock, and the only firm entitled to cash them in whenever it would think proper is Balkan Petroleum. Only when Balkan Petroleum waives this right, another party can buy the stock. Who are the stockholders of Balkan Petroleum, for who Romanians pay as much as for an IMF loan? (Savin, 2004; author's translation).

The same article series revealed that in spring 2004 (when the *Humanist Party* was still a political adversary of the SDP) *Jurnalul Naţional*, a newspa-per owned by Dan Voiculescu,[15] had started to investigate the issue. This had led to the identification of the companies' stockholders as the British firm Central Europe Petroleum (owned by Vasile Frank Timiş, who is—together with Ovidiu Tender—involved in the ecologically disastrous cyanide-mining project in Roşia Montana) and the Romanian firm VGB Invest (which counted among its associates Mihaela Ene, the sister of former SDP representative Gabriel Bivolaru, who had been convicted and impris-oned for swindling the Romanian Bank for Development out of 2,200 bil-lion ROL[16]). Later in the legislative and presidential electoral campaign, this kind of information was no longer run in *Jurnalul Naţional* and on *Antena 1*. This is explained by the fact that their owner and his political party joined the SDP side.

The pro-government Romanian media tried to maintain their position on the discursive scene mostly by quoting each other. In this way, they inflated each other's importance, hoping that the public would relate only to them and their star journalists and forget all about the critical discourses circulating in other media. However, it proved to be impossible for them to simply ignore these discourses. Therefore, as an alternative strategy they abundantly used the space available to them for disparaging their opponents. As Serge Halimi (1991) put it, the pro-government media tried to construct a *"circle of the possible and of the real,"* in which there was only room for minimized critical media discourses.

The coverage of the electoral campaign by the pro-government Romanian media was characterized by the absence of in-depth investigative journalism. In addition to this, attention was given to a wide range of other topics, including sports scandals (e.g., the exploits of soccer player Mutu, or the lawsuit filed by gymnasts against their trainers) and semi-political subjects (e.g., the scandal over the construction of the Orthodox *Church of the Nation* in Bucharest). An important segment of their campaign coverage consisted of electoral projections.

On a number of occasions the defenders of the government did turn against Traian Băsescu and his coalition. Political analyst Dan Pavel,[17] for instance, asserted that none of the two main political forces could lay a claim to ethical superiority. According to him, members of the *Yes* coalition were entangled in affairs comparable with the Petromidia refinery affair.[18] Pavel described the 2004 election in terms of a choice for the *lesser evil*. It is relevant to note here that Pavel conducted the electoral campaign for Gigi Becali, president of the small *Party of the New Generation*, which "stars" in many of the scandals contemporary Romania has known. In his article, Pavel (2004) stated:

> No competent or sane analyst can maintain that the members of one of the political parties are either all "good" or all "bad." He cannot even sustain that one of the parties or alliances is "worse" or "less bad" than another, for the simple reason that there will always be politicians that are counterexamples to the label that is used. An analyst can only claim this if he is biased and wants to influence the public opinion to vote against his declared adversaries. The fact that the SDP has, for obscure reasons, acquitted Rafo Oneşti's debts cannot be invoked as an argument by the supporters of the Liberal National Party-Democratic Party, for the simple reason that top representatives of this political force have benefited from the same privileges at Petromidia.[19] In both cases, these events can be discussed in other than ethical terms, that is, by referring to the social benefits, the long-term efficiency, the viability of one or another of the companies involved. (author's translation)

Traian Băsescu and the *Yes* coalition were continually present in all media discourses, pro-government or not. The pro-government media believed that the coalition's chances to win were slim, but at the same time Băsescu was increasingly depicted as the most committed proponent of Romanian democracy. Although this new articulation did not allow for the formulation of political claims in pro-government media that were critical towards the government, it did—very subtly—contribute to constructing an imaginary of resistance in order to put an end to Romania's undemocratic past more credible.

By creating this liberal-democratic horizon, all media discourses—deliberately or not—ended up deepening the liberal-democratic ideology. They transcended the traditional dichotomies between civil society–political society and public–private politics and, as a consequence, spread the ongoing democratic changes to ever more fields of the social. The November 2004 elections and the media discourses they generated demonstrated that there is no simple solution to the problems a young democracy has to face. They also showed that a majority of the population did not believe that a "savior" (SDP) would be able to solve these problems. On the contrary, most Romanians believed that totalitarian tendencies (manifesting themselves, e.g., through *esdeperization*) had to be resisted.

The clash between the critical (oppositional) media and the pro-government media also showed, once again, that media organizations cannot claim to speak from "*a privileged point of access to the truth*" (Laclau & Mouffe, 1985: 190). They can, however, help break down a horizon and provide discursive spaces in which the different democratic struggles gain strength within a society. They can also be instrumental in maintaining the radically open character of the social. This is exactly the role the critical media discourses in Romania played during the 2004 electoral campaign. At the same time, the articulation of these antagonisms though media discourses, even if it to a certain extent empowered the democratic struggles within (Romanian) society, cannot be seen as a miraculous route to the elimination of all inequalities.

AWARENESS AND ANTAGONISM

In order to clarify the importance of the notion of awareness, I take as a starting point Howarth's definition of discourses as "*relational entities whose identities depend on their difference from other discourses, they are themselves dependent and vulnerable to those meanings that are necessarily excluded*" (Howarth, 2000: 103). The necessity in the above quote is also a necessity that requires an understanding of the political scene and of the complex, ever-changing intellectual luggage of democratic–economic–political–social knowledge within a politically given context. Maintaining its implicit (post-)Marxist meaning, awareness is an integral part of the (discursive) understanding of a situation. In order to give meaning to a situation or event, in order to react to it, in order to actively take part in social and political struggles, an individual has to acquire (some) knowledge of the discursive frameworks that allow him or her to interpret these situations and events, and of the subject positions that allow his or her subjectivity to connect to these situations and events.

The opportunity of becoming personally involved in actions that may lead to social and political change is co-dependent on the presence of and access to discursive tools for assessing the context of (past and future) political action. From this perspective, awareness can also be seen as the opposite of the Marxist notion of alienation. The less alienated (and the less detached from emancipatory discourses) a person is, the more aware he or she is or can be. Awareness then becomes a necessary condition for supporting the socialist and radical democratic strategies defended by Laclau and Mouffe (1985). This also implies that awareness is to be seen as a *process* that can never be completed. Critical awareness thus finds itself in a complex relationship with the dominant ideology. The discursive strategies aiming for societal change also require the commitment of subjects to the process of gaining awareness, as part of the process of distancing oneself from hegemonic ideologies.

In his introduction to discourse theory, Torfing (1999) makes a case against linguistic reductionism, observing that discursive practices are not exclusively linguistic or cognitive but consist of a variety of practices that generate meaning in relation to a shared order. In linking the concept of awareness to discourse theory, I do not plead for a return to cognitive reductionism. Instead, I intend to further capitalize on the Marxist heritage in order to better interpret the role of, in this case, individual Romanian subjects and their awareness of the need for a new government after the 2004 elections — an awareness that was raised by the important but not all-structuring role of critical media discourses.

To put this differently, the notion of awareness allows us to raise questions with regard to the access to discourse. Who exactly was aware of this new imaginary that originated in the field of discursivity? The supporters of the opposition included, among many other social groups, "ordinary" citizens and journalists. These ordinary citizens were indeed aware of the discursive frameworks advanced by the opposition, but they also realized the power of public awareness, although this awareness remained tacit. However, media organizations such as *Radio Total* voiced the hope for democratization and European integration, and played an important role in raising public awareness by providing access to critical and alternative discursive frameworks. *Radio Total* (and others) translated the antagonism between the SDP and the coalition into powerful pro-coalition media discourses. As a consequence of this choice, newspapers and radio or television stations that turned a blind eye to the corruption problem lost the interest of (part of) their audience. They also lost the legitimacy to relate to the cherished social imaginary of democratization and European integration.

HAPPY ELECTORAL ENDINGS, NEW DISCURSIVE BEGINNINGS?

After Traian Băsescu became president of Romania and the coalition formed a new government, media identities changed because the interest in politics was felt to have diminished. Economics moved up the public agenda. In the meantime, the SDP continues to be an important player in Romanian politics and a specific type of SDP rhetoric[20] remains present inside and outside the discursive media arena. Post-electoral evolutions have given rise to new media configurations and new media identities. *Radio Total*, for instance, has split into *Kiss-Total* radio and *Infopro* radio. The latter became yet another part of the *Media Pro* concern (which also includes the *ProTV* station, the *Mediafax* news agency, and the *ProFM* radio station).

From a strictly political perspective, however, the dominant discourses in society have remained almost identical, because the installation of a new hegemony did not significantly change the political horizon. Paradoxically, the disappointment following the elections was generated among others by the objectivity of the media. After the elections, the dichotomy between so-called opposition media and pro-government media disappeared. Media discourses changed as well, as they became less critical and increasingly oriented towards entertainment. The disappearance of the oppositional media discourse and its constructive critical role impoverished the public sphere. After their revolutionary phase (see Hachten, 1984), the media organizations believed that the democratization process was completed and that the time had come for a return to "normality." From then on, they steered clear of any partisan role. The main consequence of this choice for a supposedly neutral position was that their potential to play a role in further democratization and in counter-hegemonic struggles also decreased (see Carpentier, 2004).

Outside the field of media discourse, corruption is now being prosecuted more often, although legal action is mainly aimed at individuals who served under or had dealings with the previous regime.[21] Maybe *esdeperization* has not completely disappeared, but its influence has diminished considerably. These evolutions show that even hegemonic practices do not create a horizon that can determine the social sphere indefinitely. Hegemonic articulations and even the various social imaginaries (such as the utopian conception that the SDP is the only party capable of leading the reforms toward the integration into the European Union) eventually become subjected to the logics of difference, which leads to their complete dismantling.

These re-articulations illustrate that existing identifications are contingent and that identities can always be subverted by other identities. The contingency of political identifications created the necessary space for political agency in the November 2004 elections. A crucial role in these elections was played by the awareness of the particularity of the horizon and by the antagonisms that destroyed the universality of the hegemonic claims. In providing publicness to these antagonisms, the opposition media played an equally substantial role.

ACKNOWLEDGEMENTS

I thank Dr. Williams Sterns of Prescott College (US) and Dr. Eric Gilder of the Lucian Blaga University of Sibiu (Romania) for their invaluable comments on earlier versions of this chapter.

NOTES

1. According to David Howarth (1998: 279) Laclau and Mouffe's discourse theory shifts the focus from a vague (or general) concept of hegemony toward the more precise (and pragmatic) notion of hegemonic practices, which are seen as unifying identities in a common (political) project.
2. In Romanian, the first letters of the party initials form the word DA (*Yes*).
3. The Romanian abbreviation is PNȚCD.
4. Some were sued for slander or libel each time they touched on the topic of corruption, while at least one journalist–Ino Ardeleanu from Timișoara–became the victim of violence.
5. As Florin Tudose put it, the local barons were "*little Ceaușescu's of the Romanian transition, ... who claimed local territories to facilitate the administration's (the central baron's) task on the one hand and to extract as much as possible from the local resources on the other. ... These epigones have privileges, always stand above the law or make up their own laws*" (Popescu, 2004). In the same interview, Tudose also explained how these barons belonged to "the Power" and how they had started their careers as powerful communist party secretaries in Ceaușescu's time.
6. Nicolae Enescu is a România Mare Party representative for Area 34 (Sibiu).
7. The article was published in *Academia Cațavencu* #10 (9-15 March 2004).

8. One example is the essay *Punctul pe I* (*Dot on the I*), written by journalist Rodica Culcer, who also co-hosts a show at the *Realitatea* television station.

9. Revolutionary formations appeared in Romanian politics after the December 1989 events. They brought together former Communist Party members (e.g., Ion Iliescu) and fellow-traveler public personalities who felt the need to get involved (e.g., the poet Mircea Dinescu).

10. Generally, opposition is a notion that refers to parties or politicians. Its use here is broader, to include the media organizations sympathetic to the opposition parties. One particular aspect should be stressed here. The SDP and the political history of its members created a particular form of continuity. Most SDP members had belonged to the lower ranks of the dissolved Romanian Communist Party's elite. They had also been prominent members of the Front for National Salvation, the first political formation after the revolution (created in December 1989) and of all its avatars ever since. Although many politicians of the other political parties that came into existence after December 1989 shared these origins, their complicity with the heritage of the communist past was less outspoken. Therefore, with Băsescu as an emblematic figure of the DP and later of the DP/LP-coalition, the "opposition" notion acquired, historically and politically, a semantic surplus. The effect of this was that all discourses favoring Băsescu and the coalition became associated with heroic political renewal and all-encompassing liberation.

11. In order to play down the importance of the SDP's communist roots, their electoral team avoided the use of the Romanian proverb "the situation is rather blue," which refers to very difficult, unpleasant or sad situations.

12. These oppositional media constituted a small but reasonably easily accessible part of the Romanian media. The role of television in making critical information available was certainly important. The most consistent criticism of the government, however, came from the printed media. The television station *Antena 1* played an ambivalent role, continually oscillating between praise and criticism of the SPD. This can be partially explained by the position of its owner, Dan Voiculescu, who was also president of a small political party, the *Humanist Party*—nowadays known as the *Conservative Party*. During the electoral period he shifted his position toward the SDP, with which he tried to establish an alliance.

13. *Rafo Oneşti* and *Carom Oneşti* are two Romanian oil refineries.

14. The Romanian abbreviation for ACSA is AVAS.

15. See also footnote 12.

16. Old Romanian Lei (ROL), now replaced by RON (New Romanian Lei). The exchange rate is 1 RON = 10,000 ROL.

17. Dan Pavel used to be a respected member of the *Group for Social Dialogue*, a group linked with liberal-democratic Romanian intellectuals. He is still a political studies professor at the prestigious State University of Bucharest, and is the author of a number of Political Studies books, such as *The Byzantine Leviathan*.

18. Only Dinu Patriciu from the *Yes* coalition came under investigation after the 2004 elections, in relation to the *Petromidia* scandal. In the *Rafo* scandal, no investigation was opened. On July 12, 2005, *ProTV* announced that there was not enough evidence in the case, and that the judges involved seemed to have been excessively zealous, for which they might have to answer to justice themselves.

19. *Petromidia* is a Romanian oil refinery.

20. The SDP rhetoric was in fact a Communist party–style rhetoric, which was characterized by the presence of dichotomies in combination with an excess of technical (and sometimes invented) terms, so that it approximated an artificial language.
21. An example is the case of the son of the influential Ion Țiriac, who was charged with drug abuse, but freed for lack of evidence. Only after the new government had been installed, the evidence was discovered in the files of the other people who were involved. Charges were then pressed against him. Ion Țiriac discussed his son's problems with both Iliescu and Băsescu. Under Iliescu, Alexandru Țiriac's name was cleared. This was not the case under Băsescu. Moreover, under Băsescu the media treated the case with greater objectivity.

REFERENCES

Antena 1 (2004) 'Amintiri din Viitor' (November 17, 2004). Retrieved May 17, 2005, from http://domino.kappa.ro/andronic/prezidentiale96.nsf/Toate/Capitole/ $File/12ziuaz.html.

Carpentier, N. (2004) *Coping with the Agoraphobic Media Professional: A Typology of Journalistic Practices Reinforcing Democracy and Participation.* CeMeSo Working Paper 2, http://homepages.vub.ac.be/~ncarpent/workpap/cemeso-02-agoraphobic.pdf.

Enescu, N. (2004) 'Nicolae Enescu — Declarație Politică Intitulați "PSD-izarea pe patru roți,"' in *Dezbateri Parlamentare, Parlamentul României.* Retrieved June 17, 2005, from http://diasan.vsat.ro/pls/steno/steno.stenograma?ids= 5638&idm=1,22.

Hachten, W.A. (1984) *The World News Prism: Changing Media, Changing Ideologies.* Ames, IA: Iowa State University Press.

Halimi, S. (1997) *Les Nouveaux Chiens de Garde.* Paris: Liber — Raisons d'agir.

Howarth, D. (1998) 'Discourse Theory and Political Analysis,' pp. 268-293 in E. Scarbrough and E. Tanenbaum (Eds) *Research Strategies in Social Sciences.* Oxford: Oxford University Press.

Howarth, D. (2000) *Discourse.* Buckingham, Philadelphia: Open University Press.

Iacob, C. (2001) 'A Party with a Vindication: The PNTCD Tells the West about Esdeperization,' *Evenimentul Zilei* (June 9, 2001). Retrieved June 16, 2005, from http://www.evenimentul.ro/local/article/20257,32,baseArticle.html.

Laclau, E. (1996) *Emancipations.* London, New York: Verso.

Laclau, E., Mouffe, C. (1985) *Hegemony and Socialist Strategy: Towards a Radical Democratic Politics.* London, New York: Verso.

Mouffe, C. (1997) *The Return of the Political.* London, New York: Verso.

Mouffe, C. (1999) 'Deliberative Democracy or Agonistic Pluralism?,' *Social Research* 66(3): 745-758.

Oprea, C. (2004) 'Radio Năstase Actualities,' *Evenimentul Zilei* (November 12, 2004). Retrieved August 28, 2005, from http://www.expres.ro/politica/ ?news_id=171429.

Patapievici, H.-R. (2004) 'A Recidivist,' *Dilema* (43) ('The Corruption Small but Stout'—5-11 November 2004). Retrieved June 29, 2005, from http://www.algoritma.ro/dilema/43/HRPATAPI.htm.

Pavel, D. (2004) 'The Theory of the Smaller Evil,' *Formula AS* (644). Retrieved August 28, 2005 from http://www.formula-as.ro/articol.php?nrrev=644& &culoarebgr=67ace2&&numecapp=Editorial&&codcapp=22.

Popescu, I.L. (2004) 'About the Local Barons or the Little Ceauşescu's of Transition,' Interview with F. Tudose, *Formula AS* (618). Retrieved June 19, 2005, from http://www.formula-as.ro/articol.php?nrrev=618&&codcap=44&&idart =5310.

Savin, N. (2004) 'The Great Swipe of Năstase's Administration,' *Evenimentul Zilei* (November 18, 2004). Retrieved August 28, 2005, from http://www. expres.ro/topstory/?news_id=171944.

Torfing, J. (1999) *New Theories of Discourse: Laclau, Mouffe and Žižek*. Oxford: Blackwell.

3

EMBEDDED IDENTITY BUILDING IN CHINESE/TAIWANESE ENGLISH-LANGUAGE PRESS NARRATIVES

Lutgard Lams

In this chapter, some central arguments from the discourse-theoretical model proposed by Ernesto Laclau and Chantal Mouffe (1985) are applied to the particular process of cultural and political identity formation in the Chinese region, with a special focus on how this process is represented/constructed in the English-language media in the Republic of China (ROC) in Taiwan and the People's Republic of China (PRC).[1] In my survey, I examined all Hong Kong (HK) handover news stories, editorials, and opinion articles over an 8-day period (from June 27 to July 5, 1997) in three English-language papers, namely *The China Post* (Taiwan), *The China News* (Taiwan), and *The China Daily* (PRC). This provided a corpus of 486 articles, 114 in *The China Daily*, 139 in *The China News*, and 233 in *The China Post*.

The results of this study[2] clearly show how ideological assumptions function in the struggle for maintaining/renewing definitions and meanings of social practices/phenomena. In the cross-strait relations between the PRC and the ROC, a discursive battle has been fought for decades. The goal of the parties involved was not only to win the hearts and minds of the

Chinese/Taiwanese community, but also to convince the international community of the validity of their respective perspectives on Chinese/Taiwanese social, cultural, and political reality. Discourse is defined by Foucault (1972: 49) as a historically specific system of meaning that shapes the identities of subjects/objects. When it comes to illustrating the role of discourse, my discourse-theoretical analysis of media accounts of the 1997 HK handover proves to be an interesting case study. My comparison between the PRC/ROC accounts will show how discourse has played a constructive role in shaping/representing this historical event.

For discourse theorists Laclau and Mouffe, too, discursive practices cannot be studied in isolation from their larger social and historical contexts. Of specific importance to them are the fundamental contingency and historicity of discursive constructions, which remain vulnerable to the onslaught of political forces that were excluded in their production and to the dislocating effects of events beyond their control (Laclau, 1990: 31-6). Laclau and Mouffe aimed to clarify the way in which political forces and social actors construct meanings within incomplete social structures open to multiple interpretations. Discourses for them include all concrete systems of social relations and practices. These systems are believed to be intrinsically political because their formation involves constructing antagonisms and drawing political frontiers between insiders and outsiders. These activities concern the exercise of power and a specific structuring of relations between different social agents. The findings yielded by my analysis of the HK handover media coverage indicate how these central components of Laclau and Mouffe's discourse-theoretical model are—in the PRC/ROC official discourse as well as in the media discourse—at work in the form of hegemonic articulations, antagonistic portrayals of us–them and the construction and maintenance of myths.

My investigation of discursive practices that constitute and maintain a certain sense of reality and an understanding of society corresponds with the two research questions Howarth (2000) suggested as criteria for the selection of empirical case studies, namely, (a) formation/dissolution of political identities; (b) analysis of hegemonic practices that endeavor to produce social myths and collective imaginaries. In line with Foucault's problematization strategy, this chapter shows how dominant discursive constructions, such as the inevitability/normality of the return of HK in particular and the reunification of China in general, are not necessary at all, but utterly contingent and political in nature. Furthermore, naturalizing particular representations of certain issues, for example by assuming that national communities need to have clearly demarcated boundaries and fixed identities, results in the expulsion of the "other" from the "domestic sphere." Likewise, I show the extent to which the narratives create room for different ways of conceiving connections between territoriality, ethnicity, and identity.

While the HK handover raised important political and economic issues, it also generated questions regarding national identity formation for HK citizens as well as for the Taiwanese population. In specific contexts (such as decolonization or redrawing of boundaries), ideological contestations are mobilized to advance preferred versions of historical reality and cultural frameworks categorizing "them" as the cultural "other" to us are rationalized and naturalized. In my discourse analysis of the HK handover stories, I concentrated on the cultural and political dynamics that unfolded in the period leading up to and following the transfer of sovereignty in terms of hegemonic identity construction and negotiation processes.

In the PRC narratives, I found the hegemonic production of a general consensus in China that reunification of all Chinese was inevitable and that the handover gave rise to overall joy, whereas in Taiwan, the theme of (re)unification was approached from different perspectives. The cultural insider–outsider frameworks in the Taiwanese English-language media not only diverged from the construction pervading the PRC state-sponsored media, but also differed between the various English-language media outlets within Taiwan. Hence, I argue that the media narratives under investigation have contributed to the (re)production of social identities and have therefore proven to be a powerful opinion-formulating instrument.

Research into discursive hierarchies exposed how powerful established ideas are reproduced and how some norm of conformity is obeyed, albeit in different degrees. My analysis demonstrates how particular language structures silently but cumulatively shape the ideas presented, molding them into established mental dispositions. The diverging coverage of a single event that was found in the three newspapers corresponds with the different points of view held by the dailies, which are themselves rooted in their own political beliefs, cultural assumptions and institutional practices—in short, in different ideological positions.

Focus on some actors and events at the expense of others encodes certain ideological positions in terms of cultural identity allegiances and assumptions about the political identity of territories, such as mainland China, HK, and Taiwan. Therefore, this study examines the discursive constructions of identities in a wider context of social structures, processes, and relations and categorizes them in three domains:

1. Relations of hegemony and domination;
2. Antagonistic constructions of us–them dichotomies;
3. Reproduction of myths pertaining to the cultural, political and historical realms of (a) collective consciousness, (b) nation-state/nationalism and clashing ideologies (communism/capitalism; autocracy/democracy), and (c) colonialism, respectively.

Because these categories are interrelated, my categorization is artificial and is used for reasons of presentation only. It allows for a clear demonstration of how the three newspapers (re)produce unequal relations between people, and create or sustain cultural and political definitions of belonging and otherness, and perpetuate myths. These three elements form an integral part of Laclau and Mouffe's discourse-theoretical approach.

THE NEWSPAPERS

Before elaborating on these three interrelated categories, some brief background information about the production context of these papers in terms of ownership and publishers, presumed readership, and the ideological and cultural environment within which the news workers operate is in order.

The China Daily was the only English-language daily on the mainland in 1997 and is widely believed to be the PRC government's mouthpiece, following the strictest rules of censorship. By contrast, the two English-language papers published on a daily basis in Taiwan in 1997, *The China Post* and *The China News* (later renamed *The Taiwan News*), are privately owned and claim to respect the journalistic rule of objectivity and not to impose restrictions on content. However, editors and copywriters contend that publishers and editors-in-chief do sometimes intervene with editorial "advice" in sensitive matters. A look into ownership (at least partially) explains why. Ever since it was founded in 1952, *The China Post* has been owned and published by the "mainlander"[3] family Huang, which has a strong Kuomintang background. *The China News* was established in 1949 by the mainlander family Wei, which also had close ties to the Kuomintang government. In 1985, a controlling share was sold to the Cultural Affairs Department of the Kuomintang (Tien, 1989: 200), but when the newspaper ran into financial difficulties again it was saved by large capital injections by I-Mei, a large food conglomerate with a strong Taiwanese identity, a process that took place from 1997 to 1999.

Both papers aim to provide a *"channel of communication between the foreign residents and the local populace"* or, as the mission statement in *The China News* has it, a *"Voice to the People and A Bridge to the World."* As this mission statement reveals, the intended readership consists of (a) foreign residents and visitors to Taiwan, (b) Taiwanese who seek an international perspective on the (world) news and/or those who want to enhance their English language skills, and (c) the international community. As is to be expected, the mainland *China Daily* also aims to win the hearts and minds of the foreign residents in China, the local Chinese, and the international community.

For the international news coverage, both Taiwanese papers rely heavily on information provided by foreign news agencies. However, this information is subjected to editorial amendments.[4] Staff workers comprise local Taiwanese as well as foreign residents. Usually, the copyeditors are native speakers of English, who report to a Taiwanese editor-in-chief.[5] *The China Daily*, by contrast, hardly uses any wire stories and relies for its foreign news coverage on its domestic news agency, Xinhua, which has a large network of Chinese correspondents overseas.

This concise sketch of the production process may not do justice to the complexity of the context in which the news workers find themselves forever fighting deadlines and in which the news outlets face various constraints, not in the least commercial pressures. However, it may already suggest some explanations for the findings that are outlined in the following sections.

RELATIONS OF HEGEMONY AND DOMINATION

As a methodological basis for the ideological analysis of media texts, a combination of several methodologies, borrowed from the field of linguistic pragmatics, critical discourse analysis and depth-hermeneutics was used. It should be noted in this context that Laclau and Mouffe's discourse-theoretical approach distances itself from the latter two analytical traditions. Laclau and Mouffe, for instance, reject a "hermeneutics of suspicion" and therefore follow Foucault's misgivings about "ideology critique." This does not mean, however, that the methodologies of these discourse-analytical traditions, with their stronger focus on the text, cannot be put to good use for showing the power of discourse in media accounts, especially since Laclau and Mouffe themselves hardly provide indications as to how to go about the empirical part of discourse investigation.

Hence, the methodological insights provided by, for example, Thompson's (1990) ideology interpretation framework were useful in compensating for this deficit in Laclau and Mouffe's discourse theory. Thompson distinguished five modes in which ideology operates: legitimation, dissimulation, unification, fragmentation, and reification. All of these modes were employed in *The China Daily*. Their presence proved to be much less salient in the Taiwanese samples.

In my analysis of the handover narratives, I examined how powerful hegemonic articulations in texts not only muffle dissenting voices, but also (re)produce unequal relations between people. Examples of discursive strategies are (a) providing labeling expressions which solidify concepts of groups; (b) assigning different semantic roles to the members of different groups, thus discriminating among them; and (c) providing an unbalanced forum to news sources and elite actors, thus strengthening the unequal distribution of power and opportunity. Identities are constantly negotiated and given competing meanings by different social actors in an environment characterized by heteroglossia, the constant interplay between different socio-ideological languages competing for dominance or hegemony (Verschueren, 1999: 238). Depending on which actors get the floor, different interpretations of social reality are presented. My study, therefore, also focused on the extent to which elite actors found access to public discourse, and on their role in the discursive management of the public mind.

There are many points of divergence between the newspapers both in the selection of views of people quoted and in the choice of news actors. *The China Post*, for example, gives primacy to the official voice of the Kuomintang ruling party at the expense of opposition views from the Democratic Progressive Party (DPP) camp. Even though *The China News* also quotes the Taiwan authorities abundantly, the DPP opposition gets a large forum and government criticism is not shunned. Therefore, it can be argued that, unlike *The China Post*, *The China News* is not a Kuomintang mouthpiece and even occasionally undermines relations of power.

By contrast, *The China Daily* (from mainland China) constructs the handover story from the point of view of those who wield power and only pro-Beijing HK citizens and selected members of the Provisional Legislative Council are interviewed. Speeches of PRC leaders, high-ranking officials, and civil servants dominate the narratives along with quotes of local as well as overseas Chinese in vox-pop interviews reverberating similar ideological messages. Dissenting voices in China or HK are muffled and different opinions in Taiwan as well as the ROC official messages to the mainland via the local and international media are conspicuously absent. My analysis thus reveals that both the mainland and the Taiwanese papers present images of overseas events in a manner congruent with the respective diplomatic policies of each regime.

ANTAGONISTIC PORTRAYALS
OF US-THEM DICHOTOMIES

Laclau and Mouffe's notions of social antagonism—exclusion and chains of equivalence—difference are useful tools to understand identity and nation-building in the Chinese/Taiwanese context. According to both theorists, an essential component of identity is that the unity of the "us" category is constructed by differentiating it from a "them." Collective identities are formed by establishing a chain of equivalence between groups composed of different individualities but facing a common opponent. As Torfing clarified, "*the logic of equivalence constructs a chain of equivalential identities among different elements, that are seen as expressing a certain sameness"* (Torfing, 1999: 301). This logic of equivalence functions within a differential system establishing a political border between opposing camps (Howarth & Stavrakakis, 2000: 11). Details of how boundaries and collective identities are constructed in the face of challenges — dislocatory events, as Laclau and Mouffe call them — in the Chinese/Taiwanese contexts are too complex to deal with in this chapter. Therefore, I limit myself to briefly exemplifying how antagonism constructs collectivities in the three areas under investigation, Taiwan, PRC, and HK, respectively.

The notion ShinTaiwanren (a new cultural concept, referring to a homogenized Taiwanese society) was created in the 1990s and means "New Taiwanese." It was thought of as the opposite of the cultural identity of mainland Chinese, which therefore functioned as the common antagonist. In fact, ShinTaiwanren is an empty signifier because it presents an amalgamation of different (ethnic and cultural) groups within Taiwan. Similarly, before 1987, when the martial law was lifted, the Tang-wai opposition movement in Taiwan was also a fragmented group of activists aspiring to different goals, as was evidenced by its disintegration into various factions in the 1990s. Originally, however, it was united by its opposition to one common antagonist, the autocratic Kuomintang government. The latter, an émigré party state, as Shiau described it, controlled the upper layers of the power structure: the government, the higher positions within the Kuomintang, state enterprises, mass media, and the education system, despite the fact that it constituted only a minority (15%) of the population (Shiau, 1999). The Chinese term Tang-wai literally means exterior to the Party (i.e., the Nationalist Kuomintang Party, the only party that was allowed during the martial law period) (Tsang, 1999: 11). The dislocatory events at the end of the 1980s revealed the Tang-wai's inner split, which led to a repositioning based on new antagonisms. Similarly, the wave of organizations within civil society, mushrooming once democratization had gathered momentum, found its origin in these various social organizations' common resistance against state domination. Between 1986 and 1988, the number of movements had risen from 5 to 12 (Chu, 1992: 105). The diversity of civil concerns underlying the common goal of transforming authoritarian rule is evident from the discussion of at least 18 social movements and civil protests[6] in 1989 by Hsiao (1992: 57-72) and Chang (1989).

By the same token, antagonism plays a major role in the reunification discourse in mainland China. PRC leaders construct an imaginary community of "a unified, great Chinese nation" threatened by separatist forces within the PRC, such as groups advocating the independence of Tibet and the Uighur community in Xinjiang Province. However, the myth of a unified Chinese nation is primarily negated by the Taiwanese regime's claim to legitimacy. In fact, the PRC's desire to unify China is constituted especially through denying Taiwanese national aspirations all legitimacy. As the island of Formosa has never been under the jurisdiction of the Communist mainland regime, this projection of a future hope onto the present and the (revisited) past as a naturalized notion of Chinese unity is a mere construction. Hence, advocates of Taiwan self-determinacy argue that this projection is tantamount to verbal annexation of Taiwan.

When applying the concepts of equivalence and differentiation to HK, one can argue that the notion of "Hong Kong identity" as an expression of its society's specific distinctiveness has also been discursively constructed by means of a rejection, in this case of HK's subordinate position with regard to both China and Britain. Yet, at the time of the handover this community comprised a variety of political and social actors with various concerns, such as the claim for speeding up the democratization process, for safeguarding press freedoms, for a better welfare system, for the protection of human rights, and so forth. The construction of a unique HK local identity as distinct from that of their new masters on the Continent served as the discursive link between these diverse concerns.

Because my research project attempted to show how social groups (us–them) are presented in discourse and how ideological discursive frames are constructed sociopolitically as a means to affirm group coherence, I first had to investigate how and when cultural and political definitions of belonging and otherness were being produced in the media narratives. I thus tried to grasp the different dimensions of Chineseness reflected in the written press and to establish how the contextual strategy of positive self-presentation and negative other-presentation manifested itself in media discourse as a means for the reproduction and diffusion of ideological references to political and cultural identities in Taiwan, China, and HK. With a view to this, I looked for modes of reporting which created *stereotyping* of specific social, ethnic and national communities in the English-language media in Taiwan and in China.

Stereotyping emerges when rich cultures and a plurality of voices and opinions are reduced to simple, monolithic representations of groups and collectivities in terms of us/them antagonisms. Inspired by the systemic-functional view of language in the tradition of Halliday's (1994) language theory, I looked at classification strategies in lexical choice when labeling groups as well as grammatical structures at the clausal level. Consistency of transitivity patterns in a particular context can point at ideological construction of a text. This type of analysis provides a semantic perspective on the ideas expressed by a clause considered as a proposition about the world in which an event, relation, or attribute is predicated of participants.

My examination of media representations resulting in the creation of negative images and stereotypes of selected groups clearly shows how representation schemes in all three papers implicitly define the various groups as the (at least potentially) "evil other." News actors (in the sense of the protagonists whose stories/speech acts are reported) are thus dichotomized into us and them. Group-related opinions about insiders and outsiders and their typical properties and actions are constructed on the basis of similar linguistic strategies, such as identification and description through relational processes, and allocation of agency, responsibility, and blame, mainly through transitivity structures.

Syntactic structures of the HK accounts in *The China Daily*, *The China Post* and *The China News* reveal an ideology that portrays the ingroup as endowed with positive attributes, whereas the outgroup is consistently associated with negative attributes. For example, *The China Daily* portrays "them" (British colonizers, colonial regimes) as primarily responsible for the humiliation of China. In contrast, "we" are generally represented as the victims of the British occupation. Other entities belonging to the outgroup are those who do not share in the patriotic fervor to reunify China under the "one country, two systems" formula. The outgroup, therefore, includes the Taiwan authorities.

A drastically different portrayal of the "us" category is found in the Taiwanese papers. This time, "we" comprises the Taiwanese authorities, who support democracy, and by extension any supporter of democracy and Taiwan sovereignty. The outgroup includes the non-democratic rulers across the Strait and any group that supports their regime (e.g., the Beijing-picked Provisional Legislative Council of the Hong Kong Special Administrative Region [HKSAR]).

Us–them constructions in the cultural realm are more complex, since I found points of convergence between the Taiwanese *China Post* and the mainland *China Daily* on the one hand, and divergences between the Taiwanese papers, *The China Post* and *The China News* on the other. In fact, the clearest ideological difference between *The China Post* and *The China News* is to be found in the portrayal of this cultural us.

For *The China Daily*, the cultural other is anyone who feels no allegiance to the Chinese identity. The Chinese are framed as a homogeneous society transcending state borders, ethnic differences, and political tensions. The cultural "us" constructed by *The China Post* is quite similar in that it includes anyone cherishing a China-centric perspective and longing for Chinese reunification. Cultural pride in being Chinese prevails and the hand -over is treated as if it were a local affair within the community of the Chinese (cultural ingroup) as opposed to the foreign colonial presence (outgroup).

However, much as the discussion of these issues in *The China Post* seems to match their treatment in *The China Daily*, the style of presentation in the former is less confrontational and its tone sounds less condemnatory. In contrast to what can be found in *The China Daily* accounts, negative predications about the colonial era are mostly balanced with positive attributions to the British colonial regime, due to the fact that the Taiwanese have a different historical view of the British legacy to HK (see later).

Moreover, the political regime in the more recent colonial HK belongs to the same political ingroup as the advocates of democracy in Taiwan. These two factors, a similar political ideology and a more comprehensive view of historical realities concerning the British administrative presence in HK, underlie the less condemnatory portrayal by the Taiwanese papers of British colonialist practices in HK.

The cultural "us" in *The China News* is composed of those who have a "Taiwan—first" outlook (i.e., the supporters of Taiwan identity). In contrast to *The China Post*, *The China News* draws a clear line between China and Taiwan. Few Chinese nationalist quotes make their way to the articles, and Chinese nationalist rhetoric is countered with disparaging remarks, criticizing it among others for exploiting the handover to imbue China with nationalist sentiments.

My survey shows that even though both Taiwanese papers *explicitly* project a middle-of-the-road point of view, in line with mainstream political thought, both papers *implicitly* encode diverging ideological positions on cultural identity allegiances and assumptions about Taiwan's political identity. When the processes implicitly generating meaning are considered, *The China News* proves to favor Taiwanism or the "Taiwan-first instead of China" concept, whereas *The China Post* remains in the camp of the old Kuomintang party, putting China's interest first and linking up the success of the HK formula with the eventual reunification of Taiwan with China.

The analysis indicates not only that the in- and outgroups are framed differently through lexical choices, but also that certain agents are promoted or disparaged through syntactical options. Varying us–them dichotomies reveal different villain–victim or villain–hero conceptual polarizations. All three papers emphasize the good points of their own political/cultural ingroup, while glossing over its negative actions. Ample structural evidence was found of positive self and negative other presentation, which constitutes a means of justifying positions and identities and of discursively legitimizing ideologies. Constructing desired mental models and social representations may eventually affect the reader's mind. This process can be countered by the reader's power to deconstruct these framings. Still, it cannot be denied that the mass media play an active role in disseminating ideology by selectively reconstructing particular opinions and representing them as if they were commonly accepted as natural.

PERPETUATION OF MYTHS

The extent to which contingent meanings within particular historical contexts are fixed and generalized in totalizing discursive constructions determines whether they will be accepted as common sense. In other words, it is the partiality of sensations which accounts for a synecdochical construction of an illusory full identity (pars pro toto). This illusory full identity (represented by Laclau and Mouffe's notion of overdetermination) starts at the level of myth and moves to the larger level of social imaginary, in which the particular is universalized. Totalizing and mystifying constructions of political and sociohistorical reality deny openness to identity and block transformational processes in historical accounts. Not surprisingly, it is precisely at critical moments in a community's history, such as the HK sovereignty transfer or the democratization process in Taiwan at the end of the 1980s and throughout the 1990s, that totalizing conceptualizations of the social reality and political identity of territories tend to be undermined and room is created for new positionings and antagonisms.

My research allows for the identification of a number of discursive strategies used by *The China Daily*, *The China News*, and *The China Post* to perpetuate myths in the cultural, political, and historical realms pertaining to collective consciousness, nation-state/nationalism, and clashing ideologies (communism–capitalism, autocracy–democracy), and colonialism, respectively. Obviously, these three notions are interrelated and cannot be seen as independent from each other. As indicated earlier, I deal with them separately for reasons of presentation only.

The Cultural Sphere

My findings demonstrate that *The China Daily* (the mainland paper) is used as an instrument to convey a mythical sense of collective and social harmony among all Chinese (in China, HK, Taiwan, overseas). A totalizing Chineseness is conjured up, denying all schisms and particularisms. The many tensions between HK Chinese and the Motherland are blotted out by the overall emphasis on festivities. Moreover, *The China Daily* suggests that HK will only achieve a state of genuine liberation with the help of the socialist mainland. Differences within the Chinese communities on the mainland, in HK and on Taiwan are thus disavowed. The handover is exploited to suppress these differences and create an image of national unity.

The nationalist strategy of promoting a sense of unity and cohesiveness also makes use of the conceptual "family" metaphor, which is strengthened by repeated confirmations through a cumulative set of related individual metaphors (e.g., "blood ties," "embrace of the motherland"). The metaphor is often used in speeches by Chinese leaders aiming to court their audiences' national identification. It readily finds its way to the Chinese media, because they publish entire speeches and duplicate their content in other news articles (i.e., they render them in disguise). As for the Taiwanese papers, *The China Post* occasionally uses the "Chinese family" metaphor, but does not label the mainland as the "mother." Significantly, the bond between both entities is said to be "brotherly," which suggests a link on an equal footing, whereas *The China Daily* echoes the PRC rhetoric of a "mother–child" relationship, which entails a hierarchy of central–local government. Congruent with its construction of cultural in- and outgroups, the Taiwanese *China News* rarely employs the Chinese family metaphor. Where it does, it mostly refers to the "motherland" in a keyed form to suggest distance.

It should also be noted that the mainland *China Daily* projects collective harmony and homogeneity as natural, thus implicitly presenting diversity as abnormal. The Taiwanese papers, on the contrary, do not exclude dissonant views of the handover in particular and of cultural allegiances in general. *The China Post* often prints reports of surveys indicating diverging opinions, and *The China News* allots plenty of space to a plurality of voices in direct quotes and interviews.

The Political Field

In this section, I distinguish among three concepts, namely: nation-state/nationalism, clashing ideologies (communism/capitalism, autocracy/democracy), and the future political status of HK.

Nationalism and the Concept of China; Taiwan as a Nation/State/ Nation-State. The analyst of nationalism who conceives of national identity as a discursive construct will have to screen the process of articulation through which particular experiences come to connote an imaginary full national identity. The nation itself is most often represented by its parts and is never perceivable as a whole (Bowman, 1994: 141). Therefore, a synecdochical representation of a nation or a community's identity can be problematic when the part does not correspond with the whole. And especially in abstract notions such as nationhood or identity, it is hard to determine the character of the whole. As Bowman argued, diverging articulations of a certain identity can have a divisive rather than a unifying effect, because they do not share a common ground on which a strong nationalist movement could be built.

In the Chinese context, when mainland Han-Chinese citizens imagine the entirety of their national community through their familiarity with a small sector of its members or conceive the character of the Chinese nation through an extension/extrapolation of their knowledge of localized customs, they will find themselves at odds with mainlanders on Taiwan. The latter may well construct their images of the Chinese nation on the grounds of their particular familiarity with different groups and customs. Similarly, ethnic minority groups within China will have differing ideas of the Chinese nation, based on their respective communal experiences. All of these communities have developed in isolation from each other, under very different sets of influences, and have as a result formed their own images of the Chinese past, present, and future.

In an already established nation, conflict is usually perceived as happening within the context of that nation, but is rarely seen as putting the existence of the nation itself into question. As long as the established national entity is not questioned, it remains a vague mythological concept. Due to this openness, a wide range of persons can identify with it. They can feel part of it without having their allegiances to it denied by exclusionary definitions. The vagueness of national identity in an unchallenged nation can be seen as the result of a passive relation to the constitutive outside (Derrida, 1976: 39-44; Laclau, 1995: 151). However, once the concept of the nation itself is threatened, the antagonistic forces obstructing its full realization have to be defined more clearly and processes of inclusion/exclusion emerge. In antagonistic situations of this kind, a collectivity can be constructed on the basis of the shared conviction that all of its members are oppressed by the same opponent. This equivalential process allows a border to be drawn between those who are denied identity (us) and others who deny it (them).

In the China/Taiwan case, this means that as long as no party clearly defines "China," an ambiguous status quo can be maintained. This is why the Kuomintang leaders prefer not to rock the boat. It also explains why Beijing authorities and reunification advocates in Taiwan feel severely threatened by those Taiwanese that offer an alternative reading of the Chinese/Taiwanese nation. Although the official cross-strait discursive exchanges remain clouded in ambiguity, many debates revolve around the definition of "China" and the drawing of its boundaries. This is the point where some members within the national entity are singled out as potential enemies. Groups that are deemed to be disruptive of national consensus are readily criminalized and ostracized.

The link with the cross-strait issue is clear: from a PRC perspective, Taiwan is framed as a renegade province and advocates of self-determination are depicted as secessionists, even though they leave multiple options (including unification) open to the Taiwan citizenry. Self-determinationists, on their turn, construct the PRC dream of reunification with Taiwan as expansionary annexation attempts. These differing viewpoints bear witness to the aforementioned processes of division and fragmentation (Bowman, 1994) or to the impossibility of society and threaten to bring about the dissolution of the national imaginary and, consequently, the disintegration of the nation itself (Laclau, 1990: 90-91).

As can be expected, the idea that reunification of all Chinese into one nation is self-evident and/or inevitable is propagated by the supporters of reunification, that is, the PRC authorities on the one hand and the former ROC regime, led by the Kuomintang, on the other. As a result, the notion of the "unified Chinese nation" has been accepted as common sense by many mainland Chinese citizens, pro-China Taiwanese and, indeed, also a sizeable part of the foreign community. My analysis shows that it is endorsed by the mainland Chinese state media propaganda, but also by *The China Post*, an implicit supporter of the Kuomintang ideology. In its perception of "culture" as coterminous with "nationhood," the Kuomintang party has always insisted on the necessity of reunification with China.

However, for those who put Taiwan first, the essence of a state is not a shared ethnic or linguistic heritage but a sense of commonality. The "new Taiwan consciousness," giving rise to "Taiwanism" and running counter to the "one great unified China" myth, is most salient in *The China News*. Even though both Taiwanese papers reject the "one country, two systems" scheme as a workable model for Taiwan, the underlying reasons for this rejection diverge. Whereas *The China Post* engages in the old Kuomintang anti-communist rhetoric, focusing on the legitimacy of the ROC regime, *The China News* adopts a Taiwan-first discourse, stating that Taiwan interests come first and that its leaders do not want to have anything to do with the PRC if it dictates a framework for the Taiwanese to live by.

The Taiwan-first notion is completely absent in *The China Post*, which privileges the frame of Chinese reunification. In this sense, the Taiwanese *China Post* and the mainland *China Daily* can be seen to pursue the same ideal of reunification on cultural grounds. Still, there are points of divergence. Whereas the mainland *China Daily* defines its Chinese nationalism in opposition to foreigners and presents a black-and-white us–them dichotomy (them being foreign rule and, by extension, an evil and decadent West), the Taiwanese *China Post*'s Chinese nationalism is less directed against an evil West and seems to aim first and foremost at winning the hearts and minds of those Taiwanese who do not think in the interest of China first. Another major difference is the political format of the proposed reunification, which according to the Chinese Communist Party has to take place following the HK "one country, two systems" scheme, imposing a hierarchical central/local government relationship. Against this, both *The China Post* and *The China News* make it abundantly clear that the Taiwanese authorities only wish to go to the negotiation table on an equal footing and reject the HK formula proposed by Beijing.

In conclusion, I can say that both the mainland *China Daily* and the Taiwanese *China Post* still believe in an imagined Chinese community and project a dream of a unified China, which in *The China Daily*'s framing is split because of Western humiliation and Taiwanese leaders. By contrast, *The China Post* attributes the division of China to ideological differences between the ROC and the Communists. In doing so, *The China Daily* engages in hegemonic discursive practices, muting voices that could deny the realization of this dream nation or undermine its myth. *The China Post*, on the contrary, openly shows that there is plurality of thought within Taiwan, even though it privileges Kuomintang party voices over DPP opposition voices.

The China Daily also leaves the vague and ambiguous nation concept unquestioned, whereas the Taiwanese papers insist on defining the nebulous term "China." In this context, the handover was a key interpretive moment, because it revealed different constructions of what "China" and "Chinese" are supposed to be. The Taiwanese community did not dodge the debate about the political and cultural meanings of these terms. Struggle over meaning opens ways to alternative frames and bears on a major aspect of social reality, namely the hegemonic process of power and dominance. The potential of hegemonic articulations depends on its spread over different discourse genres. It can be argued that the PRC discursive framing of China as a unified nation-state including all Chinese descendants of the ethnic Han-race is hegemonic, given the proliferation of the "one China" rhetoric in political speeches, media, public discourse, international media, and diplomatic discourse. The "one China" policy, which features as a prerequisite in virtually every bilateral/multilateral pact China is a signatory to, has indeed wide-ranging repercussions for international diplomacy and trade relations with the Asia-Pacific region.

The Taiwanese, however, expose the common-sense nature of the PRC construction of China with its normative frame of interpretation and try to counter the PRC's hegemonic articulation of China. *The China Post*, for example, explicitly questions Beijing's concept of China as a nation-state by disconnecting nation and state. For *The China Post* there is one Chinese nation, but there are two equal sovereign states. In other words, China is divided. *The China News* undermines both the PRC's and the Kuomintang's definition of China. It consistently juxtaposes the terms "China" and "Taiwan," carrying the implication that Taiwan is not a part of China. Furthermore, its news stories and editorials all use the referential term "China" for the mainland territory and regime, which they make coterminous with China as a cultural concept. The inference is that Taiwan has nothing to do with China and is already de facto independent.

In contrast to *The China News*, *The China Post*'s referential strategy shows a consistent use of the term "mainland China" when referring to the territory and the regime on the mainland and "China" when referring to the cultural concept. The distinction between mainland China and China implies that *The China Post* frames Taiwan as a part of China, as its official name, the Republic of China on Taiwan, suggests. *The China Daily* avoids defining China altogether.

A Clash of Ideological Systems. Assumptions about the political status of China/Taiwan underpinning the Taiwanese English-language press coverage of the handover are joined by additional background assumptions belonging to the political realm. Examples are the naturalized notion that the democratic political regime of Taiwan is to be preferred over the communist/socialist system of the PRC, and the unquestioned belief that capitalist societies automatically generate democratic systems, echoing Tory ideas expressed by British Prime Minister Margaret Thatcher at the time of the handover. The role of HK as a potential Trojan horse for the PRC is a recurrent theme in *The China News*, as is the view of Taiwan's democracy as a role model for the mainland, HK, and Singapore.

The differences between communism–capitalism, authoritarianism–democracy, and East–West are packaged in familiar Cold War language. Although *The China Post* and *The China News* have different views on matters of domestic interest, they are both committed to democratic values and show an unambiguous ideological aversion to the PRC. This framing is in line with the prevailing atmosphere at the time of the handover: for Western and Asian politicians (Clinton, Albright, Blair, Patten, Lee Kuan Yew, Lee Teng-hui, etc.), as well as for the international media, HK had become a site of ideological contestation. The PRC was once again pictured as the Cold War enemy and the villain of the Tiananmen tragedy. Britain's wealthiest colony was to be "surrendered" to the world's only remaining authoritarian (*The China News*)/communist (*The China Post*) giant. The debate about the likely erosion of Hong Kong's democracy was clad in Cold War rhetoric and was stepped up as Beijing dismantled the democratically elected Legislative Council and decided to send in People's Liberation Army forces for the handover ceremony. Not surprisingly, skepticism is present in both Taiwanese papers, even though it is often balanced by optimism about HK's future and its future economic links with Taiwan.

Hong Kong: "Their Own Masters" The myth created by the PRC that HK was to be autonomous under the one country, two systems scheme is constantly propagated by the mainland *China Daily* through its repetitive use of the metaphor that the people of HK will finally be "their own masters." The Taiwanese papers, however, question this assumption in their skepticism of the PRC's promises and expose the gradual erosion of civil liberties in HK. A *China News* editorial explicitly criticizes the "Hong Kong rules Hong Kong" myth, and adds weight to this proposition by choosing the deprecatory epithet "Beijing's puppet" for HK's chief executive, Tung Chee-hwa.

Since the 1997 handover, the much-celebrated notions of "Hong Kong autonomy" and "Hong Kong people being their own masters" have increasingly been exposed as discursive myths, among others by the participants in the week-long July 2003 demonstrations against the proposed amendments of Article 23 (an anti-subversion law) of the Basic Law. These amendments are widely viewed as having been encouraged by Beijing to prevent HK from ever becoming a source of inspiration or support for dissenting movements on the mainland (e.g., labor unions, the Falungong). The more outspoken position taken by the National People's Congress on April 5, 2004[7] made it clear that for the Chinese leadership "one country" supersedes "two systems." Arguably, the formula, which was devised by Deng Xiaoping, can at best be operational in the discursive domain, because its implementation in reality becomes impracticable as soon as "two systems" is perceived as likely to undermine "one country."

The Historical Realm

Time and space play a crucial role in the context of the handover accounts. Examples of this are the precise timing and location of the ceremonies, the fact that 1997 represents the time limit set for the handover, and the notion that the geographical repositioning of a territory implies the spatial extension of China. However, the handover gets its temporal and spatial significance especially in the wider context of attitudes toward colonialism[8] and sovereignty. The media placed the "micro" report of the handover in the "macro" context of Chinese history and inserted the present into a highly ideological perspective on the past and future. The handover activities were thus contextualized in terms of their overall historical and political significance. This resulted in different readings of Hong Kong history and British colonial rule. Myths were also created with regard to the "inevitability of Hong Kong's fate" as well as to Chinese and Taiwanese history in general.

Different Readings of Hong Kong History and British Colonial Rule. My survey reveals two different readings of HK history, refracting ideological difference between the Taiwanese papers on the one hand and the mainland Chinese papers on the other. The mainland *China Daily* essentializes colonialism by lumping together fixed ideological assumptions about colonialism in general, inspired by a post-colonial critique based on the villain–victim paradigm. Particularized perceptions about the origins of the unequal treaties as well as about racial practices in the early colonial period are at the basis of *The China Daily's* black-and-white portrayal of the HK colonial period (156 years of humiliation). One can speak of synecdochical framing here, since *The China Daily* uses a part of history as a stand-in for the entire colonial period. Its discursive fixating or freezing of particular experiences does not make any allowance for transformational historical processes. The Beijing leadership's construction of the "exercise of resumption of sovereignty" as a "retribution for a century-and-a-half of Western exploitation" is echoed by the entire mainland media machine. *The China Daily's* implicit ideological elimination of the transitoriness and variability of socio-historical phenomena through reification and legitimation processes contrasts sharply with its explicit emphasis on the historical value of the handover.

By contrast, the Taiwanese interpretation of history tends to dwell less on the early history of the colony and does not frame the handover as a retribution for a 150 years of colonial exploitation, even though it also endorses the end of colonialism. The Taiwanese media balance references to the early humiliation with a positive evaluation of Britain's more recent role in HK's development: It allowed the laissez-faire economy to flourish, established the rule of law and an efficient administration, fought corruption, and created a high degree of civil liberty. The Taiwanese papers can be said to de-essentialize the particular experience of colonialism in HK by paying attention to the positive sides of the British legacy. The British presence in HK is thus reassessed in the context of concrete and changing historical experiences. Allowance is made for historical development and the contingency/unfixity of identity.

Hong Kong's "Destiny." The sense of destiny is the dominant mood in the mainland *China Daily* accounts, which also in this respect follow the official speeches by Beijing leaders. Both *The China Daily* and the PRC official discourse continually frame the handover as an inevitable event. In doing so, they treat a transitory historical state of affairs, brought about by difficult Sino-British negotiations, as a natural occurrence, which is typical of the ideological practice of reification.

It should be pointed out that the future of HK island and the Kowloon Peninsula, which had been ceded to Britain in perpetuity through international treaties, was forcefully made to coincide with the end of a 99-year lease of the New Territories to the British Crown. That Beijing perceived and framed the return of HK to China as inevitable is clear from the way it steered the Sino-British negotiations. Although several options could have been conceived for HK, one of which was independence as in the case of other British colonies, the PRC demanded that Britain should also return the ceded HK island because Beijing perceived the international treaties as unequal and therefore invalid. Then Chinese leader Deng warned Prime Minister Thatcher that China would recover HK even if they had to take it as a barren island. This left Britain no choice. The idea of a three-legged stool (i.e., HK's participation as a third partner in the negotiations) was categorically rejected by Beijing so that HK citizens had no say in the determination of their future. The PRC's unrelenting stance hardly came as a surprise, given the fact that the first demand made by the Chinese leaders after the PRC's recognition by the UN in the 1970s was that HK be stricken from the list of British colonies. Clearly, HK was just a pawn on the chessboard of Sino-British relations. The further course of its history was designed by Beijing to be inextricably tied up with China's future.

The strong emphasis on the inevitability of HK's destiny, however, contrasts to a certain extent with the PRC leaders' belief in their ability to determine the course of history. Their conviction that they can control HK's future is made abundantly clear by their recurrent promises and unwavering assertiveness in predicting a bright future for HK thanks to the motherland's good care. By contrast, *The China Post* and *The China News* balance positive forecasts with skepticism and doubt. With hindsight, the Asian economic crisis that emerged just after the handover and the HK demonstrations in 2003 and 2004 calling for a faster democratization, render the PRC's self-assuredness of being in full control of the future ironical.

Chinese History as a Cultural Invention. The past often provides a powerful legitimation of present actions and desires. Referring to an ancient idyllic past in conjunction with a recurrent use of the family metaphor potently naturalizes the Chinese reunification discourse. Furthermore, the PRC's revival of the Opium Wars, during which HK was separated from its motherland, and the Chinese leadership's framing of the international treaties as unequal have also played a significant role in legitimating the return of HK to China.

Official accounts of history tend to perpetuate orthodox views. As a consequence, their portrayal of history has a homogenizing effect and occults historical contingency. Rawnsley (2000) rightly observed that whoever obtains the right to write history thereby gains the power to decide who are the villains and the heroes. The PRC's diplomatic isolation of Taiwan, resulting in the muffling of the latter's voice, and Beijing's hegemonic imposition of its one-China-version on the international community has effectively silenced other versions of Chinese history. *The China Daily* only tells a partial narrative of Chinese history, the one that is endorsed by the government. The Taiwanese English-language papers, on the other hand, harbor a multiplicity of views of Chinese history, even though preferred versions of Chinese/Taiwanese history implicitly underlie their accounts, as the following paragraphs explain.

Taiwanese History as Cultural Invention. Next to the PRC leadership with its hegemonic articulation of Chinese history, the Kuomintang Party on Taiwan disseminated its own particular version of Taiwanese history. The Kuomintang's cultural hegemony, which lasted from 1949 to 2000, largely determined how history was written by constructing monolithic discourses on tradition and culture. Its re-sinicizing policies silenced Taiwanese local culture for five decades. Only the landmark shift of power following the 2000 DPP's presidential election victory has broadened the horizons of historical interpretation. On June, 28, 1997, *The China News* printed a comment on its opinion page including a quote by Parris Chang, the former DPP representative in the United States, referring to the Kuomintang colonial attitude to Taiwan. This framing of the Kuomintang regime as yet another colonizer of Taiwan is part of a Taiwanese nationalist ideology. *The China Post*, on the contrary, dodges references to a foreign Chinese occupation of Taiwan, since it views Taiwan as a part of China. Its anti-independence position is cleverly clad in warnings of the real dangers involved in an independence declaration by its recurrent references to the China threat.

That historical (re-)interpretation was a hot political potato in Taiwan during the 1990s[9] is evidenced by the following quote from Wachman (1994), whose exposure of the contingency of historical constructions concurs with Laclau and Mouffe's position:

> Perhaps there is no correct view of the past or the present. There may be no truth to which one can appeal nor any way to determine who is right and who is wrong. Yet, each side dismisses the arguments of the other as a distortion of the past, a misreading of the present, a cunning effort to deceive, or a foolishly idealistic crusade. There has been very little effort to empathize with the other, to understand why others make the claims they do, or to reconcile one's own perceptions with the view of one's opponents. (Wachman, 1994: 382)

In short, history is produced and used for purposes of commodification (e.g., Hong Kong is turned into a sort of tourist attraction in the numerous articles on HK's souvenirs of the colonial past), political negotiation (different readings of history based on rivalry), and identity politics (constructing chains of equivalence [ingroup] and differences [outgroup]).

Concluding, I can say that my case illustrates that myths belonging to the cultural, political and historical realm are instrumental in forging consensus. They discursively bind members of a community together by making them aware of their shared cultural values, political interests, and histories. In all three newspapers, I find several concepts that are constantly reiterated and molded into myths. Although these are in fact congruent with the values the papers subscribe to, they are presented as commonsense universals. Rhetorical strategies of naturalizing historical and sociopolitical conditions and obscuring alternative versions of reality may have an intoxicating effect on the targeted audience.

CONCLUSION

My survey of English-language media narratives in Taiwan and mainland China about the HK handover suggests that the Taiwanese papers present a more balanced historical and political account of the sovereignty transfer than the mainland daily, although the former also engage in representational practices of highlighting and backgrounding as well as in strategies of naturalizing and myth-building. My analysis was geared towards the challenging of hegemonic discursive practices and the demystification of naturalized accounts. Examples of these are the firm belief in the supremacy of the Taiwanese democratic system and its potential as a role model for other countries (found in the Taiwanese papers), and the mainland Chinese self-proclaimed contribution to universal peace and the progress of mankind, the inevitability of China's eventual reunification, the normality of social consensus, and the victim–villain framing of Sino-British relations in the last 150 years (found in the mainland *China Daily*).

My research demonstrates how *The China Daily* conveys the PRC's official ideology, replicating the latter's sense of the Chinese cultural self, since the PRC takes culture and nationhood to be coterminous. By contrast, nationhood, national interest, and cultural assumptions are not necessarily linked in Taiwan. Although there may be consensus as to national interest, the cultural self in Taiwan is split or, put in more positive terms, there is a plurality of alternative versions of cultural identity. Because of this diversity of perspectives, no unified national cultural assumptions underlie the newspapers' narratives. It follows that the accounts of the handover can only encode the cultural values each newspaper assumes it shares with its targeted readership. Although both Taiwanese papers explicitly reflect mainstream official ROC views on foreign policy and national interest, their stories are ideologically encoded with diverging implicit messages concerning the cultural and political identity of the Taiwanese people and of Taiwan itself.

The China Post caters to the China–first readers by implicitly privileging frames of reunification with China over commitment to local Taiwanese affairs, whereas *The China News* targets the Taiwan–first audience by highlighting the theme of Taiwan identity and constructing the handover as an international affair rather than as a merely Chinese event. Domestic politics and local opinions are *The China News'* prime concern, and it consistently disconnects the fortunes of the HK formula from the future of Taiwan. *The China News* editor adopts a more tentative attitude when it comes to explicitly defending pro-independence advocates. This has to be understood against the background of the different ideological perspectives within *The China News'* production channel in 1997 (a pro-China publisher funded by a pro-Taiwan investor) and of the political climate of those years, which would have made an outright declaration against reunification politically incorrect, in other words "suicidal from an illocutionary point of view."

In line with Laclau and Mouffe's project, which aims at exposing the contingency of social identities, demystifying particularized versions of social reality, bringing to light the multitude of antagonisms and forms of oppression and thus overcoming earlier Marxist economic determinism and reductionism, my discourse-theoretical analysis of the newspapers' narratives has revealed the presence of a *"polyphony of voices"* (Bakhtin, 1981; Laclau & Mouffe, 1985: 191) within China, HK, and Taiwan. This study has demonstrated how in these three territories, several discursive identities were constructed at the critical historical moment of the HK handover in 1997. Furthermore, its results do not only pinpoint major differences in media practices between PRC and Taiwan, but also uncover divergences within the Taiwanese media community itself in its construction of social reality.

NOTES

1. By using all terms interchangeably (mainland China, PRC, China to denote the mainland and ROC, Taiwan to refer to the island) I avoid an explicit choice, which would imply a political statement.
2. Its propositions are based on findings gathered during my PhD research, which investigated the dynamic interplay of ideology and language in the media accounts of the 1997 Hong Kong (HK) handover from a comparative mainland Chinese/Taiwanese perspective.
3. *Mainlander* is a term with an ethnic connotation, referring to the people who have come to Taiwan from the mainland since 1945. The original term in Chinese, *Waishengren*, means "people from outside of the province." The term is used to differentiate this group of people from the local inhabitants who had settled in Taiwan prior to 1945 as well as the aborigines. The Chinese term for these groups is *bendiren*, meaning "locals."
4. My research findings indicate consistent divergences in the final output version of both papers' news stories originating from the same source.
5. The managing editor of *The China News* at the time of the handover was, however, a foreign newsworker with a long-standing career in journalism abroad. This editor assured me that there was little intervention on the part of the publisher except in ideologically sensitive areas (personal interview, 1999).
6. Examples of these various social movements are consumer movements, a conservation movement, a local anti-pollution protest movement, an aboriginal human rights movement, New Testament church protests, handicapped and disadvantaged welfare group protests, a Hakka rights movement, veterans' welfare protests, a women's movement, a farmers' movement, a labor movement, a teachers' rights movement, a mainlanders' home-visiting movement, and so forth.
7. On April 5, the Standing Committee of China's National People's Congress (the NPCSC) asserted that it has the sole authority to decide whether political reforms are permissible in HK. It declared that according to its interpretation of the Basic Law (the mini-constitution for HK), it has the final say about when, how, and even whether democratic reform will go forward in HK. Moreover, it ruled that requests for reforms must come from the HK Chief Executive only and not from the HK people or their elected representatives. This seems to be in violation of the spirit of Articles 45 and 68 of the Basic Law, which state that the ultimate aim of the law is the selection of the Chief Executive and the Legislative Council members by universal suffrage. In particular, Annex I states that amendments to the method of selecting the Chief Executive after 2007 shall be made by the Legislative Council with the consent of the Chief Executive, and are subject to the Standing Committee's approval only after the amendments have been made. Annex II states that methods of electing legislators not only shall be amended by

the Legislative Council with the consent of the Chief Executive, but also needs to be recorded with the NPC's Standing Committee without requiring its approval. However, another provision of that law, Article 158, does give the right of interpretation to the NPCSC rather than to an independent judiciary.

8. For a detailed and balanced account of colonial rule, see Tsang (1997).
9. The competing constructs of history in Taiwan's nation-building process are particularly salient in the controversy about the new history textbooks for junior high schools published in September 1997. The Taiwanese media largely participated in this wider societal debate, which points once again at their role in constructing sociohistorical reality.

REFERENCES

Bakhtin, M. (1981) *The Dialogic Imagination: Four Essays*. Austin: University of Texas Press.

Bowman, G. (1994) "'A Country of Words'": Conceiving the Palestinian Nation from the Position of Exile,' pp. 138-170 in E. Laclau (Ed.) *The Making of Political Identities*. London: Verso.

Chang, M.K. (1989) *Social Movements and Political Transformation* [She hui yun tung yu cheng chih chuan hua] (in Chinese). Taipei: The Institute for National Policy Research.

Chu, Y.H. (1992) *Crafting Democracy in Taiwan*. Taipei: The Institute for National Policy Research.

Derrida, J. (1976) *Of Grammatology*. Baltimore: Johns Hopkins.

Foucault, M. (1972) *The Archaeology of Knowledge*. London, NY: Tavistock.

Halliday, M.A.K. (1994) *Introduction to Functional Grammar*. 2nd ed. London: Arnold.

Howarth, D. (2000) *Discourse*. Buckingham: Open University Press.

Howarth, D., Stavrakakis, Y. (2000) 'Introducing Discourse Theory and Political Analysis,' pp. 1-23 in D. Howarth, A.J. Norval and Y. Stavrakakis (Eds) *Discourse Theory and Political Analysis. Identities, Hegemonies and Social Change*. Manchester: Manchester University Press.

Hsiao, H.H.M. (1992) 'The Rise of Social Movements and Civil Protests,' pp. 57-72 in T.J. Cheng, S. Haggard (Eds) *Political Change in Taiwan*. Boulder, CO: Lynne Rienner.

Laclau, E. (1990) *New Reflections on the Revolution of our Time*. London: Verso.

Laclau, E. (Ed)(1994) *The Making of Political Identities*. London: Verso.

Laclau, E. (1995) 'Subject of Politics, Politics of the Subject,' in *Differences* 7(1): 146-164.

Laclau, E., Mouffe, C. (1985) *Hegemony and Socialist Strategy: Toward a Radical Democratic Politics*. London: Verso.

Rawnsley, G. (2000) *Taiwan's Informal Diplomacy and Propaganda*. New York: St. Martin's Press.

Shiau, C.J. (1999) 'Civil Society and Democratization,' pp. 101-115 in S. Tsang and H.M. Tien (Eds) *Democratization in Taiwan: Implications for China*. Hong Kong: Hong Kong University Press; London: Macmillan Press; New York: St Martin's Press.

Tien, H.M. (1989) *The Great Transition: Political and Social Change in the Republic of China*. Stanford: Hoover Institution Press; Taipei: SMC Publishing.

Thompson, J.B. (1990) *Ideology and Modern Culture*. Oxford: Polity Press.

Torfing, J. (1999) *New Theories of Discourse: Laclau, Mouffe and Žižek*. Oxford: Blackwell.

Tsang, S. (1997) 'Government and Politics in Hong Kong: A Colonial Paradox,' pp. 62-83 in J. M. Brown and R. Foot (Eds) *Hong Kong's Transitions, 1842-1997*. London: Macmillan Press.

Tsang, S. (1999) 'Transforming a Party State into a Democracy,' pp. 1-22 in S. Tsang and H.M. Tien (Eds) *Democratization in Taiwan: Implications for China*. Hong Kong: Hong Kong University Press; London: Macmillan Press; New York: St Martin's Press.

Verschueren, J. (1999) *Understanding Pragmatics*. London: Arnold.

Wachman, A.M. (1994) *Taiwan: National Identity and Democratization*. Armonk, NY: M.E. Sharpe.

Arts/Film

4

THE CHANGING NATIONAL IDENTITY IN CONTEMPORARY MEXICAN CINEMA

Germán Martínez Martínez

One of the most rented movies in a video club on Earls Court Road, close to the London Underground station, is a Mexican film released in 2000, called *Amores Perros* (*Love's a Bitch*). This area of London is a popular place for temporary accommodation among backpackers from North America, Europe, Australia, and New Zealand. To a large extent, these young people are responsible for the success of *Amores Perros*. This is just a tiny example of a broader phenomenon, which has led to the description of *Amores Perros* as a "*resounding hit both in Mexico and abroad*" (D'Lugo, 2003: 221).[1] In terms of film criticism, *Amores Perros* first came to people's attention at the Cannes Festival, where it won the Critics Week Prize. After this, the film won awards all over the world.[2]

The resonance of *Amores Perros* has been different from that of other Mexican movies in the past. A recent example of this is the 1992 film by Alfonso Arau, *Como agua para chocolate* (*Like Water for Chocolate*). According to D'Lugo: "*Unlike Arau's film,* Amores Perros *does not present a clichéd Mexico for tourists*" (D'Lugo, 2003: 221). *Amores Perros* takes place in contemporary Mexico City and is a narrative of three intermingled episodes, which are not told in chronological order and where the only scene that unites most of the characters is a car crash. The first episode tells the story of "octavio and susana," in which a young man engages in illegal dog-fighting and falls in love with his sister-in-law; the second one is "daniel and valeria" about a middle-aged man who leaves his family for a model; and the last episode is that of "el chivo and maru," in which an old man, formerly a guerrilla, now a hired assassin and a tramp-like character, rediscovers the daughter he abandoned years earlier.

Alejandro González-Iñárritu, the creator of *Amores Perros*, went on to shoot his next films, *21 Grams* (2003) and *Babel* (2006), in the United States. This move is not unique, as other Mexican filmmakers have also turned to Hollywood filmmaking. The question that arises from the success of these films is whether something has changed in the Mexican imaginary that has caused these films to attract Western audiences. I suggest that, beyond issues like industrialization and modernization, there are novel discourses and identificatory forms operating in Mexican society. They are bringing Mexican identity closer to that of developed Western countries, particularly to the United States, without coinciding with it. A way of tackling this issue is to examine whether key aspects of the Mexican national identity discourse or other conditions of possibility have recently changed, leading to the emergence of the type of contemporary cinema of which *Amores Perros* is the most outstanding example. If we assume that identity discourses change over time, then we can analyze the dialectical context that encouraged the production of such films and also the contribution movies—and particularly *Amores Perros*—have made in changing contemporary Mexican identity.

This chapter thus addresses the dynamics between film and the changing identity discourse in Mexico. It focuses on the wave of cinematic production that started in the early 1990s and reached a peak of international recognition during the first years of the 21st century. I allude to the works of a few filmmakers, but dedicate most of my discourse-theoretical analysis to *Amores Perros* and its director. As was mentioned earlier, some contemporary Mexican filmmakers have been invited to work in Hollywood, on the basis of their first feature films, which are quite similar to U.S. films in terms of their capacity to attract young audiences. Having said this, the common identification of Hollywood with commercialization allows me to explain why a discursive-ideological approach is well suited to address this topic. An economy-based analysis would attribute the success of these Mexican films to the commercial decisions of filmmakers and producers, in the sense that they would be constructed as mere imitations of American models that have proven successful in attracting audiences. As opposed to this, Laclau and Mouffe's discourse theory provides us with theoretical tools that simultaneously allow an examination of filmmaking in its autonomy and of filmmaking in its interaction with cultural, political and social contexts. In this sense, even though commercial interests are at stake in the production of contemporary Mexican films, I show how the aesthetics, and therefore the filmic style, of this generation of directors has been influenced and shaped by a process of Americanization or, more precisely, by the process of close cultural interaction between Mexico and the United States, but also by Mexico's particular social development.[3]

THE HEGEMONY OF REVOLUTIONARY NATIONALISM

In terms of cinematic history, the way that leads to *Amores Perros* was not a straightforward one. First, I examine the circumstances that made *Amores Perros* possible. This evolution had three key moments: the so-called Golden Age of Mexican cinema (1940s-1950s), the presidential administration of Luis Echeverría-Álvarez (1970-1976), and that of Carlos Salinas de Gortari (1988-1994). This conceptualization allows us to study the interaction between cinema and the identity discourse that was hegemonic in Mexico throughout the 20th century, and which is now undergoing major changes.

The 1910 Mexican Revolution was followed by a period of political and social instability. This only came to an end in 1929, with the creation of a political party that united most of the struggling leaders and their factions in one political body, which could control the entire power game. This political party, organized by the Mexican presidency, ruled the country for the rest of the century, as until 2000 all of Mexico's presidents were members of this party. These administrations built their legitimacy on the hegemony of the discourse of revolutionary nationalism, which was the articulation of the social and political demands of the Revolution and the source of inspiration for the diverse policies put into practice by these governments. Consequently, *"far beyond the identifiable historical facts that its name represents, the Mexican Revolution has been, over all, a powerful ideological domination tool"* (Aguilar Camín, 1983: 11). As such, revolutionary nationalism was a discourse that was also present in socio-cultural expressions of that time. One of the core elements of the revolutionary-nationalist articulation of Mexican identity was its emphasis on the role of the United States as Mexico's historical imperialistic enemy (Bartra, 1993: 147). Moreover, as a result of the confrontation with the United States, a fundamental feature of postrevolutionary ideology was *mexicanidad*, which found its expression in diverse fields, such as the arts, political speeches, and specific policies.

After a phase of stabilization, the period from the 1940s to the late 1960s was a time of multiple accomplishments, initiated by governments that claimed to put the ideals of the Mexican Revolution into practice, as the country experienced a period of political stability and economic progress (Cosío Villegas, 1985: 170). This phase is known as the Mexican Miracle. Although the country experienced sustained economic growth from 1935 to 1970 (Cosío Villegas, 1985: 170), the Mexican Miracle was not only an economic boom. The term also referred to a series of fundamental social changes in the country. The lifestyles of Mexicans had fundamentally changed after the so-called Miracle. Starting in the 1940s, the governments of the Revolution adopted a strong policy of industrialization. Thus, the focus of the Mexican economy shifted from countryside farming to urban industrial activities. The government supported this transformation with a policy of import substitution and state economic intervention, which resulted in a *"mixed economy"* (Aguilar-Camín & Meyer, 1994: 161-162). Meyer described this mixed economy as an alliance:

> The overall economic goal, shared by the governmental and business sector of Mexico, was to use the great power of the presidency to move the country from its agrarian base and concomitantly, to export industrial products and raw materials. This ambitious project required, among many things, protective tariffs to lessen the impact of competition from cheaper and better foreign goods, mainly from the U.S. However, the long border shared by Mexico and the U.S. made it almost impossible to seal off the Mexican market from foreign goods and to impose effective controls on foreign exchange. Industrialization had to proceed almost without the market of the border states—which were linked, for all practical purposes, to the U.S. (Vázquez & Meyer, 1985: 153-154)

While articulating the government as the instigator of the Mexican Miracle, this quotation also points to the regional differences in the country and to the economic influence of the United States. Indeed, although after 1940 the economy grew at an average annual rate of more than 6%, this growth was distributed unevenly, both among social classes and between the regions of the country (Cosío-Villegas, 1985: 171). In particular, the agricultural sector and the rural peasants were left behind (Krauze, 1997a: 369). Hence, although many rural communities did not see any improvement of their social conditions, some cities flourished (at least partially) and several areas in northern Mexico developed in a way that was closely linked to the U.S. economy.

I would like to stress that these transformations changed the country over a period of several decades and, certainly, preceded events like the more intense phase of media globalization. The following data give a more detailed picture of the Mexican Miracle in sociocultural terms. The demographic evolution was important. In 1940, there were 19.6 million Mexicans; by 1977, this number had already increased to 67 million. Today, the country numbers more than 100 million inhabitants. As important as its growth, however, were the changes in the population's composition. Whereas in 1940 only 20% of the population lived in urban centers, by 1977 almost 50% of the population lived in urbanized communities. This evolution would continue over the next two decades (Aguilar-Camín & Meyer, 1994: 162-163), resulting in a majority of Mexicans becoming urbanites.

In the 1940s and 1950s, Mexican cinema was a strong industry producing a cultural export product that had an excellent reception throughout the Hispanic world, which made film appear to be part of the Miracle. These two decades constituted the so-called Golden Age of Mexican cinema. It was a period in which mainstream national movies were in tune with the identity discourse advocated by revolutionary nationalism. The industry was at what would later prove to be a peak. There was some state support, converging with entrepreneurs' investments and an efficient distribution system across Latin America (García-Canclini, 2005: 267). Skillful filmmakers of different registers, such as Luis Buñuel, Alejandro Galindo, and Ismael Rodríguez, were directing many of these films. Actresses like Dolores del-Río and María Félix; actors-cum-singers like Pedro Infante and Jorge Negrete; and comedians like Cantinflas and Tin Tan became stars throughout the Spanish-speaking world. But perhaps the most outstanding mark of this era was the popular appeal of these productions, which very often turned out to be major box-office hits. The appeal of Golden Age cinema not only left a long-lasting mark on Mexican popular culture, but also strongly influenced Mexico's image abroad, thus strengthening the hegemony of revolutionary nationalism through the creation of sources of identification. Golden Age motion pictures certainly became cultural icons, both in Spain and in the rest of Latin America. The characters of these films became archetypes and common referents for Mexicans. The *sombreros* of Infante and Negrete, their mariachi singing and the cactus environment that surrounded them still provides us with the folkloric image of the country. Also, these films continue to be part of the basic stock of several major Spanish-language television channels, and are constantly rebroadcast, even today. Consequently, they remain an important component of the common media-knowledge of its viewers. As for Mexico, by the middle of the 20th century, together with radio, cinema

> contributed to the formation of cultural citizenship [and thus] Mexicans learned to recognize themselves within an integrated whole, above ethnic and regional divisions. So Golden-Age [c]inema was not merely a prosperous commercial activity; it became that because it also played a major, imaginative role in the renewal and growth of society. (García-Canclini, 2005: 267)

However, the Golden Age came to an end, and the 1960s saw a sharp decline in both film production and the Mexican public's enthusiasm for their national cinema. The social context was hardly promising either. Starting from Echeverría's presidency, things began to change politically and economically, marking the end of the Mexican Miracle. Also, as Echeverría's policies were an attempt to re-launch revolutionary nationalism, as proof of commitment to the ideals of the Mexican Revolution, conflicts erupted with the United States: *"[B]y 1976, Mexico's economy was in crisis and its political relations with the US had deteriorated badly"* (Meyer & Vázquez, 1985: 188). Many of these issues had to do with state economic intervention.

Not only the national economy was influenced by the radical actions of the Echeverría administration, but also the academic and artistic fields:

> The cinema was to be central in Echeverría's domestic nationalistic policy. In no other presidential regime did the movie industry in general and certain filmmakers in particular receive more interest and state financial support than during the years of his regime [one of the essential factors for this being that] films could be used to promote official cultural nationalism. (Maciel, 1999: 201)

In practice, this resulted in the creation of funding institutions; the improvement of technical resources; higher salaries for actors; and the foundation of the Centro de Capacitación Cinematográfica, which even today is considered to be an outstanding film school (Maciel, 1999: 201-203).[4] Echeverría went even further when he discouraged private film producers by condemning the ideology of their films and warning them *"that the future of film production in Mexico would now be the responsibility of the state"* (Maciel, 1999: 201-202). These policies favored the careers of directors such as Arturo Ripstein, who has since created a large portfolio.

As positive as all this might sound, there were fundamental differences between the 1970s and the Golden Age. During the Golden Age, a strong connection between the general public and Mexican cinema existed. By contrast, the movies of the 1970s were mainly art films that appealed only to a minority in Mexican society. This was actually in line with Echeverría's strategy of sponsorship towards the cultural elite, which aimed at avoiding political conflicts through the co-optation of intellectuals and artists (Aguilar-Camín & Meyer, 1994: 187). Within this environment, the film industry experienced a revival, but simultaneously became almost totally dependent on the state for funding, which affected its production freedom. The strict self-censorship exercised by some film directors in order not to displease government officials, led to the production of flawed movies (Maciel, 1999: 203-205). Nevertheless, Echeverría's policies were supported by part of the intellectual elite, which was also favorable to what they considered to be *"a healthy distancing from the U.S."* (Krauze, 1997b: 743) during his presidency. In short, these events were part of an overt use of cinema for the nationalistic promotion of a revolutionary-nationalist identity discourse.

This phase of art film production was followed by long-lasting decline of the Mexican cinema industry, accompanied by ups and downs in the national economy. The film production policies of the subsequent administrations *"resulted in the near impossibility of securing production resources for filmmakers who were interested in making quality artistic movies"* (Maciel, 1999: 210). The late 1970s and most of the 1980s would witness mainly private productions *"focused on extreme violence, nudity, and degrading characters"* (Maciel, 1999: 210). Many of these movies were classified as "Adults Only," and the gap between Mexican cinema and the general public remained unbridged. In the field of cultural consumption, these were some of the first signs that indicated the end of the hegemony of the revolutionary-nationalist discourse.

THE DISLOCATION OF REVOLUTIONARY NATIONALISM

The time of change for the cinema industry, and for Mexico as a whole on a diversity of levels, would come in the late 1980s. As mentioned earlier, revolutionary nationalism was the hegemonic discourse in Mexico after the Revolution. In the 1970s and the early 1980s, factors such as the failure of the consecutive administrations to redress the economic situation and the struggle for democratization by different social and political groups increasingly undermined the prestige of revolutionary nationalism. However, revolutionary-nationalist hegemony would only come to an end following the dislocatory impact of the Salinas administration. Salinas systematically advanced a new social-liberal discourse. Emerging from the context of the end of the Cold War and the increasing trend towards globalization in the 1990s, Salinas' social-liberal discourse implied the beginning of a new phase in Mexico's relationship with its northern neighbor (Salinas-de-Gortari, 2000: 39-50). Although this opening was restricted to an economic partnership, it was in total contradiction with the revolutionary-nationalist identity discourse. Salinas, therefore, would radically reform the country's state policies and its relationship with the United States. The most eminent example of this was his signing of the North American Free Trade Agreement (NAFTA). These transformations were so radical that they led Huntington (1998: 150) to state: *"Salinas' reforms were designed to change Mexico from a Latin-American country into a North-American country."* Although Salinas' social liberalism did not manage to establish itself as the dominant discourse, it did succeed in breaking the revolutionary-nationalist hegemony. The mere fact of Mexico entering into an economic partnership with the United States produced an essential shift in the national identity discourse.

This discursive shift also had consequences for the film industry because Salinas changed the system of state control over the production of films. This time, not only art movies but entertainment films as well would be funded. Through this (structural) validation of entertainment films, audience-centeredness and pleasure became part of the articulatory chain of the social-liberal discourse, in contrast to the author-centeredness and the propagation of (a particular version of) national identity. This shift resulted in novel forms of expression in the motion pictures that were subsequently produced, as it freed the talents of people who otherwise would not have found the necessary funding. In this sense, Salinas' reforms and the evolution of contemporary Mexican cinema can be seen in light of the theoretical position outlined in the phrase: *"dislocation is the source of freedom"* (Laclau, 1996: 18). With the straightjackets of revolutionary nationalism being undermined, the opportunity for establishing new paradigms emerged. The lack of a hegemonic discourse would form the context in which the filmmakers of the 1990s would produce their movies.

Salinas' policies toward cinema were clear: *"to lessen the role of the state in the production of national films, give new impetus to co-productions, promote national and foreign exhibition of Mexican films, and help launch emerging new talent in the industry"* (Maciel, 1999: 214). As a result, *"before the [administration] ended, thirty-two directors completed their first work and exhibited it commercially. Seldom in the history of Mexican cinema have so many new directors emerged on the scene in one brief period of time"* (Maciel, 1999: 220). Among these were Alfonso Cuarón and Guillermo del-Toro. What connects Cuarón, Del-Toro, and González-Iñárritu is that the aesthetics of their first feature films eventually led them to produce movies in the United States. Interestingly, these films contain hardly any traditional or (stereo)typical Mexican signifiers. Among these movies are global products such as the third installment of the *Harry Potter* (2004) series and the award-winning *Pan's Labyrith* (2006). This could be read as a sign of the ease with which these three Mexican filmmakers relate to global audiences and markets. However, as I explore in the remaining parts of this chapter, it also suggests that their films are built on an aesthetic that is related to evolutions in Mexican society and identity.[5]

Cuarón (1961) and Del-Toro (1964) were born in a country created by the Mexican Miracle. Cuarón was born in Mexico City and would live to see the transformation of an already large metropolis into the world's biggest city, the megalopolis *par excellence*. Del-Toro was born in Guadalajara, the country's third city in terms of size, and along with Mexico City the main artistic center of the nation. Before shooting their first movies, both filmmakers directed episodes for television series for Televisa, Mexico's most important media company. Cuarón's *Solo con tu pareja* was released in 1991. This film was a romantic comedy showing middle-class characters in both modern and stereotypically Mexican surroundings. Del-Toro's vampire film *Cronos* was first screened in 1992.[6] It *"combine[d] conventions from various genres, incorporate[d] elements from Mexico's and Hollywood's cinema traditions, and blend[ed] Spanish and English"* (Stock, 1999: 268). Like *Solo con tu pareja*, *Cronos* was located in Mexico City. However, there were also important differences between the two motion pictures. Although in both actors played foreign characters, Cuarón's film was basically intended to create a comic situation commenting on the difficulties of communication. On the other hand, *Cronos'* use of the Spanish and English languages had, according to Del-Toro, the commercial goal of facilitating the film's acceptance by U.S. audiences (Stock, 1999: 278-279). Furthermore, the seemingly natural flow from one language to another in *Cronos* was complemented by subtle strategies of delocalization, such as the main character being an Argentine; a dialogue unexpectedly stereotyping Argentines and Peruvians; and even details such as the replacement of traffic signs in the center of Mexico City with signs in several languages, or the cardboard boxes of fictitious products found in an attic. All this diminished the emphasis on the local in the movie. Thus, while Cuarón represented a previously underrepresented segment of urbanized Mexican society, Del-Toro created an environment of his own. Both strategies were apparently well-accepted outside the segments of society from which Del-Toro and Cuarón originated. As diverse as they were, and together with other films, *Cronos* and *Sólo con tu pareja* were appreciated by the general Mexican public. This renewed appeal of Mexican films would not be restricted, however, to the Mexican public.

The careers of both filmmakers soon took a (for Mexican directors) rather unusual direction: Both went straight to Hollywood. Cuarón went on to direct *The Little Princess* (1995), and a new adaptation of Dickens' *Great Expectations* (1998), featuring international stars Ethan Hawke and Gwyneth Paltrow. As mentioned previously, he also directed *Harry Potter and the Prisoner of Azkaban* (2004). Nevertheless, at the British premiere, Cuarón declared that he had never heard the name Harry Potter before he had been offered the project.[7] The fact that such a commercial task was put into Cuaron's hands not only shows that the U.S. film industry had great trust in his talents as a director, but also that the producers thought he was capable of understanding and conveying the particular sensitivity of the international product that Harry Potter had become.

As for *Cronos*, it was said that it *"communicate[d] effectively with genre fans across geopolitical boundaries"* (Stock, 1999: 280). The film would actually pave Del-Toro's way to producing fantasy films in Hollywood and Spain. In the United States, Del-Toro shot the horror movie *Mimic* (1997) and the sequel to *Blade* (2002), with the world-famous action hero Wesley Snipes. In 2004, he produced an adaptation of a comic book story, *Hellboy*, with Ron Perlman, previously a protagonist in *Cronos*. In 2001, Del-Toro shot *El espinazo del Diablo* (*The Devil's Backbone*), a ghost story situated at the time of the Spanish Civil War; and in 2006 he released anothr Spanish-produced movie, *Pan's Labyrinth*, which won several Academy Awards. In 2007, both Del-Toro and Cuarón had several projects under way.

This of course points to well-exploited craftsmanship. However, my claim is that, along with González-Iñárritu, both filmmakers are representative of an ongoing process that brings important segments of Mexican urban society in tune with a number of expressions of U.S. culture. Simultaneously, through their similarity to U.S. films, these movies themselves promote that very process. However, a closer examination of González-Iñárritu's career, which shares features with Cuarón's and Del Toro's, shows that this so-called Americanization is less a product of aggressive U.S. economic influence than part of an ongoing process of changes in Mexican social reality and its national identity discourse.

SUBJECTIVITY: THE LIFE HISTORY OF A DIRECTOR AND *AMORES PERROS*

If we would subscribe to *auteurism*, then we would have to regard *Amores Perros* as a film that resembles "*the person who made it, not so much through autobiographical content but rather through the style, which impregnates the film with the personality of its director*" (Stam, 2000: 84). In this sense, the creative process of *Amores Perros* could be traced back through the career of its author and the skillful creation of a network of people that would turn a film project into a reality. Following Laclau and Mouffe's framework, a person's subjectivity is to be conceived of as an overdetermined construction through a complex diversity of subject positions and identities (director and Mexican, to name but two). The resulting unique combination guarantees individual agency. Tracing life histories then becomes one of the relevant methodologies for understanding the complexities of these identifications.

Subject positions (defined as the positioning of subjects within a discursive structure, see Laclau & Mouffe [1985]) and discourses provide the contingent building blocks for subjectivity, and should therefore not be disregarded. Mexican subjects have to negotiate their position vis-à-vis (among others) the revolutionary-nationalist identity discourse and its chain of equivalence (comprising among others discourses on the self, the United States, art and commerce, and the audiences).

Understandably, film critics have tried to trace *Amores Perros'* origins in the history of cinema, linking the film with movies that are part of their own personal cinematic culture. Less plausibly, film studies scholars have tended to disregard González-Iñárritu's life and social context. This has led to repeated assessments of many features of *Amores Perros*, such as the quick action sequences, as influences coming from the United States: "*the film does not hide its debt to a slick kind of Hollywood pop cinema ... [Amores Perros has aesthetics] easily recognizable as derived from certain foreign visual models (most notably MTV and Quentin Tarantino's Pulp Fiction, 1994)*" (D'Lugo, 2003: 221-222). When describing the opening sequence, which has a car chase in it, another critic claims that it is "*indebted to Reservoir Dogs*" (Arroyo, 2001: 39). Although I do not deny the (indirect) influence of U.S. mass media style on *Amores Perros*, I will show that these signifiers were co-determined by glocal experiences, rather than by a purely external influence.[8] This is relevant because identifying the long-lasting presence of these characteristics within Mexican culture shows us the crossroads that the country's national identity discourse has reached.

Alejandro González-Iñárritu (1963) was born in Mexico City. Early in his career González-Iñárritu made important contacts with people such as Miquel Alemán-Magni, son of one of the main stockholders of Televisa, and Miguel Bosé, son of the Italian actress Lucía Bosé and the Spanish bullfighter Luis-Miguel Dominguín. The combination of his social networking and his personal talents would boost González-Iñárritu's career as a skillful communicator in a variety of fields.

From his early 20s on, González-Iñárritu has been a successful public broadcaster. In the 1980s, he was a disk jockey at a popular radio station in Mexico City (WFM, part of Televisa-Radio). To my knowledge, nobody has so far analyzed the type of radio station González-Iñárritu worked for and which he helped to define, together with people such as Martín Hernández, another DJ, who would later be in charge of the sound production for *Amores Perros*. While most of the contemporary radio stations only played Spanish-language music aimed at the general public, WFM basically addressed a young audience, with predominantly foreign and English-language music, mainly originating from the United States. Although this does not mean that all of WFM's audience was proficient in English, it points toward its wish to identify itself not only with national music but also with music originating from the United States. This orientation was clearly different from the nationalistic tone of other radio stations, aimed at opposing foreign influences.

González-Iñárritu's work at WFM allowed him to create his own musical taste and influence the taste of his audience when he became the producer of several programs and the station's director. His choice, and that of his colleagues, was not to play commercial pop music but to broadcast a diversity of rock music styles. González-Iñárritu also explored imaginative ways to generate audience interest, such as broadcasting oral narratives. An outstanding example of these was transmitted during successive Christmas holidays and had a central character called *Pavo Asesino* (*The Killer Turkey*).

Although it narrated a complete story, it also had an open ending, which created suspense and made people await its continuation the following Christmas. These were the first stories that González-Iñárritu spread among youngsters, and they form an example of how his creative products appealed to a broad audience. These two elements positioned the WFM radio station as innovative and fresh, establishing a trend that lasted until the late 1990s. Even today, some radio stations still follow (to some extent) the style adopted by González-Iñárritu's WFM.

After this, González-Iñárritu worked for Televisa, where he became the creative director. While working there, González-Iñárritu became acquainted with several actors and actresses and with the musician Gustavo Santaolalla, who would be in charge of the original music score of *Amores Perros*. There, González-Iñárritu also came into contact with the future president of Televisa, Emilio Azcárraga-Jean, who produced a short-film segment, shot after *Amores Perros*, as part of an international collective film on 9/11.

However, the aspect of his professional career that seems most relevant to an analysis of the *Amores Perros* phenomenon is the visual work González-Iñárritu produced throughout these years. He was in charge of shooting short commercials that were meant to construct the image of the different channels affiliated with the national network. This included the production of commercials that had to convey the image of Channel 5, which was the youth channel. Its cartoons and series, although dubbed into Spanish, mainly came from the United States. The commercials González-Iñárritu shot were stories that lasted just a few seconds. As these stories had to convey their message instantaneously, the fast pace of *Amores Perros* is probably more related to these television antecedents than to U.S. cinema models. Among the images the characters of *Amores Perros* watch on television are those that González-Iñárritu produced for Televisa. In one of them we even hear his voice.

At Televisa, González-Iñárritu also attempted to launch a series in which different directors would independently shoot an episode in film format. Although the project failed, he did manage to direct the pilot program himself in 1995. The episode was called *Detrás del dinero* (*After Money*), and featured Bosé, by then a famous singer and actor throughout the Spanish-speaking world. In this one-hour film, the main character committed a bank robbery, just as one of the *Amores Perros* characters would later do. Thus, González-Iñárritu's successful radio and television experiences marked his development and revealed his ability to connect with and influence an urbanized young audience by contributing to the construction of the media's youth discourse.

The next step in González-Iñárritu's career was the foundation of his own company, called Zeta, which had three branches: audio, film, and advertising. For some time, advertising was the core business of the enterprise.

Again, González-Iñárritu would embark on visual storytelling. One of his campaigns, for Bital Bank, consisted of a number of brief stories. These shared situations and had characters that reappeared in the series, thus establishing common referents among the public, and a partial, episodic sequence. As with *The Killer Turkey*, these stories continued to be broadcast for a long time, effectively catching the public's attention.

González-Iñárritu also acquired a strong reputation as a publicist. His work environment at Zeta is shown in *Amores Perros*, with González-Iñárritu himself in a cameo appearance in the second episode, as a character arranging a magazine cover. At each step of his professional career González-Iñárritu accumulated further audiovisual narrative experience. This would mark *Amores Perros*, but not in the simplistic sense that one could claim González-Iñárritu's cinematic language equates that of television programs or promotional material. For example, although some of *Amores Perros'* sequences resemble video clips, González-Iñárritu did not shoot video clips prior to his first film. As I have demonstrated, the process was rather more sophisticated and refers more to the acquisition of aesthetic characteristics, such as tone and narrative rhythm. Furthermore, an important element of González-Iñárritu's communicational development is that he learned to be aware of his public.

THE DISLOCATION OF THE NATIONAL IDENTITY DISCOURSE

The circumstances were ready. In contrast to the Mexican art films of the recent past, *Amores Perros* was privately funded: Altavista provided 86% of the budget, the rest was financed by Zeta Films (Smith, 2003: 12). As ordinary as this might seem, this was a breakthrough, not because it was unique—as a matter of fact, it corresponded perfectly to the trend that Salinas' policies had tried to set by encouraging private production—but because it was done in an environment in which people were still reluctant to look for private funding and wanted to rely on government funding instead. For instance, just a couple of years before, and already after the Salinas administration, Ripstein said in a speech (with the Mexican president in the audience) that art films could not survive without state support and protection (Maciel, 1999: 225). This illustrates the struggle between the old revolutionary-nationalist identity discourse and the new discourse that was taking shape and aspired to replace the old discourse. A similar statement commenting on Salinas' cinema law sheds more light on this process:

The final revisions consistent with the spirit of the NAFTA, which included mass media and entertainment, did nothing to secure or expand protection for the exhibition or distribution of Mexican films. It was clear that the Salinas policies, as was the case with cinema, did nothing to enact any safeguards to protect the national culture. In actuality, these policies were designed to facilitate the expansion of U.S. investments and monopolies throughout the Mexican economy and society. (Maciel, 1999: 216)

A statement like this assumes that the state must protect national culture and that, in the particular case of cinema, it should enforce its diffusion, because—as one can already guess—national identity is seen to be threatened by U.S. interests. Within this discourse, the characteristics of Cuaron's, Del-Toro's and González-Iñárritu's movies would be understood as being based on commercial decisions that surrender to the aforementioned interests. Although *Amores Perros* was being praised at Cannes, Ripstein—who also presented a film there—publicly opposed González-Iñárritu's aesthetics by saying: "*I don't make films for idiots*" (Smith, 2003: 87). Such stances ignore both the sociocultural transformation of Mexico during its post-revolutionary period and the contemporary weakening of the revolutionary-nationalist identity discourse and its chain of equivalence.

In contrast to the perspective just discussed, the makers of *Amores Perros* did not hide their commercial intentions, which they combined with their creative aspirations. González-Iñárritu, along with screenwriter Guillermo Arriaga-Jordán and the executive producers, decided, for instance, to have a "*strong soundtrack*" (Smith, 2003: 11) with popular rock bands, as part of a coherent and powerful publicity campaign that would support the launch of the film. As D'Lugo said:

> More than mere borrowed devices from other cultures, the soundtrack affirms a substantive transnational context for the film, one in which Mexico is not simply an isolated, exotic, "other place," but a familiar urban mise-en-scène that is legible for audiences beyond Mexico. Combined with the frequent images of middle-class Mexico City, the music does much to undercut the potential exoticism of this world. It shatters the impression that this one [is] more exotic Third World narrative by suggesting a more universal urban experience. (D'Lugo, 2003: 227)

These different approaches to film production reflect the contrast between the two leading discourses. On the one hand, the stance represented by Ripstein, situated within the discourse of revolutionary nationalism, expects state intervention to provide resources for the creation of artistic goods, which are regarded by their authors and some of their consumers as contributions to strengthening national culture. On the other hand, there is the *Amores Perros* approach, which originated in the context of the dislocation produced by the Salinas regime: It accepts commercialization, while constructing novel narratives that do not regard themselves primarily as contribution to state-sponsored culture, but as private, more individualistic products, which may contribute to the elaboration of a new—and potentially hegemonic—discourse.

These implications of *Amores Perros* as a cultural event have not been noticed by nondiscursive theoretical approaches. Instead of identifying this process of change with its fundamental implications for understanding national identity, and *"despite the move away from a markedly geopolitical cinema in Latin America, critical discourse continues to privilege cultural authenticity"* as an object of analysis, and commentators *"insist upon imbuing these films with a national identity"* (Stock, 1999: 270-271). In this sense, some interpretations of *Amores Perros* force sociocultural readings on the film that seem to depend more on the commentator's idea of the real Mexico than on a close reading of the movie. Thus, it is interesting to note how the critics' readings assume that González-Iñárritu takes a number of stances that are conventionally considered progressive. In this vein, D'Lugo claims that a character mentions the alias *subcomandante Marcos* (D'Lugo, 2003: 226), comparing El Chivo to Marcos. In reality, the alias in question is never enunciated in the film.[9] Nevertheless, D'Lugo goes on to express what he thinks Marcos, the leader of a guerrilla movement of the 1990s, represents: *"Without forcing a political reading of the film, the line helps the audience recognize Martín as the saboteur of bourgeois illusions of social normalcy"* (D'Lugo, 2003: 226). Another example is found in Kantaris' attempt to read a number of Latin-American films as responses to the *"structural transformations of global capitalism"* (Kantaris, 2003: 189):

> the business of dog-fighting becomes in itself a powerful allegory for the systemic violence inherent within globalized capitalism. The owner of the dog-fighting business runs his firm according to strict and sound neo-liberal, market-oriented practice: "This is my firm [he explains], I don't pay taxes, there are no strikes or unions. Pure, clean cash." As an example of no-barriers private enterprise, of "flexible" accumulation operating with a labor force battered into passive submission, the IMF would no doubt approve. (Kantaris, 2003: 187)[10]

Perhaps these interpretations stem from what is most commonly expected from Mexican movies. As Hart pointed out: *"For many years the expectation had been that Latin-American films would take on serious social or philosophical issues and deliver a message to a blasé world"* (Hart, 2004: 190). These interpretations are ultimately founded on a dichotomy, in which on the one hand we have homogenous, underdeveloped Latin-American societies, and on the other an imperialistic international economic system characterized by (among other things) the dissemination of lifestyle paradigms through the mainstream media. Accepting this framework as relevant for the contemporary Mexican context would imply that the meanings filmmakers like González-Iñárritu convey in their films have little to do with the society they represent in their films. However,

> what happens is perhaps more pressing but much less apocalyptical. Upon insisting on cultural "penetration" (an expression that presupposes the cultural virginity of Latin America), a reverse sacralization consolidates the ideological devices of the commercial offensive. (Monsiváis, 2004: 214-215)

In other words, the apparent denunciations of globalization or Americanization take the success of such processes for granted, without problematizing the sources of change and without identifying their glocalized features. In countering the interpretations mentioned earlier, we should clarify which specific segments of Mexican society *Amores Perros* depicts. On the one hand, there is an element of diversity, as characters of different social strata are portrayed in the film. As González-Iñárritu wrote for the film's publicity campaign: "*Mexico City is ... —incredible and paradoxical as it may seem—... a beautiful, fascinating city, and that is precisely what* Amores Perros *is to me: a product of this contradiction, a small reflection of the baroque and complex mosaic that is Mexico City.*" On the other hand, however, there is an element of similarity: that of the specific type of Mexican urbanization during the post-revolutionary period. In this sense, González-Iñárritu commented in an interview: "*I am not a Mexican with a moustache and a sombrero and a bottle of tequila. ... There are millions like me. And this is the world I live in and the one I want to show*" (Patterson, 2001: 11). *Amores Perros* thus articulates a representation of the Mexicans who grew up in the heterogeneous contexts created by a process that started with the Mexican Miracle, continued with the years of economic crisis and was followed by the country's admission to NAFTA in the last decade. This context, as the very existence of the movie indicates, implies the end of the hegemony of the discourse of revolutionary nationalism.

CONCLUSION

As described earlier, Mexican society went through enormous social changes throughout the 20th century. During the last 30 years, it moved away from a form of nationalism propagated by post-revolutionary governments:

> For several years, Mexico has experienced a new era of younger customs and social expressions. The manifestation of this fact is quite visible on the walls of the cities painted by gangs, in the demographic statistics, in the entertainment industry that has successfully created child and adolescent musical groups, on the television screens, the theatres, the radio, and the bedroom walls of millions of Mexican youths. The face of this new majority that Mexico has generated in the last decades does not seem to respond either to proud Mexican traditions or to the folkloric clichés with which we attempt to comprehend them. It is a new majority, ... integrated with the perspective of modernization and approximation to the "American-way-of-life," a new majority without tradition, lay, urban, and massive, without whose social and mental history it will be impossible to comprehend the Mexico that we live in, or imagine, even approximately, the Mexico that will come. (Aguilar Camín & Meyer, 1994: 261)[11]

I would like to add to this that the so-called Americanization of Mexico is not identical to that of other countries. The overwhelming influence of U.S. popular culture can be said to be present nearly everywhere in the world. Although there is a closer link between Mexico and the United States due to the countries' geographic location and their partnership in NAFTA, the United States still constitutes the outside, for the same historical reasons that led revolutionary nationalism to identify it as the historical enemy. The United States is the other that provides the country with its identity by revealing its differences. As a consequence, Mexico is currently living a paradox, in which its constitutive outside is coming closer and closer. This seems to suggest that the future configuration of the national identities of both the United States and Mexico will be highly influenced by the relationship between the two nations.

At the same time, we should not forget that the United States is experiencing its Mexicanization, with the growing influence of the so-called Hispanic population, predominantly of Mexican origin. They already form the largest minority in the United States. With *"twelve percent of the total U.S. population in 2000"* (Huntington, 2004: 224), it is larger than the Black population and by far the fastest growing segment. This has led Huntington to claim that Mexican immigration, and the parallel process of Hispanization, constitutes a central challenge to U.S. identity. The United

States may be set to become a nation with two cultures, two languages, and two peoples (Huntington, 2004: 318). Although such an evolution, with its enormous sociocultural and political consequences, cannot be found in Mexico, this country is the main recipient of U.S. expatriates, hosting 1 million of the estimated 3.8 million U.S. citizens living outside their country (Ferguson, 2004: 209). Still, and even though there certainly are U.S. cultural influences and changes in consumption habits in Mexico[12] — of which *Amores Perros* is simultaneously an example and a promoter — the country's national culture and identity is not under the same acute pressure.

In this chapter, I have tried to show that *Amores Perros* is not only an important piece of cinema, but also a clear example of the complex identificatory interconnectedness between the United States and Mexico. This film is not the mere result of private commercial interests, but first and foremost an expression of a broader sociocultural phenomenon. The Salinas administration and the economic, cultural, political, and social transformations it instigated has had an enduring impact. García-Canclini wrote that in recent years every Mexican has to wonder if living in Mexico is a Latin American or a North-American experience (García-Canclini, 2001: 59). Another example of the end of the nationalism as it was promoted by the revolutionary-nationalist discourse is that, although there was opposition to the treaty when it was being negotiated by the Salinas administration, there is no national political party today that opposes NAFTA in its manifesto. The economic link with the United States has become a constitutive part of contemporary Mexico. The relationship between the United States and Mexico is strengthening and becoming ever more complex, and the longer-term consequences of this evolution remain to be seen. Although there is currently no hegemonic national identity discourse that successfully integrates what the United States represents for Mexican society, events such as the production and acceptance of *Amores Perros* show that the dynamic of Mexican society implies a close — but not symbiotic — connection with the United States, at least at this stage in history.

NOTES

1. For data on the profit generated by *Amores Perros*, see Hart (2004: 188).
2. Among others, at the Chicago International Film Festival; an Academy Award nomination for Film Festival and at the São Paolo International Film Festival. It also obtained prizes in Edinburgh, Flanders, Havana, Los Angeles, Tokyo, and Valdivia. In Mexico, it won the Ariel for best picture.
3. I refer to Americanization rather than globalization because, as I will explain later, the process Mexico is going through is specifically, and overwhelmingly, marked by U.S. influence.

4. Echeverria's interventionism also took the form of forcing film theaters to play Mexican films. This led to an increase in screen time for national movies from 20% in 1970 to 50% in 1974 (Maciel, 1999: 202).
5. Another example is Rodrigo Prieto, *Amores Perros'* director of photography. After *Amores Perros*, he went on to do the photography for *8 Mile* (2002), a popular youth film, featuring Eminem, employing the same techniques he had used for González-Iñárritu's film. In 2006, Prieto had an Academy Award nomination in Cinematography for *Brokeback Mountain* (2005).
6. In 1993, *Cronos* won the Critics Week Prize at Cannes.
7. Before directing this major production, Cuarón went back to Mexico to shoot *Y tu mama también* (2001).
8. Smith, too, contested these comparisons. Agreeing with one of the executive producers, he said that "*comparisons with Tarantino reveal an ignorance of Mexican cultural context, not to mention a deafness to tone.*" He concluded that "*studies of [1970s cinema] and [national soap operas] allow us to read narrative structure sympathetically for national resonance, without rushing to compare the film with over-familiar, but inappropriate, models from Hollywood*" (Smith, 2003: 30).
9. What the character actually says is: "*¿Asi como los zapatistas?*" (Like the Zapatistas?), which refers not to the followers of Emiliano Zapata during the Mexican Revolution, but to the contemporary guerrilla movement.
10. I can find no elements in *Amores Perros* that suggest dog-fighting is an allegory for contemporary capitalism. The character's income, or even profit, hardly accumulates, and can certainly not be related to "*flexible accumulation*" as conceptualized by its most important component, that is to say as increased international mobility of investment (Harvey, 1989: 338-345). Furthermore, the main weakness of this interpretation is that, in the film, dog-fighting, following Mexican reality, is portrayed as illegal. In such circumstances, not paying taxes does not relate to neo-liberalism, as opposed to state interventionism or social obligations. What the words of the character indicate is that dog-fighting belongs to the black market, or, more specifically, in talking about the Latin-American context, to the informal economy. This informal economy, which was described by De Soto in relation to Peru, but which is a reality in Mexico as well, emerged in reaction to the failure of states to establish fully fledged capitalist economies (De Soto, 1987), and not as an effect of the "*structural transformations of global capitalism*" (Kantaris, 2003: 189). This simply could not be so as the informal economy historically preceded the so-called neo-liberal reforms of the 1990s in Latin America, which fully inserted the region into global capitalism, as the latter is understood in contemporary debates.
11. I must stress that I am not presupposing the existence of a homogeneous "developed" of Mexican society. Even though, as González-Iñárritu said in his interview, the middle class, with a lifestyle similar to his, comprises millions of people, Mexican society is driven by severe social tensions that are actually addressed by *Amores Perros*. As D'Lugo (2003: 221) said, "*the contradictions of cultural modernity in contemporary Latin American society*" are a central theme of the film.
12. For instance, this is reflected in research on what Mexican moviegoers think of national cinema, as "*they see it through the comparative framework established by U.S. film. This is borne out not only by the predominance of U.S. movies ... but also [among other factors] by [the] development of aesthetic taste*" (Garcia-Canclini, 2005: 269).

REFERENCES

Aguilar-Camín, H. (1983) 'Ovación, Denostación y Prólogo,' pp. 11-19 in *Interpretaciones de la Revolución Mexicana*. Mexico City: Universidad Nacional Autónoma/Editorial Nueva Imagen.

Aguilar-Camín, H., Meyer, L. (1994) *In the Shadow of the Mexican Revolution: Contemporary Mexican History, 1910-1989* (L.A. Fierro, Trans.). Austin: University of Texas Press.

Arroyo, J. (2001) 'Amores perros', *Sight and Sound* (May): 39-40.

Bartra, R. (1993) 'Revolutionary-nationalism and National Security in Mexico,' pp. 143-172 in S. Aguayo-Quezada and B.M. Bagley (Eds) *Mexico: In Search of Security*. New Brunswick, NJ: Transaction Publishers/University of Miami.

Cosío-Villegas, D. (1985) 'The Present,' pp. 163-174 in *A Compact History of Mexico*. Mexico City: El Colegio de México.

De-Soto, H. (1987) *El Otro Sendero: La Revolución Informal*. Lima: Instituto Libertad y Democracia.

D'Lugo, M. (2003) 'Amores perros (Love's a Bitch),' pp. 220-229 in M. Díaz López and A. Elena (Eds) *The Cinema of Latin America*. London, New York: Wallflower Press.

Ferguson, N. (2004) *Colossus: The Price of America's Empire*. London: Penguin Books.

Hart, S.M. (2004) *A Companion to Latin American Film*. London: Tamesis.

Harvey, D. (1989) *The Condition of Postmodernity: An Enquiry into the Origins of Cultural Change*. Oxford: Blackwell.

García-Canclini, N. (2001) *La Globalización Imaginada*. Buenos Aires: Piadós.

García-Canclini, N. (2005) 'From the Public to the Private: The "Americanization" of Spectators,' pp. 265-276 in A. Abbas and J.N. Erni (Eds) *Internationalizing Cultural Studies: An Anthology*. Oxford: Blackwell Publishing.

Huntington, S.P. (1998) *The Clash of Civilizations and the Remaking of World Order*. New York: Touchstone Books.

Huntington, S.P. (2004) *Who Are We? America's Great Debate*. New York: Free Press.

Kantaris, G. (2003) 'The Young and the Damned: Street Visions in Latin American Cinema,' pp. 177-189 in S. Hart and R. Young (Eds) *Contemporary Latin American Cultural Studies*. London: Arnold.

Krauze, E. (1997a) *La Presidencia Imperial. Ascenso y Caída del Sistema Político Mexicano (1940-1996)*. Barcelona: Tusquets.

Krauze, E. (1997b) *Mexico. Biography of Power: A History of Modern Mexico, 1810-1996* (H. Heifetz, Trans.). New York: Harper Collins Publishers.

Laclau, E. (1996) *Emancipation(s)*. London: Verso.

Laclau, E., Mouffe, C. (1985) *Hegemony and Socialist Strategy: Towards a Radical Democratic Politics*. London: Verso.

Maciel, D.R. (1999) 'Cinema and the State in Contemporary México, 1970-1999,' pp. 197-232 in J. Hershfield and D.R. Maciel (Eds) *Mexico's Cinema: A Century of Film and Filmmakers*. Wilmington, DE: Scholarly Resources Books.

Meyer, L., Vázquez, J.Z. (1985) *The United States and Mexico* (M. Antebi, G. Benuzillo, M. Mansour, S. Watson, Trans.). Chicago: The University of Chicago Press.

Monsiváis, C. (2004) 'Would so Many Millions of People Not End up Speaking English? The North American Culture and Mexico,' pp. 203-232 in A. Del Sarto, A. Ríos and A. Trigo (Eds) *The Latin American Cultural Studies Reader.* Durham: Duke University Press.

Patterson, J. (2001) 'Aztec Cameras,' *The Guardian* (18 May): 11.

Salinas-de-Gortari, C. (2000) *México. Un Paso Difícil a la Modernidad.* Barcelona: Paza and Janés Editores.

Smith, P.J. (2003) *Amores perros.* London: British Film Institute.

Stam, R. (2000) *Film Theory: An Introduction.* Oxford: Blackwell Publishers.

Stock, A.M. (1999) 'Authentically Mexican?: *Mi Querido Tom Mix* and *Cronos* Reframe Critical Questions,' pp. 267-286 in J. Hershfield and D.R. Maciel (Eds) *Mexico's Cinema: A Century of Film and Filmmakers.* Wilmington, DE: Scholarly Resources Books.

5

ANTAGONISM AND GENRE

*Resistance, the Costume Romance
and the Ghost of Greek Communism*

N.Y. Potamitis

> The Greek people, who have suffered untold hardships, want to blot
> out—for a few hours at least—the memories of the past, and the uncer-
> tainties of the future. They demand distraction, and they'll pay for it,
> even if it means doing without some of the necessities of life. (Skouras,
> 1947: 55)

Addressing executives from RKO, Paramount, and 20th Century Fox in
1947, the Greek film producer Spyros Skouras spoke of the commercial
demand for a cinema of distraction, and in doing so revealed that the avoid-
ance of political realities in film is itself always political. His claim that
Greek cinemagoers would do without *"some of the necessities of life"* is not
simply a powerful image for the freebooting attitude underlying the explo-
sion in Greek film production in the 1950s; it makes manifest the interrela-
tionship between cinema and ideology. Skouras posited popular film within
the political domain from which he claims it provided an escape, and his
euphemistic reference to the Greek Civil War—*"the memories of the past,
and the uncertainties of the future"*—implicated cinema within a network of
violent social antagonisms, even as it attempts to dismiss them.

It should be noted that the development of the Greek domestic film industry in the 1950s coincided with a wider socioeconomic restructuring. Occupation during World War II was followed by a national conflict between communist guerrilla forces and their leftist supporters on one side, and right-wing paramilitaries, the remnants of the anti-communist regular army and its conservative British allies on the other. With the military defeat of the insurgency in 1949, the Right reclaimed political and economic dominance, ushering in an era of pro-Western capitalist expansion and anti-communist suppression. The historiography of this period, and in particular the scholarship on the bloody Civil War that catalyzed these transformations, has been articulated around a series of essentialist binary oppositions (see Close, 1993; Iatrides, 1981). The title of David Close's *The Greek Civil War, 1943-1950: Studies of Polarization*, demonstrates the centrality of this dichotomization trope to conceptions of the conflict. Approaches such as this have looked at the violent political conflicts of the post-war period in terms of objective relations between two opposed yet positive identities defined by class or race: the Right and the Left, Soviet-sponsored Communism and Anglo-American Capitalism, Hellenism and Slavism.

Following the discourse theory of Laclau and Mouffe, complemented by Žižek's work, this chapter proposes a radical deconstruction of this essentialist approach—a deconstruction that reveals how the anti-communist discourse of the Right—with its division of the social space into two opposed camps—was founded not on the establishing of *positive* identities, but on the construction of *negative* differences. "*The entire ideological discourse of the Greek ruling class,*" writes Constantone Tsoucalas (1981: 329), could "*only be formulated in a negative way*" (see also Gourgouris, 1996; Samatas, 1986). The Greek Right was a political identity constituted around both the negation of foreclosed social alternatives (socialism, agrarian reform, gender equality) and the negation of those subjects who identified with these alternatives (through censorship, imprisonment, exile, and execution; see Vervenioti, 2000; Voglis, 2000). To fully explore such a discourse requires a hermeneutic that engages with the constitutive exteriority presupposed by this double negation, and it is precisely this foundational dimension of negativity—the traumatic lack that drives all attempts at symbolic fixity—that is central to discourse theory's anti-essentialist, anti-objectivist and post-structuralist conceptual framework.

NATION-AS-LOVE OBJECT

[T]he atmosphere of the crisis went far beyond the period of fighting itself. The examination of its most striking characteristics must inevitably transcend the historical conditions of its appearance. (Tsoucalas, 1981: 319)

The anti-communist discourse of the Greek Right emerged as a purely *defensive* response to the questioning of power relations during and immediately after World War II. Through the efforts of Leftist resistance movements that were active during the German occupation, the Greek political landscape had expanded to include social groups formerly estranged from and alienated by the urban political center (see Hart, 1996; Mazower, 1993, 2000). Addressed by the wartime resistance, groups such as women, the young, and the rural poor began to re-think and re-organize their own social relations, for the first time defining themselves as politicized agents. In the aftermath of the Occupation and the violent Civil War that followed, this expansion of the political domain to include a plurality of previously excluded subject positions was rapidly perceived as a threat to the Rightist hegemony that had previously held sway. This proliferation of emerging voices was to be countered by both military opposition and ideological violence. Scholarly accounts of the Greek Civil War mark the cessation of the armed conflict in October 1949, with the scattering of the remnants of the pro-communist *Democratic Army* to Albania and Bulgaria. And yet the *political* demobilization of the Greek Left that began with its military defeat in the late 1940s, continued throughout the following decade and well into the 1960s (see Mazower, 2000). In fact, for Tsoucalas, (1981: 320) the first *"real political and ideological breach"* with the legacy of the Civil War *"did not occur until the collapse of the dictatorship of the colonels in 1974."* This ongoing political demobilization was carried out under the auspices of the State's anti-communist paraconstitution (*parasyntagma*)—established and maintained in conjunction with its official liberal constitution—through which the Right was able to institutionalize the repression and curtailment of political and civil liberties (see Pappas, 1999). While the state had won its military victory over the insurgency, it still harbored the fear of a continued threat posed by an encroaching communist ideology, what Nicos Alivizatos (1981: 228) coined, the *"theory of permanent civil war."* It was this rhetoric of permanency—of ceaseless defense against the ongoing corruption of communist influence—that legitimated the democratic Greek government's use of repressive technologies normally only associated with totalitarian regimes.

The *emergency measures* of the paraconstitution—outlawing of the *Communist Party of Greece* (KKE[1]), harassment of Leftist supporters, incarceration of political prisoners in concentration camps, anti-communist purges of the state bureaucracy, regressive education policies, expansion of the powers and functions of the military, stringent censorship legislation—enabled the state to expand its ideological discourse into a dominant social horizon. In discourse-theoretical terms, the ideology of the post-war Right was organized via polarizing logics of equivalence, which sought to reconstitute the political space into two opposed camps. It was an attempt to counter the proliferation of social and economic antagonisms—based on multiple differences in gender, geography, and generation—by recasting these myriad subject positions as equivalent to only one of two antagonistic alternatives. Ignoring political or class-based interpellations such as proletarian or capitalist, conservative, or communist, this State discourse recognized only the Nation and its enemies (Tsoucalas, 1981). Through processes of displacement and condensation, political opposition to the State was recast as opposition to the Nation. *"Greek communists were officially de-Hellenized"* (Gourgouris, 1996: 151) and so *"those that opposed the government could not be Greeks … they were simply bandits, slavo-communists, EAMoslavs, or even anarcho-slavo-communists"*[2] (Tsoucalas, 1981: 330). Communism was denounced as an alien Slavic dogma and the KKE outlawed as an organization of Soviet infiltrators whose continued presence threatened the security of the Greek Nation. Communists and Leftists were identified as Albanians and Bulgarians, nationalist shorthand connoting foreign anti-Hellenism stretching from the Occupation back to the Fallmereyer controversy.[3] Slavic speakers in Greek Macedonia and supporters of self-determination in the region were condemned as enemy separatists and a threat to the territorial integrity of the Fatherland, while opposition to the primacy of the Orthodox Church was read as support of Communist religious repression and a rejection of the tenets of the Hellenic-Christian civilization. But it was the formal integration of *ethnikofrosini* or *national conviction*—commitment to the Nation-as-love object—within the very institutional framework of State bureaucracy that did most to consolidate this recasting. Employment in the public sector, entry into higher education or even the obtaining of a driver's license were dependent on a public demonstration of commitment to national ideals. The centrality of *national conviction* to all interactions with the State meant that anti-communism moved beyond the confines of political debate. By being inscribed within the institutional apparatus of *ethnikofrosini* legislation, anti-communism could finally become entrenched within the processes of everyday social activity.

DESPITE EVERYTHING I AM GREEK

> Greeks were deeply divided into two categories: the "healthy," "clean," nationally minded *ethnikofrones*—first-class citizens—and the rest. The "rest" were the sick, non-nationally-minded miasma—the second-class—including not only communists, leftists, and sympathizers, but also anyone "disloyal" i.e. not actively demonstrating conformity and obedience to the anti-Communist state. (Samatas, 1986: 30)

As a discourse, Greek anti-communism used a metaphoric language of national health and social disease, in which the Right were physicians more than politicians. The State was committed to fighting communist infection, with *"national conviction"* serving as the criterion for the *"total exclusion of dissidents from the 'healthy and integral' national body"* (Tsoucalas, 1981: 330). And it was this image of society as a cohesive organic body—the corpus of *"nationally minded subjects"*—that became the fantasy around which the Rightist consolidation of post-war power relations was articulated. This fantasy of the organic Nation (the *ethnos*) allowed the Right to account for the disparity between its vision of society as a unified whole, and the lived reality of indeterminate conflict and struggle. With the economic exploitation, social inequality and class conflict characteristic of post-war Greece—riven with political and cultural antagonisms and still traumatized by fratricidal violence—the imagining of the Nation as an organic unity would seem impossible. Yet, the fantasy of the national body allowed society to confront this impossibility, to account for its failure to become a *"closed, homogeneous totality"* (Žižek, 1989: 127), by displacing the fundamental antagonisms that obstructed such closure onto an external corrupting element. In the case of Greece, the object-choice of this displacement was overdetermined by the country's political and economic dependency on Britain and the United States. In the context of Cold War power relations, it was the threat of the *"Soviet Union's expansionist menace"* that for the Right became the chosen symbol of foreign corruption used to mask the antagonisms dividing Greece (Tsoucalas, 1981: 329).

In the paranoiac Cold War imagination, communism becomes an external intrusion, alien to the traditional values of Greece's Crowned Parliamentary Democracy, a foreign body introducing corruption and chaos to the social fabric from outside. Following this logic to its conclusion, the removal of communist infection—its elimination from the rest of the social Body—will enable the restoration of a sense of identity. Take for example the language used in the official rhetoric of the Makronisos prison island, where Greek political prisoners were exiled for ideological reprogramming (Fourtouni, 1984: 169):

> In the great reformatory of Makronisos, among wise and benevolent teachers and healers of the soul, each man had been helped to see the light and rid himself of the terrible infection of wrong thinking, so that now they could once again take their places as nationally minded subjects on the side of the King and Queen.

Communist ideals, or even Leftist sympathies, are not alternative political opinions, but a *"terrible infection of wrong thinking"* to be cured, not by violent indoctrination, but by *"healers of the soul."* The success of *ethnikofrosini* in defining communism as a foreign body, both alien and antithetical to the essential nature of the Greek Self, is evident in these comments from an army Major, again from Makronisos: *"I was a Communist,*

too, but I got over it. For, despite everything I am a Greek" (Hart, 1996: 261).
Again, we are back within corporatist discourse. Communism is a virus that
attaches itself to the social Body from without, and like any other infection,
the Body can expel it and recover from its effects. It is possible to *"get over"*
communism and retrieve the irrepressible nationalist core of the ethnikofrones lying beneath the discarded remnants of an alien ideology. For,
"despite everything"—despite religious differences, despite political dissent,
despite class antagonism—*"I am a Greek."* It is clear that we are dealing
with a discursive field that articulates the conflict not in terms of opposing
political positions but as a question of commitment to the Nation-as-love
object. This profession of faith in national ideals was institutionalized in the
form of the *dhiloseis*—the repentance declaration and loyalty oath. Through
this formalized statement of national love, the stigma of national disloyalty
defining the non-*ethnikofrones* could be removed, thereby restoring the
imagined unity of the national Body (Voglis, 2000: 76):

> I renounce the Communist Party for the completely anti-Greek meth-
> ods that it employs and I am ashamed for having been its follower. I
> assure you that in the future I shall lead my life as a true-born Greek,
> faithful to the patrimonial national heritage, which a few evil so-called
> Greeks tried to ruin. I call on all the misguided young to follow my
> example.

The declaration of repentance was circulated amongst the various repressive
and ideological state apparatuses: prison authorities, legal authorities such as
the Public Prosecutor's office, the Ministry of Justice, municipal authorities,
church authorities, and the media. Its circulation across the socio-symbolic
domain imposed upon the signatory the symbolic humiliation and social
stigmatization necessary to retroactively articulate communism as a shame-
ful moral error and anti-communism, therefore, not as a political position
but as a moral injunction (see Voglis, 2000; Hart, 1996).

We see an identical retroactive articulation of honor/shame dichotomies
in the redefinition of post-war gender identities. And again this moral matrix
acts to efface the socio-economic, political and class character of such subject positions. For example, women who had been involved in the Leftist
resistance and could therefore be considered emancipated from both traditional gender roles and domestic social spaces were derogatorily labeled
"Bulgarians," "women of the streets" and *"whores"* in everyday speech,
propaganda literature and political songs (see Hart, 1996; Fourtouni, 1984;
Vervenioti, 2000). This sexualization of political activism and social autonomy conflates a double symbolic negation of nationality and morality. Within
this discourse, a subject position of politicized gender difference is recast as
a transgression of both national and familial honor in which these women

are re-domesticated—albeit negatively—as bringers of *"'shame' for the Nation and their families"* (Vervenioti, 2000: 113). This negation then serves to legitimate the subjection of Leftist women to actual sexual and symbolic violence upon which such shame/honor dichotomies are reliant. At the hands of Rightist security forces, paramilitaries and local vigilante groups, women who had been active in the Resistance had their heads shaved as a visual marker of moral turpitude, or were raped by aggressors that considered them already dishonored by their political activities. It is these subsequent acts of obscene violence that retroactively establish the subject position of the shamed non-*ethnikofrones*, by enacting onto the women's bodies the conditions of physical violation and emotional humiliation upon which such a fantasy of honor-bound national-commitment is predicated.

Right-wing hegemony was therefore articulated through twin mechanisms of condensation and displacement, mechanisms that recast political positions as issues of social and national commitment. With the criminalization of the Left, we see the displacement of political conflicts onto social conflict, with class antagonism displaced onto the terrain of law and order. State historiography inscribed the Civil War not as a conflict between opposing political factions, but as a *"bandit war"* (*symmoritopolemos*) waged by the authorities against violent criminals. Political opposition to the Right is re-defined and displaced as criminality directed against the State. However, through an additional process of condensation—through *ethnikofrosini* legislation and its rhetoric of *"national-mindedness"*—the Right could merge political acquiescence with national allegiance, and inscribe both within the institutional form of the State apparatus. And so, opposition to the State is recast as aggression against the Nation, and the communists become not merely criminals, or even traitors; their lack of love for the Nation means they are ultimately recast as simply not Greek.

For an illustration of the centrality of the Nation-as-love object to the dominant anti-communist discourse and its attendant sexualization of the symbolic space, let us turn to the popular film genre of the resistance movie.[4] Operating under a system of conservative self-censorship, the Greek film industry depicted the wartime resistance in accordance with State ideology: as a spontaneous national movement based on the activities of patriotic citizens supported by British allies and coordinated from abroad by the Greek government in exile. Within this Rightist discourse, wartime resistance was imagined as consensual, collective, and conservative, with any internal conflict stemming not from ideological differences between the Left and Right, but from the seditious activities of communist insurgents. These representations of resistance are structured by a dual stranded defense of national borders against two foreign enemies: Nazi fascism and Soviet communism. As an alien dogma, the attempted communist monopolization of the resistance movement undermines the resistance ideal of national autonomy, and thus must be resisted as vehemently as the more overt threat to the integrity of the Nation posed by the Axis invaders. The 1946 Novak Film production *Unconquerable Slaves*, and Finos Film's 1949 feature *The Final Mission* both illustrate this figuring of resistance unified in its opposition to two threats. And it is this second threat—the destabilizing activities of the communists— that is represented within the diegesis by the figure of the collaborator.

Both films invest in the promulgation of a discursive imagining of the enemy that conflates political, sexual and national identities. The political is displaced onto the libidinal, and the libidinal condensed with the national, with collaboration and resistance articulated as opposite responses to the Nation-as-love object. Resistance emerges as an ideologically sanctioned dis- play of national love expressed through emotional sacrifice, the forfeiting of sexual gratification, and the subsuming of personal desire to the needs of the community. Conversely, collaboration is associated with a prioritization of characters' own sexual desires—desires often expressed as corrupt or per- verse—and therefore antithetical to the demands of the Nation. For example, in *Unconquerable Slaves* the activities of the resistance cell are undermined by the presence of a prying neighbor, whose inquisitiveness and obsequiousness arouse suspicion. Eventually, he threatens to inform on the group unless one of the girls, played by Elli Lambetti, acquiesces to his unwanted advances. Following an attempted rape, the neighbor proceeds to the Nazi authorities, and the resistance leader is left with no option but to shoot him before he betrays the group and their mission. In stark contrast to the patriotic ideals of bravery and loyalty shared by the resistance, the collaborator is revealed to be cowardly, morally corrupt, and sexually depraved. While the neighbor seeks to blackmail the young girl for the fulfillment of his own sexual cravings, the girl and her friends in the cell actively suppress their romantic feelings for the greater good of the resistance. Again, love of the Nation supersedes all other emotional bonds. Similarly, *The Final Mission* demonstrates the extent of wartime collaboration in its presentation of a Quisling figure working in a liaison capacity alongside the Nazi authorities. Here again, the figure of the collaborator is portrayed negatively, both in terms of his actions and through his visual presentation. Where the sordid neighbor of *Unconquerable Slaves* is a squat leering toad-like figure, the toadying informant of *The Final Mission* is a diminutive oily character with slicked down hair and a snake-like appear- ance. The ugliness of the characters mirrors their behavior, with the torture sequence of *The Final Mission*—in which a young maid is brutally whipped and beaten by the Nazis—depicting the Greek collaborator as a sadistic voyeur, looking on in obvious sexual excitement. The sexual depravity of the figure of the collaborator is a corollary to his moral corruption and his rejec- tion of the Nation-as-love object. And it is this rejection of national ideals that posits the figure of the collaborator, not as a fascist sympathizer—as we might expect from the point of view of the Left—rather, from within the Rightist discourse of national-mindedness, the collaborator embodies the paranoid construction of the communist enemy within.

As we have seen, the dominant ideology of the post-war Right privileges the signifier of the Nation, to the point where the remaining signifying elements of the discourse establish meaning only in relation to this signifier-in-dominance. The Nation is the semantic knot that ties together the various independent constituents of the discursive terrain over which the ascendant Right sought to assert authority. It functions as a nodal point (Laclau and Mouffe, 1985), the Lacanian *point de caption* quilting what Žižek calls "*the multitude of 'floating signifiers,' of proto-ideological elements*" (1989: 87), stopping up and fixing their semantic sliding. And it is over authority of this stabilizing and structuring signifier that ideological struggles are fought. Defining the Nation as the organizing center of discursive articulation retroactively determined all other identities within the new structure of meaning constructed around it. Janet Hart illustrates how control of this key-signifier could shift from one bloc to another and how the faction conquering dominance could take control of the superseded subject position by retroactively redefining it. As we have seen, the act of symbolizing wartime resistance is illustrative of this symbolic re-articulation. "*To have been in the resistance,*" writes Hart, "*whose stated goals had been 'national self-determination' (ethniki avtodhikisi) and 'people's power' (laokratia) was now to be officially reclassified as 'antinational' (anti-ethnikofrosin)*" (1996: 141). The Nation functioned as the discursive signifier-in-dominance and the establishing of authority over its symbolic articulation was fundamental to the ideological struggles in the post-war political domain.

The centrality of the Nation as this key-signifier is manifest in the post-war state's obsessive recourse to the symbolic mandate of the fatherland (*patrida*), the spiritual—if not always geographic—home of the Greek *ethnos*. The efficacy of the concept of the *patrida*—through which the ideological subject is tied to the name-of-the-father*land*—and the history of its use stretches across the ideological terrain of Greek Nation formation. From the *Memoirs* of the nineteenth-century revolutionary Makriyannis to the fascist propaganda and sloganeering of the Metaxas dictatorship, the call of the *patrida* has been fundamental to the interpellation of the Greek social subject. The *patrida* functions as the symbolic agency in whose name the power elite can claim to speak, and through whose authority they can legitimate their continued enforcement of political and constitutional restrictions. And it is in response to the symbolic call of the *patrida* that the ideological subject relinquishes his own interests and submits to the law of castration embodied by the threat of state violence. It is of no surprise, then, that the post-war regimes should look to the *patrida* to legitimate the repressive ideological technologies of their paraconstitution. For example, the most serious offence for a civil servant as laid down in official codes of practice was not incompetence, or corruption, but "*lack of faith in the Fatherland, lack of faith in national ideals*" (Samatas, 1986: 48). Read in reverse, this bureaucratic rubric provides the definition of *ethnikofrosini*, for what is national-mindedness if not an expressed *abundance* of faith in the fatherland, in national ideals? As we have seen, defending the territorial integrity of the fatherland from the threat of communist expansionism provided the pretext for the introduction of a permanent state of emergency. Thus it was that faith in the fatherland became not only a political slogan but also a call for the state to restructure the bureaucratic, military and educational apparatus in its own defensive image. And just as the name of the fatherland unifies the political space of the right-wing regime by occupying the structural position of the symbolic mandate, so similar procedures operate within popular film. While we have seen how the wartime resistance movie highlights the libidinal economy of Greek anti-communism, it is the popular costume romance genre with its melodramatic plotlines and pastoral nostalgia that most vividly demonstrates the centrality of the paternal metaphor for narrative and ideological closure.

MILKMAIDS ON THE HILLSIDES

> It is in the name-of-the-father that we must recognize the support of the symbolic function, which from the dawn of history has identified his person with the figure of the law. (Lacan, 1977: 67)

As a cinematic genre, the costume romance, or *foustanella* as it was colloquially termed, emerged in the infancy of Greek cinema, but did not impact significantly upon film production until 1956. In that year, three adaptations of *The Shepherdess' Lover*—a nineteenth-century bucolic melodrama—signaled the return of the genre and posited it squarely within a cultural arena defined by its pervasive nostalgia for an imagined national past. During the 1940s, for example, Seferis appropriated nineteenth-century folk culture in his three lectures on the *Memoirs* of Makriyannis, the folk-romance *Erotokritos* and the naïve painter Theofilos. In the Academy, the study of folk history and culture enjoyed a brief resurgence during the early 1950s. One example of this new corpus of work was Hatzimichali and Benaki's two-volume study of the history and form of *Hellenic National Costumes*, completed and published between 1948 and 1954. In addition to, and in conjunction with, this renewed interest in folk costume was the establishment during the 1950s of a large number of popular folk dance troupes, whose repertoires consisted of regional songs and dances. In terms of its own narrative origins, the *foustanella* itself emerged out of such still popular sources as nineteenth-century folk song, melodrama, and operetta. In addition to these nineteenth-century antecedents, the *foustanella* also drew heavily on contemporary narrative models. The genre borrowed elements from the romantic plot of the woman's film or "weepy," as well as from crime movies and even the

Hollywood Western. Whatever its particular trappings, the narrative tended to focus on the romantic trials of a rural love-couple often transgressing social boundaries or disobeying parental edicts in the name of love.

In drawing on a variety of cinematic codes and structuring them around a central romantic core, the *foustanella* promised its audience "*tears and excitement*" in a highly intertextual melodrama full of passion, conflict and the threat of violence (Mitropoulou, 1980: 117). The past as constructed in the costume romance was a place in which transgression, disobedience and romantic passion could all be safely enjoyed as part of the nostalgic pleasure offered by the film. For example, Dinos Dimopoulos' 1958 film *Astero* (director Dinos Dimopoulos, writer Alekos Sakellarios, producer Finos Film) presents a melodramatic narrative that revolves around the identity and origin of the eponymous heroine played by Aliki Vouyouglaki. Yet it is with the father-figure of Mitros (Titos Vandis) that the responsibility for establishing the film's initial deadlock and the power to resolve it both reside. Abandoned as a baby, Astero was raised in the household of a wealthy land-owning shepherd, Mitros, where she now lives and works as his servant girl. Ignorant of her origins or the identity of her parents, Astero hopes to find stability in marriage to her childhood sweetheart, Mitros' son Thimios (Dimitris Papamichael). Mitros, however, demands that his son's prospective wife bring in a dowry befitting his social status, and so violently opposes the proposed marriage. Prohibited from formally becoming part of the only family she has ever known, and unwilling to marry the alternative husband Mitros has chosen for her, Astero flees the village but is eventually found hiding in an underground cavern by Thimios and his father. Astero has clearly descended into a state of madness. At the sight of the young girl in such a pathetic state Mitros breaks down.

Astero's conception of the world has collapsed and she is forced to create a hysterical fantasy of family life in which she can participate despite her poverty. Abandoned by her lover and his family, alone and with no possessions, Astero retreats into a fantasy identity in which her desire for a sense of security and belonging can be fulfilled: "*I don't have a father, a mother did not give birth to me [...] My mother is the earth, and the trees are my brothers.*" Astero's "*family romance*"—which in this sequence finds verbal articulation—is visually emphasized throughout the film as an affinity with nature. The opening shot of the movie follows Astero and Thimios as they run playfully through a wooded glade. She whispers her love for Thimios to a flower, and later wears blossoms in her hair. Astero even takes pleasure in bathing naked in the river, and when she is spotted hides nymph-like in the undergrowth. It is in these visual associations, and in the poetry of her hysterical monologue, that Astero's attempts to resolve the question of her true origins are articulated. Enlightenment, however, does not arrive until the film's dramatic closing sequences. Distraught at the pathetic sight of the young girl and racked with guilt, Mitros finally tells the young lovers the story of Astero's origins. Conceived out of wedlock to a wealthy neighboring villager, Astero was secretly given to Mitros to be raised as his own. In return he was given money to help feed and clothe the child and was to take charge of her inheritance until she came of age. However, he stole Astero's birthright and used it to transform himself from a lowly farmhand into one of the wealthiest landowners in the village. Mitros' crimes are therefore twofold. Not only is he guilty of disenfranchising the girl by stealing her economic inheritance but also of stealing her symbolic inheritance. In withholding Astero's true identity from her, Mitros has barred her entry into the symbolic order. Therefore, the only recompense the father can offer is to allow her a place within the social network of his own family. By giving Thimios his blessing to marry Astero, Mitros resolves the conflict he himself had created by obscuring Astero's identity and the film moves towards a resolution in full accordance with the romantic logic of its narrative matrix. Thus the significance of Mitros lies not simply in his status as head of the household and *tselingas*; the wealthiest and most influential landowner in the village. As the figure that holds the key to the narrative enigma, he occupies a central role within the structural organization of the filmic fabula. Through this condensation of domestic, social, and narrative roles, the paternal authority of the biological father is transformed into the patriarchal authority of the symbolic Father; an authority that does not derive from any biological mandate but from the assumption of a structural position within the wider symbolic network.

And so we return to the Nation-as-paternal metaphor, as nodal point; the structural position that fixes meaning in a given ideological field. Through the repressive ideological technology of the *ethnikofrosini* legislation, *"faith in national ideals"* was inscribed within the political infrastructure, and as such the Nation concept was now itself radically politicized. In terms of such ideological maneuvering, national commitment could no longer be taken for granted; it had to be proved, which meant adhering to state definitions. It is clear then that the Rightist regime was able to successfully consolidate itself by means of an ideological discourse the fundamental premise of which was the conflation of national identity with its own class interests. Yet, as we have seen in relation to the shifting symbolization of the Resistance, the success of the *ethnos* as the *point de capiton*—the way it inscribes the values of opposing discourses into the social imaginary—is due not to its positivity—its fullness as a symbol—but to its emptiness. As such, its function is a negative one: to delimit, to deny and to denounce. Greek Communists were *"officially de-Hellenized"* (Gourgouris, 1996: 151), since in the rhetoric of the Right those who opposed the state opposed the Nation and were, therefore, simply not Greeks. Thus the Nation-as-nodal point enables the development of a twofold negation of identity by the state: the negation of alternative values, meanings, and interpretations, and the negation of collective identities articulated around those alternative positions.

According to Laclau and Mouffe, this process of exclusion enables a discursive formation to constitute identities, by allowing it to establish itself in opposition to an antagonistic force external to it. Thus we see that the State discourse of national conviction establishes an ever-expanding series of excluded elements—what Laclau and Mouffe would call a chain of equivalence. These excluded elements are linked in a relationship of sameness whose only common denominator is their very exclusion from the discourse of national conviction. As the chain of equivalence expands to include not only Communist guerrillas and EAM activists, but also pacifists, political critics of American aid, agrarian-rights campaigners, republicans, Leftist trades-unionists, Slavophone Macedonians, progressive educationalists, and atheists, it becomes self-evident that the only common ground between these disparate elements is their being discursively articulated as anti-Hellenic. The signifier Nation is emptied to the point where it becomes meaningful only when confronted with a discursive exterior, that is, it is eventually only this oppositional relationship between elements that determines their significance.

It is clear, then, that the identities we are concerned with here are not positive, essential entities, but require determination through the key signifier to achieve a semblance of positivity. It is their articulation within a discursive field that inscribes them anew in accordance with the nodal point, that sign "*to which 'things' themselves refer to recognize themselves in their unity*" (Žižek, 1989: 95-96). For example, the social subject's identification with the symbolization of the Nation does not simply follow from accepting "national ideals"; neither does it come from an adherence to the ideals of the state. It comes at the point at which the subject recognizes the ideals of the state *as* the ideals of the Nation. Thus the Nation—the imagined community of social subjects—emerges not from any positive content of its own "Nation-ness," but only at the point when "real" social subjects identify their lived experiences with the imagery of Nationhood. Again, the costume romance and its nostalgic *mise-en-scène* provide an illustration of this process of inversion. Rather than strive for an accurate representation of the past through a rigorous attention to historical detail, the *foustanella* favors a visual aesthetic that produces an imaginary approximation or *feel* of the past. Elements of costume and décor—while procured from antique shops, folk museums or private collections and therefore authentic in themselves— would often be juxtaposed with items from wildly differing historical periods or geographic regions. The end result is what Sue Harper in her studies of British bodice-rippers has called a "*chaotic amalgam—an opened cache of objects with uncertain meaning but available 'beauty'*" (Harper, 1987: 180). This visual overlaying of folk artifacts such as dresses, spinning wheels, and shepherd's crooks—as with the cinematic reworking of theatrical figures, folk heroes and cultural stereotypes—creates a sense of cultural familiarity and nostalgia. In an aesthetic mélange of Ottoman and fin-de-siècle Greece, the films offer a *mise-en-scène* of an imagined national past, in which histor-ical images, folk motifs and popular archetypes are reduced to decorative elements. The costume romance is a clear illustration of what Seferis calls *"the folklore side of art"* — a superficial emphasis on the identificatory signif-icance of surface details: *"the local costumes, the foustanellas, the milkmaids on the hillsides"* (Seferis, 1982: 5). It is from the overlapping of these cultur-al markers that the *foustanella* constructs a nostalgic *bricolage* of the Nation. And it is here that the anti-essentialist inversion takes place. Identification occurs not when the audience recognizes some essential national identity within the imagery of the films, but when it begins to identify with the empty motifs of the filmic imagination. It is not that the cinema projects a sense of national identity, but that the identification with a particular vision of the Nation is projected upon the cinema. As Slavoj Žižek argues in rela-tion to the culture industry tropes of America: *"the point is not that Coca-Cola 'connotes' a certain ideological experience-vision of America (the fresh-ness of its sharp cold taste); the point is that this vision of America itself achieves its identity by identifying with the signifier 'Coke'"* (1989: 96). So also with the rural landscapes, traditional costumes and folksong of the *fous-tanella*. These romantic motifs do not reflect a particular vision of national identity — popular values and traditions are rooted in the very soil of the Nation; virtue resides with the common people — instead it is this populist ideology that identifies with the imagery of the *foustanella*.

Returning to the ideological discourse of the Right, it is the negative inversion — the identification with the national body — that offers both an escape from the trauma of civil war anticommunism and the legitimization of its continued presence. Through the mediation of "national conviction," the signifier "Greek" remains unchanged, but its signified, what it alludes to, is radically altered, radically politicized. By identifying with the position *"for, despite everything I am a Greek,"* the *ethnikofrones* are *"obliged already to have forgotten"* (Anderson, 1991: 200) not simply an alternative political position, but the violent repression of that position by the state. The subject's ideological complicity resides in the fact that behind this refusal to remember is the impossibility to forget. The trauma of a fratrici-dal class conflict can be escaped only through the comfort offered by the image of a cohesive national Body. And yet this national Body is itself no more than the fantasy of an essential and apolitical "Greekness" within the institution of a state-defined and class-oriented national rhetoric. It is the subject's paradoxical act of *"remembering-to-forget"* (Bhabha, 1991: 93), of ignoring its own complicity within the politics of *"national conviction"* that ultimately secures it within its ideological orbit. The *ethnos* is the fantasy through which the subject can protect itself behind a timeless, apolitical, and unifying identity, despite its knowledge that this identity is nothing but a contingent, partisan and divisive ideological construct.

DOOMED TO WALK THE NIGHT

[R]eality is not the "thing itself," it is always-already symbolized, constituted, structured by symbolic mechanisms—and the problem resides
in the fact that symbolization ultimately always fails, that it never succeeds in fully "covering" the real, that it always involves some unsettled,
unredeemed symbolic debt. This real (the part of reality that remains
non-symbolized) returns in the guise of spectral apparitions. (Žižek,
1994: 21)

Once essentialism is abandoned, social subject formation becomes a process
where identities are mutable, their articulation contingent on the discursive
mechanisms of difference and equivalence, condensation and displacement.
The fact that identities are no longer given but articulated, that they achieve
coherence through a process of discursive mediation and negotiation, opens
up space for the deconstruction of these articulations and the uncovering of
alternative meanings suppressed by the dominant ideology and buried
beneath the layers of its symbolization.

   In her work on post-war Greek cinema, Maria Stassinopoulou has
endeavored to show how certain films offer narrative alternatives to their
overtly Statist ideologies. For example, Stassinopoulou argues that central to
the *foustanella* is the narrative *"conflict with the father."* It is evident from
the above discussion of *Astero* that the structuring of the narrative resolution around the figure of the father imposes a conservative order on the
unfolding fabula, emphasizing a return to the stability of the status quo.
Stassinopoulou claims that while such popular films demonstrate *"an
oppressive ideology"* in terms of their manifest content, it is possible to discern in them *"an underlying divergent narrative"* in which *"the infallibility
of the father figure is often questioned"* (Stassinopoulou, 1997: 7). For example in a typical narrative configuration, the 1959 film
Sarakatsanissa/Sarakatsani Girl (director and writer Orestis Laskos, produced by C. Maniatis) questions paternal authority through an exploration
of the romantic tribulations of a young love couple. The plot follows the
struggles of a young man and woman from opposing sides of a Sarakatsanni
village split into two factions. The fissure dividing the village—symbolized
by a river running through its center—is an obvious reference to the political schism of post-war Greek society. The film highlights a narrative structure in which the constitution of the love couple requires parental reconciliation (see Stassinopoulou, forthcoming). In her discussions of
Gerakina/The Falconress (directed and writen by Orestis Laskos, produced
by Chrisma Film, 1959) Stassinopoulou draws attention to the narrative elements that highlight an alternative to the film's dominant ideological rhetoric. *Gerakina* follows the persecution of the film's star Giorgos Foundas, a

romantic fugitive hiding out in the mountains as local law enforcement forces hunt him down for a murderous crime of passion. Describing *Gerakina*, Stassinopoulou writes (1997: 8):

> If the film is read as an allegory of the political situation it seems obvious that while the defeat of the Left is nonnegotiable, the winner is called to recognize his responsibility in starting and perpetuating the conflict. He is also called to stop persecution of the people related to the initial conflict and also to re-integrate the persecuted in society if political and social harmony is to be reached.

In our reworking, what begins as an undermining of the "infallibility of the father" becomes a radical questioning of the law of the Father, prompting not the reworking of family structures but the far more incendiary interrogation of the social order. It is important to note that the ability to recognize these "divergent narratives" is not reliant on the critical distance offered by a contemporary vantage point. Stassinopoulou states that the original audiences of these films were often fully cognizant of the dissenting voices hidden within them, and in the case of *Gerakina*, the outlawed KKE even sent "*small parties to applaud at the 'right' moments*" (1997: 12). And yet, during the 1950s, the emergency measures and State censorship prevented the Greek film industry from actually producing a single film that directly tackled the violence of the Civil War. Instead, a repressed narrative of filial conflict returned within the films, as a concealed voice articulating a desire for reconciliation and social cohesion. As one can see, revealing repressed meaning that yields to close reading allows us to dispel the view of popular film as mere distraction or the simple reflection of a dominant world-view. Obviously, our interpretative schema is akin to Freudian dream-analysis, in which a distinction is made between the manifest text of the dream and its latent dream-content. Freud's analysis, however, always involved a third step: a move beyond the hidden meaning of the dream-thoughts to a concern with the actual *form* of the dream through which the thoughts were articulated.

Moving then to this third structural level—what Freud termed the "dream-work"—we can observe that the "divergent narratives" of *Astero*, *Sarakatsanissa* and *Gerakina* all contain allusions to the struggles of the Civil War, allusions characterized by a spectral, ghostly quality. They consist of a series of images that are both present and absent, clearly discernible and yet not quite there. The spectral nature of these phenomena is manifest in the motifs through which they are articulated. In *Astero*, it is Vouyouglaki's disenfranchised eponymous heroine who represents the defeated and dispossessed Resistance, barred from entry into the symbolic domain of the national imaginary. When she finally descends into madness, Astero is found hiding in a mountain cave where she enacts her hysterical monologue before Mitros and Thimios. The local villager who leads the two men to Astero talks of her as a witch or spirit and indeed, when she appears, dressed only in her torn white wedding gown and with blossoms in her bedraggled hair, she takes on a dryadic appearance. The vacant stare and ghostly timbre of her voice, along with the expressionistic lighting of the underground cavern, all add to the spectral nature of her appearance. Similarly, in *Sarakatsanissa* the divided hamlet—a microcosmic manifestation of the national schism—is described, by a ghostly voice-over that never finds embodiment within the filmic diegesis, as *"a strange village unlike any other in Greece."* It is literally a blot on the landscape, a grotesque apparition that is both uncanny and strangely recognizable, a vivid realization of an impossible image. In *Gerakina*, the figure that embodies the persecuted Left is a mountain-dwelling fugitive who flits in and out of the narrative, leaving no trace of his presence behind him. His spectral nature is established even before he actually appears on the screen. Initially, we only observe two villagers discussing the exploits of the murderous "ghost," a fleeting menace that haunts the countryside. His first visual appearance comes in the form of a flashback. One of the village girls, another Astero, retells the account of her first meeting with the ghost, who appeared before her as she lay sleeping on the mountainside. The third manifestation is only as an acousmatic trace. As she prepares for bed, we see Maro—the ghost's sister—recognize the sound of her brother's flute as he plays in the distance. Finally the ghost makes his way down to the village to surprise Astero. He enters the frame from a hidden position behind the camera. The effect is that of materializing before the young girl. This series of apparitions and half-glimpsed appearances all clearly mark out the spectral nature of the film's allusions to the defeated Resistance.

These spectral apparitions serve as reminders of what Žižek would call an *"unsettled, unredeemed symbolic debt"* (1994: 21). For what is a specter or ghost if not *"someone who went unburied or was badly buried"* (Chion, 1992: 195)? It is evident that the consolidation of a right-wing hegemony necessitated the denial of any form of symbolic burial to the defeated Greek communists. While the actual and political death of the Communist guerrillas came with their military defeat by the Greek State and its western allies in October 1949, this event was unaccompanied by any form of symbolization. Here we can draw a parallel with another specter: the ghost of Hamlet's father, who was murdered by his own brother. He represents, in particular for Lacan, *"actual death unaccompanied by symbolic death"* (Žižek, 1989: 135). Old Hamlet dies un-shriven, *"without a settling of accounts,"* and this is why he must return *"as a frightful apparition until his debt has been repaid"* (Žižek, 1989: 135). Greece, like Hamlet's Denmark, is *"rankly abused"* by one brother's usurpation of power through the murder of his sibling. Thus, communism is doomed *"to walk the night"* as a ghostly apparition. The state rhetoric of national conviction and defense of the

fatherland obscured the real nature of the Greek Civil War behind its ideological machinery, denying the very possibility of a Greek communism. No
reconciliation could be made with communist Greeks, since by definition no
"nationally minded" Greek could be a communist. And so the specter
emerges at the point where symbolization fails, where the striving by an ideology for total closure overreaches itself. It is here that something is left
unsaid. And it is this unsayable remainder that the Rightist discourse seeks
to efface and which takes on the form of the specter. This is the return of the
"primordially repressed," that which has been foreclosed from the national
imaginary of the bourgeois regime. For society to conceive of itself as a self-
enclosed whole, the dissension, discord and dislocation resulting from economic and social exploitation must be effaced. Only through the displacement of these antagonistic struggles onto an external enemy—communism—can the political space be constructed as a cohesive and united whole,
but this displacement never fully succeeds. There is always a specter coming
back to haunt society.

   This specter emerges out of the inevitable failure of the fantasy of
national conviction. Yet this should not be understood simply as the emergence of traces of a suppressed alternative political identity, the return of
which has been suppressed by the dominant power's official history. This
would amount to misrecognizing our ghost. In the final analysis, the specter
does not represent the Greek Left as such—the motifs of the *foustanella* we
have discussed do not give body to the politically repressed Communist
voice—for it is not Communism as a positivity that threatens rightist hegemony, but Communism in its structural position as the defining boundary
of that discourse. We are concerned not with *Communism-as-Communism*
but with *Communism-as-anti-Hellenic*, and as such we could just as easily
speak of the ghost of Greek atheism, or the ghost of Slav Macedonia. In the
final analysis, we are concerned not with the particularities of a hidden identity suppressed and dominated through a particular discourse, but with the
fact that all discourse and all identities are constituted through relations of
suppression and domination. We witness this continued haunting of the
Greek social imaginary in the words of philosopher Ann Cacoullos: *"what
outsiders who come to Greece fail to understand is that Greece in the 1990s
is still trying to get over the civil war of 1945-50"* (cited in Horton, 1997: 69).
In her distinction between outsiders and insiders, Cacoullos highlights the
constitutive functioning of frontiers, of an encounter that has yet to be overcome and continues to haunt the socio-symbolic field. Ultimately the Civil
War is the fantasy-object that constitutes Greece as a symbolic structure,
again through its emptiness rather than through its fullness. The Civil War—
this harshly contested subject of political, cultural and historiographic conflict—is the traumatic event that ultimately embodies nothing but *"a certain
void."* It does not represent or introduce antagonism or dislocation within
the symbolic structure in any positive sense, but is in itself only a retroactive

effect of this attempted structuring. It is in this sense that the Civil War functions as Greece's fetish, a fantasy of traumatic violence that gives body to a constitutive lack in the symbolic order and that serves to obfuscate the fact that essentially *"there is nothing 'behind' the fantasy,"* that ultimately the social fantasy of the Civil War *"is a construction whose function is to hide this void, this 'nothing'"* (Žižek, 1989: 133). And it is this void that we perceive in the schism that divides victor and vanquished, the disenfranchisement of a lost identity and the persecution of defeated alternatives, all of which are to be fleetingly glimpsed in the spectral forms of the rural phantasm in *Sarakatsanissa,* the witch-like dryad in *Astero,* and the ghostly fugitive in *Gerakina.*

ACKNOWLEDGEMENT

I would like to thank Helen Ferguson for her invaluable comments and careful reading of various drafts of this chapter.

NOTES

1. *Kommounistiko Komma Elladas.*
2. EAM (*Ethniko Apoleftherotiko Metopo*) was the National Liberation Front established in 1941 as a coalition of communist, socialist and agrarian groups to organize mass-participatory resistance to the German Occupation.
3. In 1835, the German historian Jacob Philip Fallmereyer (1790-1861) gave a lecture before the Bavarian Academy of Sciences on the racial and cultural inheritance of the Peloponnesian Greeks. Fallmereyer argued that their genealogical origin was in fact Slavic and that all traces of ancient Greek racial continuity had been obliterated by the Slavic invasions of the fifth century A.D.
4. Films such as *Adouloti sklavoi/Unconquerable Slaves* (directed and written by Bion Papamichael, Novak Film, 1946), *Ta Paidia tis Athinas/The Children of Athens* (directed by Takis Bakopoulos, written by Ion Daifas, I. Pergantis, 1947), and *I Teleftaia apostoli/The Final Mission* (directed and written by Nikos Tsiforos, Finos Film, 1949).

REFERENCES

Alivizatos, N.C. (1981) 'The "Emergency Regime" and civil liberties, 1946-1949,' pp. 220–228 in J.O. Iatrides (Ed) *Greece in the 1940s: A Nation in Crisis.* Hanover: University Press of New England.

Anderson, B. (1991) *Imagined Communities.* London, New York: Verso.

Bhabha, H.K. (1991) 'A Question of Survival: Nations and Psychic States,' pp. 89–103 in J. Donald (Ed) *Psychoanalysis and Cultural Theory.* London: Macmillan.

Chion, M. (1992) 'The Impossible Embodiment,' pp. 195–207 in S. Žižek (Ed) *Everything You Always Wanted to Know about Lacan (But Were Afraid to Ask Hitchcock).* London: Verso.

Close, D.H. (1993) *The Greek Civil War, 1943-1950: Studies of Polarization.* London, New York: Routledge.

Fourtouni, E. (1984) *Greek Women in Resistance: Oral Histories.* New Haven: Thelphini.

Gourgouris, S. (1996) *Dream Nation: Enlightenment, Colonization, and the Institution of Modern Greece.* Stanford: Stanford University Press.

Harper, S. (1987) 'Historical Pleasures: Gainsborough Costume Melodrama,' pp. 167–196 in C. Gledhill (Ed) *Home Is Where the Heart Is.* London: British Film Institute.

Hart, J. (1996) *New Voices in the Nation: Women and the Greek Resistance 1941-1964.* London: Cornell University Press.

Horton, A. (1997) *The Films of Theo Angelopoulos: A Cinema of Contemplation.* Princeton: Princeton University Press.

Iatrides, J.O. (Ed) (1981) *Greece in the 1940s: A Nation in Crisis.* Hanover: University Press of New England.

Lacan, J. (1977) *Écrits. A Selection,* translation Alan Sheridan. London, New York: Tavistock Publications.

Laclau, E., Mouffe, C. (1985) *Hegemony and Socialist Strategy: Towards a Radical Democratic Politics.* London: Verso.

Mazower, M. (1993) *Inside Hitler's Greece: The Experience of Occupation.* New Haven, London: Yale University Press.

Mazower, M. (Ed) (2000) *After the War Was Over: Reconstructing the Family, Nation, and State in Greece, 1943-1960.* Princeton, Oxford: Princeton University Press.

Mitropoulou, A. (1980) *Greek Cinema* (in Greek). Athens: Thymeli.

Pappas, T.S. (1999) *Making Party Democracy in Greece.* London: Macmillan.

Samatas, M. (1986) 'Greek McCarthyism: A Comparative Assessment of Greek Post-Civil War Repressive Anticommunism and the U.S. Truman-McCarthy Era,' *Journal of the Hellenic Diaspora* XIII (3 & 4): 5–75.

Seferis, G. (1982) *On the Greek Style.* Athens: D. Harvey.

Skouras, S.D. (1947) 'Greek "Patrons Want Good Films,' *Motion Picture Herald* March 15, 1947: 55.

Stassinopoulou, M. (1997) 'Why Don't Our Films Show Greek Reality?,' unpublished.

Tsoucalas, C. (1981) 'The Ideological Impact of the Civil War,' pp. 319–341 in J.O. Iatrides (Ed) *Greece in the 1940s: A Nation in Crisis*. London: University Press of New England.

Vervenioti, T. (2000) 'Left-Wing Women between Politics and Family,' pp. 105–121 in M. Mazower (Ed) *After the War Was Over: Reconstructing the Family, Nation, and State in Greece, 1943-1960*. Princeton, Oxford: Princeton University Press.

Voglis, P. (2000) 'Between Negation and Self-Negation: Political Prisoners in Greece, 1945-50,' pp. 73–90 in M. Mazower (Ed) *After the War Was Over: Reconstructing the Family, Nation, and State in Greece, 1943-1960*. Princeton, Oxford: Princeton University Press.

Žižek, S. (1989) *The Sublime Object of Ideology*. London: Verso.

Žižek, S. (Ed) (1994) *Mapping Ideology*. London: Verso.

6

CHILEAN TRAUMATIZED IDENTITY

Discourse Theory and the Analysis of Visual Arts

Hernán Cuevas Valenzuela

The work of social theorists Ernesto Laclau and Chantal Mouffe, although highly influential in poststructuralist Social Sciences, Cultural Studies, and the Humanities, has so far been rarely used in a systematic study of (popular) culture.[1] Although such an ambitious task cannot be accomplished in a single chapter (or even a book), my contribution aims to show that some major categories of discourse theory can be fruitfully applied in order to interpret and understand cultural objects (works of art). The case I discuss here is that of the monumental mural painting *Memoria Visual de una Nación* (*Visual Memory of a Nation*), by the renowned Chilean artist Mario Toral.[2]

The key categories of discourse theory are very useful analytical tools for carrying out political and cultural analyses for two main reasons: first, they take into account the interconnectedness of meaning and the social; and, second, they do not reject but rather admit the tension between the realm of *the political*, or antagonism; and the realm of hegemonic politics, or order. From this perspective, any practice, including art, can be politicized because the dimension of antagonism, the political, has no specific place in the social and can potentially manifest itself in any relation (Mouffe, 2001: 100). Hence, the distinction between political and non-political practices—including artistic practices—loses its sense:

> One cannot make a distinction between political art and non-political art, because every form of artistic practice either contributes to the reproduction of the given common sense—and in that sense is political—or contributes to the deconstruction or critique of it. Every form of art has a political dimension. (Mouffe, 2001: 100)

My goal in this chapter is to analyze the political dimension of the mural painting *Memoria Visual de una Nación* by Mario Toral, which is the largest work of its type in Latin America, more than 1,200 square meters in size. This monumental mural painting is located in the most important and crowded underground station in Santiago de Chile, covering its main walls.[3] Its production has been made possible by a public–private partnership called MetroArte.

In this chapter, I focus on national identity as the result of identity formation (identification) and on the discursive construction of meaning, in both the production and the reception of a visual work of art. I analyze a particular section of Toral's mural, the panel *Los Conflictos*, which deals with a series of political conflicts. In doing so, I pay particular attention to the discursive representation of the military coup of September 11, 1973. My chapter also contains an analysis of the reception of the mural by three young Chileans. In the final section, I elaborate my own interpretation as a researcher of the *Memoria Visual de una Nación* mural.

THE BREAKDOWN OF DEMOCRACY AND THE IDEA OF NATIONAL RECONCILIATION IN *MEMORIA VISUAL DE UNA NACIÓN*

The *Memoria Visual de una Nación* mural can be seen as a visual representation of the history and identity of the Chilean nation from its early beginnings to the present. Next to this central theme, there are subthemes, such as the forces of nature; real and fantasy landscapes; poetry; the ocean; the meeting of cultures; the popular; and the traumatic conflicts in Chilean history. The mural also expresses admiration for humanism through the use of the human figure. This mural is a daring project because it avoids clichés and does not give in to the temptation to present an unproblematic version of Chilean history. Toral's painting is neither a juxtaposition of clichés nor an attempt to uphold a myth of cultural coherence. For him, Chilean national identity is not only the result of shared values, experiences, and origins. Just as important are the divisive experiences, the antagonisms and conflicts and the unresolved traumas. In my view, the mural represents national identity less as a coherent entity based on shared values that cement society—a common vision not just in conservative social thought—than as a historical construct built on the basis of conflicts, traumas, and divisions defined by antagonisms. From this perspective, a national cultural identity can be seen as a combination of shared elements and values on the one hand, and antagonism and divisive points of concern on the other.[4] Once, Toral wrote:

> It was impossible for me to avoid some sad episodes and events for our country. Those episodes are real, they happened, and if left aside the represented would not be Chilean history but a fairytale. (Philips, http://www.philips.cl/artephilips/autores/toral.htm).

Following Lacanian psychoanalysis, Laclau (1994) considered identity to be constitutively split because it is based on a constitutive lack.[5] I also view trauma and lack as constitutive of Chilean national identity. Toral seemed to share that intuition when he stated that *Memoria Visual de una Nación*

> represents scenes that divided the Chilean people during their history; violent and bloody events, tragic divisions that we—their descendants— have inherited and that tear us apart as citizens of a common land in which we should live in peace. (Toral, 1999a)

The lack at the heart of identity has to be filled through processes of identification: *"one needs to identify with something because there is an original and insurmountable lack of identity"* (Laclau, 1994: 3). Although a united and reconciled Chilean nation is an impossibility, it remains a strong aspiration with which we identify. *Memoria Visual de una Nación* represents such an impossible aspiration to fullness as a plenitude of the nation. Toral's concern is about the constitution of a Chilean Nation, understood as a collective of persons endowed with rights and sharing the same land as their homeland (Toral, 1999a).

The experience of nationality and identity in Chile is particularly traumatic, due to a past rich in conflicts that still divide the population. The northwestern panel of Toral's mural, named *Los Conflictos (The Conflicts)*, is mainly about the political antagonisms and conflicts in the history of the Chilean republic (see Fig. 6.1). Images of pain and suffering in red and dark colors are predominant. Besides Toral's talent as a muralist, his affinity with the sensibility of expressionism makes him eminently suited for representing such events. Indeed, his painting contains references to Goya's *Caprichos* and other Goya paintings, such as *El tres de Mayo de 1808: los fusilamientos en la Montana del Principe Pio*[6] as is evidenced by the composition of the section on the execution of Portales by firing squad.[7] Similarly, Picasso's *Guernica* and Eisenstein's 1925 film *The Battleship Potemkin* are alluded to in the frieze *La Masacre de Santa María de Iquique* (*The Massacre of Santa Maria de Iquique*). There is also a possible link to neo-expressionist painters such as Helmut Middendorf and his images of bombed cities[8]—particularly in the La Moneda section. Another reference are the murals and early works of the Ecuadorian painter Oswaldo Guayasamin, with their emphasis on deeply human feelings like suffering and anger—for example in his collections of giant and harrowing hands and faces. Last but not least, there are connections with Fritz Lang's 1927 film *Metropolis* in the section *Vida y muerte en las minas del Carbón* (*Life and Death in the Coal Mines*), where alienated and exploited workers are depicted in a way reminiscent of Lang (see fig. 6.1).

THE WORK OF REPRESENTATION: THE MURAL PAINTING, LA MONEDA, AND PHOTOGRAPHY

My contention is that, when referring to the 1973 coup, Toral's painting does not signify the event itself but rather a representation of the event—more precisely: the event as it has been mediated through well-known photographs.[9] In order to show this, I first analyze a famous picture of the La Moneda bombing.

Common sense assumes that photographs, because of their iconic character, have a straightforward meaning. As Fiske (1990) stated, the photographic image tends to elude the contingency of meaning. Its realism seems to guarantee its objectivity as a mirror of reality, reflecting truthfully, honestly, without intrusion. In reality, however, the photographic text is entwined in intertextuality, so that its meaning is unfixed. The meaning of the photograph is contingent, open to interpretation, and therefore also to political intervention. In short, the photograph has no true and unique meaning. Truth claims with regard to the interpretation of the photographic image are no more than strategic moves, attempts to hegemonize its meaning. As Stuart Hall (1991: 152-3) stated:

> In any event, the search for their "essential Truth"—an original, founding moment of meaning—is an illusion. The photographs are essentially multiaccentual in meaning. No such previously natural moment of true meaning, untouched by the codes and social relations of production and reading, and transcending historical time, exists.

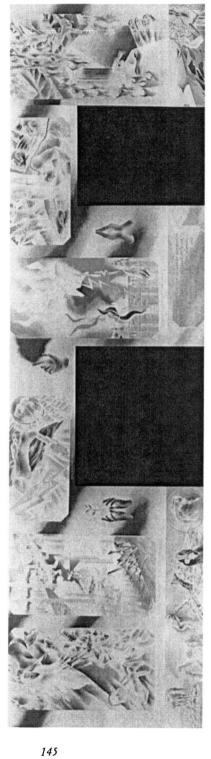

FIG. 6.1. Panel *Los Conflictos* (*The Conflicts*), by Mario Toral (1999).

145

Political interventions concerning images and photographs usually try to fix
their meanings by anchoring them in wider discursive chains. This is exactly what has happened with the pictures of the La Moneda bombardment and
fire. These have been interpreted in highly diverse ways. As a consequence,
the same image (see Fig. 6.2) is given captions and headings by different people and groups that blatantly contradict each other. The web site of one
Britain-based Chilean human rights organization published the picture in
question under the title: *11th of September: coup d'État.* The same web site
states:

> In 1973, the military led by Augusto Pinochet overthrew the democrat-
> ically elected government of President Salvador Allende, installing a
> military dictatorship that lasted until 1990. (Memoria Viva, http://www.
> memoriaviva.com/)

A very different interpretation of the same image is provided by the Chilean
Anti-Communist League: *La Moneda in flames: the only way to free the
Nation from Marxism* (The Chilean Anti-Communist League, http://www.
geocities.com/CapitolHill/Congress/1770/11-september-1973.html).

This illustrates how an image can be interpreted in different ways,
because the actual event presented in the picture is defined differently in dif-

FIG. 6.2. The La Moneda bombing (1973).

ferent discourses. But what is discourse? Laclau and Mouffe (1985: 105) defined discourse as a "*structured totality*" produced by "*articulatory practices.*"[10] One should not confuse the commonsensical notion of discourse as speech or language with this rather technical meaning, which refers to the "*meaningful field*" that pre-exists and makes possible any singular "*perception, thought or action.*" As a consequence, the discourse-theoretical notion of discourse goes beyond the distinction between linguistic and extra-linguistic (Laclau, 1993). Through discourse, empirical objects, events and identities are constituted as discursive objects.[11] Hence, what is usually taken to be "*objective reality*" is actually a social and discursive construct. Discourse can also be seen as providing us with "*a viewpoint*" that enables us to describe the "*totality of the social life,*" and that makes our world intelligible and our experience of it meaningful (Laclau, 1993: 433; 435). An empirical discourse is a "*relatively unified and coherent organization of meaning*" that is "*historically constructed*" in contingent and conflictive political processes (Sayyid & Zac, 1998: 260). With regard to the subject at hand, we can say that the September 11, 1973 event is discursively constructed either as the tragic end of Chilean democracy or as the nation's liberation from Marxism. The meaning of September 11, 1973 or of its representations in pictures or paintings depends on the structuring function of the discourse that signifies it.

How does the structuring function of discourse work in this case? The contradictory interpretations of the photograph of the La Moneda bombing are made possible by the openness of signs to a variety of discursive articulations (Evans & Hall, 1999; Hall, 1991). What we call reality, including social relations and the experienced world, is culturally mediated and therefore overdetermined.[12] Hence, for discourse theory, external entities or events are never given as independent essences with inherent meanings. Meaning arises only in a process of symbolical and imaginary mediation. Consequently, the 1973 coup has no inherent and objective meaning waiting to be discovered and articulated (Laclau & Mouffe, 1985: 98). The multiple and often contradictory meanings that one finds connected with it have been bestowed on it by discursive practices of articulation.

Articulation is a recurrent discursive practice that aims to produce meaning, to signify. It takes place in a heterogeneous, amorphous and potentially infinite domain of signification called the field of discursivity (Laclau & Mouffe, 1985: 111). Articulation links dispersed *elements* from that field and transforms them into *moments* belonging to a signifying chain that fixes their meanings. Laclau and Mouffe (1985: 105) defined articulation as "*any practice establishing a relation among elements such that their identity is modified as a result of the articulatory practice.*" In other words, articulation is a redescription in which discursive elements are disarticulated and appropriated from other discourses. However, the results of articulation are fragile. The meanings it produces are unstable, partial and temporary. This feature of

FIG. 6. 3. *1973. The Bombing of La Moneda*, detail of the panel *Los Conflictos* (*The Conflicts*), by Mario Toral (1999).

articulation is of paramount importance in discourse theory and is a condition of possibility for hegemonic politics. Hence, the meaning of September 11, 1973 remains open to contestation, disarticulation and new hegemonic articulations.

The image referring to the 1973 coup and the breakdown of democracy is significantly located in a central position in the *Los Conflictos* panel (see Fig. 6.3). In my view, the iconic nature of the image tends to determine or constrain its meaning. The bombing of the building seems to be used essentially as a metaphor for the breakdown of democracy. La Moneda is the heart of the executive power and therefore symbolizes the core of the Chilean democratic institutions. The iconic representation of the burning palace is clearly inspired by the historic television images and photographs with which generations of Chileans have lived since 1973.[13] This point is crucial because it makes the representation of the 1973 events strikingly different from that of other events depicted in the mural, most of which are situated in imaginary spaces. This representational strategy can be framed as an attempt to positivize and objectivize the discursive construction of the event so as to evade controversy. In my view, however, the objectivist nature of the representation does not make it neutral: The image is still constructed as a highly contentious and traumatic event.

Toral's depiction is not based on personal memories of the La Moneda bombing, but on widely disseminated and well-known images. In my view, this is coherent with the whole logic of his mural, which both derives from and strengthens the collective memory rather than the artist's personal and intimate recollections. However, there is a certain iterability at work here. The representation of popularized images is twisted, although it is still recognizable through a *"minimal remainder"* (see Culler, 1982, on iterability). Let me break down a few of these variations, beginning with the perspective. The panel presents a frontal view of a section of the façade. The scale, too, is modified. The image in the mural shows dramatic details of the bombing in a close-up rather than the usual panoramic view of explosions, smoke, and dust seen from a side angle. Another intervention has to do with the representation of the jet fighters. There is no photographic representation that shows the planes and the building together, because the distance between the two was too great. However, everyone remembers the documentary images of fighters approaching the civic area of Santiago's city center. Here, the building is brutally attacked by obscured planes, resembling black hawks or lightning. A third variation is the dramatization of the image through the collapse of the flagpole. The falling flag symbolizes the pain of the Chilean nation and the collapse of its democracy. In fact, as one of my interviewees stated, it also symbolizes the end of an era of institutionalized popular progressivism in the world—of which Chilean politics since the 1920s had been a local manifestation.

In addition to these interventions, we should also consider the symbolic role of the *hands* surrounding the representation of La Moneda. Most of them are folded in prayer or shaking other hands. The folded hands appeal to a religious code to express hope for national reconciliation. The hand with the raised finger can be traced back to Leonardo da Vinci's famous and ambiguous *St. John the Baptist* and to other religious paintings in which the main character points to the mystery of Heaven. Another Christian symbol is that of the Hand of God.[14] Furthermore, the hand gesture on the left is clearly inspired by the typical representations of the Lord of the Divine Mercy. The mural refers to the conflicted Chilean reality and the fundamental division of its people and, at the same time, to the universal task of constructing a civilization characterized by peace and happiness. The fantasy of a national reconciliation seems therefore to be the main theme of the section. The reconciled nation is evoked through a permanent presence-through-absence. Moreover, the representations of these painful events from Chilean history can be read as a national narrative that transcends the particularities of each event when we oppose the divisions they evoke to the imaginary scenario of a reconciled Chile. Here we find a *quasi*-religious concept of socio-political reconciliation. By contrast with the strictly religious meaning of reconciliation, which drew on the idea of unity as well, reconciliation here mainly means peace as a sublime state in which antagonism is overcome. This is not an accident or a representation typical of Toral only. Both religious (Silva, 1986) and political leaders (Aylwin, 1992; Foxley, 2003) extensively used religious symbols and figures of unity and reconciliation when talking about the re-democratization of Chile during the 1980s and 1990s. As opposed to Paul's reduction of all social differences,[15] the image here is of a state of peace, achieved through moral improvement. As in the Reign predicted by Isaiah, differences do not disappear. What changes is the logic of the interactions.[16] Toral's view supports the hope for tolerance, not the utopia of social homogeneity.

These symbols and signifiers of reconciliation and consensus function as nodal points (Laclau & Mouffe, 1985) or empty signifiers (Laclau, 1996) that structure and join otherwise isolated and contentious elements. They are key moments in the practice of articulation, which consists of *"the construction of nodal points and empty signifiers] which partially fix meaning"* (Laclau & Mouffe, 1985: 113). In this particular case, these empty signifiers/nodal points are supported by a particular fantasy: the fantasy of the wholeness and plenitude of the community.[17]

Despite the will for reconciliation the *Los Conflictos* section bears witness to, its unveiling proved to be a controversial event. We have to remember that it took place in the beginning of 1999, in a conjuncture of polarization over Pinochet's detention in London. The unveiling of the mural was met with virulent criticism, especially from a number of right-wing leaders. The reasons for this controversy far exceeded the Pinochet affair. The mural stirred up memories of fearful times.[18] Fear was a condition, a result and a justification of the military coup and the new regime's subsequent consolidation. As we saw, some view military authoritarianism as a response to the threat of a revolution and a communist takeover. For others, fear was the result of military repression and political persecution. Generally, one can say that Chilean authoritarianism aimed to put an end to uncertainty, insecurity, and disorder. Consequently, the promotion of order and national values formed the basis by means of which it tried to legitimate itself. During the post-authoritarian period, the fear from the past formed the backdrop of the consensual politics and the discourse of national reconciliation. As was said by a former minister of defense of that period, trauma was the underlying motivation of what was called *"the lessons from history."* The stability of the new democracy, social peace and governability required the elite to learn those lessons (Fernández, 1998).

The *Los Conflictos* panel assembles discursive elements and symbols of different and sometimes contradictory ideological narratives. It refers to the execution by firing squad of the 19th century conservative ideologue and Minister Diego Portales — but also to the mass slaughter of native people in southern Chile and of saltpeter miners and their families in the northern Atacama desert in Santa Maria de Iquique, to the inhuman exploitation in the coal mines and to the political prosecution under the *Ley Maldita* (*Damned Law*), which banned the Communist Party and was used to prosecute leftist leaders. The way Portales is represented, the dimensions he is given, his hieratic posture, and the presence by his side of a spiritual force suggest his superior nature. Traditional historiography portrays Portales as the ideologue of the so-called Conservative Republic (Edwards, 1936; Vial, 1981-1987). Most other episodes in the panel are central to Marxist or anti-oligarchic historiography (Villalobos, 1980; Vitale, 1993-1998; Vitale et al., 1999). The reference to the 1891 civil war and President Balmaceda's suicide[19] is more ambiguous, because these events have been articulated by both elite and anti-oligarchic narratives. Placed in the context of this ambiguous series of events, *1973. The Bombing of La Moneda* tends, in my view, to be framed by an anti-oligarchic narrative.[20]

The major political achievement of Toral's northern panel is its critical exposure of the predominant political discourse, which focuses on the idea of Chile as a homogenous society and a unified and monolithic nation. In contrast to this, Toral's representation of Chilean national identity stresses conflict and division.[21] His work intervenes in the struggles over, among other things, the history of Chilean democracy, the role of oppression and social struggles, the role of key figures in the history of the republic and the 1973 coup. In doing so, Toral negotiates between the dominant conservative historiography and counter-hegemonic leftist versions of the past.

In Toral's representation, Chilean cultural identity is best understood as the provisional result of a conflictual process. The term reconciliation pre-

supposes the existence, at a given time in the past, of a unity that was broken. Although this moment may be purely fictional, it can have real discursive effects. Thus, we can say that Chilean contemporary identity is built not
only on the basis of shared elements in the fantasies surrounding Chilean
national identity, but also on the basis of the conflicts, divisions, traumas and
antagonisms that constitute key divisive points in Chilean national culture—
which is exactly what we can expect when we consider the question of identity formation from the point of view of contemporary Lacanian theory
(Laclau, 1994; Laclau & Zac, 1994; Stavrakakis, 1999; Žižek, 1990, 1994).
The traumatized society of Chile requires the fantasy of a national reconciliation to keep itself together.

I asked myself if the La Moneda painting in the mural is as open to
interpretation as are the photographic images. With this question as a starting point, I will analyze the reception of the mural by three people in the
next section.

THE RECEPTION OF THE MURAL

A discourse-theoretical analysis in the cultural field[22] should pay attention
not only to the characteristics of the empirical discourse(s) under analysis,
but also to the circuit connecting production and reception. Discourse is
produced for someone. It is encoded, brought into circulation and decoded.
Discourse interpellates subjects, who (if it is successful) identify with it.
Hence, my aim here is to analyze the meanings encoded in Mario Toral's *Los
Conflictos* panel and its active reception by a small number of viewers. In my
view, meaning is produced in both the production and reception phases of
communication (Hall, 1993). The potential support for, or resistance to, the
dominant discourse on consensus and national reconciliation in Chile is a
matter for empirical analysis. The *Los Conflictos* panel allows me to address
the construction of the conflicting meanings of the Chilean democratization
process—the breakdown of democracy, authoritarianism, and re-democratization—and of the collective memories these processes have produced. The
panel in question is ambiguous. On the one hand, it bravely represents controversial political issues such as mass slaughter, exploitation, political
repression, and political violence, and more generally the breakdown of
democracy and the human rights abuses that took place at different times in
the republican history of Chile. On the other, it fails to produce a radically
critical counter-hegemonic interpretation of Chilean history. This is so
because Toral's *Memoria Visual de una Nación*, through its negotiated reading of social antagonisms that have marked Chilean history, finally supports
the dominant discourse on national reconciliation of the Chilean elite of the

1990s. In what follows, I examine how the mural is read by three Chilean youngsters.

Presenting the Participants' Backgrounds

My aim in this section is to present an analysis of the reception and interpretation by three young Chileans of Mario Toral's *Memoria Visual de una Nación* and, more specifically, of the section of the *Los Conflictos* panel depicting the September 11, 1973 events. In doing so, my research question is the following: What is your interpretation of the work of art under analysis and the events it depicts? These interviews are illustrative of types of readings and have no further pretension than to expand the range of the research. Hence, there is no claim for (statistical) representativeness. Still, I do claim that these readings contain no accidental or unstructured impressions. They are typical in the sense that they represent patterns of understanding that are available in present-day Chilean culture.

O (28 years old) is a leftist female plastic artist. Her family background is coherent with that. Both her parents are socialist voters and health service professionals. According to O, her parents were, at one time, strongly committed to the public health model. She studied arts as a postgraduate in Britain. She told me that her family lived in a climate of fear during her childhood. She remembers how her father, an intellectual left-wing sympathizer, hid his books out of fear. She also has memories of her parents' friends having to go abroad. As a teenager, she was never allowed to take part in political activities that her parents considered dangerous. Only later on, during the 1990s, could she take part in politics at the university, but she never got involved as a real activist.

L (27 years old) is from a middle-class background. Originating from southern Chile, he studied in Santiago. L went to the United Kingdom as a postgraduate. Both his parents have higher education degrees. L's father held a position in a state security service during the dictatorship, but L was ambiguous and proved unwilling to talk about this.

As could be expected, the particularities of social background, culture, personal experiences, and political identifications had their impact on the interpretations of each participant. I expected that the main independent variable[23] would be their political identification. However L, the right-wing respondent, recognizes that his experiences at the University in Chile and abroad have changed his view of the breakdown of democracy and the legacy of the military regime. He appears to be more critical than could be expected, especially with regard to the human rights issue.

However, his views of the Allende government are critical as well. In both the interview and his interpretation of the *Los Conflictos* panel, he presented Allende's government as suffering a deep *"legitimacy crisis,"* which he regarded as the key factor in the breakdown of Chilean democracy. This statement was backed up with a solid knowledge of history and politics. He almost seemed to be trying to make an academic point. However, after our conversation had become more confidential, he started to tell me about his family life during those years. This highly personal account of the period stressed his feeling of insecurity—a feeling that was also brought to light by studies of collective memory and public opinion surveys. He told me that "*[i]n those days his father went to University with a gun ... every day ... there was such a fear ... and that he experienced sometimes real threats. Because of his German background—he learned Spanish after speaking fluent German—he was usually called: 'Hey, Nazi, go back to Germany!' And his mother was usually harassed for being the only right-wing person in her school. She told me she was once taken by her hair and shouted at ... 'Right-wing bitch' ... she was exposed to everyone in school.*"[24]

S (22 years old) comes from an upper middle-class background. Both her parents are professionals and right-wing voters. They were strong supporters of Pinochet. She studies in Chile and participated in a brief educational exchange in Britain.

S, too, has an ambiguous position toward the Pinochet regime. Because of the family environment in which she grew up, she "*cannot judge badly any supporter of Pinochet.*" And she added that she cannot even hate Pinochet himself. She also holds ambiguous views of the effects of the Agrarian Reform, saying that it "*appears unfair to lose inherited land due to a political program.*" She talked extensively about the damage done to former landowners (*terratenientes*) during the Allende years. Therefore, her family is grateful to Pinochet, because "*he gave the land back ... the same land Allende took away from my family.*" Talking about the legitimacy of the land ownership, she evaded the question of underproduction (one of the well-known arguments in favor of the Agrarian Reform) and stressed her father's affection for the countryside and his land. Following this, she put this rhetorical question to me: "*Is it fair to take it?*" Here, then, areas of clear contradiction appeared, because she strongly supported redistributive policies. Her point was also that she tried to explain why so many Chileans had good reasons for supporting the Pinochet government.

When discussing the human rights issue, however, she was clearly against the systematic disappearances, repression, and torture of that era. She added that many people, including her own mother, had only recently become aware of these atrocities. However, she added, "*they are still in contradiction ... thanking Pinochet but beginning to criticize some aspects of his government [such as human rights abuses].*"

Interpretations of *1973. The Bombing of La Moneda*

L's interpretation was ambiguous: To him the image meant *"the end of a popular process of democratization"* and at the same time *"an action to some extent justified because of the excesses of the socialist regime."* In other words, this single image of the bombarded presidential palace evoked conflicting memories and statements about the breakdown of democracy and subsequent authoritarianism. The monumental dimensions of the image and its title — *1973. Bombardeo de La Moneda* — make it a significant section. All participants associated the image with authoritarianism and human rights violations. On the syntagmatic level, the combination of images representing historical events belonging to a narrative of national conflicts — remember the panel's title: *Los Conflictos* — contributes to anchoring the message and limiting its polysemic potential by inhibiting the production of new readings (for this, see Fiske, 1990). On the same metonymic or syntagmatic level, one should also look at the combination of elements in the image (Nichols, 1985). This combination is crucial for the work of signification. For instance, L was very aware of the combination of *"planes, the falling flag, the broken flagpole, flames, the building set on fire"* as elements that emphasize dramatic and negative feelings toward the military action. In addition, he found it very difficult not to relate the images referring to the so-called Ley Maldita, which show the repression and torture in prison camps under the military government in the late 1940s, to the major narratives on the conflicts.

Reconciliation

A further significant aspect of the syntagmatic axis lies in the combination of images of conflict with various hand gestures. All three participants, even right-wing sympathizer L, interpreted these images as traumatic and violent rather than glorious. When L and S mentioned other ideological elements, they did so as a disclaimer, or to relativize their main statements, as for instance when L stated he *"justified the coup to a certain extent."* With regard to the hands, however, they came up with ideas like *"consensus, agreement, rationality"* and *"reconciliation."* Obviously, the hands and their gestures signified togetherness, reconciliation and peace to them. The preferred reading suggests the termination of conflict through a civil handshake or a religious reconciliation. Nonetheless, both L and S were quite skeptical about the possible realization of this reconciliation. L even considered such a *"utopia"* to be a straightforward *"impossibility."* For him, the term consensus *"is like trying to impose a rational agreement ... that is what the shaking hands inscribed within geometrical lines mean to me.*" O stated that "*the hands are relevant here ... they are oversized in relation to all other elements ... and are far more metaphorical and interesting than the figurative images.*" According to O, they mean "*agreement, peace and reconciliation.*"

As I suggested earlier, the image of the La Moneda bombing condenses two opposite narratives and, as a consequence, gives rise to very mixed feelings: pain and suffering on the one hand, glory and joy at the triumph over the Marxist enemy on the other. Thus, the image becomes a symbol of the differences dividing the Chilean people. L agreed with this view, suggesting that the broken post and the falling flag signified the failure of Chile to become a unified nation. To him, reconciliation seemed to be an unrealizable utopian dream.[25] S expressed the view that the failure to bring about reconciliation is due to the fact that, from the beginning, this reconciliation was an elitist maneuver, a ruse, a *charade*. She considered it an attempt to mask reality, to maintain the *status quo* and hold on to power.

All three participants saw the image of the La Moneda bombing as less problematical and critical than I had expected. S stated that although the "*content of the picture is truthful and critical,*" it was in fact less "*annoying and stressful*" than could have been anticipated:

> Nobody can deny the fact that the Armed Forces attacked the governmental palace and a Government that was democratically elected. That could be an interpretation. However, these are historical facts, impossible to deny; they are true and the image in the mural is in fact supported by the media coverage of the time of the event ... it cannot be denied whatever the different perspectives it might give rise to ... this is, thinking about the attack as a reasonable and justifiable act or exactly its opposite ... [Now] it does neither annoy our senses nor disturb our view ... it can be tolerated by anyone who does not feel guilty because it is simply something that everyone knows has happened . . .

S told me that she often "*passes by the mural*" and that she has never "*given it attention until now.*" In this sense, my role as a researcher asking questions and confronting the participants with a set of images to be interpreted is not to be neglected, because I induced the participants to tell stories that otherwise would never have emerged. The interviewer should see himself as a *coaxer*, working close to the production phase[26] (Plummer, 1995: 20-21), but not necessarily favoring the producer's preferred reading (i.e., in this case, Toral's reading of the panel as a plea for national reconciliation).

Elaborating on her own lack of attention for the mural, S expressed the conviction that the mural's location in a "*high-traffic area*" prevents it from having a critical impact. According to her, this location "*made it acceptable for powerful groups*" precisely because it "*passes unattended.*" In our conversation, we also came to the conclusion that the massiveness of the work, the shape of the room, and the distribution of the space it was in, make it difficult to see it in a single viewing. In order to look at it in detail, one needs time to walk around the different platforms of the underground station.

O, also reflecting on the mural's location, said that *"it is interesting that a mural, which is a public work of art, has been located in another important work as it is in an underground train station, which is also a public space that belongs to everyone and to none in particular."* However, on the point of its critical impact, she hesitated. According to her, *"the Orozco and Rivera murals"* had a *"powerful impact"* because *"they were talking about their time"* whereas Toral's mural was *"less effective in mobilizing disclosure [destape], revolt and protest"* because of its *"time distance"* with regard to current Chilean experience. According to her, *"the publicity of those images ... does not secure their critical edge."* She also emphasized the metaphorical character of the hands, as symbols of *"reconciliation,"* condensing both a *"religious"* sense and a *"political one."* I personally agree with her reading of some of the gestures relating to *"prayer"* and *"compassion"* as being displaced to mean *"agreement."* S also made the remark that one of the gestures was a kind of civic *"shake of hands,"* which was different from the other, more religious gestures. It relates to *"politics and the place of power"* in a mood of national reconciliation. The relation between two sets of symbolisms (i.e., the religious discourse on sin, forgiveness, and reconciliation on the one hand, and the political and civic discourse on reconciliation on the other) was successfully explored as an underlying structure in the mural that seemed to give meaning and shape to the attempts to achieve consensus and peace in the period of political transition.[27]

L seemed to agree with this remark when saying that the *"praying hands ... inscribed in a geometrical figure mean a rational trend towards political and social reconciliation."* He then asked a rhetorical question: *"Does this mean consensus and a sensible search for democracy?"* His own answer was that such democratic consensus seemed a *"utopian reconciliation between an increasingly diverse, divided and uneven Chilean nation; not only in its material sense but also in its spiritual one, which seems to be the basis of the patriotic feeling of belonging."*

The readings of my participants show that for them these images did not work as effective symbols of reconciliation, because they lacked the capacity to articulate or negotiate the different views of the process. On the one hand, they find themselves confronted with images of conflict, on the other, there are hands symbolizing reconciliation. Between the two, there is an irresolvable tension. At the level of visual representation, the mural constitutes a coherent attempt to express hope for a possible reconciliation following past conflicts. Looking at the actual readings of my three participants, I had to conclude that this preferred reading is far from being realized consistently. The panel proved to be more of an *"open work"* than I had expected (Eco,

1999). In the catalogue accompanying the mural, Toral himself wrote that he presented these images of *"tragic"* events that *"divided Chileans during their history"* as truthful representations (Toral, 1999a). His argument seems to refer primarily to *"rendering real history ... in full"* and to a hope for a future of *"peaceful coexistence"* (Toral, 1999a, 1999b: 31-32), rather than to a determination to provoke, criticize, break the silence, and lift the veil.

Whatever reading we prefer, the image invites us to reflect about a divisive past. In this sense, it causes a dislocation that prevents the discursive closure of the dominant discourse and reveals the impossibility of its attempt to ultimately reconcile the nation and erase all antagonisms and political frontiers within it (Laclau, 1990).

CONCLUSION

Articulation is a key category of Laclau and Mouffe's social theory, and can be seen as a major contribution to the theory of hegemony. Its potential field of application is wide, extending beyond the domain of political speeches and documents into architecture, arts, rituals and all other fields of human action. The discourse-theoretical analysis of works of art for purposes of political research seems to hold great promise. Cultural and artistic practices frequently result in the expression of collective traumas, fantasies and anxieties that remain unexpressed in other fields. This is a good reason for analyzing visual expressions of discourse. Such an analysis is especially fruitful for the exploration of the affective dimension of discursive meaning-construction, which is frequently supported by a fantasy structure. As Lacanian psychoanalysis teaches, fantasy—although symbolically structured—stems from the realm of images, the Imaginary.[28] Phantasmatic visual expressions—like those in *Los Conflictos*—provide easier access to the passions and traumas involved in discourse.[29]

Discourse theory's radical constructivism takes seriously the contingency of signifieds and the constitutive lack at the heart of the identity of social agents:

> Society and social agents lack any essence, and their regularities merely consist of the relative and precarious forms of fixation, which accompany the establishment of a certain order. This analysis opens up the possibility of elaborating a new concept of articulation, which would start from the overdetermined character of social relations. (Laclau & Mouffe, 1985: 98)

This starting point allows us to elaborate a social theory that views the construction of meaning as a political process, combining articulation and hegemonization. This is a radical starting point, which demands from us that, when undertaking empirical analyses, we take contingency seriously, connecting these ontological premises with an ontic questioning of empirical problems. From this perspective, I have focused on the question of identity formation and the lack in identity, rather than on defining identity as pregiven. For this purpose, Lacanian theory proved to be helpful. Therefore, rather than stressing commonalities, I have tried to pay particular attention to the constitutive role of the divisions, traumas and conflicts that seem to tear Chilean national identity apart.

Similarly, while exploring discourse, I have emphasized its processual nature in relation to the production and reception of meaning, instead of considering discourse as a set of statements that require the study of its morphology to reveal its meaning. I (modestly) draw on the premises of reception studies as practiced by Cultural Studies scholars from the 1970s on in order to show the contingency of the articulation of Chilean cultural and political discourses around the signifiers reconciliation and consensus. Hence, reception studies are a must if we want to show that interpellation often fails and discourse is contingent and inherently dislocated.

The mural *Memoria Visual de una Nación* fosters and encourages a consensual reading of the recent history of Chile. It strategically uses symbols and images of reconciliation and consensus as nodal points/empty signifiers in structuring meanings. The efficiency of such symbols relies on a fantasy structure, around which images and concepts of unity, harmony, nation, republican values and national identity circulate. Such signifiers are embedded in the discourses that produce the meanings of those images. Moreover, there is a certain economy of enjoyment that draws on fantasy to support these meanings. The quasi-religious images of reconciliation suggested by hand gestures are what reunites the Chilean nation. They represent national unity, as a state in which divisions have been overcome, and which is built on a fantasy of harmonious unity of the nation as a whole. This leads to the construction of an imagined community that attempts either to eclipse the dimension of social antagonism or to reconcile it in an imaginary scenario.

Still, the images of the mural make social antagonism visible, and present it as constitutive of the identity and history of Chile. The presence of an enemy of the Chilean community is still implied. In *Los Conflictos*, the threat to the phantasmatic scenario is precisely the internal conflict, the split of the identity of the Chilean nation, the divisive events of the past and the possible reproduction of such divisions in times to come. The solution to this threat is a phantasmatic reconciliation, the hope of which is suggested through the images of the hands, which suggest the potential to overcome conflict through reconciliation. They point to the idealized scenario of the reconciled nation as an imagined community.

Consistent with evidence collected in previous research, I have found here that contemporary discourses on democratization, nation and identity in Chile prove to be highly intertwined. Indeed, the signifiers reconciliation, unity and consensus, and the narratives about wounds in the soul of the nation and about the need to overcome conflict, foster forgiveness and learn the lessons from the past—all of which were key themes of the elite discourse of the 1990s—are also very evident in the panel *Los Conflictos*, although they are transcoded here into a visual register.

The application of the concepts of discourse theory to art is fruitful because it stresses the political aspects of artistic production, which are too often overlooked. Furthermore, art seems to be a very interesting field for the application of Laclau and Mouffe's concepts. This move seems to be facilitated by discourse theory's linguistic and Gramscian inspiration, which allow it to combine questions of meaning and politics in very interesting and enlightening ways.

NOTES

1. There are a few interesting discussions, centering especially on the category of articulation (Slack, 1996; also see Stuart Hall, 1997). This mainly adds to the credit of Stuart Hall.

2. The Chilean artist Mario Toral (1934-) studied in Santiago (Chile), Montevideo (Uruguay) and Paris (France). From his early years on, he has traveled through Latin America, Europe, and the United States. He has successfully taken part in several art biennials and was granted various international awards. His works have been exhibited all around the world and have been bought by some of the most important museums and collectors. During the years of the Pinochet government, he lived in New York and Spain, returning to Chile only in 1992. From that moment on, he became involved in the formation of new generations of artists at the Pontifical Catholic University of Chile and at Finnis Terrae University (Chile).

3. *Muralismo* is a particular style, a visual practice with its own rules, codes, history, and traditions. It includes both forms of high art and popular expressions. Whatever level we look at—fine art or ordinary popular culture—muralism is defined as public art (i.e., art about public issues frequently located in public places). In Latin America, it did have an ideological impetus—something very evident in the influx of Marxism and nationalism, as represented by the works of the Mexican masters Rivera, Orozco, and Siqueiros. There is also a history of muralism in Chile. Siqueiros was in exile in Chile between 1941 and 1942. In this period, he made the marvelous *Mural de la Escuela México* in the Chilean city of Chillán. This is an example of an early influence of *muralismo* on generations of Chilean artists like Gregorio de la Fuente. A second strand of mural painting that has influenced Toral's work is the Chilean political and popular *muralismo*

from the 1960s and 1970s, which was executed by collectives such as the communist *Brigada Ramona Parra* (BRP).
4. Archer (1997) criticized monadic and *"consensual"* conceptions of culture. Laitin (1988) coined the term *"points of concern,"* by which he meant those social problems and worries that, although conflictive, seem to constitute a shared concern for the whole society or community. For their part, Laclau and Mouffe's (1985; see also Laclau, 1994) notion of antagonism helps us conceive the formation of identity as a contentious process that requires demarcations and frontiers.
5. This psychoanalytical argument can be traced back to the trauma of the primal loss of the original abundance of unity with the mother (Fink, 1995). Nonetheless, one has to be cautious when applying such a notion to social analysis, because *"primal loss"* itself can be considered a myth, produced by the castration/alienation at entering the symbolic order—not an origin, not something primal therefore.
6. Here, I consider expressionism as an artistic *sensibility* rather than as a proper avant-garde movement. Hence, I do not want to suggest that Goya is a fully fledged expressionist, but rather that he, Guayasamin and Toral (and Middendorf, who is in fact a neo-expressionist), despite their not being members of the avant-garde movement of the first third of the 20th century, share a common expressionist *sensibility*.
7. Diego Portales was an important minister. He is seen as the politician who created the conditions for order, stability, and progress in the Chilean Republic during the 19th century.
8. See for instance his *Flugzeug, Traum, Kopf* (1983).
9. In this respect, reflections on the visual mediation of our experiences in societies of mechanical—and now digital—reproduction may well apply. Consider, for instance, Guy Debord's following quotation from his classic *The Society of the Spectacle* (1977): *"In societies where modern conditions of production prevail, all social life presents itself as an immense accumulation of spectacles. Everything that was directly lived has moved away into a representation."*
10. Laclau and Mouffe (1985) used, indistinctively, the categories of discursive formation and discourse. Sometimes Laclau (1990, 1993, 2000, 2004) also used the terms structure, symbolic order, or system of differences.
11. An alternative definition: *"discourse or discourses refer to systems of meaningful practices that form the identities of subjects and objects"* (Howarth & Stavrakakis, 2000: 3-4). This definition stresses the constitutive aspect of discourse.
12. The term overdetermination has its origin in psychoanalysis. Freud used it to account for dream work and the processes of condensation and displacement. Althusser used it to account for the "imaginary" character of social relations and the mediated—overdetermined—character of social formations. According to Althusser, empirical and essential entities and social relations are never directly given to our experience. Instead, they are always-already symbolically mediated. This of course holds for the Althusser of *For Marx* (1969) and *Ideology and State Apparatuses* (especially the first part) (2000 [1971]).
13. A research survey of 2003 (Fundación Futuro, 2003) shows that the coup still is the most defining or marking event of Chilean history across the generations.

Nonetheless, for younger generations other events—like the 1988 plebiscite or the detention of Pinochet—were considered more important. This marking effect of the 1973 coup is also emphasized by the participants. Moreover, while living abroad I have noticed that these images have also been used by international media (see Strasma, 2003).

14. The figure of the Hand of God has traditionally been used in Christian iconography for representing God the Father, his actions, creation, miracles, and his presence in the history of mankind.

15. *"There is neither Jew nor Greek, there is neither bond nor free, there is neither male nor female: for ye are all one in Christ Jesus"* (Galatians, 3, 28).

16. *"The wolf also shall dwell with the lamb, and the leopard shall lie down with the kid ... They shall not hurt nor destroy in all my holy mountain ..."* (Isaiah, 11, 6-9).

17. The relation between nodal point, empty signifier, and fantasy is a dynamic area of current research for discourse theorists (Glynos, 2001; Stavrakakis, 1999). About the distinction between nodal point and empty signifier, see Laclau (2004), where he stated they have the same referent but stress different functions. Whereas nodal point stresses the joining together and structuring aspect, empty signifier stresses the representation of an impossibility. Laclau did not use the term fantasy. Nonetheless, he agreed that there are commonalities with his concept of empty signifier (personal communication).

18. Lechner (1990) talked about a *"culture of fear."* Similarly, Silva (1999) developed the idea of social fears in relation to different traumatic experiences of the diverse social sectors of Chilean society.

19. The 1891 Civil War was a marking conflict in Chilean history. The national project of President Balmaceda clashed with interests organized in the Congress. The armed forces were divided and a second government based in the north was established. Balmaceda's party eventually was defeated. Isolated, he committed suicide instead of surrendering to his opponents.

20. Indeed, one participant of the reception analysis, L, a well-educated person in the field of history, was quite aware of this selection of events, which he regarded as *"popular"* (populist). Nonetheless, as is seen here, the other two participants regarded the particular section on the bombing of La Moneda as less controversial.

21. This is in line with data provided by diverse surveys regarding Chile's divided political culture (Huneeus, 2003).

22. Here I use the field concept as it is used by Bourdieu to delimit a certain area of the social for the purpose of analysis. By invoking Bourdieu, this attempt does not run the risk of falling into the structural division of the social, nor of establishing relations of determinism between parts of the social.

23. I am using the term cautiously as a metaphor, because of its logical-positivistic and explanatory connotations. The latter have little to do with my own ontological and epistemological interpretive position.

24. Following Karen O'Reily's advice (personal communication), I distinguish between quotations that come from my fieldnotes made during informal conversations and quotations from the participants' written or recorded statements. Whenever possible, I tried to keep my account as close as possible to the participants' exact words when taking notes. The quotations in this section draw on my own notes.

25. I wonder to which extent he is conscious of the fantasy structure of the discourse on national reconciliation in post-Pinochet Chile.
26. I do not claim that, as a researcher, I have a privileged insight into Toral's intentions, but rather that as an interviewer I partially structure the meaning produced by the interviewee when selecting the problems to be discussed.
27. Lira and Loveman (1999) discussed the meanings of reconciliation. The religious model mentioned here is one of the paradigms within which reconciliation acquires meaning.
28. I am referring to the Imaginary and the Symbolic in their Lacanian sense here. I am not using the term symbolic in its conventional sense, in which symbolic images would be taken to mean images that stand for something else.
29. This is not alien to everyday political experience. Indeed, it is obvious that visual symbols work as global and synthetic representations in electoral campaigns. Such symbols conflate both cognitive and affective dimensions of political signification. They establish a political map for voters (cognitive framing function), showing who are the allies/friends and who are the enemies/contenders. I contend that in the case of Chile during the period studied here, visual symbols, like those that are deployed in public works of art like Memorieo Visual de una Nación, are also politically important.

REFERENCES

Althusser, L. (1969) 'Marxism and Humanism,' pp. 221-231 in *For Marx*. London: Allen Lane/The Penguin Press.

Althusser, L. (2000) 'Ideology and Ideological State Apparatuses (Notes towards an Investigation),' pp. 100-140 in S. Žižek (Ed.) *Mapping Ideology*. London: Verso.

Archer, M. (1997) *Cultura y Teoría Social*. Nueva Visión, B.A.

Aylwin, P. (1992) *La Transición Chilena: Discursos Escogidos 1990-1992*. Santiago de Chile: Andrés Bello and Secretaría de Comunicación y Cultura, Ministerio Secretaría General de Gobierno.

Chilean Anti-Communist League, http://www.geocities.com/CapitolHill/Congress/1770/11-september-1973.html. Downloaded on February 2, 2005.

Culler, J. (1982) *On Deconstruction: Theory and Criticism after Structuralism*. New York: Cornell University Press.

Debord, G. (1977) *The Society of the Spectacle*. New York: Zone Books.

Eco, U. (1999) *Obra Abierta*. Barcelona: Ariel.

Edwards, A. (1936) *La Fronda Aristocrática en Chile*. Santiago: Ediciones Ercilla.

Evans, J., Hall, S. (1999) 'What is Visual Culture?,' pp. 1-8 in J. Evans and S. Hall (Eds) *Visual Culture: The Reader*. London: Sage.

Fernández, M. (1998) 'El Sistema Politico Chileno: Características y Tendencias,' pp. 27-51 in C. Toloza and E. Lahera (Eds) *Chile en los Noventa*. Santiago de Chile: Presidencia de la República-Dolmen Ediciones.

Fink, B. (1995) *The Lacanian Subject: Between Language and Jouissance*. Princeton, NJ: Princeton University Press.

Fiske, J. (1990) *Introduction to Communication Studies*, 2nd ed. London: Routledge.

Foxley, A. (2003) El Alma de Chile, *La Segunda* - September 12.

Fundación Futuro (2003) 'A 30 Años del Golpe Militar,' Estudio de Opinión, http://www.fundacionfuturo.cl/estudios_pub.php?id=35&valor=1. Downloaded on February 2, 2005.

Glynos, J. (2001) 'The Grip of Ideology: A Lacanian Approach to the Theory of Ideology,' *Journal of Political Ideologies* 6(2), 191-214.

Hall, S. (1991) 'Reconstruction Work: Images of Post-war Black Settlement,' pp. 152-164 in J. Spence and P. Holland (Eds) *Family Snaps: The Remaining of Domestic Photography*. London: Virago.

Hall, S. (1993) 'Encoding, Decoding,' pp. 507-517 in S. During (Ed) *The Cultural Studies Reader*. London: Routledge.

Hall, S. (1997) 'The Work of Representation,' pp. 13-64 in S. Hall (Ed) *Representation: Cultural Representations and Signifying Practices*. London: Sage Publications in association with the Open University.

Howarth, D., Stavrakakis, Y. (2000) 'Introducing Discourse Theory and Political Analysis,' pp. 1-23 in D. Howarth et al. (Eds) *Discourse Theory and Political Analysis: Identities, Hegemonies, and Social Change*. Manchester: Manchester University Press.

Huneeus, C. (2003) *Chile, Un País Dividido. La Actualidad del Pasado*. Santiago: Catalonia.

Laclau, E. (1990) *New Reflections on the Revolution of our Time*. London: Verso.

Laclau, E. (1993) 'Discourse,' pp. 431-437 in R. Goodin and P. Pettit (Eds) *The Blackwell Companion to Political Philosophy*. London: Blackwell.

Laclau, E. (1994) 'Introduction,' pp. 1-8 in E. Laclau (Ed) *The Making of Political Identities*. London: Verso.

Laclau, E. (1996) *Emancipation(s)*. London, New York: Verso.

Laclau, E. (2000) 'Identity and Hegemony,' pp. 44-89 in J. Butler et al. (Eds) *Contingency, Hegemony, Universality: Contemporary Dialogues on the Left*. London: Verso.

Laclau, E. (2004) 'Glimpsing the Future: A Reply,' pp. 279-328 in S. Critchley and O. Marchart (Eds) *The Laclau Reader*. London: Routledge.

Laclau, E., Mouffe, C. (1985) *Hegemony and Socialist Strategy. Towards a Radical Democratic Politics*. London: Verso.

Laclau, E., Zac, L. (1994) 'Minding the Gap: The Subject of Politics,' pp. 11-39 in E. Laclau (Ed) *The Making of Political Identities*. London: Verso.

Laitin, D. (1988) 'Political Culture and Political Preferences,' *American Political Science Review* 82(2): 589-593.

Lechner, N. (1990) 'Hay Gente que Muere de Miedo,' pp. 87-101 in N. Lechner (Ed) *Los Patios Interiores de la Democracia*. Santiago: FCE.

Lira, E., Loveman, B. (1999) 'Derechos Humanos en la Transición 'Modelo': Chile 1988-1999,' pp. 339-374 in P.Y. Drake and I. Jaksic (Eds) *El Modelo Chileno: Democracia y Desarrollo en los Noventa*. Santiago: LOM.

Memoria Viva, http://www.memoriaviva.com/. Downloaded February 2, 2005.

Mouffe, C. (2001) 'Every Form of Art has a Political Dimension,' Chantal Mouffe interviewed by Rosalyn Deutsche, Branden W. Joseph and Thomas Keenan, *Grey Room* 2 (Winter 02): 98–125.

Nichols, B. (1985) 'The Analysis of Representational Images,' pp. 43-68 in J. Corner and J. Hawthorn (Eds) *Communication Studies: An Introductory Reader*. London: Edward Arnold.

Plummer, K. (1995) *Telling Sexual Stories: Power, Change and Social Worlds*. London, New York: Routledge.

Sayyid, B., Zac, L. (1998) 'Political Analysis in a World without Foundations,' pp. 249-267 in E. Scarborough and E. Tanenbaum (Eds) *Research Strategies in Social Sciences: A Guide to New Approaches*. Oxford: Oxford University Press.

Silva, P. (1999) 'Collective Memories, Fears and Consensus: The Political Psychology of the Chilean Democratic Transition,' pp. 171-196 in K. Koonings and K. Kruijt (Eds) *Societies of Fear: The Legacy of Civil War, Violence and Terror in Latin America*. London: Zed Books.

Silva, R. (1986) *El Alma de Chile*. Santiago, Chile: Cieplan.

Slack, J.D. (1996) 'The Theory and Method of Articulation in Cultural Studies,' pp. 112-127 in D. Morley and K.H. Chen (Eds) *Stuart Hall: Critical Dialogues in Cultural Studies*. London, New York: Routledge.

Stavrakakis, Y. (1999) *Lacan and the Political*. London: Routledge.

Strasma, M. (2003) 'History in its Walls: La Moneda, Memory, and Reconciliation in Post-authoritarian Chile,' paper presented at FLACSO Chile, 5th of August 2003.

Toral, M. (1999a) *Memoria Visual de una Nación*. Metroarte.

Toral, M. (1999b) 'El Grandioso Mural Incomodo de Mario Toral,' an interview with José Miguel Varas, *Rocinante* 2(7).

Vial Correa, G. (1981-1987) *Historia de Chile (1891-1973)*. 4 Vols. Santiago: Santillana del Pacífico.

Villalobos, S. (1980) *Historia del Pueblo Chileno*. Santiago: ICHEH.

Vitale, L. (1993-1998) *Interpretación Marxista de la Historia de Chile*. 6 vols. Santiago: Lom.

Vitale, L. et al. (1999) *Para Recuperar la Memoria Histórica: Frei, Allende y Pinochet*. Santiago: Lom.

Žižek, S. (1990) 'Beyond Discourse Analysis,' pp. 249-260 in E. Laclau (Ed) *New Reflections on the Revolution of our Time*. London, New York: Verso.

Žižek, S. (1994) 'Introduction: The Spectre of Ideology,' in S. Žižek (Ed) *Mapping Ideology*. London: Verso.

Ads

7

A DISCURSIVE CRITIQUE
OF McJOB

*Putting Laclau, Mouffe, and Bakhtin
to Work*

David M. Boje

Yue Cai

This chapter narrates how activists overcame McDonald's corporation's resistance to putting the word McJob in the dictionary, making use of the theoretical tools of Laclau, Mouffe, and Bakhtin. Laclau and Mouffe (1985: 112) made the point that discourse is never safe from foreign or external elements. This became painfully clear (at least to McDonald's) when the word McJob was at the center of a discursive struggle that constituted an invasion of a corporately dominated discursive structure. In 2005, McDonald's found a way to strike back and invoked a narrative of how a McDonald's CEO— Ray Kroc—rose to the top from being a milkshake machine salesman. A similar case is that of its newest CEO, Charlie Bell, who recently died from colorectal cancer (on January 15, 2005 in Australia[1]). He had been a burger-flipper and a worker at McDonald's since the age of 15.

The 11th edition of Merriam-Webster's Collegiate Dictionary, published in June 2003, defined McJob as *"a low-paying job that requires little skill and provides little opportunity for advancement."* In 2003, BBC News presented stories that defined the word McJob in a similar way.[2]

McDonald's, on the contrary, advertises their jobs as opportunities that *can* lead to advancement because they are a first step for those lucky crew members (counter people) who someday will own a franchise.

Jim Cantalupo, McDonald's former CEO, called the McJob definition a *"slap in the face"* to the 12 million people who work in the restaurant industry, and demanded that Merriam-Webster dish up something more flattering.[3] The BBC reported Cantalupo as saying he dismissed the definition as *"an inaccurate description of restaurant employment."* In an open letter to Merriam-Webster, Cantalupo said: *"more than 1,000 of the men and women who own and operate McDonald's restaurants today got their start by serving customers behind the counter."*[4] The former CEO launched a public relations campaign printing his open letter in *Nation's Restaurant News* (November 3 edition), in which he said: *"[we] are all about opportunity for hundreds of thousands of Americans."*

CNN reported that Walt Riker, a spokesman for McDonald's, said the Oak Brook, Illinois-based fast-food giant is also concerned that McJob closely resembles McJOBS,™ the company's training program for mentally and physically challenged people.[5] *"McJOBS is trademarked and we've notified them that legally they are an issue for us as well,"* Riker said.[6] In a follow-up story, a Merriam-Webster's company spokesperson said they would keep the McJob definition. *"For more than 17 years 'McJob' has been used as we are defining it in a broad range of publications,"* the company said, citing everything from *The New York Times* and *Rolling Stone* to newspapers in South Africa and Australia. Arthur Bicknell, a spokesman for the Springfield-based publisher, said: *"Words qualify for inclusion in the dictionary because they are widely and commonly used in a broad range of carefully edited sources."*[7] The relevance of these stories is that McDonald's Corporation would not be able to retain the meaning of McJOB™ (its training program label) and avoid the forces of social opinion to make McJOB into a corporately alien word, in the elastic environment of social heteroglossia.

Similar definitions of McJob have been found outside of the Merriam-Webster Collegiate Dictionary, for example in the American Heritage Dictionary, the Oxford English Dictionary (OED), Webster's Dictionary (published by Random House), American Heritage (Houghton-Mifflin) and Dictionary.com. McJob was defined in the OED as: *"A job, usually in the retail or service sector that is low paying, often temporary, and offers minimal or no benefits or opportunity for promotion."*[8] The OED entry includes a 1986 story in *The Washington Post*, *"about an unstimulating, low-paid job with few prospects, especially one that was created by the expansion of the service sector."*[9]

The term McJob was coined by the Canadian novelist Douglas Coupland in his 1991 novel *Generation X* to describe *"A low-pay, low-prestige, low-dignity, low-benefit, no-future job in the service sector frequently considered a satisfying career choice by people who have never held one"*

(1991: 5). Coupland's surprised reaction to McDonald's delayed action was: *"I've always kinda wondered why the highly litigious McDonald's never went ape on this one years ago."*[10] In 1997, *The Independent* reported that the OED was advised by its lawyers not to include McJob in its dictionary, but OED ignored the lawyers and printed the word anyway. Shortly after, the British courts reached a verdict in the McLibel Trial in the United Kingdom, and José Bové was prosecuted for his action of dismantling a McDonald's in France.

MCJOB'S EMBEDDEDNESS
IN A DISCURSIVE STRUCTURE

According to Laclau and Mouffe, subjects are incorporated in a discursive structure in which they occupy a certain position. Every subject position is, by definition, a discursive position (Laclau & Mouffe, 1985: 115). Subjects cannot be the sole origin of social relations. More specifically, being a McDonald's worker is also a discursively constructed position, based on always-specific articulations within an infinite range of other possible subject positions (Laclau & Mouffe, 1985: 116). McDonald's construct the acceptability of being a McDonald's crew member by embedding labor in the narrative of "work hard" and "you too can become a McDonald's owner or even a CEO some day." However, McDonald's is just one of the many institutions that structure the discursive position of the McDonald's worker. Other types of institutions include unions, sociologists, newspapers, and so forth. There is an ensemble of significations attributed to the new word McJob discussed in this chapter, which goes beyond the control of McDonald's. Diverse forms of discursive subject positions are created, from negative (dead-end, low-pay, temp) all the way to unlimited advancement (the heretic dream of free market capitalism). Each of these representations is founded on a fiction, on a presence that is at a certain level *"something which, strictly speaking, is absent from it"* (Laclau & Mouffe, 1985: 119). Here, how various institutions articulate McWork is what particularly interests us.

If the meaning of McJob is constructed through language, then the antagonistic relationship between subject positions articulated by various institutions and social movements co-determines this discursive structure. The meaning of the word McJob is a discursive rebellion to the worker-subject positions constructed by McDonald's Corporation since 1948, at the time when car-hops were fired and replaced by counter order takers (Boas & Chain, 1976). The McDonald's brothers were not the first to Taylorize the fast-food industry, but they remain the most cited exemplar. Since then, the

McDonaldization of work has spread to other industries. Ritzer's (1993/2002) thesis is that McDonaldization spreads its recipe for the organization of work (its routinization, calculation, efficiency, and control) to other industries, including banking, real estate, travel agency, car rental, and so forth.

EMPTYING WORK

Laclau described how empty signifiers are structured around an empty place. The *"un-systematicity of the system"* (Laclau 1996: 40) we are dealing with here is McDonald's production/work system. Specifically, McDonald's workers did not have a (public) voice of their own (or the help of a union) to articulate their own subject positions far beyond the realm of the private. It was mainly the corporation that spoke for its workers. This lack of direct representation, limiting the narrative capacity of the workers with regard to their working conditions, meant that McDonald's corporation was able to fill the empty signifier McWork with significations that masked and excluded the materiality of working conditions, wages, and other issues. McDonald's discourse managed to (over)determine the signification of part-time fast-food restaurant work for more than five decades. This intense claim on the empty signifiers, which led to an absence of differential content (Laclau, 1996: 43), is exactly what is called a hegemonic project.

Opposition to this work system (see Boas & Chain, 1976; Leidner, 1993) was organized by social activists and embedded in the various subject positions signified by McJob. In the case of McJob, it took a decade to find a signifying content that would be a wake-up call for society to redefine the narrow corporatist perspective and allow integrating emancipation in the definition of McWork. The McDonald's workers have yet to present their own voices and objectives, and fill in the gap left by the no-more hegemonic corporate claim on the empty signifier McWork. Historically, whenever workers did organize themselves, McDonald's Corporation either used RAP (Report, Acceptance, Perform) sessions to dissuade them from supporting the initiative in question or if necessary to fire them, and as a last resort the corporation would close the franchise and reopen a new store just down the street. The fact that most workers are temporary and that there exists a high turnover is actually an advantage for the corporation in keeping unions from taking a hold. In short, it took a long time before social activists could gain any advantage in this kind of hegemonized encounter. Eventually, their resistance managed to rearticulate the definition of McWork and has left the corporation to imagine new strategies in the hegemonic game. McDonald's claim on the empty signifier McWork is no longer exclusive. What is common knowledge about work at McDonald's has been transformed through new articulations, and reflected in new meanings in the dictionaries. The age of uncontested hegemony of McDonald's mask has been eclipsed by a postmodern, loosely unified coalition of social movements ranging from unionization to slow food.

However, McDonald's does spend close to $1 billion a year on advertising itself as the pinnacle of the free market. Jobs at McDonald's are said to give workers freedom, opportunities for growth, which is the first step to individualism. These millions of dollars are still used to present to all American teenagers (and workers) the discourse that working at McDonald's (would) provide(s) them with growth opportunities. Globally, McDonald's presents itself as a wonderful place to work, where everyone can make a career out of his job.

ADDING BAKHTIN TO THE EQUATION

At a time when he was living in a cooperative, Bakhtin produced a book that was authored by Voloshinov: *Marxism and the Philosophy of Language* (1973); 90% of this book is Bakhtin's writing. The final part of Bakhtin's (1981) *Dialogic Imagination*, written 1934-1935, continues his project of amending Marxism with an alternative philosophy of language.

At issue is the Marxist (critical theory) study of material conditions of labor, production, and consumption, which aims to analyze the manufacture of corporate masks through dramaturgy and narrative or even through the aesthetics of architecture and decor. The words, gestures, and images produced in this context are not ideologically neutral (Bakhtin/Voloshinov, 1930/1973: 9). The corporate mask is an instrument of production and consumption; it refracts and reflects the production and consumption process; one reality (chronotope) reflects another reality (another chronotopicity of time/space).

In the debate on "idealist philosophy" and "idealist social psychology," ideology has been located within individual or social consciousness. It is viewed as some kind of inner effect, rather than being located in the semiotics of material conditions, embodied in the materiality of signs (Bakhtin/Voloshinov, 1930/1973: 10-13). Workers' and consumers' consciousness is filled with ideological signs, through social interaction, a consciousness nourished by the material facts of production and consumption. The middle ground of the debate (is identity internal consciousness or material semiotics?), where we can also find Laclau and Mouffe's work, would focus on how signs are social (intertextual), how consciousness is shaped by the materiality of signs. At the same time, Bakhtin/Voloshinov (1930/1973: 13) is/are quite definite: "*Individual consciousness is not the architect of the ideological superstructure, but only a tenant lodging in the social edifice of ideological signs."*

One example of this can be found in McDonald's expansion to China. During the first 3 years of McDonald's in China, the government was, to a certain extent, restringing the entering of this new model of modernization. Watson (2000) argued that McDonald's is an outpost of American culture. It offers authentic hamburgers to young people eager to forget that they live in a tiny colony on the rim of Maoist China. The word "fast" in fast food refers not to the consumption of the food but to its delivery (Watson, 2000). In China, restaurants have been turned into a place where one cannot only get a meal, but also spend time with friends and family.

BAKHTIN AND McJOB

McJob is what Bakhtin (1981: 277) termed a spectral ray-of-light, a social word, filling McDonald's with alien words, value judgments, and accents as the spectral light passes, penetrates, and surrounds the identity of McDonald's. McDonald's sparkles with alien McJob words, calculated accents, in an elastic environment full of dissonance and dialogized processes.

Bakhtin/Voloshinov (1930/1973: 10) make(s) the point that *"everything ideological possesses semiotic value."* The McDonald's worker, holding a McJob, is the embodiment of the ideological sign. Then a dictionary contests the corporate image of romantic work for teens and older workers, connecting McDonald's to a style of work it spends millions on to convince us that it is otherwise.

The McDonald's Corporation is a sign system deployed in global society, linked to the material conditions of fast-food labor processes and slaughterhouse production. McDonald's constructs an affirmative identity using marketing and standardized speech acts (the infamous greeting), the predictability of fast food in the Golden Arches, and so forth. McJob manufactures a corporate identity that goes against McDonald's official corporate discourse.

At one level, McDonald's corporate sign system is a very sophisticated and effective mask (of labor processes and animal slaughter), a manufactured identity ready to be handed to the public. At the same time, McDonald's is incredibly naïve. The corporate naiveté (unrealistic views) with regard to novelistic conditions of dialogized resistance to McDonaldization is absolutely stunning. Bakhtin (1981: 279) referred to the "Adam" myth, the idea that the verbal world is unqualifiedly "virginal," so that a word like McJob could really be purged from public discourse. In reality, McJob is embedded in a dialogized elastic environment.

A dialogized image of corporate counteridentities that occurred in the McJob saga shows how the image can unfold with dynamic complexity, and how deep and engulfed it is in the elastic environment of what is here called the "novelistic organization." McDonald's has moved from being the paradigmatic role model of epic entrepreneurship (the proverbial Ray Kroc story, which is retold in many strategy case books) to being the model of novelistic multiplicity of images and counterimages.

For Bakhtin (1981: 276), the environment is elastic. In it, words like McJob enter a process of living dialogic interaction that shapes their meaning, individualizes them and gives them stylistic shape. McJob enters a word-shape-shifting, elastic environment, not a linear information-processing one. This is where information-processing theories lack explicatory force to adequately model utterances and "elastic environments"; and they certainly do not allow tracing the materiality of discourse (from a critical theory perspective). Utterance theory, for example, overlays words with *"qualifications"* making them *"open to dispute," "charged with values,"* and *"already enveloped in an obscuring mist"* (Bakhtin, 1984: 276) that defines the elastic environment.

Through social action, McJob took on a stylistic profile with semantic layers that made the McDonald's Corporation, despite all its advertising dollars, its 30,000 outlets and nearly 500,000 workers in 121 nations, lose control over its sense-making process. The word McJob took on physical and physiological appearances in a set of disparate historical movements, in a socially specific elastic environment.

Foes of McDonaldization focus on the McJob (deskilling of work) and on the environmental waste from McDonald's 30,000 outlets (Ritzer, 1993/2002). Yet, to McDonald's defense, it should be added that the ethnographic evidence (Talwar, 2002) shows that in some outlets, the labor process is not deskilled, workers are cross-trained, and there is a good deal of multitasking (which is contrary to the deskilled identity of work, as signified by McJob).

CONCLUSION

McDonald's has had a close encounter with Bakhtin's *"treasure-house of language"* and found that reverting to a simplistic information-process open system theory is not up to the verbal dynamics of social heteroglossia. McDonald's is a veritable Tower-of-Babel inventing McWords to shadow its labor process (and animal slaughter): McDonaldland, McCheese, McDouble, McDrive, McExpress, McFlurry, McHero, McKids, McMenu, McNugget, McOz, McPollo, McRoyal, McScholar, McWorld and McJO.

Activists—inspired by Coupland's (1991) introduction of the word McJob—managed to disarticulate and reclaim the empty signifier McWork from McDonald's hegemonic discursive order. McJob was soon joined by other counter-words such as McDonaldization, McLibel, and McSpotlight, McUniversity, McWar, and so forth.

Both corporation and social activists use what Bakhtin (1981: 279) termed "*artistically calculated nuances*" in the living social discourse. From Laclau and Mouffe's perspective, both societal actors are confronted by the impossibility to exhaust the infinite field of discursivity, its permanently present potential for rearticulation and the elastic environmental dialogism of the McWords, as each position is an anticipation of corporate or activist answers, part of the living conversation between McDonald's and the foes of McDonaldization that has occurred since the early 1970s.

In the words of Mr. Coupland, who co-opted the McJob word for a different purpose: "*Let me speak up for the millions of Scots ... everywhere in expressing our annoyance at McD's for taking our surname prefix 'Mc' and turning it into a cheesy signifier for tasteless globalized pap. Thanks guys.*"[11]

NOTES

1. January 16, 2005—"Former McDonald's CEO Charlie Bell Dies of Cancer" http://www.usatoday.com/money/industries/food/2005-01-16-bell-obit_x.htm?csp=34.
2. BBC, November 9, 2003 http://news.bbc.co.uk/1/hi/world/americas/3255883.stm.
3. ABC Business News On Line, November 12, 2003 http://abclocal.go.com/kabc/business/111203_nw_mcjob.html.
4. BBC, November 9, 2003 http://news.bbc.co.uk/1/hi/world/americas/3255883.stm.
5. "McDonald's McJOB Trademark Lapsed in February 1992, and Was Declared 'Dead' by the United States Patent Office." http://www.theregister.co.uk/2003/11/11/merriamwebster_explains_disappearing_mcjob/.
6. 'McDonald's first registered the term on May 16, 1984, as a name and image for "training handicapped persons as restaurant employees." http://kornet.nu/blindhona/arkiv/000632.html.
6. CNN, November 10, 2003—"McDonald's not Lovin' 'McJob' Dictionary Definition" http://www.cnn.com/2003/SHOWBIZ/books/11/08/mcjob.dictionary.ap/.
7. CNN, November 11, 2003—'Merriam-Webster says 'McJob' is Here to Stay' http:// www.cnn.com/2003/SHOWBIZ/books/11/11/offbeat.mcjob.ap/.
8. Dictionary.com On Line http://dictionary.reference.com/search?q=mcjob.

9. On November 12, 2003, *The Washington Post* ran a 1986 opinion piece "McJobs Are Bad for Kids." http://abclocal.go.com/kabc/business/111203_nw_mcjob.html.
10. The Globe & Mall On Line, November 22, 2003 http://www.evalu8.org/ static-page?page=review&siteid=5280.
11. The Globe & Mall On Line, November 22, 2003 http://www.evalu8.org/ static-page?page=review&siteid=5280.

REFERENCES

Bakhtin, M. (1981) *The Dialogic Imagination: Four Essays by M.M. Bakhtin* (C. Emerson and M. Holquist, Trans.). Austin: University of Texas Press.
Bakhtin, M. (1984) *Problems of Dostoevsky's Poetics* (C. Emerson, Ed. and Trans.). Manchester: Manchester University Press.
Boas, M., Chain, S. (1976) *Big Mac: The Unauthorized Story of McDonald's*. New York: E.P. Dutton.
Coupland, D. (1991) *Generation X: Tales for an Accelerated Culture*. New York: St. Martin's Press.
Laclau, E. (1996) *Emancipation(s)*. London: Verso.
Laclau, E., Mouffe, C. (1985) *Hegemony and Socialist Strategy: Towards a Radical Democratic Politics*. London/New York: Verso.
Leidner, R. (1993) 'Making Fast Food: From the Frying Pan into the Fryer/Dishing It Out: Power and Resistance among Waitresses in a New Jersey Restaurant,' *American Journal of Sociology* 98(4): 942-944.
Ritzer, G. (1993/2002) 'The McDonaldization of Society,' *Journal of American Culture* (6): 100-107.
Talwar, J.P. (2002) *Fast Food, Fast Track. Immigrants, Big Business and The American Dream*. Boulder: Westview.
Voloshinov, V.N. (1973/1930) *Marxism and the Philosophy of Language*. NY/London: Seminar Press Limited.
Watson, J.L. (2000) *China's Big Mac Attack*. Foreign Affairs.

8

DECONSTRUCTING
A PORTUGUESE CITY

Cement, Advertising, and the Hegemony of "Green Growth"

Anabela Carvalho

Despite widespread interest in the impact of globalization on social and cultural life, the daily existence of individual citizens remains largely molded by particular experiences of space, the community and the city. As the physical traits of urban geographies create both possibilities and constraints in terms of sociability, work, mobility, leisure, and so on, they can be viewed as an important constituting factor of local culture and identity. However, the processes of constructing space and living in it are fundamentally dependent on the particular meanings that are assigned to it and that are constantly reconstructed. The *"urban experience"* (Harvey, 1989) is therefore fundamentally constituted by discourse.

The purpose of this chapter is to read the Portuguese city of Braga using some critical tools from the work of Ernesto Laclau and Chantal Mouffe (especially 1985). I argue that "development" and "green growth" are two important nodal points that have fixed the meaning of the social at different historical moments. While environmental concerns were excluded from the "development" project, green has, in the last few years, become the focus point of new political and business articulations that sustain their hegemonic positions.

"Nature" and the "environment" have recurred in a variety of discursive contexts to sustain the city council's project for the city. As these signifiers became increasingly eroded, they turned into empty signifiers allowing for all sorts of discursive uses in constructing and reinforcing the hegemonic position of local powers. "Green" has been arbitrarily employed by developers to fix the meaning of space and continues to be a key symbol in a profit strategy that paradoxically destroys what it attempts to market. This chapter pays particular attention to political propaganda and advertising as articulatory practices that contribute to a particular perception of space and a particular identity of subjects.

I start by reviewing (some of) the literature on discourse, urban politics and, more particularly, visions of what a city is or should be about. The ensuing discourse-theoretical analysis of the historical context in which a particular form of hegemonic politics emerged in Braga will help explain the chains of equivalence it has constructed and the meanings it has attached to the built and natural environments. Next, I discuss the system of alliances that Braga's mayor has entered into and forms of resistance to the city council's hegemonic project. This is followed by an analysis of the recent discursive (re)construction of environmental issues and the development of a green growth hegemonic discourse. The chapter ends with a reflection on consumption, place identity, and citizen identity.

DISCOURSES OF URBAN GOVERNANCE

Urban governance involves a continuous rebalancing of three main elements: social relations, economy, and nature/environment. These elements have a varying weight in steering the process of production and reproduction of space. Most recent research points out that there are currently three dominant discourses expressing different configurations of society–economy–environment in contemporary urban governance: the social inclusion discourse, the growth discourse and the sustainability discourse.

The social component of urban politics, which at particular historical moments lay at the foundation of many visions of urban future, has with the weakening of the welfare state lost some of its prominence in policymaking. However, research has emphasized the continued importance of the relations between spatial organization and issues of social inclusion–exclusion and distribution (e.g., Madanipour, Cars & Allen, 1998; Mortensen, 1995). In European and especially in American cities, the social conditions of impoverished neighborhoods form a striking contrast to the materially affluent lifestyle of other neighborhoods, with all the implications this has for education, employment, and citizenship in capitalist societies. In addition to this, the increasingly multicultural character of many cities in the (de-) industrialized world has raised pressing questions concerning ethnicity and spatial justice (e.g., Harvey, 1973, 1996). Over the last few years, proposals for participatory forms of governance have gained momentum. In many cases this has led to a democratic renewal, with citizens being granted more and better access to decision-making circles and with various forms of empowerment (e.g., Forester, 1999).

Urban policy around the world today is largely influenced by a new "growth discourse" (e.g., Jonas & Wilson, 1999). In a context of increased mobility, labor restructuring, and "globalization forces," decision makers emphasize the need to attract investment and capital to cities.[1] They claim cities have to aim at being competitive in a highly competitive economic environment. And in order to be competitive, they must—according to this discourse—attract entrepreneurial individuals and projects.

The new urban politics (Cox, 1993) and the *entrepreneurial city* (Hall & Hubbard, 1998; Harvey, 1989) are associated with a market-driven logic of accumulation. "Competitiveness" and "wealth" are the main signifiers in this discourse, which is promoted by growth coalitions composed of developers, state agencies, representatives of municipal governments and others. Public authorities often subscribe to a laissez-faire philosophy with regard to the free market (see Vojnovic, 2003).

Cities have, undoubtedly, an enormous environmental impact at all levels. Resource usage and generation of negative environmental effects are spatially concentrated and generally higher per capita in cities than in rural zones. Given the large pressures cities put on environmental systems and the awareness of the finite possibilities of the latter, significant attempts have been made to decrease the damage cities cause to nature. Whereas traditionally urban spaces were viewed as a break with nature, attention has progressively turned to forms of co-existence between city and ecology. Interest has been growing not only for the role of *the city in ecology,* but also for that of *ecology within the city* (Næss, 2001)—in other words, for the nature of nature within the city.

The environmental demands of urban spaces and the challenges and possibilities created by the interweaving of natural and built environments have led to a sustainability discourse, which attempts to reconcile economic growth, environmental protection and social concerns (e.g., Frey, 1999; World Commission on Environment and Development, 1987). This discourse is behind many regulations regarding transportation, land-use planning, waste management, and so on, which have been developed at local, national, and international levels. However, the ongoing withdrawal of the state from a range of governance processes and a tendency toward transferring responsibility for addressing environmental problems to the citizen or

private institutions may complicate attempts to resolve the present environmental crisis.

This chapter illustrates the potential of the analytical concepts formulated by Laclau and Mouffe for understanding how particular discourses come
to be hegemonic and how they are reconfigured through practices of
(re)articulation. The analysis of the historical development of urban governance in Braga demonstrates the contingent nature of meaning and identities
and shows how positions of dominance are (re)constructed within differential systems set up by discourse.

BRAGA: THE DEVELOPMENT PROJECT
AND ITS CHAIN OF EQUIVALENCES

Braga is a medium-sized city situated in the Minho region of northwestern
Portugal. With a population of 164,192 (2001 census), it is the third largest
city in the country. Braga's recent history has been irrevocably marked by
the fact that its municipal government has since the mid-1970s been controlled by one single party and, in fact, by one single person. Mesquita
Machado, the mayor of Braga, first came to power in 1976 and was re-elect-
ed seven times on a Socialist Party ticket. Not long ago, he suggested that he
might run again in the 2013 elections (Praça, 2002a).

Through the ongoing articulation and disarticulation of ideas and values
in the discourse he uses, Mesquita Machado has sustained a particular project for the city that has shaped its physical expansion and influenced the
lifestyles and identities of its citizens. In order to understand Braga's particular form of hegemonic politics, one needs to trace the social and political
circumstances in which it became dominant. This will also help explain how
antagonistic frontiers (Laclau, 2000) were constructed and managed.

We start with a short overview of the city's history. Taking over the
Celtic town of Bracai in the third century BC, the Romans made Bracara
Augusta the capital of the Gallaecia region. After changing hands between
the Suevi, Visigoths and Moors, Braga got a *foral* (city charter) in the 16th
century. Between then and the 18th century, the city knew a period of
intense Catholic development, with the construction of numerous churches,
convents, and monasteries. With its numerous sites of religious devotion,
Catholic administrative centers, and institutions for the study of theology,
Braga is even today considered a center of Catholicism. From the 19th century onward, the intent to modernize the city led to intense road construction activity, which reshaped the city's geography. However, local authorities lacked an integrated long-term vision for the city and consequently
failed to implement adequate planning policies (Bandeira, 2002).

For about half of the 20th century, Portugal was ruled by the *Estado Novo*, a fascist dictatorship that was overturned by the 1974 revolution. Political oppression, limitation of the freedom of expression, and very low levels of education characterized Portugal under Salazar. The legacy of the *Estado Novo* was an impoverished country, which was run economically according to a logic of self-sufficiency and that therefore mainly relied on agriculture. Since 1974, however, Portugal has changed tremendously. Initially, the country made a turn to the political left. However, it has so far been ruled almost exclusively by governments led either by the Socialist Party or by the Social Democratic Party (center-right). The 1986 entry into the European Union was a key moment, which brought huge structural funds to the country and gave a very significant impetus to the economy.

The revolutionary context of the mid-1970s opened up a series of possibilities for the reconfiguration of the social. However, demonstrating the *"impossibility of all 'objectivity'"* (Laclau, 1990: 182), the 1974 political transformation brought only a partial (re-)fixation of social relations and identities. The carnation revolution, as it became known, paved the way for democratic pluralism, the unfolding of identity struggles, the redistribution of wealth, and the realization of many other ideals. However, the radicalization of the political field (Mouffe, 1993) in the first years after the revolution, was followed by a process of disarticulation of many aspects of the revolutionary project. Progressively, the country became a standard neoliberal democracy.

The political and economic context of the mid-1970s was favorable to the constitution of an urban project of material growth and social inclusion. Mesquita Machado articulated this context into a system of relations centered on the idea of city development. "Development" became synonymous with a variety of aspirations and struggles. It came to represent, *inter alia*, the improvement of economic conditions, decent housing, and mobility for everyone.

"Development" was transformed into a nodal point (i.e., a signifier capable of fixing the meaning of a number of other signifiers in a chain of equivalence). From the mid-1970s onward, it linked builders and residents, rich and poor, apparently unifying their interests. It became associated with a "free-for-all" vision of material accumulation and transformation of the physical space. In the 1980s and 1990s, the construction industry boomed, with a large number of small and medium-sized companies being created in this sector and in associated ones. Construction was to a large extent unregulated, due to a lack of concerted planning strategies and the municipal government's permissiveness.[2]

A comparison can be made between Mesquita Machado's project and the growth discourse that was discussed in the previous section. A study by Wilson and Wouters (2003) of three rust-belt cities in the American midwest sketched the outlines of a discourse picturing the *"entrepreneurial develop-*

er as a civic salvationist" able to guarantee the future of the city: "*The developer is presented in the discourse as an omniscient, wise, grass roots individual whose energy and entrepreneurial spirit knows no bounds*" (Wilson & Wouters, 2003: 124). A similar view underpins a 2002 statement by then Prime Minister António Guterres that, thanks to the "*vision, daring and prestige*" of Mesquita Machado, Braga "*ha[d] known an unmatched development*" and was a "*reference for the rest of the country*" (Praça, 2002b).

From early on, Braga's city council discursively constructed "development" as a project of social inclusion and promoted a policy of affordable housing through the acquisition of building land in various areas of the city. Combined with the dynamics of the private market, this policy led to mid-size apartment buildings mushrooming all over the city in a case-by-case management of available space. A lack of coordinated planning combined with the sociopolitical values of the time resulted in the sacrifice of a number of public facilities such as parks, gardens, and other leisure and cultural infrastructures. Inexpensive housing increased population flows into the city, which in their turn were seized on as an economic opportunity by further speculative development operations.

As can be inferred from the previous discussion, "development" also came to signify social democracy and solidarity. In a leaflet distributed in 2001 to the inhabitants of Braga, the mayor claimed that "*we have a democratic occupation of the city, where all the socio-economic groups cohabitate, where all have a place.*" This was contrasted with other cities and their "*ghettos …, which are unconcealable wounds*" ('Braga, Terra Solidária,' n.d.). Mesquita Machado finished with an appeal for everyone to join him in seeking "*more development, more justice and more solidarity.*"

The comparison with other cities that was made earlier is also quite prominent in another leaflet of the same period. In this leaflet, Mesquita Machado listed a series of firsts in his city in comparison with others. The text emphasized the city's "*development, which we all feel proud of*" ('Braga, Terra de Progresso,' n.d.). In a further extension of the chain of equivalence, "development" was thus equated with ideas of inter-urban competition.[3]

The spatial design of Braga—and the lifestyles of its citizens—have been strongly marked by the construction of roads, which also became associated with progress and development. At the time the city's outer beltway was completed, the mayor addressed Braga's inhabitants in a leaflet claiming "*everyone (without exception)*" was proud of this achievement. Figure 8.1 shows a city council street billboard with the picture of a system of overlaid roads and overpasses and the slogan "*Braga: uma aposta de sucesso*" (*Braga—a successful bet*). Pictures of the many road systems in and around Braga were also used in many other media to promote the city.

In the last three decades, mobility by car has been greatly facilitated, in a predict and provide-type of approach that has led to continually increasing traffic (see Evans, Guy & Marvin 1999).[4] The new parts of the city are

FIG 8.1. *"Braga uma aposta de sucesso"* billboard.

intersected with fast roads running close to residential areas. In contrast, life has been made difficult for pedestrians and impossible for cyclists. In order to increase traffic flow, crosswalks and street lights have, in many cases, been replaced by overpasses, which prove to deter many people and result in a high number of pedestrians being hit by cars when trying to cross the road unsafely.

The hegemony of the development project subverted differences between car drivers and pedestrians, and between car drivers and cyclists. The car driver hybrid (Urry, 2004) was constructed as the default subject position and the specific needs and rights of others were not acknowledged. By means of a comparable logic of equivalence, wealthy people and the disadvantaged, too, were subsumed under the same discursive categories. In reality, there are striking differences between the living conditions of social groups in Braga and issues of social justice in the city remain underdiscussed (see Harvey, 1973).

The billboard in Fig. 8.1 and others that are discussed here have to be read in the context of local social and economic history. For a long time, construction was essentially *contra* nature. This should be understood against the backdrop of a history of deprivation in the villages and small towns of the region that many of those who moved to the city had known by experience. The living memory of the lack of adequate shelter, sanitation, water, electricity, and road access created a desire for progress and material possessions.

In Laclauian terms, we can locate nature on the other side of the antagonistic frontier of the development project (i.e., on the same side as lack of mobility, isolation, and poverty). In summary, it can be said that the central chain of equivalence of the discourse sustaining this project included, among others, material growth, social inclusion, (auto)mobility, and inter-urban competition.

As suggested previously, "development" became an empty signifier capable of symbolizing anything (Laclau, 1996),[5] and a nodal point of a hegemonic project. Thomassen (2005: 10) argues that hegemony analysis should inquire

> which signifier takes up the task of representing the whole. While this is ultimately contingent, it is not arbitrary. The particular signifiers are not *equally* able or likely to take up this task because it takes place in an already partly sedimented terrain permeated by relations of power.

"Development" has certainly been a powerful signifier in the social, economic, and political context of Braga. However, as is seen further on in this chapter, even this discourse has been reconfigured for it to be able to maintain its hegemonic position.

THE INDETERMINATE CHARACTER
OF POLITICAL IDENTITIES

Mesquita Machado defined himself as a *"pragmatic man, interested in the principles of democracy and solidarity"* (cited in Feio, 1995a: 39). Pragmatism is a way of thinking and acting that is more concerned with solving problems and obtaining results than with principles or values. It is an apparently neutral position. However, the identification of problems and the pragmatic solutions found for them are never neutral. In this section, we examine the open-ended nature of political identities by reviewing the particular kind of coalitions that Braga's mayor has developed and their role in the hegemonic politics of the city.

Gramsci's (1971) understanding of hegemony can contribute to an analysis of the system of relations Mesquita Machado and a variety of other actors in the city have constructed. By entering into alliances with certain individuals and institutions, the mayor has repeatedly attempted to create consensus and often succeeded in doing so, thus managing to dilute contestation and marginalize opposition. An example of this is that, in this traditionally very Catholic city, the socialist council entertains exceptionally good relations with the Church. A number of key figures in the ecclesiastical hierarchy continue to play a very influential role in the city, and no visible conflicts between the Church and the council have arisen. In fact, an effective form of power-sharing between two potentially colliding entities has been reached.

This relationship is well known to city residents and plays a role in political consciousness. It has mainly been forged in the backstage of public life, but occasionally emerges in the public sphere. For example, in February 2002, a coalition of local groups and personalities organized a tribute to Mesquita Machado on the occasion of his 25 years as mayor of the city. This coalition included, among others, the University of Minho, the Industrial Association, the Red Cross, Sporting Clube de Braga (the city's soccer club), and many representatives of the Church. It thus formed a clear expression of the complex and highly open system of pacts the mayor has created. The following excerpt from *Público*, a national newspaper of reference, illustrates the particular role of church authorities in this:

> It is a tribute clearly "blessed" by the conservative and powerful Church of Braga. It suffices to note that almost half the institutions in the [organizing] committee are associated with the Church, from Universidade Católica to Cabido Metropolitano, Misericórdia, Irmandade de Santa Cruz and Confrarias do Sameiro and Bom Jesus. ('Uma 'união local',' 2002)

In Gramscian terms, one can say that, while the Catholic Church used to be a pillar of Salazar's dictatorial regime, it has now become part of the city council's hegemonic project by entering into an alliance with it. The local government's system of alliances has taken other unexpected forms. After the 2001 local elections, a Communist Party representative who had often publicly criticized the mayor and his management of the city was invited to be part of the mayor's team. For Bloco de Esquerda, a left-wing party coalition, this meant the *"weakening of the left in Braga."* It called the resulting union a *"baroque marriage"* between the communists and the *"unilluminated despotism which rules the city"* with the blessings of the Church ('BE-Braga,' 2002). As was noted by Gitlin (1980: 256), *"only by absorbing and domesticating conflicting values, definitions of reality, and demands on it, in fact, does [a given 'frame'] remain hegemonic."*

DISCURSIVE RESISTANCE TO BRAGA'S HEGEMONIC PROJECT

Despite the electoral success of the council's political project, the city's cultural meaning has been fixed only partially. Moreover, several social agents have pointed out the non-necessary character of the relations put in place by the hegemonic project. As one of the city's leading musical artists put it:

> [Braga] could be a pleasant medium-sized European city, with gardens, squares, tree-lined streets, small local shops, lively neighborhoods, diverse cultural activity [and] a convivial atmosphere, and I see it transformed into a giant and arid suburb [which is] dissected by fast roads [and] where the automobile is king. (Adolfo Luxúria Canibal, 2001)

Political parties from the opposition have long criticized Mesquita Machado's way of running the city. A Christian Democrat Party candidate described it as a *"closed-up form of management which is not inclined to stimulate and accept civic participation; a management marked by a concubinage with 'vested interests,' which did not invest in the quality of living of the population."* (Miguel Macedo in Feio, 1995b: 43) Miguel Portas, one of Bloco de Esquerda's national leaders, stated that *"Braga's city council is a builders' union"* (Monteiro, 2001).

Civic organizations, too, have repeatedly challenged the chain of equivalence created by the city council by pointing out the problems its policies have caused. ASPA, an association for the defense of the built and natural heritage created in 1976, has been very active in denouncing the council's negligence toward—or even active destruction of—historic buildings, archeological sites and the natural environment.[6] Part of ASPA 's discursive resistance to Mesquita Machado's hegemony has taken place in *Diário do Minho*, a local daily newspaper.[7] Illustrative of the complex and fragmented nature of Braga identities is that the Catholic Church owns this newspaper. Although many influential members of the Church express support for the mayor, other representatives of the same institution create space for critical voices.

Aggregating a number of people with highly diverse social and political positions, ASPA is an example of how social movements can assemble a wide variety of people around ideas or values and thus transcend class consciousness or party affiliation (see Laclau & Mouffe, 1985: 159-171).

Braga's mayor maintains an extremely conflictual relationship with ASPA. He actually considers ASPA the main force of opposition to his power and his feeling has been described as one of *"hate"* for this *"prime enemy"* (Lemos, 2001).[8] Mesquita Machado has repeatedly accused ASPA of *"doing politics,"* as if politics were a narrow strip of the social accessible to political parties only and outside of which subjects do not have the right to express their differences. The following excerpt from an interview granted to *Público* is a good illustration of how the mayor discursively constructs this view:

Mesquita :   [ASPA] had better turn itself into a political party. Then
Machado   it would play straight.

Público: But ASPA has members from all ideological walks, from the far left to the far right . . .

| Mesquita: | It's a group of friends. Everyone knows it. |
| Machado | ('ASPA devia formar um partido,' 2002) |

Here, Mesquita Machado deliberately creates confusion as to the organization's standing, which is a rhetorical practice he commonly uses. Another example is the discussion surrounding the plans for Quinta dos Peões,[9] which brought together the main opposition parties and several non-governmental organizations. In his reaction to their criticism, the mayor claimed that it came from a *"minority strip"* that was *"not representative of the population of Braga"* (Lima, 1999). Other forms of resistance or dissent have regularly been dismissed by the mayor as being anti-town (i.e., as the local equivalent of antipatriotic behavior).

Composed mainly of young graduates from the University of Minho, Projecto BragaTempo attempted to boost debate on a number of public matters concerning the city. In 2001 and 2002, it organized a series of meetings to discuss spatial planning, architecture, mobility, and other urban policy domains. The city council was invited to take part, but chose to completely ignore the events. After a few years, Projecto BragaTempo moved its focus to politically less sensitive domains such as the promotion of cultural and/or artistic initiatives. In the meantime, it seems to have ceased its activities altogether.

Throughout the years, several civic associations in Braga have been forced to put an end to their activities or to tone them down, clearly as a consequence of anti-democratic oppression. Arco-Íris, Fórum Bracarense and Braga Para a Democracia are examples of civic organizations that appear to have recently vanished. The political struggle entered upon by these groups was seen as a threat to the city council's hegemonic position. There are reports of the council adopting measures like a *"takeover"* by people committed to the *"system"* (see 'Quando ser associação cívica,' 2002). For example, the local branch of Quercus—one of the most active nationally organized environmental organizations—is now weakened, because its leader has become a municipal government employee.

In democratic societies, the media are supposed to be a forum for pluralistic debate. Braga's local press could therefore be expected to host alternative discourses. In reality, part of the local press actually contributes to reinforcing the city council's domination. *Correio do Minho*, the city's other daily besides *Diário do Minho*, was governed and financed by the council between 1982 and 1999. Although the newspaper has been privatized since and now belongs to a group composed of journalists and a businessman, the director (now turned co-proprietor) and the editorial line remained the same. Not surprisingly, *Correio do Minho* invariably depicts the local authorities favorably and contributes to strengthening their hegemonic politics. The biography of Costa Guimarães, the director of *Correio do Minho*, is in itself highly revealing. He used to be a journalist for *Comércio do Porto*, a Porto-based newspaper, in which he was very critical of Braga politics—until Mesquita Machado invited him to head *Correio do Minho*. A similar case is that of a previously incisive journalist of *Diário do Minho*, who is presently a press aid to the mayor. The city council's Gramscian logic of "buying" people into its hegemony seems to have found universal application in Braga.

THE NEW GREEN GROWTH DISCOURSE

Presenting continuous physical expansion as desirable, the development discourse subverted the differences between, among others, builders and citizens, present (construction) and past (heritage), growth and nature. At present, Braga's skyline is dominated by concrete (see fig. 8.2). The rapid rate of construction has put enormous pressures on the land surrounding the city and has caused high environmental, visual, and aesthetic costs.

Despite the huge expansion of the built environment in the last three decades, not one single park or even sizeable garden has been laid out. Green areas remain limited to roundabouts and to the small strips of land between roads and apartment buildings. Braga and its surroundings also face a number of other environmental problems. Rio Este, the small river that runs through the city, has been walled for many kilometers, so that houses and roads could be constructed on its banks. The river is very polluted by open sewage pipes discharging themselves into it in several parts of the city.

In the last few years, faced with the discursive resistance discussed above and with the increasing visibility, in the media and in other arenas, of discourses advocating the protection of nature and the environment, the city council has attempted to engulf these discourses by presenting itself as a pro-green agent.

A first example illustrating this tendency is that, for some time now, the council has been promoting the Janela florida (Flowery window) and Varanda florida (Flowery balcony) competitions, in which awards are put up for homeowners with appealing flower displays. Significantly, these events are organized by the council's Environmental Department and are discursively constructed, through press releases and council publications, as proxies for environmental policy in the council's public communication.[10]

In a recent news release, the city council legitimated its plan to build a park—which is to be given the paradoxical name Urban Park—in the northern part of Braga as follows:

> In a global world, where competition for generating and attracting development initiatives and projects has to be assumed as a strategic goal, cities have to build urban facilities necessary for the construction

FIG 8.2. New residential areas, Braga.

of a "friendly" environment. The Urban Park of Braga, which includes multifunctional equipments with sports, economic and leisure facilities, is integrated in a vast green area and served by a modern road network. It brings new infrastructural and logistic capacities to the city that contribute decisively to the consolidation of Braga as a pole of development of the peninsular northwest, and increases capacity for the organization of events, attraction of business initiatives and development of sports and tourist activities. (Gabinete de Comunicação da Câmara Municipal de Braga, 2005)

This excerpt illustrates the merging of the growth discourse discussed earlier (and the high value it places on competitiveness and entrepreneurialism) with a green discourse. In the resulting discourse, the environment is seen not just as *helpful* in the creation of growth, but as *constitutive* for it.

Modes of articulation of the economy and the environment or wealth, and nature are being reconfigured, as noted by While, Jonas and Gibbs (2004: 554), who claimed that *"the relation between urban entrepreneurialism and the search for an urban sustainability fix is becoming a necessary rather than contingent condition of the contemporary political and economic form of urbanization in capitalism."* They hold that any urban sustainability fix meets a number of contextual pressures such as economic imperatives, regulatory drivers, public legitimation pressures, intensified interurban competition, and the neoliberal restructuring of the state. In Laclauian terms, we can argue that the link between entrepreneurialism, sustainability, and the other aspects listed is discursively created and that, as a consequence, the sustainability discourse is a purely contingent construction. Meanings are fixed through particular articulations between different objects in a particular sociocultural context.

In the discursive construction of Braga's city council, deep environmental issues like the flows of people or transportation policies related to the park and its facilities are not acknowledged or debated. On the contrary, the council emphasizes that the park is surrounded by a good road network and thereby discursively constructs the privately owned car as the preferred means of mobility. This is made possible culturally by the local history of the development project.

One of the city council's favorite promotional devices are street billboards. Here, too, the tendency is to subsume nature to the council's ruling discourse. One of the recurrent slogans in the council's ads is: "*É bom viver em Braga*" (*It's good to live in Braga*). It often appears in combination with the city council's coat of arms and/or with its acronym or designation in full. In the examples in Fig. 8.3 and 8.4, the council is associated with two hypermarkets. This association between political power and the business sector is naturalized by the system of relations created by the development discourse, the message being that the municipal government brings consumption facilities to the city's residents.

In Fig. 8.5, the message that greenery makes Braga a good place to live in is conveyed by the picture that was selected for the ad, the green stripe at the bottom and the logo on the lower left side (the word Braga with leaves on top).

An analysis of these forms of communication shows that the frontiers of the development discourse have been gradually redrawn so as to absorb nature. Turned into a new central signifier, greenery has not only been made compatible with but has become constitutive of growth.

FIG. 8.3. Feira Nova billboard.

FIG. 8.4. Sign posted in Carrefour hypermarket soon after it was built.

FIG. 8.5. "*É bom viver em Braga*" billboard.

THE ARTICULATION OF "NATURE" WITH THE CONSUMPTION OF SPACE

The discourse of the business sector in the city of Braga shows signs of a reconfiguration similar to the one that has taken place in the political field. Given the purposes of this chapter, the construction industry and its advertising practices constitute a highly interesting object of study. The construction industry, too, frequently uses street billboards as an advertising and communication instrument, which can be explained by the fact that they are placed strategically vis-à-vis the product and the mobility routines of consumers (Gonçalves & Pires, forthcoming a, b). Because of the spatial relations they share with the land and the surrounding buildings and their particular embeddedness within an architectural setting, the articulations made on street billboards have a significant power in the construction of place identity.

The rapid growth of the construction industry has resulted in an excessive offer on the housing market. In 2001, there were 70,268 houses for 164,192 inhabitants, with an average occupation of 2.3 people per house. More than 10,000 houses were unoccupied, with approximately 6,000 being offered for sale or rent (Coentrão, 2004). Notwithstanding this, the construction industry is still very active, with new buildings emerging all the time and often left unfinished because the firms building them run into financial difficulties. In a context of immense competition and faced with (some) criticism because of the lack of green space, the construction industry has responded by appropriating nature as a sales argument, as is shown in the examples discussed next.[11]

The billboard in Fig. 8.6 is divided in two distinct parts, roughly corresponding with a division between image and text. The left part shows a picture of a forest with a number of very large trees. The dominant green color is enhanced by orange tones in the leaves of some of the trees and on the ground. On the right part, a text in green letters against a white background reads:

FIG. 8.6. Quinta da Reguenga billboard.

Come and get to know the ideal house for your family.
Quinta da Reguenga (Reguenga Farm)
Your farm in the center of town
Visit the model house

In Portuguese, the term quinta carries positive connotations, referring as it does to a property with farmland and a distinguished house, often a manor, belonging to an aristocratic or wealthy family. Following demographic changes and the modernization of agricultural practices, many quintas have been sold to developers.

The land where this project was being developed used to be part of a quinta. However, there are no traces of what it once looked like. As the picture demonstrates, there is no resemblance between the actual referent and the promotional ad, all the less so because the site is surrounded by apartment buildings. What we find here is a marketing attempt to evoke a past and a spatial history that have paradoxically been deleted by the product that is being marketed—the new development. Moreover, even in the (recent) past, the area would have looked more like an agricultural zone than like the scene in picture. The selected picture is therefore totally arbitrary. Its interest lies in its attempt to fix the meaning of the space and of the experience of living in that space through their association with an idealized green environment.

A similar analysis can be made of the ad in Fig. 8.7. Put up in a rather built-up area next to a hypermarket and a shopping mall, it reads "*Espaços quase florestais*" (*Spaces that are almost like forests*[12]). Above this text is the picture of a set of very modern terraced houses. Again, the trees depicted in

FIG. 8.7. "*Urbanização Bouça da Fonte*" billboard.

the ad do not exist and are unlikely to sprout in the surrounding tarmac. The choice of the marketing strategy may again be motivated by the name of the place: Urbanização Bouça da Fonte (Fountain Wood Development). Bouça is a common designation in Minho for a plot of land covered with trees. This may have held for the site in a relatively distant past. In a more recent past, however, it was used for farming.

In Fig. 8.8, the ad is for *"small condominiums surrounded by a large green area."* The natural environment is encapsulated in the figure of a bird (belonging to a species that is not common in the region) resting on a tree branch. As the area is still being developed, it is not clear how much of a green area there will actually be, but it should be noted that the apartment buildings will be next to a four-lane road. Most of the green will probably be in the surrounding hills (i.e., far away, relatively inaccessible, and offering visual pleasure only).

Laclau and Mouffe's (1985: 166) *"critique of the category of unified subject, and the recognition of the discursive dispersion within which every subject position is constituted"* provides a useful conceptual background for the analysis of the combination of subject positions in the ad shown in Fig. 8.6. It appeals to the family (wo)man who is interested in material well-being and in the social status linked to exclusive ownership, and who is at the same time fond of nature. Consumption is presented as the way to realize all of these aspirations. Indeed, in most societies, consumption practices have become a central dimension of social subjectivities. Identity tends to become largely defined by commodities and their symbolic value. House ownership (including features of the house such as size, location and design) has arguably become one of the main status symbols.

FIG. 8.8. Minho Investe billboard.

Alluding to the impact of discourses on consumption, Laclau and Mouffe (1985: 163-4) have pointed out the following:

> the dominant discourses in consumer society present it as social progress and the advance of democracy, to the extent that it allows the vast majority of the population access to an ever-increasing range of goods. ... Interpellated as equals in their capacity as consumers, ever more numerous groups are impelled to reject the real inequalities which continue to exist.

Advertising is one of the central cultural phenomena associated with consumption in present-day societies. It has a profound influence on the construction of meaning. Marketing strategies for the articulation of commercial identities have been so successful that, in some cases, the product has become a *"mere filler for the real production: the brand"* (Klein, 2000: 21). The imagery created by brands like Apple and Calvin Klein evokes powerful associations with social values, lifestyles, and desires. The conceptual and semiotic dimensions obliterate the materiality of the product. In the last few years, advertisers have understood the symbolic potential of nature and the environment and taken hold of these signifiers, turning them into commercial tools. "Green advertising" and "green public relations" are now multi-million dollar businesses in advanced capitalist societies (Nakajima, 2001).

In the cases examined here, nature is commodified by the advertising discourse and turned into a desirable possession coming with the acquisition of a house. However, there is a fundamental irony in these examples, since the marketing device used by developers is in fact destroyed by them. Referring to a similar process, Linder (2003) pointed out how the semiotic value of global warming has been reworked by advertising in ways that, ironically, serve to promote consumption and traveling. This illustrates the contention made by Nash (2002) that the *"constitutive undecidability of [the] articulation [of different signifiers] means that re-signification is always a possibility."*

Several recent studies help understand the fundamental unfixity of the signifier "nature." There is, as was theoretically and empirically illustrated by Macnaghten and Urry (1998), no single nature. The term has come to represent a variety of things. Which meaning will be assigned to it depends on the particular system of discursive and social practices it functions in. What we have today is a variety of contested natures. In a world that has been profoundly reshaped by human activity, nature is, materially and symbolically, no longer simply the spontaneous/natural environment, but is deeply embedded in social, cultural and economic systems. This is why Castree (2000: 28, emphasis in original) maintained that the production of nature is *"a continuous process in which nature and capital co-constitute one*

another in temporally and geographically varied and contingent ways."
Moving a step forward, Dingler (2003) proposed a discursive understanding
of nature that transcends the dualism between the symbolic and the material and conceptualizes nature as the result of power relations.

The political and commercial articulations of nature and the environment discussed here can be related to a wider discursive context, in which
"sustainable development" has gained a hegemonic character. Over the last
decade, "sustainable development" has become a mainstream concept forging a new consensus that is supposed to end conflicts between economy,
society and the environment (e.g., Torgerson, 1995; World Commission on
Environment and Development, 1987). Environmentalism, which had
emerged as an important social struggle aiming to expose man's antagonistic
relation to nature and to promote less exploitative ways of dealing with
nature, has in many respects been captured by a variety of social forces that
have discursively reconstructed it to reinforce a whole range of projects.

PLACE IDENTITY AND CITIZEN IDENTITY

Laclau and Mouffe (1985: 111) emphasized that *"identities are purely relational"* and that *"there is no identity which can be fully constituted."* All
identities are permanently open to reconstruction. This holds for individuals and institutions but also for other entities, including places. As suggested earlier, the identity of the city of Braga has been shaped and re-shaped
through discursive practices that were themselves permanently evolving.

There is a growing awareness, among researchers and decision makers,
of the importance of discursive practices in defining what a city stands for.
Avraham (2000), McCann (2004), and Skillington (1998), among others, discussed the role of the media in the construction of the meanings of cities.
Mazanti and Pløger (2003: 309) stated that *"[c]oncepts such as place identity
and place of belonging [now] play a central role in current urban planning
and urban regeneration programs."* Policymakers have attempted to
*"(re)shape the reading and interpretation of the social and physical mean-
ings"* of given communities through such strategies as *"historicization and
aestheticization"* (Pløger, 2001: 68).

Personal identities are developed and transformed within a system of
relations between various elements, including space. In fact, spatial experiences are an important dimension of subjectivity. On the one hand, personal views and perspectives influence one's understandings of space; on the
other hand, the experience of space plays an important part in identity construction. Research has shown how, for instance, practices of daily mobility
constitute gender (Law, 2002) and how ethnic identity and citizenship are

negotiated through spatial experiences (Secor, 2004). People use, perceive and make sense of space in complex ways. Their "readings" of the city and of their place in it depend on the constraints and possibilities associated with the physical space but also on various forms of symbolic mediation.

In short, space plays an important role in the definition of one's personal identity. This also implies that political and commercial discourses on space are constitutive not only of space identity but also of personal/citizen identity. As was argued earlier, the slogan *"É bom viver em Braga"* (*It is good to live in Braga*) and the city council's promotional/legitimating discourse it belongs to have played an important part in the council's hegemonic practices. In addition to this, we can say that, through the use of street billboards and other communication technologies, the council has attempted to fix the meaning of the social by subjectifying the urban experience: *"é bom ..."* is a discourse conveying appreciation, which is a personal experience.

By displaying these ads in a variety of locations and discursively linking itself to a number of different aspects of life, the city council has sought to "naturalize" its message. Evoking Laclau and Mouffe, Bowman (2002) noted the following:

> [F]or as long as the struggle persists, it will be immensely important to each side of the struggle to reiterate a certain meaning for these events, in order that, over time, and through the "regularity in dispersion" of these reiterations, the meaning which best serves the cause will become consolidated and sedimented as "true" in the minds, or imaginary, of as many people as possible.

As seen here, real estate advertising aligns itself with the new political discourse by articulating "growth," "nature" and "consumption." Figure 8.9 shows another example of how political and commercial discourses concur to construct the identity of Braga and Braga's citizens. The billboard displays an advertisement with the picture of a man showing the drawing of a heart on his palm and the slogan *"Braga no coração"* (*Braga in the heart*). The ad is for a shopping center (with the significant name Braga Park), which is situated next to a hypermarket and accommodates 80 shops, 11 restaurants, a 7-screen movie theater, entertainment facilities, and free parking space. Shopping opportunities are the reason to love Braga. Or, differently put: if you love Braga, you ought to love shopping/consumption.

Mesquita Machado has claimed that Braga is the *"Portuguese city with the highest level of quality of life"* (cited in Feio, 1995a: 40). A recent European Union Urban Audit Perception Survey (European Commission, 2004) appears to confirm that most Braga inhabitants feel that way. The survey was conducted in January 2004 to measure how the quality of life was perceived in 31 European cities. Braga ranked fifth in terms of people's general satisfaction with living in the city. Despite all problems in areas like

FIG. 8.9. *"Braga no coração"* billboard.

health care, public transport, and cultural facilities, life in Braga was experienced as satisfactory by 95% of its residents. Even satisfaction with green spaces was relatively high, since about a dozen cities scored worse than Braga in this field. Most people considered that it is easy to find good housing at a reasonable price in Braga. When asked whether they believed that, in the 5 years to come, their city would become more pleasant to live in, the Braga respondents again placed their city in the top five of the selected European cities.

The results of this survey should not be overstated or generalized, as is illustrated by the fact that they are contradicted by another study, which was undertaken in Lamaçães (a new development in the city) and which showed that 66% of the people living in the area would like to move away in the years to come (Lima, 2001). There are cracks in the apparent inclusiveness of Braga and antagonisms are inscribing themselves onto various discursive surfaces, such as part of the local press, the communication of a number of non-governmental organizations and public meetings organized by political parties from the opposition. Nevertheless, the articulatory practices of the municipal government and business agents seem to have been very effective in fixing a particular meaning of Braga as a social totality.

CONCLUSIONS

In this chapter, the relation between urban politics, space, and identity has been re-examined by means of analytical concepts advanced by Laclau and

Mouffe. It is easy to understand that political discourse plays a constitutive role with regard to urban spaces. A particular articulation of the various dimensions of (life in) the city is embodied in all kinds of spatial arrangements, as we have been able to demonstrate in the case of Braga. In their turn, decisions on spatial design have significant and long-lasting implications for urban experiences. Individuals, groups, and classes and the relations among them are, in multiple ways, affected by the decisions that are made on the configuration and uses of space.

At a higher level, this chapter has attempted to understand the relational and contingent nature of meaning and identity in urban spaces, and how these function within a hegemonic logic that is characteristic of all political systems. First of all, spatial features, both built and natural, can only be understood by situating them within the system of relations set up by discourse. We have seen how the development discourse of Braga's city council created a particular form of intelligibility for the city and how place identity was defined and redefined within that horizon of meaning. At the same time, the subject positions and the identity of Braga's citizens were also reconstructed by that particular discourse. We can therefore say that the development project established a mutually constitutive relation between the identity of the space and the identity of citizens/inhabitants of that space.

Second, contingency is a fundamental trait of any hegemonic project. As *"[t]he moment of the 'final' suture never arrives"* (Laclau & Mouffe, 1985: 86), the constitution of a hegemonic order is an ongoing process. Meaning is constantly renegotiated through changing articulations and disarticulations. As a consequence, the *"sense of every social identity appears constantly deferred"* (Laclau & Mouffe, 1985: 86). The overwhelming dominance of the political position of Braga's city council is to a large extent explained by its capacity to adapt and extend the chains of equivalence created by its discourse. As seen here, it has redrawn the antagonistic frontier defined by the development discourse so as to include nature in its hegemonic project. Its current green growth discourse eludes the fundamental conflict between economic growth and the environment, and unites different actors and agendas. The unfixity of the signifier nature has allowed for many types of re-articulations. Commercial discourses, for example, have so emptied the meaning of the term that it can be made to stand for "nature as it" (supposedly) "existed in the past." These new discursive structures redefine the identities of places and citizens.

Reconciling the aspirations of different communities and social actors in designing a city, town, or village, while enhancing the inhabitants' sense of belonging and allowing for the coexistence of differences is a difficult but ever-pressing mission for planning powers. Spatial and urban design thus holds some of the greatest challenges for a pluralist democratic politics. The recent "communicative turn" in urban planning (e.g., Fischer & Forester, 1993; Forester, 1999; Healey, 1997) is based on a normative program for improving planning practice through argumentation and pluralistic debate. This perspective is associated with a belief in the possibility of finding a rational consensus among people (rational being viewed as synonymous with objective and necessary). However, conflicts between values and the uneven distribution of knowledge and power in the interaction between social actors always compromise this idealized Habermasian process of communicative rationality. Laclau and Mouffe (2001: xviii) maintained that *"it is vital for democratic politics to acknowledge that any form of consensus is the result of hegemonic articulation, and that it always has an 'outside' that impedes its full realization."* According to them, this is the *"very condition of possibility"* (Laclau & Mouffe, 2001: xviii) of the democratic project.

Cities face a number of social, economic and environmental pressures and demands that are associated with various types of antagonisms. Competing forces constantly struggle for hegemony. As was noted by Mouffe (1993), the idea of a totally consensual polity in which the wishes of all are taken into account is a dangerous utopia, because it conceals and suppresses conflicts of values and positions. By deconstructing the operations of hegemony and helping understand the open-ended nature of social struggle, Laclau and Mouffe's work forms an important contribution to the "radicalization" of urban democratic politics.

NOTES

1. The growth discourse is often associated with the world city discourse (see Flowerdew, 2004).
2. A similar process also occurred at the outskirts of other cities and towns along the Portuguese coast, where the majority of the population lives.
3. Pride of the city is a recurrent theme in the city council's discourse.
4. This is particularly serious in a country where car transportation has increased exponentially in the last few years and alternatives are, in most cases, unavailable or inadequate. Besides congestion, pollution, and other problems associated with the car culture, Portugal faces the problem of excessive greenhouse gas emissions, as the country has already exceeded the Kyoto Protocol limit it had accepted for 2012.
5. In a comparable analysis, Jeffares (2004) showed how *"flourishing neighborhoods"* became an empty signifier in the dominant discourses of the British city of Birmingham.
6. See www.aspa.pt. The destruction of Palacete Matos Graça to create space for a luxurious condominium and the damage that is likely to be done to the historical site of Sete Fontes following the construction of a road and a new development are recent examples of the council's negligent attitude toward the architectural heritage.

7. Especially through *"Entre Aspas,"* a regular contribution to the paper by the association, but also by acting as a source of journalists from *Diário do Minho*.
8. Hegemonic articulations define enemies as a threatening outside that contributes to unifying those within the discursive boundaries.
9. Quinta dos Peões is a farm in front of Universidade do Minho that used to be a part of the National Ecological Reserve. A 1999 deal between the city council, a developer, and the university resulted in the removal of that status, so that a construction permit could be issued for part of the site and the rest could be given to the university in concession. In the past, various alternative proposals for this stretch of land had been advanced, including the creation of a botanical garden.
10. The city council clearly values the role of local media in its attempt to retain domination. Like other city councils, Braga's increasingly invests in the management of its communication with the press and in its public relations (Costa, 2004). The glossy magazine *Braga Agora*, which is directed by the director of *Correio do Minho*, is also being used for promotional purposes by the municipal government.
11. The very names of a number of companies and buildings embody this tendency to present everything as "green" (verde in Portuguese): Norverde, Verdizela and Habitat 2000 are just a few examples.
12. Free translation.

REFERENCES

'Adolfo Luxúria Canibal: Inquérito' (2001, 17 January) *Público*.
'Aspa Devia Formar um Partido' (2002, 23 February) *Público*.
Avraham, E. (2000) 'Cities and their News Media Images,' *Cities* 17(5): 363-370.
Bandeira, M. (2002) *O Espaço Urbano de Braga: Obras Públicas, Urbanismo e Planeamento (1790-1974)*. Unpublished PhD thesis, Braga: Universidade do Minho.
'BE-Braga Critica o 'Casamento Barroco'' (2002, 26 January) *Público*.
Bowman, P. (2002) 'Laclau, Mouffe and Post-Marxism.' Downloaded on 16 April 2005 from http://www.roehampton.ac.uk/hacs/cs/articles/BowmanLaclau Mouffe.htm.
'Braga, Terra de Progresso' (n.d.). Leaflet.
'Braga, Terra Solidária' (n.d.) Leaflet.
Castree, N. (2000) 'Marxism and the Production of Nature,' *Capital and Class* (72): 5-36.
Coentrão, A. (2004, 7 March) 'Quatro Principais Cidades do Distrito de Braga têm Mais de 22 mil Casas Desocupadas,' *Público*.
Costa, C. (2004) *O Impacto das Câmaras Municipais na Imprensa Regional. Um Olhar sobre os Dois Jornais Diários da Cidade de Braga*. Unpublished master's dissertation, Braga: Universidade do Minho.
Cox, K. (1993) 'The Local and the Global in the New Urban Politics: A Critical View,' *Environment and Planning D: Society and Space* 11: 433-448.

Dingler, J. (2003) 'The Discursive Nature of Nature: Towards a Postmodern Concept of Nature.' Paper presented at a conference entitled 'Does discourse matter? Discourse, power and institutions in the sustainability transition,' Hamburg, 11-13 July.

European Commission (2004) 'Urban Audit Perception Survey: Local Perceptions of Quality of Life in 31 European Cities.' Downloaded on 17 March 2005 from europa.eu.int/comm/public_opinion/flash/fl_156_en.pdf.

Evans, R., Guy, S., Marvin, S. (1999) 'Making a Difference: Sociology of Scientific Knowledge and Urban Energy Policies,' *Science, Technology & Human Values* 24(1): 105-131.

Feio, R. (1995a) 'Eng. Mesquita Machado Garante: "Braga no Caminho Certo,"' *Roteiro Braga* (95): 39-41.

Feio, R. (1995b) 'Dr. Miguel Macedo Defende: "Qualidade de Vida é o Mais Importante,"' *Roteiro Braga* (95): 42-43.

Fischer, F., Forester, J. (1993) *The Argumentative Turn in Policy Analysis and Planning*. Durham, NC: Duke University Press.

Flowerdew, J. (2004) 'The Discursive Construction of a World-class City,' *Discourse & Society* 15(5): 579-605.

Forester, J. (1999) *The Deliberative Practitioner: Encouraging Participatory Planning Processes*. Cambridge, MA: MIT Press.

Frey, H. (1999) *Designing the City: Towards a More Sustainable Urban Form*. London, New York: E and FN Spon, Routledge.

Gabinete de Comunicação da Câmara Municipal de Braga (2005, 21 June) 'Complexo de Piscinas Olímpicas de Braga.' Press release sent as unrequested e-mail to some inhabitants of the city.

Gitlin, T. (1980) *The Whole World is Watching: Mass Media in the Making and Unmaking of the New Left*. Berkeley: University of California Press.

Gonçalves, H., Pires, H. (forthcoming, a) 'A Paisagem Urbana e a Publicidade Exterior. Um Cenário Vivo na Configuração da Experiência do Sentir.' Proceedings of the 2nd Iberian Congress of Communication Sciences.

Gonçalves, H., Pires, H. (forthcoming, b) '"Viagens na Minha Cidade": Interpelações da Publicidade Exterior.' Proceedings of the 2nd Iberian Congress of Communication Sciences.

Gramsci, A. (1971) *Prison Notebooks*. New York: International Publishers.

Hall, T., Hubbard, P. (1998) *The Entrepreneurial City: Geographies of Politics, Regime, and Representation*. Chichester: Wiley.

Harvey, D. (1973) *Social Justice and the City*. London: Edward Arnold.

Harvey, D. (1989) *The Urban Experience*. Oxford: Basil Blackwell.

Harvey, D. (1996) *Justice, Nature and the Geography of Difference*. Oxford: Blackwell.

Healey, P. (1997) *Collaborative Planning: Shaping Places in Fragmented Societies*. Basingstoke: Macmillan.

Jeffares, S. (2004) 'Interpreting the Rhetoric of Community Planning: Discourse Theory and the Role of the Empty Signifier 'Local Visioning'.' Paper prepared for the 54th Political Studies Association annual conference, University of Lincoln, 5-8 April. Downloaded on 18 March 2005 from www.psa.ac.uk/cps/2004/Jeffares. pdf.

Jonas, A., Wilson, D. (1999) *The Urban Growth Machine: Critical Perspectives Two Decades Later*. Albany: State University Press of New York.

Klein, N. (2000) *No Logo*. New York: Picador.

Laclau, E. (1990) *New Reflections on the Revolution of Our Time*. London: Verso.

Laclau, E. (1996) *Emancipation(s)*. London: Verso.

Laclau, E. (2000) 'Constructing Universality,' pp. 281-307 in J. Butler, E. Laclau and S. Žižek, *Contingency, Hegemony, Universality: Contemporary Dialogues on the Left*. London: Verso.

Laclau, E., Mouffe, C. (1985) *Hegemony and Socialist Strategy: Towards a Radical Democratic Politics*. London: Verso.

Laclau, E., Mouffe, C. (2001) *Hegemony and Socialist Strategy: Towards a Radical Democratic Politics*. 2nd edition. London: Verso.

Law, R. (2002) 'Gender and Daily Mobility in a New Zealand City, 1920–1960,' *Social & Cultural Geography* 3(4): 425-445.

Lemos, J. (2001, 30 January) 'A Inimiga Principal,' *Público*.

Lima, T. (1999, 16 December) 'Partidos e Associações Cívicas Unidos Pela Quinta dos Peões,' *Público*.

Lima, T. (2001, 3 Abril) 'Maioria dos Habitantes de Lamaçães Deseja Mudar de Casa,' *Público*.

Linder, S. (2003) 'The Transformation of "Global Warming" from Public Policy Problem to Cultural Sign, and Back Again.' Paper presented at a conference entitled 'Does discourse matter? Discourse, power and institutions in the sustainability transition,' Hamburg, 11-13 July.

Macnaghten, P., Urry, J. (1998) *Contested Natures*. London: Sage.

Madanipour, A., Cars, G., Allen, J. (1998) *Social Exclusion in European Cities: Processes, Experiences and Responses*. London: Jessica Kingsley.

Mazanti, B., Pløger, J. (2003) 'Community Planning: From Politicised Places to Lived Spaces,' *Journal of Housing and the Built Environment* 18(4): 309-327.

McCann, E. (2004) '"Best Places": Interurban Competition, Quality of Life and Popular Media Discourse,' *Urban Studies* 41(10): 1909-1929.

'Mesquita Machado quer Braga Capital Europeia da Cultura' (2001, 19 November) *Público*.

Monteiro, E. (2001, 4 February) '"Câmara de Braga é Sindicato de Construtores," Acusa Portas,' *Público*.

Mortensen, N. (Ed.) (1995) *Social Integration and Marginalisation*. Frederiksberg: Samfundslitteratur.

Mouffe, C. (1993) *The Return of the Political*. London: Verso.

Næss, P. (2001) 'Urban Planning and Sustainable Development,' *European Planning Studies* 9(4): 503-524.

Nakajima, N. (2001) 'Green Advertising and Green Public Relations as Integration Propaganda,' *Bulletin of Science, Technology & Society* 21(5): 334-348.

Nash, K. (2002) 'Thinking Political Sociology: Beyond the Limits of Post-Marxism,' *History of the Human Sciences* 15(4): 97-114.

Pløger, J. (2001) 'Millennium Urbanism—Discursive Planning,' *European Urban and Regional Studies* 8(1): 63-72.

Praça, A. (2002a, 23 February) 'Não Será Irrealista Candidatar-me em 2013,' *Público*.

Praça, A. (2002b, 24 February) 'A Minha Recandidatura em 2013 Pode Assustar Alguma Gente,' *Público*.

'Quando ser Associação Cívica é um Problema' (2002, 29 January) *Público*.

Secor, A. (2004) '"There is an Istanbul that Belongs to Me": Citizenship, Space, and Identity in the City,' *Annals of the Association of American Geographers* 94(2): 352-368.

Skillington, T. (1998) 'The City as Text: Constructing Dublin's Identity Through Discourse on Transportation and Urban Re-development in the Press,' *British Journal of Sociology* 49(3): 456-473.

Thomassen, L. (2005) 'From Antagonism to Heterogeneity: Discourse Analytical Strategies.' Essex Papers In Politics and Government. Sub-Series In Ideology and Discourse Analysis 21. Downloaded on 20 June 2005 from www.essex.ac.uk/government/Essex_Papers/IDAno21_thomassen.pdf.

Torgerson, D. (1995) 'The Uncertain Quest for Sustainability: Public Discourse and the Politics of Environmentalism,' pp. 3-20 in F. Fischer and M. Black (Eds) *Greening Environmental Policy: The Politics of a Sustainable Future*. London: Paul Chapman.

'Uma 'União Local' com a Benção da Igreja' (2002, 23 February) *Público*.

Urry, J. (2004) 'The "System" of Automobility,' *Theory, Culture & Society* 21(4/5): 25–39.

Vojnovic, I. (2003) 'Governance in Houston: Growth Theories and Urban Pressures,' *Journal of Urban Affairs* 25(5): 589-624.

While, A., Jonas, A., Gibbs, D. (2004) 'The Environment and the Entrepreneurial City: Searching for the Urban "Sustainability Fix" in Manchester and Leeds,' *International Journal of Urban and Regional Research* 28(3): 549-569.

Wilson, D., Wouters, J. (2003) 'Spatiality and Growth Discourse: The Restructuring of America's Rust Belt Cities,' *Journal of Urban Affairs* 25(2): 123-138.

World Commission on Environment and Development (1987) *Our Common Future*. Oxford: Oxford University Press.

ICT

9

AN(OTHER) ENEMY

The Representation of Otherness in Video Game Culture

Evangelos Intzidis
George Prevedourakis

In those days, I thought that when the game was up
The prince would be far, far away—
In a limestone suburb, on the promenade at Nice,
Reduced in circumstances but well enough provided for.
In Paris, he would hardly require his private army.
The Jockey Cap might suffice for café warfare,
And matchboxes for APCs.

—James Fenton (1981)

Video games characteristically combine multiple modes of representation (images, discourses, genres, and styles/voices) through which both the "self" and the "other" are imagined, constructed, and articulated. This scheme of self and other in video game culture, and especially in the video game that is examined in this chapter, runs parallel to the formation of collective national identities — "we" — in opposition to a distinctive "them." It does not distinguish between opponents who fight for different political and social visions, but creates a black-and-white distinction between two sides ("us" and "them"), thus creating a discourse that transforms the opponent into the *"utterly evil enemy"* (Laclau, 1977; Mouffe, 2000). This distinction between "the good we" and "the evil them" (e.g., terrorism, Iraq — see also Chapter 1, in this volume) creates new moral majorities, such as neo-conservative republicanism, coalition forces, the New Europe, and so on.

As was pointed out by Mouffe (1999), pluralistic democratic systems are capable of transforming competitive relations into antagonistic relations through the formation of collective identities that are sustained by alternative democratic programs. When, however, these collective identities (us/them) are removed from the antagonistic political sphere of pluralistic democracy and displaced into the field of morality, the opponent is transformed into an enemy that has to be eliminated at all cost. This moralistic approach blurs the democratic differentiation among social classes, institutions, and citizens by emptying the political field of its meaning and canceling out differences between popular identities. As a result, society is viewed as an undifferentiated and amalgamated whole (Laclau & Mouffe, 1985).

In contemporary gaming culture, the relation between the good us and evil them creates enemies through empty signifiers such as freedom, security, which in the context of the game are given a specific meaning through the particular discursive context. This material character of every discursive structure (Laclau & Mouffe, 1985) is present in video games in the form of the different multimodal practices the game uses to construct meaning.

THE NARRATIVE OF THE
FIRST-PERSON SHOOTER

In war video games,[1] and more particularly in First-Person Shooters, the gamer has to assume an imagined identity (a soldier, a special agent, etc.) in order to confront an equally imagined other. Video games rely on discursive production, as they (visually, textually, sonically) convey meaning through narratives, combining filmic, literary, and textual modes of representation. War video games employ a series of multimodal means (verbal/written texts, audiovisual modes of representation) through which the setting (space, time, and identities) and the system of rules are created. Simultaneously, however, this "unreal-visualized" setting draws on an existing political and historical narrative in which the gamer is constantly positioned. Hence, the gamer finds him- or herself in a predetermined context made up of carefully selected elements borrowed from and reflecting a specific political and historical reality (e.g., the Vietnam War, World War II, Iraq, etc.). This setup allows for the creation of an undifferentiated good "us" confronting an equally undifferentiated evil "them."

The First-Person Shooter that is discussed here consists of two separate games with the following titles:

1. *Medal of Honor—Frontline* (inspired by D-Day, Operation Market Garden, and a series of other World War II battles).
2. *Medal of Honor—Rising Sun* (inspired by World War II battles in the Pacific, including the attack on Pearl Harbor).

In both titles, the gamer plays the role of an American marine. Although the *Medal of Honor* series consists of a wide range of titles with different representations of the protagonist-agent (see e.g., *Medal of Honor—Underground*[2]), we can limit ourselves to a discussion of the two games just mentioned because the fundamental characteristics of narration, aesthetics and discursive representation are identical in the whole series. In these games, the user is briefly introduced to the historical setting of the conflict (World War II) and is given a series of assignments that have to be carried out successfully for the mission to be accomplished. Once the actual game begins, the character the gamer has chosen is supposed to march through the battlefield (cities, landscapes, enemy facilities, etc.), confronting hundreds upon hundreds of enemy troops. Every level-mission is followed by a short film (in a documentary fashion) in which the real protagonists of the war are presented along with historical data and images.[3] The game also abounds in texts and historic speeches, which contain highly interesting elements for a discourse-theoretical analysis. For now, let us observe how the first-person character has to proceed in order to obtain its medal on the narrative battlefield.

The first-person is structured as an empty space and given substance by the voices of the program-game (i.e., by the fantasy in which the gamer plays the role offered to him or her by the game's semantic universe). The fantasy scenario fills in the gap left by the absence from the game of a social structure by providing pleasure in the extermination of the other.

Once the gamer takes on the role of the agent-protagonist, he or she enters the field of a pregiven and fixed narration. The gamer becomes an object of the narration, a speechless protagonist constantly reproducing meanings, values, and significations within a predetermined semantic universe of rivalry and annihilation. Reflection on the violence hidden in the predrawn dividing lines is absent. The game's narrative positions the players, the enemy, and the violence between them in the undifferentiated *cul-de-sac* of a "*steadily repeated reality.*" However, in Feldman's (1991: 13) words:

in a political culture the self that narrates speaks from a position of having been narrated and edited by others—by political institutions, by
concepts of historical causality, and possibly by violence. The narrator
speaks because this agent is already the recipient of narratives in which
he or she has been inserted as a political subject. The narrator writes
himself into an oral history because the narrator has already been written and subjected to powerful inscriptions.

In this perspective, facts do not have objective meanings. They are always
already engulfed in narration, framed, and reproduced by discourse.
However, the narrator (but also, outside the context of the game, the citizens) can decide to create a moment in which identities are articulated
around different political programs, challenging this *cul-de-sac* and trading in determinism for openness and contingency (Mouffe, 2000; Žižek,
2001).
  Commenting on Ricoeur's theory of narration, Feldman (1991: 15)
observed: *"The fact is not what is happening. A fact is something that can
become the object of narration. In other words, the existence of any knowledge is always located within the context of a specific social reality that supports this knowledge."* Culture (including gaming culture) cannot be studied
in isolation from social accounts and narratives. It is embedded within the
macrocosm of social and political accounts, constantly reflecting the signified elements of narration.
  Narration in video games, one could argue, is a free-flowing process,
open to the user's own decisions and actions, subject to change and circumstances, an interactive product of the game's interactive essence. The various
assignments can be accomplished in various ways. For example, the door of
an underground compound in which—ironically enough—weapons of mass
destruction are produced can be opened either by using the handle or by
throwing a grenade. Just as in real life, every task can be carried out in different ways, each of which leads to different consequences. One could therefore be inclined to say that the narrative process is open-ended. In reality,
this narrative freedom is an illusion, because the players' decisions and the
manners in which they perform their specific tasks cannot effectively change
the course of narration. Players are constantly required to follow a pregiven
set of rules, which is always located within a prearranged setting level with
predefined objectives or aims.
  Hence, the object of the narration is forced to go along with the narrative. Constantly framed by the historic narration on the one hand, and by
the game's overall structure and methodology (tasks, goals, missions) on the
other, the gamer is embedded in an inescapable narrative context. The gamer
indulges in the *"illusion of narrative freedom"* for the sake of the game (i.e.,
for the sake of the pleasure in exterminating the evil other).

BODY, SPACE AND REPRESENTATION
OF SELF

As the first-person agent advances through the battlefields of Europe or the Pacific, all he or she sees is him- or herself as an arm holding a weapon. This image is familiar to everyone who has ever played this type of video game. The arm of the agent is an extension of the self and a synecdochical representation of a body. In a more detailed narrative analysis, however, the gamer is also a reader. Hence, the body of the agent is the body of the reader. The gamer's perception is defined by an invisible and hidden narrator—the programmer who decides to contract or expand space and/or time during the narrative process. The agent-hero knows exactly what the gamer-reader knows (i.e., nothing more and nothing less than what the programmer has allowed to be known, to become narrated, and thus to become a fact).

The void between the hand of the hero and the rest of his body (which remains unseen) is filled in by the body of the gamer. However, which body is this? It is the body the gamer chooses to project, created by his or her imagination. It is a borrowed, chimerical body, just as virtual as the hero. The gamer enters the battlefield with a well-seasoned body, with the toned biceps and rough physique of a special forces hero, borrowing his or her imagined body-identity from the wide range of images with which we have become familiar over the years, supplied as they are by action movies and live news broadcasts, comics and magazine pictures. At the moment the gamer enters the battlefield, all he or she has is an arm and a weapon, along with a cause and an assignment. The gamer chooses to project a body fitting his or her identity as a hero. Whether the gamer's real physique is that of a soldier able to destroy the entire Nazi war machine is of no importance in the role-playing involved in the gaming process.

At the same time, however, the gamer is presented with visual representations of his or her imaginary body for action both in the introduction to the game and in the animated segments between the various levels. The marketing package that comes with the game contains pictures of the protagonist-hero and detailed biographies of the hero and of the allies the hero comes across on his missions. This means that the gamer can choose from a pregiven index of existing bodies and identify him- or herself with the body he or she will "be" on the historic battlegrounds. The combination of this imaginary projection of various stereotypical archetypes found in media culture and the gamer's actual identification with the agent-hero's specific character prompts the gamer to create a persona, slipping into and momentarily adopting another body. In doing so, the gamer becomes someone else, because the actual fight takes place in the imaginary realm of narration. It is not the gamer's real body that participates in this virtual conflict. The gamer

participates in the narrative process through the mediation of a digital persona, which finds its *raison d'être* not in the respective personas but in the
presence of hostile bodies. Just as a battleground is not a battleground if
there is no one to battle against, the existence of the hero's body presupposes the symmetrical existence of incarnated, "bodified" enemies.

An interesting aspect of the visual representations of the body in these
games (visualities) is the representation of the enemies' death. When an
enemy dies, he (enemies are always masculine) is immediately disembodied,
because he evaporates the moment he touches the ground. As a consequence, the gamer is not given the opportunity to become aware of the consequences of his or her acts. When the gamer returns to a place on the battlefield where enemies have died, the dead bodies have disappeared. Dead
enemies have no place in the continuity of the narration. The same holds for
the tragedy of war. This means that the agent can feel morally and ethically
justified in pursuing the war by all means, because he or she never comes
face to face with the lasting consequences of his or her actions.

Often in First-Person Shooters, the protagonist-agent exchanges words
and phrases with his enemies. In our games, the enemy addresses the hero
using negative epithets and offensive phrases. He also often refers to the
hero's nationality or to the side the hero is on ("*Amerikaner!*" or, more generally, "*Ally!*"). As a consequence, and irrespective of his or her real national identity, the gamer is constantly identified with the protagonist-hero.
Whether the gamer is Greek, German, or Philippine, once he or she plays
the game, the gamer assumes the identity of an American soldier. Later in
this chapter, we observe that this identity is supposed to connote "security
and justice," implying that the agent-hero should be perceived as a heroic
(American) guarantor of "security" to the "free world." The gamer moving
within a particular level can occasionally eavesdrop on conversations taking
place between enemy troops. However, never in the actual play is the gamer
presented as a speaker. The only way in which the gamer can speak is
through firearms and bullets. The gamer has to speak on his or her own
behalf, lending his or her voice to the speechless hero.

Space and time are in a direct relationship with the acoustic-musical
environment of the narration, which constantly provides the action with the
necessary mythical and heroic background. In this respect, the game can be
seen as a reconstruction of famous war films. It uses the same musical-
descriptive patterns as for instance *The Bridge on the River Kwai* or *Saving
Private Ryan*. As a matter of fact, the game can be viewed to a certain extent
as a reconstruction of these well-known films. It offers the gamer a chance
to participate in Steven Spielberg's representation of the June 1944 landing
in Normandy, or in battles fought by Oliver Stone's platoon in the jungles
of Vietnam (although the game is set in the jungles of Guadalcanal). This
filmic dimension is reinforced by the montage of historical movie fragments
between the various levels as well as by the animated films in which the

gamer receives orders (the rules of the game) from his or her officers and is thus introduced to the next level.

The filmic segments are only a part of the discursive dimensions of the game that entrench a series of meanings into a specific unity. The game's virtual reality is constructed by a discourse which (together with the corresponding ideology) defines the agent's identity. As G. Kress (1989: 6) contended: *"the discourses are inclined towards exhaustion and condensation, that is, they try to explicate not only a sector of immediate interest over an institution, but increasingly wider fields of interest, ... A discourse colonizes the social world in an imperialistic manner assuming the angle of an institution."*

The gamer creates a universe of conceptions, norms, beliefs, and attitudes that give his or her role substance. The signaled is equated with the signified in a one-and-only signification. This signification is constantly associated with certain key stereotypical elements, such as homeland, security, democracy, freedom, and so on. The subject is an empty space, a vacant territory that acquires its identity thanks to such articulations. In this case, the gamer's identity is created by an imagined body in a digitally reproduced space. Moreover, before the shooting starts, the gamer is expected to take upon him- or herself the role and the accompanying morals and aesthetics of the protagonist-hero. That role always fits within a single and unified reality. The allies (and hence also the hero-agent) are presented as possessing clearly delineated particular identities with salient idiosyncrasies and fixed characteristics. Both within the actual game (where the hero occasionally meets and interacts with his fellow combatants) and in the leaflets one finds in the package, each allied character is introduced by means of a short biography, a nickname and a list of his accomplishments and particularities.

All the gamer's allies have different accents, different origins—there are Scots, French, Irish, Americans, and so on—and different skills in battle. The enemy, on the other hand, is presented as vague, homogeneous, massive, and rigid. When the enemy attacks the hero, he does so in indistinct hordes. As an individual, he is always stereotypically portrayed as an evil torturer and an inhabitant of an evil empire. The entire "moral framework" of the game, the causal web that motivates and justifies action, is based on the classic good-versus-evil matrix, a popular type of identity construction the use of which stretches from Hollywood's box office hits to public speeches of prominent political leaders:

> Identity-types (e.g., masculine vs. feminine, straight vs. gay, middle vs. working class, children vs. adults, White vs. Black, etc.) tend to reproduce low-dimensional and highly biased oversimplifications of the high-dimensional space of diversity-by-degree of possible patterns of human self-presentation through action. This favors the power of those who benefit from illusory political alliances, which group together different coalitions as members of the "mainstream" or "majority" or dominant

category in each case, even though it is only this small powerful minority, which is always included in all these coalitions. Every such reduction of the cultural model of human diversity results in the creation of
one "superior" group categorically contrasted with all other "naturally
inferior" groups, whatever the prevailing rhetoric of equality or democracy. (Lemke, 2003: 71)

As mentioned earlier, the strange and distant other is portrayed as bringing
danger and insecurity, whereas the reliable and well-known we is projected
as the guarantor of safety and democracy—for both the other and the we.
This is in line with Vivienne Jabri's (1996: 74) assertion:

Social identity and categorization emerge from cognitive processes
which seek coherence and positive self-imagery producing in their
instantiation such social consequences as stereotyping, social judgment,
and conformity, all of which are constitutive of the conflict process and
the legitimization of violence.[4]

This type of representation reinforces the us-versus-them distinction that
typifies narratives of conflict.

THE DISCOURSES OF A PERPETUAL PAST

Discursive practices are closely linked with the systems of social hierarchy
within which they become organized, but also with the identity or self-aware-
ness of the individuals enmeshed in these systems (Fairclough & Wodak,
1997; Fairclough, 2000). In other words, there is a whole range of discursive
practices—of means, that is, that produce and ascribe meaning through language—which are closely connected with the standpoints of specific social
and cultural groups. In our case, the hero's beliefs and ideology within the
universe of the game are conveyed through a series of audiovisual, textual and
digital discourses. These discourses are essentially political, because they
ascribe meaning to the gamer's actions and to the overall causal environment.[5]
For Laclau (1977), the term discourse refers to the entirety of the phenomena
that socially produce meaning. The main body of Laclau and Mouffe's argumentation is directed against the classic conception of the subject as a positive
entity, a substance that is always-already given and to which the social process
is subordinated. Against this, Laclau and Mouffe maintain that each social and
historical context is characterized by a series of specific subjective standpoints
(feminist, ecological, democratic, etc.), the meaning of which is not pregiven
but permanently modified as a result of articulatory practices.

In the following example, we examine how the gamer's moral universe is constructed through such articulatory processes, which formulate the patriotic-heroic discourse of the game. Laclau and Mouffe's analytical and theoretical toolkit for the study of identity construction plays a central role in this analysis.[6]

Discourse is not confined to the realm of language. In the words of Norman Fairclough et al. (2004: 2):

> As a medium for the social construction of meaning, discourse is never solely linguistic. It operates conjointly with vocal and visual elements (depiction, gesture, graphics, typography), in the context of meaning-laden architectures, with the semiotics of action itself and with music and other extra-linguistic auditory signs. Its form is constrained by the media through which it moves.

Hence, a discourse consists of all the practices and processes of the social sphere that generate meaning.

For Laclau and Mouffe, human reality is discursively articulated. Their constructivism considers society itself as the unfinished product of our constructs. In this context, Laclau and Mouffe hold that the structuring of discourses, the conjunction of elements into a unified whole of meaning, makes use of so-called nodal points. Articulatory practices result in the construction of nodal points that partially fixate meaning. The partial character of this fixation follows from the constant overflow of every discourse from the infinity of verbalizations and textualizations.

The always temporary fixation of meaning in a specific articulatory practice often seeks to define identities in the antagonistic social field. Hence, a discourse frequently strives for hegemony. A hegemonic discourse can be defined as the framework that allows for the creation of temporary identities and not as the inevitable, predetermined result of social processes (Laclau & Mouffe, 1987). In a pluralistic democratic context, hegemony has to do with the mobilization of pathos for democratic goals and not with the evacuation of pathos from the public sphere. Every conception of the citizen corresponds to different views of society (liberal, conservative, radical, democratic, etc.), while each one strives to hegemonize its own idea of the "common good." Democracy requires these different and often conflicting types of political identification. From the angle of agonistic pluralism, the distinction between us/them does not imply that one pole is to be destroyed or demonized but, on the contrary, that different political ideas and programs have to be given the chance to confront one another in a battle for hegemony.

In this chapter, we seek to explore how a particular video game reinterprets and relocates discourses on World War II in order to fit in with the contemporary (post-9/11) context (i.e., in order to reflect the current hegemonic political narrative that legitimates among others the war on Iraq and the fight against international terrorism).

Our aim, therefore, is not to "deconstruct" the significance of the U.S. intervention during World War II or to downplay the historical significance of the textual discourse we examine. What we want to do is study how this discourse is being relocated in the present. Words addressed to the soldiers of D-Day are, with remarkable ease, recontextualized to fit in the contemporary context. The phrase "Security for the Free World" (used by General Eisenhower at the beginning of D-Day and quoted in the introduction to the game) functions as an empty signifier, which is displaced from the ideological and political context of World War II to the context of contemporary ideology and history.

At the same time, the video game's aesthetic and linguistic discourse is rich in multimodal means that play a prominent role in the discursive construction of identities. Exploring the ways in which the identity of enemies and allies are constructed within the context of a contemporary video game by displacing World War II discourses is the primary aim of this concluding part. By drawing on the field of discourse theory, we intend to highlight the social semiotics of hegemony through the multimodality of new technologies as they are used in gaming culture. Clearly, the gaming industry has become an important commercial sector, which has given rise to a global-scale culture in which people of all age groups and professional and social class partake. Our textual analysis intends to show that this culture is eminently political in its — quite blatant — notions and meanings, and that its discursive practices reproduce elements of our contemporary social and political context.

Eisenhower's Open Letter to US Troops before D-Day
(Introduction to the game *Medal of Honor — Frontline*)

You're about to embark upon this great crusade for which we have striven these many months. The eyes of the world are upon you. The hopes and prayers of liberty-loving people everywhere march with you. In company with our brave allies and brothers in arms in many fronts you will bring about the destruction of the German war machine, the elimination of Nazi tyranny over the oppressed people of Europe, and security for ourselves in a free world. Your task is not an easy one — your enemy is well-trained, well-equipped and battle-hardened. He will fight savagely. I have full confidence in your courage, devotion to duty and skill in battle. We will accept nothing less than full victory. Good luck and bless us all who seek the blessings of Almighty God upon this great and noble cause.

At a primary level, we can point out the following elements:

- Element 1: *"liberty-loving people"*
- Element 2: *"brave allies and brothers in arms"*
- Element 3: *"the German war machine"*
- Element 4: *"tyranny"*
- Element 5: *"oppressed people of Europe"*
- Element 6: *"security for ourselves in a free world"*
- Element 7: *"your enemy"* (why not *"our enemy"*?)
- Element 8: *"duty, skill in battle"*

Beside the primary-typical distinctions of the "you-versus-them" type, there is another set of binary links that discursively signal the identifications and the ideological context of the text:

1. *"You"*: *"eyes of the world"*
2. *"We"*: *"oppressed people of Europe"*
3. *"Our security"*: *"liberty-loving people"*
4. *"Our allies and brothers in arms"*: *"the German war machine"*

The depersonalized enemy (*"the German war machine"*) is contrasted with a highly personalized "we" (our *"allies and brothers in arms"*), which is also normatively charged with a series of adjectives (honored and skilled, characterized by devotion and duty). The enemy has no such qualities, because he is presented in an impersonal and undifferentiated manner that selectively highlights his ruthless and brutal nature (*"tyranny,"* he *"will fight savagely,"* etc.). However, the enemy is also associated with a number of positive qualities (*"your enemy is well-trained, well-equipped, and battle-hardened"*), but these are embedded in a negative discursive context. The courage and devotion to duty of the U.S. military along with their skill in battle is contrasted with an enemy that fights *"savagely."* The phrase *"he will fight savagely"* contrasts with the phrase *"you are skillful,"* although the "you" will also fight *"savagely"* if this is needed to obtain *"full victory."*

The letter follows a "you" > "we" > "our" > "your" pattern. However, toward the end, it is suddenly personalized: *"I have full confidence in your powers."* The same also applies for the enemy (from *"the German war machine"* and *"Nazi tyranny"* to the phrase *"He will fight savagely"*). These addresses serve the purposes of demonization, according to the we-good / them-evil pattern. The we-good has the duty to annihilate its entirely evil opponent. In accordance with the aforementioned articulatory practice, this strategy connects the establishment of security and freedom with the extermination of the other.

At a second level of analysis, we find an antithesis between the elements *"security for ourselves in a free world"* and *"oppressed peoples of Europe."* This statement advances "security" as a nodal point and presents the *"brave allies"* as the guarantors of that security, which appears to be first and fore-most security *"for ourselves."* However, this goal is achieved by reclaiming freedom for others, namely the *"oppressed peoples of Europe."*

It is interesting to point out that the game was released at a time when the international political situation was changing rapidly following the 9/11 attacks, the subsequent war on terrorism, and the conflict in Iraq. It is hard not to see a connection between the game's ideology and current trends in contemporary global and U.S. politics. In fact, this connection is established by the game itself, through its emphasis on the similarity of the attacks Japan conducted against the United States in 1941 with the terrorist attacks of 9/11. Interestingly, the following abstract is furnished in the form of a doc-umentary following the completion of the first mission.

> Abstract (audio + visual) in *Medal of Honor—Rising Sun* (film shown after the completion of mission 1)
>
> December 7th, 1941. The United States suffers one of its most devastat-ing surprise attacks with 2,403 dead. With its once invincible Navy deci-mated, America is forced to join the conflict in Europe and Asia. Prior to Pearl Harbor, the Japanese war machine had swept across China, cutting off American aid, and then pressed on to Burma with militant persist-ence. At home, Japan was building up a seemingly superior naval fleet led by some of the world's largest aircraft carriers. But admiral Yamamoto's prediction had come true. The aftermath of the day of infamy had indeed awakened the sleeping giant that was America. As the emperor's armies march toward the Philippines, the United States takes action.

Which normative, political, and esthetic horizon is the contemporary gamer directed to via this text? Which images and meanings does this fragment tend to evoke in the international political context of the present day? Let us try to answer these questions by analyzing how the gamer is steered toward specific interpretations of the situation he or she finds him- or herself in.

CONCLUSION: THE PAST AS PRESENT

> Power is activated in the place where discourse and action have not been disjoined, where words are not used to disguise intentions but to reveal realities, and where actions are not used to violate and destroy, but to restore relations and to create new realities. (Arendt, 1986: 273)

The gamer in the First-Person Shooter games, which are based on historical facts (such as those inspired by the battles of World War II), inhabits a sys-tem where Nazi tyranny is constantly equated with global terrorism and the

allied effort with the effort to defeat terrorism. Past discourses are populis-
tically displaced to and reactivated in present discourses. Of course, the discursive recontextualization we describe here is not only found in video game
culture. In fact, it is also typical of dominant political discourses of the present day. A typical example is a speech President George W. Bush gave in
Normandy in May 2004, on the occasion of the 60th anniversary of D-Day:

> On this day in 1944, General Eisenhower sat down at his headquarters
> in the English countryside and wrote out a message to the troops who
> would soon invade Normandy. "Soldiers, Sailors and Airmen of the
> Allied Expeditionary Force" he wrote, "the eyes of the world are upon
> you. The hopes and prayers of liberty-loving people everywhere march
> with you."
>
> Each of you receiving a commission today in the United States military
> will also carry the hopes of free people everywhere. As your generation
> assumes its own duties during a global conflict that will define your
> careers, you will be called upon to take brave action and serve with
> honor. In some ways, this struggle we're in is unique. In other ways, it
> resembles the great clashes of the last century—between those who put
> their trust in tyrants and those who put their trust in liberty. Our goal,
> the goal of this generation, is the same: We will secure our nation and
> defend the peace through the forward march of freedom.
>
> Like the Second World War, our present conflict began with a ruthless,
> surprise attack on the United States. We will not forget that treachery,
> and we will accept nothing less than victory over the enemy.
>
> Like the murderous ideologies of the 20th century, the ideology of ter-
> rorism reaches across borders, and seeks recruits in every country. So
> we're fighting these enemies wherever they hide across the earth.
>
> Like other totalitarian movements, the terrorists seek to impose a grim
> vision in which dissent is crushed, and every man and woman must
> think and live in colorless conformity. So to the oppressed peoples
> everywhere, we are offering the great alternative of human liberty.
>
> Like enemies of the past, the terrorists underestimate the strength of free
> peoples. The terrorists believe that free societies are essentially corrupt
> and decadent, and with a few hard blows will collapse in weakness and
> in panic. The enemy has learned that America is strong and determined,
> because of the steady resolve of our citizens, and because of the skill and
> strength of the Army, Navy, Marines, Coast Guard and the United
> States Air Force.

And like the aggressive ideologies that rose up in the early 1900s, our enemies have clearly and proudly stated their intentions: Here are the words of al Qaeda's self-described military spokesman in Europe, on a tape claiming responsibility for the Madrid bombings. He said, "We choose death, while you choose life. If you do not stop your injustices, more and more blood will flow and these attacks will seem very small compared to what can occur in what you call terrorism."

In all these threats, we hear the echoes of other enemies in other times— that same swagger and demented logic of the fanatic. Like their kind in the past, these murderers have left scars and suffering. And like their kind in the past, they will flame and fail and suffer defeat by free men and women.

In this speech, Bush paraphrased Eisenhower's letter and thus displaced it to the post-9/11 context. Equating terrorism with Nazism and the attack on Pearl Harbor with the 9/11 attacks, Bush reproduced stereotypical representations of the enemy. Bush's speech tends to exhaust the antithetical dyad of free versus oppressed, so that the past gives off *"echoes of other enemies in other times."* In this context, the war against Nazi Germany can and should be seen as similar to the contemporary war on terrorism, because both conflicts are basically about an unambiguous choice between democracy and tyranny.

Rereading Hegel, we remember that the moments the mind seems to have left behind are, deep down, always present. When we play this video game, the process of constant rearticulation makes us rediscover moments the project of rationalism had destined for oblivion. The demonizations conjured up by the game's moral narratives are characteristic of influential contemporary articulatory practices that equate security/freedom in the present era with security/freedom in the World War II period.

NOTES

1. The games discussed in this chapter are:
   Electronic Arts Games 2002. *Medal of Honor—Frontline.* Platform: Playstation2. Publisher: LucasArts.
   Electronic Arts Games 2003. *Medal of Honor—Rising Sun.* Platform: Playstation2. Publisher: Eidos.
2. In this game, we come across a female agent-hero, as the gamer is to assume the identity of a woman fighting for the French Resistance.
3. For a detailed description and a review of the games, see http://www.gamespot.com/ps2/action/medalofhonorfrontline/index.html?q=Medal+of+Honor

4. Vivienne Jabri (1996) examined this discursive structuration of war by concentrating on the construction of identity through dominant discourses (discourses reflecting social dominance). Jabri combined structuralist and individualist approaches, defining war as a social continuity, through the application of Giddens' structuration theory and his concept of the *"duality of structure."* In this context, war is ceaselessly reproduced through shared intersubjective meanings and images as well as social institutions, which serve a war-legitimizing purpose.
5. For a detailed study of the political characteristics of video games (design and context), see: 'Does gameplay have politics?' by Jonas Heide Smith (2004), at http://www.game-research.com/art_gameplay_politics.asp
6. See also Howarth et al. (2000: 1-18).

REFERENCES

Arendt, H. (1986) *The Human Condition (Vita Activa)* (S. Rozanis, G. Likiardopoulou, Trans.). Athens: Gnosi.

Fairclough, N. (2000) *New Language, New Labour*. London: Routledge.

Fairclough, N. et al. (2004) 'Introduction,' *Critical Discourse Studies* 1(1): 1-7.

Fairclough, N., Wodak, R. (1997) 'Critical Discourse Analysis,' pp. 258-284 in T. van Dijk (Ed) *Discourse as Social Interaction: Discourse Studies Volume 2*. London: Sage.

Feldman, A. (1991) *Formation of Violence: The Narrative of the Body and Political Terror in Northern Ireland*. Chicago: The University of Chicago Press.

Fenton, J. (1981) *Dead Soldiers*. Oxford: Sycamore Press.

Howarth, D., Norval A., Stavrakakis, Y. (Eds) (2000) *Discourse Theory and Political Analysis*. Manchester: Manchester University Press.

Jabri, V. (1996) *Discourses on Violence*. Manchester: Manchester University Press.

Kress, G. (1989) *Linguistic Processes in Sociocultural Practice*. Oxford: Oxford University Press.

Lemke, J.L. (2003) 'Language Development and Identity: Multiple Timescales in the Social Ecology of Learning,' pp. 68-87 in C. Kramsch (Ed) *Language Acquisition and Language Socialization*. London: Continuum.

Laclau, E. (1977) *Politics and Ideology in Marxist Theory: Capitalism, Fascism, Populism*. London: New Left Books.

Laclau, E., Mouffe, C. (1985) *Hegemony and Socialistic Strategy. Towards a Radical Democratic Politics*. London: Verso.

Laclau, E., Mouffe, C. (1987) 'Post-Marxism without Apologies,' *New Left Review* (166): 79-106.

Mouffe, C. (1999) 'Deliberative Democracy or Agonistic Pluralism?,' *Social Research* 66(3): 745-758.

Mouffe, C. (2000) *The Democratic Paradox*. London: Verso.

Smith, J.H. (2004) 'Does Gameplay have Politics?' Downloaded on August 1, 2005, from http://www.game-research.com/art_gameplay_politics.asp.

Žižek, S. (2001) *On Belief*. London: Routledge.

10

THE "OUTSIDE" INSIDE US

Antagonisms and Identities in Taiwanese Online Gay Forums

Yow-Jiun Wang

The 1990s witnessed the emergence of a new wave of identity politics in Taiwan, a growing capitalist society. Although identity became a major factor of political mobilization, the locus of activism partially shifted from the street to a variety of other discursive spaces, in which the production of a strategic and coalitional collective identity was on the main agenda. In the field of nationalism, a cross-ethnicity national identity was manufactured; in local aboriginalism, "the indigenous" had been proposed as a new frontier to integrate disparate tribes into a unified force; in the Les-Bi-Gay movement, the new category "*tongzhi*" is under construction, aiming to encapsulate as many sexual minorities as possible.

The emerging activisms coincide with the advent of the global fever of Internet communication. The new information and communication technology (ICT) is said to have a worldwide impact on cultural, social, political, and economic landscapes. In the field of social research, the Internet has been well explored in its interactivity, virtuality, connectivity, digitality, anonymity and hypertextuality, to name just a few aspects. Its possible influences on social movements have been particularly noted (e.g., Arnold & Plymire, 2004; Harcourt, 2004; Kahn & Kellner, 2004; Kellner, 1997; Lax, 2004; Lin & Cheng, 2001; Warf & Grimes, 1997). The new ICT is considered contributory to democratic practices in this field by facilitating the circulation of dissident and marginal/critical voices, campaign publicity and information distribution, and social mobilizations, as well as by offering new spaces and mechanisms for radical political organizations.

Forming part of local identity politics that have arisen in the Internet age, the Les-Bi-Gay activism (generally known as the *tongzhi* movement) is the only one in Taiwan that builds up its discursive power through new ICTs. Because they first appeared in the early 1990s, local internet forums dedicated to Members of the Same Sex (MOTSS) have become the major recruitment networks of the movement as well as the primary discursive space for the lesbian/gay community (Hong, 2000; Huang, 1997; Kefei, 1995). So far, there are more than 80 major local MOTSS forums scattered around (mostly campus-based) bulletin board systems and Web sites. Working hand in hand, the movement and the community forums have organized a series of campaigns aimed at destigmatization and civil rights. They have also largely contributed to the discussion of the *tongzhi* identity as the public identity of the movement. During the past decade, the construction of a shared identity has been at the crux of the movement: via identity engineering, the subject of activism has advanced from an other-defined marginalized sexual group to a self-defined radical social force that has progressively articulated other sexual minorities into the body of the movement.

The fortuitous convergence of identity-oriented social activism and new ICTs, embodied in the *tongzhi* movement, provides a vantage point for an inquiry into Laclau's and Mouffe's identity approach in the context of a new discursive space. In embedding an Internet research project within a discursive identity approach, this inquiry also holds the promise of shedding new light on the influence of ICTs on contemporary social movements, beyond what current studies have explored. To tackle these questions in an empirical study, this chapter examines MOTSS speech practices in relation to the construction of the *tongzhi* identity. The focus of this discourse-theoretical analysis is placed on the antagonistic and articulatory aspects of identity building: We look at how antagonism is transformed into a constructive force that allows a hegemonic *tongzhi* identity to crystallize in the contemporary Taiwanese Les-Bi-Gay movement. This antagonism, as is argued, has been contingently rearticulated in grassroots-oriented MOTSS forums and ironically turned into a dividing force that underlies intragroup confrontations.

Given the microscopic nature of the case study, it is imperative to triangulate a new methodology that makes feasible the application of Laclau and Mouffe's approach to these new questions. The following pages are aimed at bridging the gap between Grand Discourse Theory and microscopic discursive practices. To begin, I map out the approach of discourse theory to identity and link it with sociolinguistic methods for discourse analysis. The case study continues with an introduction to the *tongzhi* movement and the question of its identity, followed by an analysis of MOTSS performance based on the triangulated methodology. In doing so, I hope to broaden the applicability of discourse theory, which may be connected to other discourse-analytic tools in future case studies. Furthermore, this case study is expected to shed light on the democratizing potential of the Internet, which has been widely discussed, although few insights have been given from the perspective of radical democracy as articulated by Laclau and Mouffe.

ARTICULATING AN ANTAGONISTIC IDENTITY IN INTERNET-BASED DISCURSIVE SPACE: SEARCHING FOR A NEW METHODOLOGY

Laclau and Mouffe's discourse-theoretical approach to collective identity, as formulated in their *Hegemony and Socialist Strategy* (Laclau & Mouffe, 1985/2001), is marked by the emphasis on its antagonistic, contingent, and hegemonic aspects. To map out their idea of collective identity that paves the way for their project of a pluralist democracy, a number of concepts drawn from Marxism and poststructuralism, notably Gramsci's hegemony, are radicalized. An identity can be constituted only when there is an antagonizing "other" that blocks one's full identity by showing its limits, and when these limits can be transformed into "frontiers" of identity construction. Moreover, in a pluralist/radical democracy, where the loci of a multiplicity of political struggles are no longer confined to class, the subject is not to be limited to one single fixed category, but instead opened up to a new synthesis traversing multiple (activist) subject positions, articulated on the basis of a shared cause. The new synthesis as a contingent totality is a "hegemonic formation," partially fixed around one or more nodal points—privileged discursive points that hold together a signifying chain.

The formulation of a partially fixed identity as described here is underpinned by Laclau's and Mouffe's critical reading of Althusser's overdetermination and Derrida's *différance*. Basing themselves on Althusser's assertion that everything in the social (as a symbolic order) is overdetermined, both discourse theorists advance their argument of the impossible fixity (i.e., the lack of an essence) of social relations. The idea that identity is overdetermined is linked up with Derrida's argument of the absence of a center or (in Derrida's jargon) "transcendental signified." Laclau and Mouffe, however, did not fully adopt the formulation of *différance*, in which meaning is said to be infinitely deferred in sign substitutions (Derrida, 1978: 278-293, 1982: 1-27) Instead, they contend that meaning must be at least partially fixed before it can be subverted. What a discourse aims for is indeed to construct a center, or a nodal point to fix meaning (Laclau & Mouffe, 1985/2001: 112-113).

To throw light on the way in which a partially fixed identity is constructed, Laclau and Mouffe developed their concept of articulation by modifying the Foucauldian view of "regularity in dispersion" in discourse formation. This idea refers to the fact that a discursive formation is constituted according to certain logic, which accounts for its relative regularity (a common theme and style, and shared concepts). According to Laclau and Mouffe, this process needs "certain contexts of exteriority." These account for the logic of equivalence and its "totalizing effect": every element is articulated as part of one totality against another. In so doing, the original differential character of the elements is subverted and replaced with a shared one defined by its negative relation to a common outside (i.e., the differential moments become equivalents in the sense that they are all different from the outside; Laclau & Mouffe, 1985/2001: 127-134).

This argument lies at the heart of Laclau's and Mouffe's definition of antagonistic, hegemonic identity. As they defined it, antagonism is the impossibility of fully constituting an identity due to the presence of the "other," an external force that negates or blocks the identity in question (Laclau & Mouffe, 2001: 125). In Laclau's later work (Laclau, 1990: 17), the other is referred to as the constitutive outside. It antagonizes as it denies one's full identity; the presence of the outside is, however, also constitutive of the identity because it renders its limit, and thus also its boundary, visible. Antagonism can be mutual: A constitutive outside can itself be turned into the antagonized inside once its outside-ness is recognized and resisted. Moreover, it is as much contingently constructed as the antagonized "inside" is, because both are part of the social and unavoidably belong to the field of overdetermination.

By virtue of the Marxist turn, the political aspect of discourse theory is brought to light. Where a social identity is discursively constructed against a constitutive outside and the constitutive outside is equally subject to construction, identity is no longer the locus of logic but of politics (i.e., it is open to struggles aimed at fixing its meaning through discursive processes). This is the point where Laclau and Mouffe directed their discourse theory toward the field of radical democracy, and where the Gramscian concept of hegemony is radicalized. The idea of a historic bloc in Gramsci's original format—a number of historic forces or sectors unified by a collective will—is explored and re-conceptualized into that of *hegemonic formation*, the pivot of Laclau and Mouffe's identity-oriented democratic project. A hegemonic formation is a partially fixed totality of equivalent elements, constructed around a number of nodal points. In Laclau and Mouffe's new formulation, the ideas of hegemonic formation and subject positions have come to replace historic bloc and historic forces (or sectors) in Gramsci's theory of hegemony. In

transforming Gramsci's historic bloc theory into a theory of hegemonic formation, Laclau and Mouffe abandoned his conception of a dichotomically
divided political space. This makes it possible for a radical democratic struggle to move away from the singular, class-oriented center into the field of a
pluralist democracy defined by a multiplicity of frontiers (Laclau & Mouffe,
1985/2001: 127-138). These frontiers are drawn in accordance with the limits experienced by antagonized identities. To be strategic, frontiers that
demarcate hegemonic formations are "*essentially ambiguous and unstable,
subject to constant displacement*" (Laclau & Mouffe, 1985/2001: 134).
Besides, in articulating various forces into a new formation, the articulating
force itself is faced with redefinitions in accordance with the changing identity of the hegemonic formation (Laclau & Mouffe, 1985/2001: 138-139).

In embedding their political project in discourse theory, Laclau and
Mouffe have remained fairly vague with regard to the way articulatory practices actually operate in discursive production. Conceived in the pre-
Internet age, their approach offers no insight into the new scenarios brought
forth by participatory, grassroots-oriented media. In order to bridge the
methodological gap and apply the grand discourse theory to a microscopic
analysis of cultural production, it is essential to have at least a few analytical
tools at one's disposal. One possible approach is inspired by critical discourse analysis. It advances the selective reading of cases while emphasizing
the broad field of aspects to be analyzed, ranging from lexical choices, textual forms, distribution of speaking turns, structures of argumentation to
generic structures (Fairclough, 1995: 7).

Given the interactivity of Internet forums, a turn to sociolinguistics
seems to provide the answer here. Ethnographers of communication (e.g.,
Gumperz & Hymes, 1972; Hymes, 1977; Saville-Troike, 1989) suggest that
the focus of a sociolinguistic analysis of speech phenomena should be placed
on the aspect of *cultural patterning*: not only the utterances per se but also
the way they are produced should be included in the analysis. The domain
of cultural patterning consists of speech participants, settings, channels,
forms, contents, and, as is stressed in this case study, the norms of interaction. In order to better explore the aspect of interactive patterning, we draw
on a more specific analytic category. The interaction in internet forums consists of a series of "follow-ups," messages that are produced in response to
one or several previous posts. From a functional perspective, follow-ups are
similar to "turns" in a conversation, although they can be more organized at
the textual level. According to Sacks (1992: 555-58), there is a relation of
"next position" between conversational turns. A next position is the position made available by the current speaker to whomever intervenes as the
immediately following speaker. A variation of next positioning is "sequential positioning," in which a given utterance refers to prior (but not adjacent)
utterances via "sequential techniques," such as the citation of prior utterances in the first words of a conversational turn, or the use of markers that

indicate speakers' positions. In both functions, the turns of later speakers are related to and in effect opened up by the previous ones.

By adopting these analytic categories, we can make a detailed analysis of the process of articulatory practices in quasi-conversational discursive productions. As argued here this process tends to become apparent in contestations among MOTSS participants. In accentuating the next/sequential positioning, we are looking at the relatedness of utterances as well as the constructiveness of turn-taking, due to which discursive elements are brought up, articulated, and transformed into moments of an evolving formation.

TONGZHI: MOVEMENT AND IDENTITY

The public identity of the local Les-Bi-Gay movement emerges in 1992, concomitant with the first *Tongzhi* Film Festival. The word *tongzhi* (or *tung-ji*, as it is pronounced in Hong Kong dialect) was first introduced into gay discourses in Hong Kong as a translation for queer. Originally, it denotes comrade, while the first part of the word *tong* is equivalent to the word same in English and the second part generally takes on the meaning of will as in collective will. Its implied connotation of solidarity is considered essential in the early years. This new identity is well acknowledged by local activists, gender researchers, younger generations of the lesbian/gay community, and, unsurprisingly, the media.

The emergence of the self-constructed collective identity marks the beginning of a movement that aims to transform a stigmatized, other-defined social minority into a self-defined, active cultural group. A few landmark events are the first campus-oriented Gay and Lesbian Awakening Day (GLAD) and the establishment of a nationwide student lesbian/gay union in 1995, a series of de-stigmatization street actions from 1996 onward, the setting-up of the leading activist task force Front for *Tongzhi* Citizenship in 1996, the lobbying for gay rights in the 1998 mayoral elections and the 2000 presidential election, and the organization of the annual festive events *Tongzhi* Civil Rights Movement from 2000 onward, including the 2003 and the 2004 gay pride parades. Before these actions took place, social perceptions of the sexual group in question were mainly built on biased media representations relating to small crime (e.g., male prostitution), pathology, psychiatry, and, since the 1980s, the AIDS epidemic. During this "dark age," lesbians and gays were generally referred to as *tong-xin-lien* (same-sex love(r), the Chinese equivalent for homosexuals/homosexuality). The discursive power to define the gay subject was firmly held by criminologists, pathologists, psychiatrists, and epidemiologists (Wu, 2001). In these discourses, *Tong-xin-lien* was first labeled as an abnormality and later as a threat to society, especially because it was blamed for the spread of HIV (Huang, 2000). It should be noted that the signified of *tong-xin-lien* were males rather than females. Besides the pathological/psychiatric name, other stigmatizing labels, such as *zen-yao* (homo-freak, a dysphemism for transvestites) in the 1970s or *glass* (an earlier gangsters' jargon word for ass) up to the 1980s were used to refer to male gays. In contrast, labels for lesbians were scarce. In fact, before the advent of the 1990s *tongzhi* movement, lesbians used to be nearly invisible in public discourse and media representations.

The stigmatizing element of the term *tong-xin-lien* gradually fades away as the movement unfolds; it is sometimes comfortably adopted by lesbians/gays for self-naming, despite its lack of political correctness for some. Meanwhile, in the wake of the translation of northern American and western European gender studies, English terms such as gay, bi, and lesbian (and its Chinese variation, *ladzi*, equivalent to les) begin to appear in popular discourses and daily conversations. Differences between lesbians, gays, and bisexuals receive greater emphasis. Another locally constructed identity *cooer* (cool child) was proposed in 1994, with the publication of a special issue of an alternative journal, introducing queer theories to local readers. The term *cooer* is coined in order to translate and localize queer studies and is well accepted as the Chinese equivalent for queer. According to its advocates, *cooer* embodies the spirit of sexual transgression. It denies "normality" in sexuality and embraces sexual minorities, including sexual workers and sadomasochists. Unlike the Western experiences, in which queer politics tend to be contradictory to traditional, citizenship-oriented gay activism, the Taiwanese *cooer*/queer school and *tongzhi* activists have been working closely together as strategic partners in organizing major events (Chi, 1997).

These new identities constitute part of the *tongzhi* community. Stretching its discursive frontiers, the *tongzhi* movement has articulated a wider range of subject positions marked by sexuality, including gay, les, bi, as well as transgender, transvestite, and more recently, sadomasochist, into its activist identity. The trajectory of the shifting *tongzhi* identity can be traced in the themes of the aforementioned *Tongzhi* Civil Rights Movement events. In the first 3 years, the movement was reserved for lesbians and gays. However, in 2003, two other sexual minorities, bisexuals and transgenders, were subsumed. In the 2004 Taiwan Pride *tongzhi* parade, the coalitional identity was further expanded as the sadomasochist group, BDSM Company, joined the party. The strategic stretching of identity frontiers is thematized in the official announcement of the 2004 parade. The collective action defines *tongzhi* as both "dissident citizens" and "diversified subjects" and declares that the diversified subjects (encapsulating a number of sexualities) is totalized as a "combating coalition" not on the basis of similarity but on the common difference from the "*normal, mainstream, heterosexual moralities and bodily-determined gender divisions, etc., that have long existed in the 'straight' society*" (Taiwan Pride, 2004). In other words, it is by contrasting them with the dominant, "straight"-based moralities—the antagonizing force, or the hegemonic constitutive outside that marginalizes sexual minorities—that these minorities are totalized into the *tongzhi* community, while their pre-articulated differential characters are subverted. The formation of this strategic, coalitional activist subject represents a case of "a counter-hegemonic hegemony." It is counter-hegemonic in its opposition to the dominant (or hegemonic) moral system in mainstream society. In the meantime, it aspires to become a hegemonic formation in Laclau and Mouffe's sense, because it attempts to fix the meaning of the *tongzhi* identity in creating a chain of equivalence (i.e., in turning a number of antagonized sexual minorities—as subject positions—into equivalents that constitute the totality of the *tongzhi* community).

The move to create a new activist subject entails the construction of a new antagonistic relationship. In taking the *"normal, mainstream, heterosexual moralities and bodily-determined gender divisions, etc."* as the constitutive outside, *tongzhi* identity has crossed the old frontier that was drawn by the binary opposition homosexual/heterosexual. In accordance with Laclau and Mouffe's (2001: 138-139) findings, the expansion of the *tongzhi* identity shows that a hegemonic formation can embrace an opposing force (e.g., the likely-to-be-heterosexual-based BDSM) when it accepts the parameter of articulation used by the articulator (*tongzhi* community). New articulations frequently lead to the subversion and redefinition of the original identity of the articulating force. In the experience of the *tongzhi* movement, the identity has shifted from being based on the homosexual/heterosexual antagonism to being constructed through the difference between "heterodox, marginalized sexualities" and "mainstream, middle-class sexual moralities."

The redefined *tongzhi* identity that functions as the nodal point of the current lesbian/gay movement, has been created through a series of articulatory practices. As depicted earlier, these practices may occur at the level of activism within the movement itself, in which the identity is shaped and reshaped via a series of collective actions, such as the *Tongzhi* Civil Rights Movement events, and publicized through documents such as the aforementioned official announcements. However, as is seen here, they may also occur at the level of "grassroots knowledge" among the community membership, whose everyday interactions may facilitate the proliferation of its meaning. Still, the polysemy of the identity is not primarily based on "self-descriptions," but rather results from different understandings of its constitutive outside. In MOTSS forums, the major site of grassroots knowledge among the lesbian/gay community, the "outside" is defined primarily as the "heterosexual hegemony." During the past decade, MOTSS speeches on the subject have constituted a paradigm in which the term heterosexual hegemony is co-constructed as the nodal point of discourses on the antagonizing force that marginalizes the *tongzhi* community. Owing to the communicative environment of asynchronous internet forums, the process of co-construction is marked by spontaneous and unorganized interpersonal interactions, which are saturated with conflicting viewpoints and constant contestations. Within these confrontations, the outside–inside difference is brought up, debated, and re-articulated. The following pages examine this process closer.

ARTICULATION IN CONTESTATION

Historically, MOTSS forums have functioned as the major site of discourse production by the lesbian/gay community. On the one hand, they are collective strongholds/dissident media against antagonizing forces/mainstream media, in which protests against stigmatizations and repressions can be voiced. Since the earlier days, when local gay activism first started to rock the system, MOTSS forums have been the major space where the gay community fought against anti-homosexual forces that appeared in the forums as metaphorical gay-bashing or as a reaction to gay discourse (Huang, 1997; Kefei, 1995). At the same time, they are the sites where individual positions are registered. MOTSS forums work as platforms where life experiences, views, opinions, and ideas intersect and, not surprisingly, often clash with each other. Despite a common appeal to solidarity, there are no homogeneous "gay values" or "gay viewpoints." Efforts aimed at pinning down "gay essence" or "gay spirit" (e.g., being anti-war) are usually dismissed. Neither can the quest for the collective good guarantee compromises between MOTSS participants. In MOTSS forums, long discussion threads are mostly the product of vehement disagreements among the discussants. As a local *cooer* writer noted, these spaces have allowed internal differences and discontents to emerge, as they serve to facilitate dialogues between different subject positions (Hong, 2000).

The confrontation of positions and the clash of viewpoints create opportunities for contesting and henceforth reconstructing discourses concerning identity issues. Among these discourses is the popular discourse of heterosexual hegemony. Having first appeared in tw.bbs.soc.motss (the major local MOTSS forum) in 1995, the term is one of the MOTSS buzzwords that have filtered down from academic to grassroots discussions: Thanks to enthusiastic intermediaries, fashionable concepts, and jargons—such as Freudian psychoanalysis in the earlier days or, more recently, discourses of "erotic subjectivity"—have been introduced to the community and localized as grassroots knowledge. Apart from a few well-drafted introductory posts, the term is by and large used to define everyday situations, including among others, daily practices in relation to existing social/legal/medical systems. More significantly, it emerges when there is disagreement among discussants and when some of them are accused of complying with the mainstream system.

The disagreements arising in discussions on heterosexual hegemony reveal the divergent trajectories of *tongzhi* identification among the community. One of the common pleas in MOTSS speech is to remove the mark of the *tongzhi* community. Statements in this vein usually appear in response to biased media representations manifesting a hierarchical sexual order. Heterosexuals (as the dominant majority) are generally viewed as the prime, normal, or—as Laclau put it—unmarked human beings. In contrast, homosexuals are antagonized as abnormal or marked (Laclau, 1990: 32-33). The quest for removing the mark is underpinned by the argument that homosexuals/*tongzhi* are not different from heterosexuals except in their sexual orientation and that, therefore, their quality as human beings should not be depreciated. The following statement in a much-echoed post represents this point of view:

> homosexuals are also human. We contribute to the world and bring warmth to people, *same* as other people. ... They [heterosexuals] are not of a higher class, and we are not of a lower one. We are equally good, in terms of integrity, abilities, and contributions to the world. (March 26,1998, tw.bbs.soc.motss; italics added)

An opposite way of responding to the biased sexual order is to accept the negation and turn it into the vantage point on which a positive *tongzhi* identity is built. In this fashion, *tongzhi*/homosexual becomes a self-differentiated, rather than an other-differentiated category. The mark, or the limit defining what is normal, is turned into the frontier of an antagonistic *tongzhi* identity, self-defined by its difference from the normal, principal order. Somehow, this new form of identity construction does not fall into the heterosexual-suppressor–homosexual-the-suppressed dualism of the past; rather, it explores the possible field of identity construction by investing the implications of its constitutive outside. This tendency becomes manifest in the discourse of the heterosexual hegemony in everyday MOTSS speech.

The MOTSS understanding of the term heterosexual hegemony has long gone beyond the earlier definition that sees it as "*an oppressing system that designates sex for procreation*" (Jao, 1997: 174). Instead, it is freely articulated with other elements originating from various contexts. For instance, in a series of discussions on the 2003 Iraq war, some discussants attempt to build a relation between "the hegemony of the American" and "the hegemony of the heterosexual" by naming heterosexuals "the war wagers" and the dominators of world order. However, apart from such "expansive" interpretations, MOTSS discourse on heterosexual hegemony is more often related to sexuality. As noted previously, it is most often used when the advocates of "difference" and the supporters of "sameness" clash. These clashes, as is seen soon, allow for the emergence of next positions favorable to the occurrence of articulatory practices that ultimately reshape the concept of heterosexual hegemony and consequently change the outside–inside difference and its boundaries.

A 2000 discussion thread on incest in tw.bbs.soc.motss exemplifies the way in which the heterosexual-hegemony discourse is brought up, contested, and reconstructed. The discussion is an instance of the long-term MOTSS debates on the relationship between the *tongzhi* community and social moralities. It is initiated when a post reveals the writer's personal experience of having a homosexual relationship with his brother. A debate on the propriety of incest, based on the case at hand, is triggered after a series of comments on the case that emphasized ethical considerations. In the post containing these comments, the participant, Noodle Cat, defines incest as an act deviating from *lun-chang*, the existing social norms/order, or the normal human relationship in Confucian ethics. The assertive speech of ethics constitutes an opportunity for reflection on the position of *tongzhi* in normal morality. Another respondent contradicts the ethical view by connecting incest and homosexuality in terms of their marginalized positions in mainstream sexual moralities. The term heterosexual morality pops up in the debate for the first time:

> . . . Against *lun-chang?* Sounds quite familiar . . .
> Isn't it the way in which we homosexuals are diminished by the heterosexual hegemony/chauvinists, the anti-homosexual, and the homophobic? "You homosexuals are against *lun-chang!*" "Abnormal!" (Toshiko, December 18, 2000)

The articulation of *lun-chang* with heterosexual hegemony sparks off an exchange focusing on *tongzhi* identity and heterosexual hegemony. In response to the articulation of *lun-chang* with heterosexual hegemony, participant Frankenstein asks *"what the position of* tongzhi *shall be once it dislocates the heterosexual-based values."* This response to Toshiko's post gives the latter the opportunity to elaborate on his understanding of the *tongzhi* position. In answer to Frankenstein's question, Toshiko refers to *cooer*/queer theories. This is his argument:

> Do we need to build another hegemony ... after we break with the heterosexual hegemony that regulates people with so-called *"lun-chang,"* "family values," "social order," etc ... I would say, instead of emphasizing "norms" or "orders," we should learn to respect "pluralism." Isn't this what we *cooer* can identify with best? (December 18, 2000)

The reference to the *cooer*/queer spirit brings forth a further questioning into the essence of that spirit and of the *tongzhi* space. The floor is then taken by Sea, another *cooer* advocate, who defines the heterosexual hegemony as a system of binary oppositions that demarcates the normal from the abnormal while diminishing the latter. In contrast, *cooer* embraces the abnormal as part of us, including bi, transvestite, incest, sadomasochism, and any other *"sexual minorities who have been marginalized by the system."*

In facilitating the unfolding debate, the mechanism of next position paves the way for articulatory practices that link *lun-chang* (i.e., Confucianism), "social order," and the "system of binary oppositions" to the "heterosexual hegemony." Meanwhile, a chain of equivalence between *tongzhi, cooer,* pluralism, and *"any sexual minorities marginalized by the system"* is suggested. By virtue of situational articulation, furthermore, the imported concept of the heterosexual hegemony is localized, whereas indigenous elements (e.g., Confucianism) are contingently included in the chain.

To further examine the contingency of these articulatory practices in MOTSS communication, we look into another common theme of MOTSS discussions pertinent to the heterosexual hegemony speech—the "CC gay"–"Man" dichotomy in the *tongzhi* community. In this series of discussions, the "heterosexual hegemony" is no longer concerned with mainstream sexual moralities; rather, it is the male body that is at stake. Discussions regarding the prevalent biased aesthetics preferring masculine gay bodies have been recurring in MOTSS forums. The focal points of these discussions are usually the diminished status of CC gays (local MOTSS jargon for "sissy" gay) as well as the possible power relationship behind the theory of male beauty. The "mainstreaming" of bodybuilding and the preference for masculinity are feared to be creating a marked category, namely the CC gays, within the community. Moreover, it is cautioned that the "CC-phobia" indeed embodies the *tongzhi* community's subjection to the heterosexual hegemony, marked by phallocentrism and the worship of manliness.

A few 1997 discussions represent early MOTSS practices that articulate the elements "worship of masculinity," "phallocentrism," and the "mainstream" into the chain of the "heterosexual hegemony." GG, in citing a celebrity, urges the *tongzhi* community to rethink the bodybuilding fashion that *"reduces the beauty of* tongzhi *to the beauty of muscles"* (October 30, 1997, ntu.bbs.motss). This reductionism is described as *"a colonized aesthetics among male* tongzhi*"* in an immediate follow-up from participant Bi, whose view is countered by Major's questioning on *"what a pre-colonized aesthetics should be,"* while rejecting the accusation of reductionism. Participant NG then takes the floor and answers the question by pointing to the "exclusiveness" and the "macho"/"sissy" hierarchy underlying the preference. In response to this comment, Major demands intra-group consensus by posing another question: "*Is it proper to create internal struggles within the* tongzhi *camp on this issue, when we are still fighting against the domination of the heterosexual society?*"

The questioning of the propriety of internal struggles over the issue facilitates the position taken by Bi, who takes the opportunity to state his understanding of the power relationship implicated in the biased values concerning gay bodies. In so doing, he first articulates the element hegemony with the "*preference for masculinity*":

> the prevalent aesthetics cannot be so overwhelming if it hasn't been reinforced and *hegemonized*. ... A new minority (e.g., CC gays, less-muscular gays) is brought forth concomitantly when such a *hegemony* takes form . . . (October 31, 1997, ntu.bbs.motss; italics added)

The articulation of preference for masculinity and hegemony is elaborated in later interactions between Major and Bi. The former denies the theory of hegemony and argues about the long-existing history of these preferences. This argument paves the way for Bi's articulation that builds on the connection between the heterosexual system and mainstream gay values:

> *heterosexual* publications have been playing the "educatory" role for *tongzhi* in presenting the "masculine males–feminine females" binary. It is hard to tell when we have started to take on these values. ... However, what is undeniable is that once the values become the *mainstream* (in our community), there is a *hegemony*. ... (November 1, 1997, ntu.bbs.motss; italics added)

As shown previously, within the next positions created by questioning and dissenting utterances, a new chain of equivalence is progressively building up, in which the preference for masculinity, the mainstream gay values, and the heterosexual hegemony are paralleled. This chain is affirmed in a thread of later discussions dealing with the same subject, in which earlier postings are cited as starting points for sequential speech positions. For instance, tw.bbs.soc.motss participant Rodo defines the category mainstream gay in reference to the masculine/CC gay debates. He depicts the subgroup mainstream gays as those who believe they are improving the collective image of *tongzhi* by living up to mainstream values (i.e., earning good salaries, building bodies, dressing properly, and practicing other professional middle-class lifestyles). They fear that their efforts may be wiped out due to the "bad image" of CC gays. Owing to these fears, they "*collaborate with the heterosexual hegemony and suppress their own folks.*" The assimilation of the heterosexual hegemony into mainstream gay values has in effect stigmatized CC gays, "*those who wear the original colors of* tongzhi." He concludes the post with a plea for internal pluralism, in which *"plural/unfettered gay bodies are respected"* (December 22, 1997, tw.bbs.soc.motss).

In aligning the preference for masculinity with the heterosexual hegemony and calling mainstream gays collaborators of that hegemony, the post suggests an opposition between the antagonizing force—mainstream gays/collaborators of the heterosexual hegemony—and the antagonized—CC gays/the wearers of the original colors of *tongzhi*. The former is the unmarked, whereas the latter is the marked. The demarcation is similar to the aforementioned articulation in the incest discussion, in which the heterosexual hegemony also works as the nodal point of the discourse of the antagonizing force (Confucianism/normal social moralities). In that case, the intra-group antagonizing force (i.e., Confucian gays) marginalizes deviant sexualities, epitomized here by incest.

No matter how the intra-group division is drawn—between masculine/mainstream gays and CC gays, or between moralist gays and immoral gays—the discourse of an internal heterosexual hegemony implies the breaking up of the traditional boundary of *tongzhi* identification. In an ideal vision, *tongzhi* as a totality is greater than the sum of lesbians and gays. The *cooer* speakers (in the first case study) advocate, and the latest development of the *Tongzhi* Civil Movement aims for, a *tongzhi* identity that is expanded into a coalitional identity for all sorts of sexual minorities—in Laclau and Mouffe's terms: into a hegemonic formation that articulates all sexual minorities into a chain of equivalence, sustained by its shared difference vis-à-vis heterosexual hegemony. The case studies exemplify the way in which the conceptual outside is substantiated through articulatory practices, by virtue of which new frontiers of *tongzhi* identity (amorality/emancipated body), transformed from its limits rendered visible in antagonism (immorality/stigmatized body), are constructed. However, as seen in these case studies, the antagonism that enables the frontiers to emerge does not emerge outside the MOTSS community, but within it. As the forums are virtually exclusive for gays and confrontations are therefore mostly intra-group, the accused practitioners of the heterosexual hegemony are simultaneously the collaborating insiders (moralist/mainstream gays), rather than the embodiment of straight society. In other words, the borderlines differentiating us from them actually cut across the sexual group marked by homosexuality. The heterosexual hegemony, the constitutive outside of antagonistic *tongzhi* identity as embodied in the aforementioned divisions, is inside us.

The outside-in-the-inside-ness of an antagonistically constructed *tongzhi* identity in MOTSS experience manifests a possible drawback for a hegemonic project rooted in counter-hegemonic antagonism. As Laclau and Mouffe noted, the identity of the articulating force cannot remain unchanged after articulation (Laclau & Mouffe, 2001: 139). This tendency is reflected in the shifting definitions of *tongzhi* identity in the course of the *tongzhi* movement, as the activist subject is expanding. It should be noted

that the post-articulatory identity may exclude what was originally included as the result of the modification of its meaning. Unsurprisingly, this is
often met with discontent from those who are excluded in the new situation.
Furthermore, an identity project based on antagonism may risk internal
struggles, when consensus over the objective of antagonism is yet to be
reached, and the objective is tainted by the internal differences over the
issue. The two case studies represent some of the most common MOTSS
struggles over the definition of *tongzhi* identity: Once the system of the outside is articulated and the outside inside us designated, an intra-group antagonism becomes unavoidable. In the first case study (questioning whether
gender liberation can be stretched to encompass sexual liberation), the supporters of the original borderline and the detractors of the identity expansion are labeled as moralists, oppressors, heterosexual hegemony reproduc-
ers (i.e., as agents of the constitutive outside). Likewise, an antagonism
between us (the original gays) and the other in us (the mainstream gays) is
clearly defined in the second case study. Both the theory of internal antagonism and the legitimacy of a *tongzhi* identity based on antagonism are contested and resisted, whereas the accused internal outside express anxiety for
possible exclusion through the new definition ("*Are you claiming 'being
womanish' is the original color of* tongzhi? *Do I deserve the name of oppres-
sor for my preference for masculinity?*" (December 22, 1997, tw.bbs.soc.
motss), "*Isn't it another chauvinism to differentiate* tongzhi *by this logic?*"
(October 31, 1997, ntu.bbs.motss).
    These scenarios to a certain extent manifest the problems of pure partic-
ularism, which Laclau tackled in his later works. A pure particularism—an
identity project embedding a particular identity entirely in its differential
relation with others—runs the risk of sanctioning existing differential systems that underlie current social antagonisms. In contrast, a radical, antagonistic opposition, instead of simply aiming to invert the oppressor-
oppressed relationship (as pure particularism tends to), strives to turn the
form of oppression into a universal other toward which the antagonism is
directed. In other words, the ultimate goal of a hegemonic project is not to
reproduce the older differential system marked by exclusion and subordination; rather, it aims to subvert the system and meanwhile seeks for certain
universal values that create a common ground for the development of individual groups co-existing in a global community (Laclau, 1995, 1996: 20-35).
The inside–outside struggles in MOTSS communities as depicted in the text
accurately reproduce the differential relations in which the antagonistic
tongzhi identity is rooted. What may be beyond the foresight of Laclau and
Mouffe is that an identity project initiated on the basis of antagonism, as the
case study exemplifies, is not necessarily immune from the drawbacks of
pure particularism. Moreover, the antagonism may, as shown, end up bringing forth internal exclusions and thenceforth producing the outside inside us.
This tendency, as far as this case is concerned, seems unavoidable: in coun-

tering heterosexual hegemony, a strategic essentialism that entails the domination of (and hence struggles over) the meaning seems to be the answer. Ergo, internal confrontations are perhaps a necessary agony in the current stage of the movement, which may or may not be progressing toward Laclau and Mouffe's radical democracy or the universalism envisaged by Laclau.

CONCLUDING REMARKS: WHAT CAN WE EXPECT FROM GRASSROOTS/DIALOGIC ARTICULATORY PRACTICES?

The case studies demonstrate how MOTSS discussions are sucked into the spiral of the heterosexual hegemony discourse and consequentially reconfigure the discourse. Via situational articulatory practices, new chains of equivalence, pivoting round the nodal point heterosexual hegemony, are constructed. Based on these chains of equivalence, the frontiers of a collective identity are reconstructed: an amoral *cooer-tongzhi* arises against normal sexualities, whereas an original, emancipated *tongzhi* body compares with the straight-based view of male bodies. The discourse-theoretical analyses also suggest that these articulatory practices tend to emerge in the confrontations of different viewpoints; these confrontations do not only render clear the crux of the problem but also facilitate the speech positions for elaborative discursive construction. Nevertheless, the new chains are not necessarily well embraced by the speech community; on the contrary, discontents surface when, because of this new articulation, some insiders are turned into outsiders, a process that is viewed as antagonizing.

These case studies see MOTSS forums as spaces for discourse production at a grassroots level. The symmetric relationships and interactive mechanisms among participants permit the weaving of viewpoints into a discourse of collective identity, while a privileged voice or a predominant force is absent. However, the grassroots orientation does not guarantee their isolation from the influence of elite/activist discourses. As indicated, the forums have been distribution centers of mediated gender discourses via the animation of cultural intermediaries. The concept of the heterosexual hegemony is an academic import, as is the *cooer*/queer discourse. Some posts in the first case study appear as patchworks of the influential 1997 publication *Queer Archipelago*, the first Taiwanese book aimed at localizing queer studies. One *cooer*/queer MOTSS advocate hints at her or his source of knowledge in advising the moralist gays to update their understanding of *tongzhi* issues by reading books or attending gender studies seminars. The 1997 CC gay discussion series is sparked off by a MOTSS participant's reflection over a *tongzhi* celebrity's comment on gay glossies, published in a major newspaper. These are signs that indicate a dialogic relationship between MOTSS/ grassroots speech and elite discourses.

This intertextuality does not, however, imply a necessary hierarchical relationship between grassroots and elite discourses. Resistance to speeches of noted scholars or to fashionable academic thought is common in MOTSS forums. The 2000 incest discussion is a fine example of this resistance. Whereas the *cooer*/queer speakers display familiarity with gender discourses and academic jargon (e.g., transgression, eros, subjectivity, etc.), supporters of existing moralities distance themselves from theory and emphasize practical social conditions. Some even indicate the power-knowledge-ness in the *cooer*/queer advocates' constant turning to academic sources. Apart from being critical, the local MOTSS discursive practices prove to be creative and go beyond merely reproducing existing discourses, as is evidenced by the expansion of the heterosexual hegemony discourse from sexuality to body issues.

Despite it being a major recruitment network of gay activism, the local MOTSS community is not explicitly affiliated to activism. The grassroots membership's proposal for an all-embracing sexual minority-based *tongzhi* identity, represented by the *cooer*-queer voice in the 2000 incest discussion, turned up long before activists promoted the same idea in the 2003/2004 parades. This, however, does not imply that MOTSS necessarily operates in the vanguard of hegemony formation. As a matter of fact, MOTSS participation has its reactionary side as well: the "conservative"/"moralist" camp has been raising objections to an all-inclusive *tongzhi* identity, marked by a series of intense debates on the *Tongzhi* Civil Rights Movement events since 2000.

These attributes of MOTSS participation suggest its intermediary role in the hegemonic formation of *tongzhi* activism. On the one hand, it facilitates the popularization and reconstruction of elite/activist discourses, via which a shared understanding of—if not a consensus on—the antagonistic collective identity is built-up at the grassroots level. On the other hand, it is also implicated in intra-group confrontations, which has overshadowed the counter-hegemonic struggle when an overall consensus of the *tongzhi* community is seen as essential among the membership.

A final reflection on the issue concerns the propriety of defining MOTSS forums as an absolute grassroots discursive space. The current *tongzhi* activism thrives on campus, and so do MOTSS forums. A few leading activists in the field (e.g., the organizer of the Front for *Tongzhi* Citizenship) used to be early devotees of MOTSS participation; in some more elite-oriented forums, participants may include postgraduates, cultural workers, and even semi-anonymous university teaching staff (Hong, 2000: 98). The inherent elite orientation of MOTSS forums has prevented them from being radically grassroots, despite their accessibility and horizontal interaction patterns. At the end of the day we are looking at relatively grassroots articulatory practices, which can hardly reach beyond the frame of elite/activist discourses.

REFERENCES

Arnold, E.L., Plymire D.C. (2004) 'Continuity within Change: The Cherokee Indians and the Internet,' pp. 254-264 in D. Gauntlett and R. Horsley (Eds) *Web. Studies,* 2nd edition. London: Arnold.

Chi, T. (Ed) (1987) *Queer Archipelago: A Reader of the Queer Discourses in Taiwan.* Taipei: Meta Media. Published in Chinese.

Derrida, J. (1978) *Writing and Difference* (A. Bass, Trans.). London, Henley: Routledge, Kegan Paul.

Derrida, J. (1982) *Margins of Philosophy* (A. Bass, Trans.). London, New York, Toronto: Prentice Hall.

Fairclough, N. (1995) *Critical Discourse Analysis: The Critical Study of Language.* London: Longman.

Gumperz, J., Hymes, D. (Eds) (1972) *The Ethnography of Communication. Directions in Sociolinguistics.* New York: Holt, Rinehart and Winston.

Harcourt, W. (2004) 'World Wide Women and the Web,' pp. 243-253 in D. Gauntlett and R. Horsley (Eds) *Web. Studies,* 2nd edition. London: Arnold.

Hong, L. (2000) 'The End of Identity Politics and its Insufficiency,' pp. 89-106 in J. Ho (Ed) *From Queer Space to Education Space.* Taipei: Rye Field. Published in Chinese.

Huang, H.-Y. (1997) 'Dissident BBS in TANet,' Paper presented at the Information Technologies and Social Transformation 1997 Conference. Retrieved July 16, 2003, from www.ios.sinica.edu.tw/pages/seminar/infotec2/info2-14.htm. Published in Chinese.

Hymes, D. (1977) *Foundations in Sociolinguistics: An Ethnographic Approach.* London: Tavistock Publications.

Jao, Y.-N. (1997) 'Building a new Map for Eroticism,' pp. 147-160 in T.-W. Chi (Ed) *Queer Archipelago: A Reader of the Queer Discourses in Taiwan.* Taipei: Meta Media. Published in Chinese.

Kahn, R., Kellner, D. (2004) 'New Media and Internet Activism: From the "Battle at Seattle" to Blogging,' *New Media & Society* 6(1): 87-95.

Kefei (1995) 'Building Gay Nation on the Net: The Development of Taiwanese MOTSS Boards,' *Po Weekly* 23 (November). Published in Chinese.

Kellner, D. (1997) 'Intellectuals, the New Public Spheres and Techno-politics,' *New Political Science* 41-42 (Fall): 169-188. Retrieved January 1, 2005, from http://www.qseis.ucla.edu/faculty/kellner.

Laclau, E. (1990) *New Reflections on the Revolution of Our Time.* London, New York: Verso.

Laclau, E. (1995) 'Subject of Politics, Politics of the Subject,' *Differences: A Journal of Feminist Cultural Studies* 7(1): 146-164.

Laclau, E. (1996) *Emancipation(s)*. London, New York: Verso.

Laclau, E., Mouffe, C. (1985/2001) *Hegemony and Socialist Strategy: Towards a Radical Democratic Politics*. London, New York: Verso.

Lax, S. (2004) 'The Internet and Democracy,' pp. 217-229 in D. Gauntlett and R. Horsley (Eds) *Web. Studies*. London: Arnold.

Lin, H., Cheng, L.-L. (2001) 'Social Movement Goes Online: An Exploratory Analysis on the Internet Experience of Taiwan's Social Movements,' *Taiwanese Journal of Sociology* (25): 111-156. Published in Chinese.

Sacks, H. (1992) *Lectures on Conversation, Volumes I and II*, edited by G. Jefferson. Cambridge, MA, Oxford: Blackwell.

Saville-Troike, M. (1989) *The Ethnography of Communication: An Introduction*. Oxford: Basil Blackwell.

Taiwan Pride (2004) 'Event Theme.' Downloaded from http://twpride.net/2004.

Warf, B., Grimes, J. (1997) 'Counterhegemonic Discourses and the Internet,' *The Geographical Review* 87(2): 259-274.

Wu, T-S (2001) 'The Representation of Tongzhi in Newspapers: An Analysis of the Recent Fifteen-year Coverage on Homosexual Issues,' pp. 89-116 in J. Ho (Ed) *Tongzhi Research*. Taipei: Chuliu. Published in Chinese.

11

DOWNLOADING AS PIRACY

Discourse and the Political Economy of the Recording Industry

Benjamin De Cleen

Music downloading has been a hot issue ever since the Napster hype at the end of the 1990s. Popular media and academics (e.g., Burkart & McCourt, 2003; Garofalo, 1999, 2003; Liebowitz, 2002, 2003; Oberholzer & Strumpf, 2004) have written extensively about the phenomenon, and analyzed its success and consequences for the music industry. The purpose of this chapter, however, lies on a different level. Instead of focusing on the economic aspects of downloading, it studies the discourse of one of the most important participants in the downloading debate: the International Federation of the Phonographic Industry (IFPI). My argument is that the realm of the discursive is crucial to understanding the recording industry in the "age of the Internet," not only because it shows which rhetoric is used by the recording industry in its fight against illegal downloading, but also because discourse is an important element in the reproduction of the capitalist recording industry.

The analytical framework is based on concepts and methods developed within critical discourse analysis (predominantly Fairclough, 1992, 2003) and within Laclau and Mouffe's (1985) discourse theory. As Philips and

Jørgensen (2002: 160-162) point out, non-discourse analytical approaches can be of help in gaining a preliminary understanding of the discourse under scrutiny and in discerning discourses in the material to be analyzed. The discourse-theoretical framework is therefore supplemented by critical political economic analyses of the recording industry.

The choice for critical political economy is informed by the focus on power relations that critical political economy shares with critical discourse analysis and discourse theory. The focus of this chapter is on the realm of the discursive, whereas critical political economy relies on economic factors for explaining the (re)production of capitalism. However, the analysis of the discourse of IFPI, the largest recording industry lobby organization, will make use of sensitizing concepts developed in critical political economic analysis. These sensitizing concepts will suggest *"what to look for and where to look"* (Ritzer, 1992: 365) in the discourse under study.

The first section deals with the political economy of the recording industry in general and in the context of the Internet specifically. The sensitizing concepts developed in this section—copyright and piracy—form the point of departure for a second section that, after presenting the organization, analyzes IFPI's discourse on the Internet. The next section takes this analysis to a more abstract level via the analysis of two specific discourses IFPI uses in its discourse on piracy. The last two sections deal with competing discourses on the Internet. One section argues that the online music industry serves as an economic imaginary through which the Internet is incorporated into a capitalist discourse, while the final section concerns IFPI's response to alternative discourses on music and the Internet.

THE POLITICAL ECONOMY
OF THE RECORDING INDUSTRY

A large portion of the debate on music downloading (e.g., Liebowitz, 2003; Oberholzer & Strumpf, 2004) focuses on the effects downloading has on music sales. Although the studies of this issue arrive at different conclusions, they all share a concern with the viability of the recording industry's present structure and do not question the structure itself. Consequently, they cannot constitute the basis for an analysis of the recording industry's discourse and of the ideological assumptions on which it rests. Critical political economic approaches—focusing on the power relations in the production, distribution, and consumption of cultural products in a capitalist industry (Hesmondhalgh, 2002: 55)—constitute a more fruitful point of departure.

From a political economy viewpoint, the main objective of cultural industries in a capitalist society, such as the recording industry, is to accumulate capital. As Mosco (1996: 140-141) argues, commodification—the process of transforming use value (the value deriving from the satisfaction of a human want or need) into exchange value (the value based on what the product can command in exchange)—is of vital importance to achieving this goal. However, cultural industries take their distinctive character from the products they trade in. Garnham (2000: 55-58; see also Hesmondhalgh, 2002: 19-22) distinguishes a number of characteristics that complicate the commodification process of cultural products. First, cultural products traditionally have high production costs and low reproduction costs (Garnham, 2000: 55). For example, recording a CD is rather expensive, copying it is cheap and easy: Virtually the entire cost of a CD arises when making the original master tape (Burnett, 1996: 40). Second, cultural products are semi-public, they are *"non-rival in use"* (Garnham, 2000: 57): *"the act of consumption by one individual does not reduce the possibility of consumption by others"* (Hesmondhalgh, 2002: 19). Cultural products are not naturally scarce and as a consequence, the transformation of use value into exchange value can be endangered by free-riders (Garnham, 2000: 57) or—in the recording industry's terminology—pirates. Third, demand for cultural commodities is very unpredictable (Garnham, 2000: 55).

Cultural industries use different strategies[1] in dealing with these characteristics (see Garnham, 2000: 55-58; Hesmondhalgh, 2002: 19-22). In order to extract exchange value, the recording industry limits access to music by artificial means. One way of limiting and controlling supply is through vertical integration. An example of this is the creation by major record companies of their own distribution channels through which they try to control the number of available copies of a particular piece of music in a certain place at a certain time (Robinson, 1992: 16). Another strategy is to limit access to the means of reproduction. However, such control is never absolute. One only needs to think of the widespread personal use of CD writers and taperecorders. In the course of the development of the cultural industries, copyright laws have been adopted, granting rights holders the exclusive rights on reproduction. Copyright can be considered a response to the free-rider problem and is crucial for the process of commodification of cultural products. It is the foundation of the recording industry and of immense value for all cultural industries (Christiaanse & Dolfsma, 1999: 3; Towse, 2001: 1-9). Copyright is also one of the keys to understanding the controversy about downloading and a fruitful starting point for an analysis of the recording industry's discourse on the Internet.

The second sensitizing concept is piracy. The term music piracy points to a contradiction between the characteristics of music and its commodification in a capitalist industry. According to May (2000: 42, cited in Soderberg, 2002), this contradiction lies at the heart of any political economy of intellectual property. In the recording industry, it has been sharpened by the possibility of downloading music through the Internet. This makes copying easier and cheaper (Liebowitz, 2003: 16) and thus affects the industry's control over the means of reproduction. However, the Internet also holds opportunities for record companies, for instance by giving them the possibility to make the consumer pay for every use of a copyrighted work (including the uses that are traditionally considered fair use) through digital rights management (Litman, 2001: 83-84; Towse, 2001: 141-143).

In fending off the threats and exploiting the opportunities created by the development of the Internet, record companies have developed a number of strategies. These strategies can be mapped by means of Lessig's (2000: 85-99) model for the regulation of human behavior (in cyberspace). Lessig discerned four regulators that both constrain and enable (by loosening constraints that are placed on the individual) the behavior of individuals. These are, the law, the market, architecture, and norms. On the basis of this model, the recording industry's battle against downloading can be said to deploy the following four strategies:

1. A legal strategy consisting of legislation (lobbying for stronger copyright protection) and litigation (Burkart & McCourt, 2003: 337-339).
2. A market strategy trying to provide an alternative for "illegal" downloading.
3. A technological strategy trying to counter the loss of control that record companies suffered from the introduction of the Internet, and to tighten control in comparison to the level of control exercised before (Lessig, 2002: 1799). Examples are digital rights management and copy protection.
4. A normative/moral strategy trying to influence norms regarding intellectual property in order to stop people from "stealing" music via the Internet.

These four strategies are interdependent. Technological measures are, for instance, supported by lobbying activities to secure government support for the recording industry's investment in these measures (Bettig, 2003: 7; Lessig, 2000: 43-60). When copy protection was introduced, it was accompanied by strong lobbying for laws prohibiting the circumvention of this technological barrier to copying music and distributing it via the Internet (Digital Media Project, 2004: 33). These four strategies have a double goal: to incorporate music distribution via the Internet into the existing industry structures and to defend the traditional model of physical distribution of music (Leyshon, 2005: 199).

Each of these strategies can be considered a way of dealing with the contradictions that are inherent to commodification and that have been sharpened by the development of the Internet. I emphasize the importance of discourse in dealing with these contradictions. Clearly, rhetoric is crucial for lobbying with legislative bodies and for public campaigns denouncing downloading. However, discourse should not be reduced to a mere strategic tool, as is often the case in critical political economy. Indeed, discourse is constitutive, not only of the strategies discussed here, but also of the political economy of the capitalist recording industry in general. This is made clear by looking at the recording industry's discourse on music distribution via the Internet.

COPYRIGHT AND PIRACY ON THE INTERNET: IFPI'S PROPERTY DISCOURSE ON MUSIC

Together with its American counterpart, the Recording Industry Association of America (RIAA), the IFPI is the world's largest lobbying organization of the phonographic industry. It represents some 1,450 producers and distributors of music in 75 countries, including all major record companies (IFPI, 2004a). This gives IFPI considerable power in lobbying with such legislative bodies as the World Trade Organization, the European Union (EU) and national governments, and in negotiating with other industrial bodies (Laing, 1993: 28). IFPI plays a crucial role in the aforementioned strategies that record companies adopt vis-à-vis the Internet. It is also the source of information on music sales. In short, IFPI holds a very powerful position in the public debate.

Despite its importance for the music industry, IFPI has hardly been the object of academic inquiry. This is not to say that IFPI remains unmentioned in literature on the music industry. However, it is usually only referred to as the source of most figures on music sales (e.g., Christiaanse & Dolfsma, 1999; Liebowitz, 2003; Poel & Rutten, 2003). Hardly any attention is given to IFPI as an industrial interest group (i.e., as a promoter of specific economic interests). This is problematic because it may result in academics incorporating industry discourse and ideology into their own accounts of the music industry (Harker, 1997: 47). Still, a few authors (e.g., Frith, 1993; Harker, 1997, 1998) *have* made valuable contributions to the study of discourses on copyright in the music industry. Others (e.g., Bettig, 1997, 2003; Litman, 2001; May, 1998, 2003) have reflected on the discourse of copyright in general.

The empirical material consists of IFPI press releases issued between January 1, 1999 and April 30, 2004.[2] Press releases are an essential tool in the external communication that is of course crucial to IFPI's activities as a pressure group.[3] The corpus only includes press releases in which reference is made to the Internet.[4] In addition to this, speeches by IFPI representatives and ifpi.org and ifpi.be web pages also have been included, which makes it possible to confront IFPI's more general definitions of copyright and piracy with its discourse on the Internet.

As has been argued, copyright and piracy are central to an understanding of the political economy of the recording industry. They also function as nodal points—privileged signifiers that fix the meaning of other signifiers in a discourse (Laclau & Mouffe, 1985: 112)—in IFPI's discourse on the Internet.

Copyright

As a recording industry organization, IFPI carries out a wide range of tasks related to copyright. IFPI lobbies for copyright laws, takes legal action against copyright infringements, plays a role in the development of technological means of copyright protection and tries to convince the public that "*piracy is theft.*" In doing so, IFPI draws on the legitimations of copyright associated with different intellectual property traditions: Anglo-Saxon copyright and European author's right. Whereas the first emphasizes the moral and natural right of the author to his or her work, the latter stresses the need for legal protection as a means of stimulating creativity (Grosheide, 1986: 1-2; Hugenholtz, 2000: 2; Vivant, 2001: 1-3). May (2003) traced these justifications of copyright to distinct "*material property-related narratives.*" The first, typical of Anglo-Saxon copyright, is tributary to a Lockean view of property, which is seen as a reward for the effort that is put into the improvement of nature. Property rights, then, are considered a means of stimulating individual effort. The second narrative is tributary to the Hegelian view that links property rights to the individuality of the creator. This is reflected in the European author's rights system, in which authors have inalienable moral rights to their works.

IFPI draws on the Anglo-Saxon copyright rationale for contending that copyright encourages the creation of cultural works. This assumption is central to IFPI's lobbying for copyright legislation and legitimates many of its other practices. In a section of its Web site entitled Copyright and creativity, IFPI's (2004b) definition of copyright says that:

> Copyright provides that the rights holders determine whether and how copying, distributing, broadcasting and other uses of their works take place. This gives talented people the incentive to create great works, and entrepreneurs the economic reasons to invest in them. Copyright has underpinned an extraordinary modern economic success story, accounting for tens of millions of jobs worldwide. The dramatic growth of the artistic, cultural and other creative industries in today's major economies would have been impossible without the strong levels of copyright protection that those countries have developed over many decades.

In this passage, IFPI does not merely emphasize the benefits of copyright for both culture and the economy, but also presents strong copyright laws as a condition *sine qua non* for cultural industries to thrive. This argument is used on all legislative levels. However, exactly *which* economy or culture is said to benefit from the recording industry's activities varies, depending on whether the targeted organization is national, European, or global.

The author's rights narrative is somewhat less visible, but plays a significant role in IFPI's discourse, too, as IFPI links the interests of record companies with those of artists (who have a more favorable image than record companies). Artists and record companies are represented as sharing the same needs and suffering the same perils. This is achieved through establishing relations of equivalence between both parties, for example by means of frequent references to *"artists and record companies."* In this way, the diverging interests of artists and record companies and the possible conflicts between them are repressed.[5] Often, IFPI even seems to speak on behalf of the artists. The record company pressure group presents itself as fighting for the rights of authors, a lobbying strategy that—according to Ewing (2003)—has been central to developments in copyright law favoring third parties since the birth of copyright. This apparent consensus is also created through the incorporation of artists' voices. Without exception, the artists quoted are supportive of IFPI positions, often actively so by attending IFPI lobbying activities (as was done by among others The Corrs and Jean-Michel Jarre). Artists with diverging opinions are never mentioned. Through this discursive strategy, differences are suppressed and a consensus is suggested (Fairclough, 2003: 42). The use of terms like "the creative community" (e.g., IFPI et al., February 13, 2001) and "the copyright community" (e.g., IFPI, June 26, 2001) is another element that helps create relations of equivalence and downplay divergences between the interests of artists, record companies and other players in the recording industry. In what follows, I argue that this effect is also achieved through a logic of equivalence that *"consists in the dissolution of the particular identities of subjects within a discourse by the creation of a purely negative identity that is seen to threaten them"* (Howarth, 2000: 107). In this case, this negative identity is referred to as *piracy*.

Piracy

The introduction of *piracy* as a term in intellectual property debates is said to date back to around 1700, when London stationers used it as a label for infringements on the printing privileges the Crown had granted them (Kretschmer, 2000: 206). In the context of the cultural industries, the term piracy is used as a metaphor denoting copyright infringements. Through the use of the term piracy, copyright infringements are presented as acts of theft and robbery.

Today, like copyright, piracy is part of the discourse of the cultural industries. In IFPI's discourse, both signifiers are intimately linked. This is because their articulation draws upon the same *"material property-related narratives"* (May, 2003). Where copyright is conceived of as a means of stimulating creativity, piracy is represented as a *"disincentive"* to creativity (e.g., IFPI, December 1, 2000) that *"stunts the development of new talent"* (IFPI, May 21, 2003). In denouncing unauthorized uses of music, IFPI also draws on the tradition of author's rights and the *"scent of holiness"* (Grosheide, 1986: 1-2) surrounding authors and their creations within that tradition.

The use of the term piracy to denote music downloading is part of a longer term evolution that dates back to the 1980s, when it was used for condemning home taping (Frith, 1993: 2). This led to a broadening of the meaning of piracy to include noncommercial forms of copying. However, in IFPI's discourse, the move to include not only "commercial piracy" but also "individual piracy"[6] has not been completed yet, as is reflected in the different definitions of piracy in IFPI press releases and on ifpi.org. The IFPI Web site (IFPI, 2004c) states the following:

> The term of piracy is generally used to describe the deliberate infringement of copyright on a commercial scale. In relation to the music industry it refers to unauthorized copying, and in this context, falls into 3 categories:
>
> - Simple piracy—is the unauthorized duplication of an original recording for commercial gain without the consent of the rights owner. . . .
> - Counterfeits—are copied and packaged to resemble the original as closely as possible. The original producer's trademarks and logos are reproduced in order to mislead the consumer into believing that they are buying an original product.
> - Bootlegs—these are the unauthorized recordings of live or broadcast performances. They are duplicated and sold—often at a premium price—without the permission of the artist, composer or record company.

In IFPI's general definition, piracy denotes infringements on copyright that are commercial in nature. In all three categories, reference is made to selling the pirated music. This means that peer-to-peer file-sharing, which is cost-reducing instead of profit-making (Scott, 2001), does not fall into the categories identified by IFPI. However, in IFPI press releases on downloading it is continuously referred to as "Internet piracy". In IFPI's discourse on the Internet, every unauthorized use of music is labeled as piracy, including those uses that do not serve a commercial goal.

Authorization is a key signifier in IFPI's discourse on music distribution via the Internet. Every use of copyrighted material that is not authorized (by the copyright owners) is referred to as piracy. As a consequence, the scope of the term exceeds the uses of music that are prohibited by law. A comment on the EU Enforcement Directive (IFPI et al., January 30, 2003) states that "*the proposal creates a two-tier system of enforcement where some types of piracy are acceptable and others not.*" This statement implicitly constructs copyright as an absolute property right, and piracy as a term referring to all practices that are in defiance of this absolute property right. In other words, IFPI's discourse rests on the ideological assumption that music *is* property. This assumption forms the basis of IFPI lobbying for stricter copyright laws on the Internet, which are said to protect existing property rights rather than create new ones. It also grounds the representation of music piracy not as an infringement of legally defined (and thus finally contingent) copyrights, but as the theft of an inalienable property. In IFPI's discourse, the law should prevent this and the owners of music should be given the possibility of defending their property against pirates by every (legal, technological, etc.) means necessary.

In the articulation of this discourse, intellectual and physical property become intertwined. The chain of equivalence is established positively by representing copyright as a property right that implies absolute control over music, for instance through referring to "*the fundamental right ... of the copyright holders to choose how their music is distributed*" (IFPI, May 9, 2001). It is also constructed negatively, through frequent references to the stealing/piracy of music. By defining copyright infringements as stealing/piracy, copyright itself is established as a property right. It is even treated as a property *per se*, as is evidenced by references to "copyright owners" and "copyright theft."

As May (2000: 42, cited in Söderberg, 2002) argued, this property discourse is a way of dealing with the contradiction between the characteristics of music and its treatment as scarce property that lies at the heart of the commodification of music. Presenting downloading (and other forms of "individual piracy") as stealing is an attempt to convince the public that not paying for music is (morally and legally) wrong, which has been the core argument of the recording industry's "information campaigns" for years (see Frith, 1993: 2).

The next section deals in more detail with two discourses IFPI draws on in the construction of piracy as a threat to the recording industry and to society in general: a biological and a militaristic discourse of criminality.

CAPITALISM AND PIRACY: THE CONSTRUCTION OF A CONSTITUTIVE OUTSIDE

Although the previous sections dealt with copyright and piracy separately, this section argues that the two signifiers depend on one another for their meaning. It is useful here to turn to Laclau and Mouffe's (1985: 135-136) use of the Derridean concept of the constitutive outside. According to Laclau and Mouffe's discourse theory, a discourse establishes its limits by excluding a radical otherness that poses a threat to the discourse. The different elements of a discourse are linked not by an underlying essence but by a common threat: the constitutive outside (Torfing, 1999: 124-125).

In this way, piracy serves as a shared threat that is crucial in linking the interests of record companies with those of authors and artists. At the same time, the signifier is used to lump together illegal practices that serve a commercial goal and practices that constitute an alternative to the existing system and are not motivated by commercial gain. Through the use of the term piracy, the differences between these practices are repressed. The excluded elements function as the constitutive outside of the capitalist discourse on music. What they have in common is *"their negation of the discursive formation in question"* (Torfing, 1999: 124). By referring to this common element, the differences between the practices are supressed. Their meaning is reduced to the threat they represent to the capitalist system of intellectual property.

The relation between piracy and copyright is an antagonistic one. Antagonism, however, is not a relationship of pure and simple negation. It is precisely through antagonism that the meaning of both signifiers is constituted. Piracy is equated with copyright infringements and thus depends on the existence of copyright—and vice versa: it is because piracy exists that (a stronger) copyright is necessary. Similarly, the "copyright community" is constituted through its opposition to a shared "other": pirates.

The antagonism under consideration is discursively constructed by associating all practices that do not fit into the capitalist model of music distribution with a chain of equivalences that further includes the following: "piracy," "illegal," "wrong," "illegitimate," "unauthorized," "without permission," "free," "unfair," "stealing," "infringing," and opposing it to the recording industry (on- and offline) and its chain of equivalences, which contains terms like "legal," "legitimate," "right," "authorized," and so on.

Furthermore, IFPI draws on two discourses for representing piracy as a threat to the capitalist recording industry: a medical/biological discourse representing the capitalist recording industry as an organism of which the health is endangered by external threats; and a militaristic discourse representing piracy as an external aggression the industry has no choice but to respond to. Both discourses are combined in the following extract (IFPI, October 1, 2003):

Jay Berman, Chairman and CEO of IFPI said: "Despite some healthy signs that a legitimate online music business is now taking hold, the music industry continues to suffer from the unauthorized file-sharing and commercial piracy. We are responding to this decisively, however: on the physical piracy front, seizures of discs rose four-fold last year; on the Internet piracy front, the U.S. industry is leading a highly effective global public awareness drive on the legal risks of file-sharing; and on the new business front, a marked change in the landscape is visible as a number of legitimate online music sites take hold."

By describing the strategies against "illegal" downloading as forming part of a battle, piracy is represented as a homogeneous threat and not as a series of isolated actions by individuals. In this way, the gravity of the situation is emphasized. Moreover, through the use of a militaristic discourse, piracy is articulated as an attack on an innocent recording industry, which is obliged to respond in legitimate self-defense. Fairclough (1992: 130) argued that militaristic metaphors function to represent criminals as being *"at war"* with society, and society as having to *"mobilize its forces"* to *"fight them off."* Also, as Logie (2003) pointed out, the use of war metaphors for the industry's actions against downloading reinforces a capitalist discourse of intellectual property by articulating *"military conflicts over real [i.e. material, BDC] property as exemplary."*[7] As will be shown here, the use of militaristic metaphors is not the only way of establishing an analogy between intellectual and physical property.

The articulation of health and disease in IFPI's discourse is based on a core capitalist ideological assumption. A situation of economic growth is healthy and natural. A stagnation or decline in (in this case: music) sales is a symptom of disease. This disease is attributed to external factors such as the different types of piracy, which according to IFPI's head of enforcement (Grant, 2003) constitute *"an epidemic"* (again, a homogeneous threat). Industry-internal factors such as the kinds of music that are available, the long life cycle of the CD, or high pricing are not taken into consideration. It is continuously emphasized that *"demand is strong"* (IFPI, April 14, 2000), even if this *"surging growth has been at the cost of having consumers who are not actually paying for it"* (Berman, 2002). IFPI presents the decline in music sales as a crisis[8] *in* and *not of* the recording industry, a strategy that according to Jessop (2004: 167) prevents the opening up of a discursive space for radical changes.

In this fashion, IFPI's discourse functions ideologically by providing what Laclau (1990: 63-63) called a social imaginary—*"a horizon in the sense that it is not one among other objects, but rather the condition of possibility for the emergence of any object"* (Torfing, 1999: 115). A social imaginary constructs the world as a set of essences, and ignores that these supposed essences are the (naturalized) results of political decisions (Torfing, 1999:

116). In IFPI's discourse, the contingent nature of the existing copyright system is disavowed and the system of intellectual property is articulated as the legal confirmation of the pre-existing reality that music *is* property. This natural, healthy, normal situation is presented as being under threat of external aggressions, epidemics, and attacks.

Before turning to IFPI's nonrecognition of alternative discourses, the next section analyzes the online music industry as an *"economic imaginary"* (Jessop, 2004: 162) through which the Internet is incorporated into a capitalist discourse on music.

THE FUTURE'S BRIGHT, THE FUTURE'S COPYRIGHTED: THE ONLINE MUSIC INDUSTRY AS AN ECONOMIC IMAGINARY

In conceptualizing the relation between capitalist and noncapitalist practices on the Internet, good use[9] can be made of the distinction introduced by Jessop (2004: 162) between the *"actually existing economy"* and *"the economy."* Whereas the former refers to the chaotic sum of all economic activities,[10] the latter is *"an imaginatively narrated, more or less coherent subset of the 'actually existing economy.'"* This subset and others are constituted by economic imaginaries that develop when *"economic, political and intellectual forces seek to (re)define specific subsets of economic activities as subjects, sites, and stakes of competition and/or as objects of regulation and to articulate strategies, projects and visions oriented to these imagined economies"* (Jessop, 2004: 163).

As shown earlier, IFPI's discourse discredits alternative practices on the Internet in favor of *"formal (profit-oriented, market-mediated) economic activities"* (Jessop, 2004: 172). Using Jessop's terms, the whole of activities on the Internet can be seen as constituting the actually existing economy, while only some of them fit in with the economic imaginary of the online economy that is constructed by IFPI's discourse.

The online music industry is presented as safeguarding the *"right way to use the Internet"* (IFPI, October 28, 1999) and the desired future of the Internet:

> The future of music on the Internet lies not in infringing copyright, but in developing secure services that respect copyright. That is the way consumers are going to get the music they want in the myriad of new ways that the Internet makes possible. (IFPI, June 26, 2001)

The online economy is crucial in IFPI's lobbying for strong copyright legislation on the Internet and for a stricter enforcement of copyright laws dealing with "Internet piracy." In its lobbying strategy, the online economy is
presented as being both inevitable and dependent on measures prohibiting
"Internet piracy." For these combined arguments to be successful in lobbying with governments, the imaginary of the online economy is linked to a
discourse of globalization. Not meeting the desires (presented as "needs") of
the record companies is presented as causing an economic and cultural dis-
advantage to the region represented by the organization lobbied with, as is
clear from this comment on the EU Copyright Directive (IFPI, May 23,
2000):

> The final result would be tremendous uncertainty at a time when the
> European music industry is striving to develop legitimate e-commerce,
> get on-line and compete globally. The music industry urges the Internal
> Market ministers not to go down this path, which will create obstacles
> to conducting business on-line and set the European content industries
> back in their efforts to create a secure framework for electronic com-
> merce. It would be ironic if Europe, which allegedly values its cultural
> heritage so highly, provides a lower level of protection than the U.S.

In this fashion, the global online economy serves as an imaginary by means
of which which IFPI integrates the Internet into the (global) capitalist ideology. This imaginary is important in strategies reproducing the political
economy of the recording industry. It is, however, not the only imaginary
offering a construction of the Internet. The next and final section of this
chapter looks at IFPI's reaction to competing imaginaries of the Internet.

"ILLEGAL FILE-SHARING": IFPI AND ALTERNATIVE DISCOURSES ON THE INTERNET

According to Flichy (2001), the online or "new" economy is just one of the
"technological imaginaries" (along with the information superhighway, the
scientific community's view of the Internet, a utopian Internet community,
etc.) that are constitutive of the development of the Internet. The imaginary
of the new economy, Flichy (2001: 223-251) argues, is central to the commercialization of the Internet. However, it is not the only possible discourse.
   Alternative discourses on peer-to-peer-downloading conceptualize the
Internet in a way that clearly diverges from its conceptualization by IFPI. In
these discourses, the Internet is not (merely) a capitalist distribution channel. Some (Barbrook, 1998; Burnett & Marshall, 2003: 186-188) describe

peer-to-peer file-sharing (in itself a term with a positive, democratic connotation) as belonging to a gift economy. Others (Kollock, 1999: 221-222;
Poster, 2001: 57-58) reject this classification, because the participants in an
Internet-mediated peer-to-peer network remain anonymous. This is incompatible with the reciprocity that is fundamental to a gift economy, in which
every participant returns the gifts he or she receives because he or she feels
obliged to do so. For this reason, they prefer the term *economy of sharing.*

Irrespective of these differences in terminology, one can say that the distinctive feature of a gift economy or an economy of sharing is that no
exchange value is extracted from the system, which of course makes these
economies radically different from the capitalist economic system. For the
recording industry, this difference becomes especially relevant when music
created *within* the recording industry is distributed via the Internet. This
amounts to the decommodification of commercial music (Burnett &
Marshall, 2003: 188), for as we have seen, file-sharing and downloading are
not aimed at making a profit: Their goal is to reduce costs (Scott, 2001). In
radical contrast to the capitalist system of music distribution, peer-to-peer
networks do not depend on the successful extraction of exchange value.
IFPI's discourse on the Internet and the strategies record companies adopt
vis-à-vis the Internet can be interpreted as reactions to this decommodification.

It is clear that these discourses constitute a threat to the dominance of
the capitalist intellectual property discourse on music promoted by IFPI.
IFPI, therefore, tries to delegitimate and discredit these discourses.
However, in reacting to these alternative discourses, IFPI's discourse is
inevitably influenced by the discourse of sharing it criticizes. This is among
others evidenced by its use of the term *file-sharing.* As a signifier mainly
associated with pro peer-to-peer discourses, which present downloading as
sharing, it is incorporated into IFPI's discourse, which equates downloading
with stealing. The incorporation of the term into a property discourse shows
its pervasiveness in debates on peer-to-peer downloading. IFPI does, of
course, use different discursive strategies, aimed at discrediting the discourse
of sharing or at least at distancing itself from that discourse.

In IFPI's reaction to the rival discourse of sharing, attribution is always
vague: It refers for instance to the *"free side"* (e.g., IFPI, February 6, 2004)
or to *"the publicists of unauthorized file-sharing"* (IFPI, December 19,
2003). As Fairclough (2003: 48) showed, such nonspecific attributions make
it difficult to challenge what is being attributed. There certainly is no real
dialogue with advocates of peer-to-peer downloading. Alternative discourses are only incorporated for the purpose of discrediting them.

In some cases, file-sharing is put between quotation marks to make clear
that the term originates from an alien discourse and that IFPI rejects the
(positive) connotations these signifiers have there. Quotation marks are also
a way of discrediting the signifier:

unauthorized "file-sharing" harms the artists, songwriters, musicians, record labels and everyone else involved in making the music that users want to "share." (IFPI, August 14, 2003)

Another strategy consists of forging new semantic relations by associating file-sharing with elements from IFPI's capitalist discourse on downloading. When talking about *"illegal file-sharing"* (IFPI, March 30, 2004), for example, IFPI incorporates file-sharing into its intellectual property discourse that defines file-sharing as theft. At the same time, however, it leaves room for legal use of file-sharing services by explicitly referring to *illegal* file-sharing.

A similar way of disarticulating file-sharing from the discourse of sharing in order to discredit it, is the use of the term *"file-stealing"* (IFPI, March 30, 2004). In this fashion, IFPI depreciates the discourse of sharing by removing the positive connotations associated with sharing entirely and replacing them with the negative connotations associated with stealing.

CONCLUSION

Nature. Essence. Innate. The way things are. This kind of rhetoric should raise suspicions in any context. It should especially raise suspicions here. If there is any place where nature has no rule, it is in cyberspace. If there is any place that is constructed, cyberspace is it. ... There is certainly a way that cyberspace is. That much is true. But how cyberspace is, is not how cyberspace has to be. There is no single way that the Net has to be; no single architecture defines the nature of the Net. The possible architectures of what we call "the Net" are many, and the character of life within those different architectures is diverse. (Lessig, 2000: 24-25)

The focus of this chapter is on the role of discourse in the reproduction of the political economy of the recording industry in the "Age of the Internet." Starting from a political economy analysis, copyright and piracy were outlined as sensitizing concepts, which were subsequently developed using discourse theory as a framework. In other words, the meaning of these signifiers was not derived from the political economy analysis but analyzed in their concrete articulation within IFPI's discourse, in which copyright and piracy function as nodal points (Laclau & Mouffe, 1985: 112) fixing the meaning of other signifiers in the discourse on the Internet. Both signifiers are articulated as elements of a property discourse on music that has hegemonic and essentialist ambitions, because it is unwilling to recognize that the existing system of intellectual property is the result of political decisions (see

Torfing, 1999: 116) and therefore by no means the only possible way of organizing music distribution via the Internet.

The acceptance of this property discourse (and of the biological and militaristic metaphors that support it) blocks the articulation of alternative discourses—not just those that refuse to treat music as property, but also those formulating alternative ways of valorizing music on the Internet (inside or outside a capitalist system—e.g., the *Creative Commons*), for example, by extracting advertising revenue from websites or from software used to gain access to peer-to-peer networks. IFPI's discourse thus leaves very little room for changing the business model of the recording industry.

In order to think about the creation and distribution of music in a more open fashion, it is necessary to criticize the ideological assumption that music is property. Copyright must be conceived of as one possible means to achieving an end, rather than as the inevitable basis or affirmation of property rights over music. Resisting IFPI's property discourse on music and formulating alternatives is important because, as Flichy (2001: 8) argued, "*technological imaginaries*" are an integral part of the development of a technological system like the Internet. As IFPI attempts to assimilate the Internet to the system of intellectual property, its discourse is part of what Bettig (2000: 6) called the "*enclosure of cyberspace*" by copyright owners.

Counter-tendencies do remain possible, as is evidenced by the formulation of alternative discourses on the Internet such as the discourse on the Digital Commons, defined by Murdock (2004) as "*a linked space defined by its shared refusal of commercial enclosure and its commitment to free and universal access, reciprocity, and collaborative activity,*" and the discourse of sharing associated with, for instance, peer-to-peer networks. These alternative discourses are of paramount importance for the resistance to the all-encompassing ideology of intellectual property and the enclosure of cyberspace, and therefore also crucial for preserving the diversity of life on the Internet.

NOTES

1. Hesmondhalgh (2002: 19-22), inspired by Garnham, defines five strategies: offsetting misses against hits through a repertoire; concentration, integration, and co-opting publicity; artificial scarcity; formatting through stars, genres, and serials; loose control of symbol creators, tight control of distribution and marketing. This discussion is limited to those strategies that are most relevant to the issue of music downloading.
2. Ninty-two press releases issued by IFPI International, IFPI Europe, and IFPI Belgium have been analyzed.

3. Press releases are not only directed to the general public. They are also a way for IFPI to communicate its operations to its members.
4. This is interpreted very broadly. The corpus includes the press releases dealing with actions against downloading or with legal alternatives, as well as those dealing with the application of copyright law to the Internet. It also includes two press releases on CD copy protection, because copy protection devices are supposed to render impossible the conversion of digital music on CDs to the MP3 format (ripping).
5. The same goes for the competition between record companies. As a pressure group, IFPI stresses their common interests and suppresses possible conflicts, for instance between majors and minors. The fact that it speaks in the name of "the recording industry" also functions to stress its own importance.
6. This terminology is the fruit of the changing meaning of piracy, as commercial piracy would have been pleonastic and individual piracy would not have been labeled as such.
7. Logie (2003), therefore, regrets the use of war metaphors by advocates of peer-to-peer-networks.
8. A "crisis" that in itself is an important element of its discourse as it serves to legitimate action against that which is argued to have caused the crisis.
9. Albeit with the necessary precautions: we should be careful not to fall back into a discursive–non-discursive dichotomy. Within my framework, "actually existing economy" refers to a diversity of practices that are discursively excluded from "the economy."
10. Defined by Jessop (2004: 162) as those activities "*concerned with the social appropriation and transformation of nature for the purposes of material provisioning.*" When applied to the recording industry, this definition should be broadened to include activities concerned with immaterial production.

REFERENCES

Barbrook, R. (1998) 'The High-Tech Gift Economy.' Retrieved June 10, 2005, from http://www.hrc.wmin.ac.uk/theory-hightechgifteconomy.html.

Berman, J. (2002) 'Presentation by Jay Berman: JP Morgan Seminar.' Retrieved January 3, 2004, from http://www.ifpi.org/sitecontent/press/inthemedia07 .html.

Bettig, R. (1997) 'The Enclosure of Cyberspace,' *Critical Studies in Mass Communications* 14(2): 138-157.

Bettig, R. (2003) 'Copyright and the Commodification of Culture,' *Media Development* (45)1: 3-9.

Burkart, P., McCourt, T. (2003) 'When Creators, Corporations and Consumers Collide: Napster and the Development of On-line Music Distribution,' *Media, Culture and Society* 25(3): 333-350.

Burnett, R. (1996) *The Global Jukebox: The International Music Industry*. London, New York: Routledge.

Burnett, R., Marshall, P.D. (2003) *Web Theory: An Introduction*. London, New York: Routledge.

Christiaanse, E., Dolfsma, W. (1999) 'Global Electronic Channels in the Music Industry.' Retrieved March 10, 2004, from http://www1.fee.uva.nl/pp/ echristiaanse/publications/christiaanseDolfsma1999.pdf.

Digital Media Project (2004) 'ITunes: How Copyright, Contract, and Technology Shape the Business of Digital Media: A Case Study–Green Paper v.1.0.' Retrieved April 5, 2004, from http://cyber.law.harvard.edu/media/ uploads/53/GreenPaperiTunes03.04.pdf.

Ewing, J. (2003) 'Copyright and Authors,' *First Monday* 8(10). Retrieved November 27, 2003, from http://firstmonday.org/issues/issue8_10/ewing/index. html.

Fairclough, N. (1992) *Discourse and Social Change*. Cambridge: Polity Press.

Fairclough, N. (2003) *Analysing Discourse: Textual Analysis for Social Research*. London/New York: Routledge.

Flichy, P. (2001) *L'Imaginaire d'Internet*. Paris: Éditions La Découverte.

Frith, S. (1993) 'Music and Morality,' pp. 1-21 in S. Frith (Ed) *Music and Copyright*. Edinburgh: Edinburgh University Press.

Garnham, N. (2000) *Emancipation, the Media and Modernity*. Oxford: Oxford University Press.

Garofalo, R. (1999) 'From Music Publishing to MP3: Music and Industry in the Twentieth Century,' *American Music* 17(3): 318-354.

Garofalo, R. (2003) 'I Want My MP3: Who Owns Internet Music?,' pp. 30-45 in M. Cloonan and R. Garofalo (Eds) *Policing Pop*. Philadelphia: Temple University Press.

Grant, I. (2003) 'Piracy is not a Victimless Crime (Speech at European Parliament, April 23, 2003).' Retrieved April 17, 2004, from http://www.ifpi.org/site-content/press/inthemedia10.html.

Grosheide, F.W. (1986) *Auteursrecht op Maat*. Deventer: Kluwer.

Harker, D. (1997) 'The Wonderful World of IFPI: Music Industry Rhetoric, the Critics and the Classical Marxist Critique,' *Popular Music* 16(1): 45-79.

Harker, D. (1998) 'It's a Jungle Sometimes: The Music Industry, the Crisis and the State.' Retrieved November 15, 2003, from http://www.mediamusicstudies.net/tagg/others/harker1.html.

Hesmondhalgh, D. (2002) *The Cultural Industries*. London, Thousand Oaks, New Delhi: Sage.

Howarth, D. (2000) *Discourse*. Buckingham, Philadelphia: Open University Press.

Hugenholtz, P.B. (2000) 'Copyright and Freedom of Expression in Europe,' pp. 343-363 in R.C. Dreyfuss, H. First and D. Leenheer Zimmerman (Eds) *Innovation Policy in an Information Age*. Oxford: Oxford University Press.

Jessop, B. (2004) 'Critical Semiotic Analysis and Cultural Political Economy,' *Critical Discourse Studies* 1(2): 159-174.

Kollock, P. (1999) 'The Economies of Online Cooperation,' pp. 220-239 in M.A. Smith and P. Kollock (Eds) *Communities in Cyberspace*. Londen, New York: Routledge.

Kretschmer, M. (2000) 'Intellectual Property in Music: A Historical Analysis of Rhetoric and Institutional Practices,' *Studies in Cultures, Organizations and Societies* (6): 197-223.

Laclau, E. (1990) *New Reflections on the Revolution of our Time*. London: Verso.

Laclau, E., Mouffe, C. (1985) *Hegemony and Socialist Strategy: Towards a Radical Democratic Politics.* London: Verso.

Laing, D. (1993) 'Copyright and the International Music Industry,' pp. 22-39 in S. Frith (Ed) *Music and Copyright.* Edinburgh: Edinburgh University Press.

Lessig, L. (2000) *Code and Other Laws of Cyberspace.* New York: Basic Books.

Lessig, L. (2002) 'The Architecture of Innovation,' *Duke Law Journal* 51(6): 1783-1803.

Leyshon, A. (2005) 'On the Reproduction of Musical Economy after the Internet,' *Media, Culture and Society* 27(2): 177-209.

Liebowitz, S. (2002) 'Policing the Pirates in the Networked Age,' *Policy Analysis* 438. Retrieved April 7, 2004, from www.cato.org/pubs/pas/pa-438es.html.

Liebowitz, S. (2003) 'Will MP3 Downloads Annihilate the Record Industry? The Evidence so Far.' Retrieved June 15, 2003, from wwpub.utdallas.edu/~ liebow-it/intprop/records.pdf.

Litman, J. (2001) *Digital Copyright.* New York: Prometheus Books.

Logie, J. (2003) 'A Copyright Cold War? The Polarized Rhetoric of the Peer-to-Peer Debates,' *First Monday* 8(7). Retrieved November 27, 2003, from http:// first-monday.org/issues/issue8_7/logie/index.html.

May, C. (1998) 'Thinking, Buying, Selling: Intellectual Property Rights in Political Economy,' *New Political Economy* 3(1): 59-79.

May, C. (2003) 'Digital Rights Management and the Breakdown of Social Norms,' *First Monday* 8(11). Retrieved November 27, 2003, from http://firstmonday. org/issues/issue8_11/may/index.html.

Mosco, V. (1996) *The Political Economy of Communication.* London, Thousand Oaks, New Delhi: Sage.

Murdock, G. (2004) 'Building the Digital Commons: Public Broadcasting in the Age of the Internet' (The 2004 Spry Memorial Lecture). Retrieved June 2, 2005, from http://www.com.umontreal.ca/spry/spry-gm-lec.htm.

Oberholzer, F., Strumpf, K. (2004) 'The Effect of File Sharing on Record Sales: An Empirical Analysis.' Retrieved April 7, 2004, from http://www.unc.edu/~ cigar/papers/File-sharing_March2004.pdf.

Phillips, L., Jørgensen, M. (2002) *Discourse Analysis as Theory and Method.* London: Sage.

Poel, M., Rutten, P. (2003) 'Impact and Perspectives of Electronic Commerce: The Music Industry in the Netherlands.' Delft: TNO-STB. Retrieved June 15, 2003, from www.oecd.org/dataoecd/49/2/2072953.pdf.

Poster, M. (2001) *What's the Matter with the Internet?* Minnesota: University of Minnesota Press.

Ritzer, G. (1992) *Sociological Theory.* New York: McGraw-Hill.

Robinson, D.C. (1992) 'Of the People? The Case of Popular Music,' pp. 114-136 in V. Mosco and J. Wasko (Eds) *Democratic Communications in the Information Age.* Toronto: Garamond Press.

Scott, B. (2001) 'Copyright in a Frictionless World: Toward a Rhetoric of Responsibility,' *First Monday* 6(9). Retrieved December 1, 2003, from http://firstmonday.org/issues/issue6_9/scott/index.html.

Söderberg, J. (2002) 'Copyleft vs. Copyright: A Marxist Critique,' *First Monday* 7(3). Retrieved November 27, 2003, from http://firstmonday.org/issues/issue 7_3/soderberg/index.html.

Torfing, J. (1999) *New Theories of Discourse: Laclau, Mouffe and Žižek*. Oxford: Blackwell.

Towse, R. (2001) *Creativity, Incentive and Reward: An Economic Analysis of Copyright and Culture in the Information Age*. Cheltenham/Northampton: Edward Elgar.

Vivant, M. (2001) 'Droit d'Auteur et Copyright: Quelles Relations?' Downloaded on May 26, 2004 from http://droit-Internet-2001.univ-paris1.fr/pdf/vf/Vivant_M. pdf.

IFPI Material

IFPI (October 28, 1999) 'Recording Industry Aims Global Crackdown on Internet Pirates.' Retrieved April 19, 2004, from http://www.ifpi.org/site-content/press/19991028.html.

IFPI (April 14, 2000) 'Recorded Music Sales up 1.5% in 1999.' Retrieved April 19, 2004, from http://www.ifpi.org/site-content/press/20000414.html.

IFPI (May 23, 2000) 'Music Industry Warns that Draft Copyright Directive Will Pull the Plug on the On-line Market.' Retrieved April 19, 2004, from http://www.ifpi.org/site-content/press/20000524.html.

IFPI (December 1, 2000) 'Music Industry Hails EU Crackdown on Piracy.' Retrieved April 19, 2004, from http://www.ifpi.org/site-content/press/20001201.html.

IFPI, GESAC (Groupement Européen des Sociétés d'Auteurs et Compositeurs), GEIE (Groupement Européen représentant les Organismes de Gestion) (February 13, 2001) 'MEPs Urged to Make a Stand for Creativity.' Retrieved April 19, 2004, from http://www.ifpi.org/site-content/press/20010213.html.

IFPI (May 9, 2001) 'Music Copyright Holders Offered Songbird, the First International, Publicly-available Napster Search Tool.' Retrieved April 19, 2004, from http://www.ifpi.org/site-content/press/20010509.html.

IFPI (June 26, 2001) 'Statement by Jay Berman, Chairman and CEO of IFPI, on Aim/Impala/Napster Announcement.' Retrieved April 19, 2004, from http://www.ifpi.org/site-content/press/20010626.html.

IFPI, BSA (Business Software Alliance), MPA (Motion Picture Association), IVF (International Video Federation), ISFE (Interactive Software Federation of Europe), FIAPF (International Association of Film Producers Associations), IMPALA (Independent Music Companies Association), FEP (Federation of European Publishers) and GESAC (European Grouping of Societies of Authors and Composers) (January 30, 2003) 'EU Enforcement Directive Falls Far Short of Providing Urgently Needed Tools to Tackle Piracy.' Retrieved April 19, 2004, from http://www.ifpi.com/site-content/press/20030130.html.

IFPI (May 21, 2003) 'Music Sector Calls for Fans to go Online with Pro-music.org.' Retrieved April 19, 2004, from http://www.ifpi.com/site-content/press/20030521.html.

IFPI (August 14, 2003) 'Germany Launches First National Pro-music Website.' Retrieved April 19, 2004, from http://www.ifpi.com/site-content/press/20030814a.html.

IFPI (October 1, 2003) 'Global Sales of Recorded Music Down 10.9% in the First Half of 2003.' Retrieved April 17, 2004, from http://www.ifpi.com/site-content/press/20031001.html.

IFPI (December 19, 2003) 'IFPI Response to Netherlands Supreme Court Judgement on Kazaa.' Retrieved February 3, 2004, from http://www.ifpi.com/site-content/press/20031219.html.

IFPI (February 6, 2004) 'IFPI Welcomes Australian Action Against Kazaa.' Retrieved April 17, 2004, from http://www.ifpi.org/site-content/press/20040206.html.

IFPI (March 30, 2004) 'Recording Industry Starts Legal Actions Against Illegal File-sharing Internationally.' Retrieved April 25, 2004, from http://www.ifpi.org/site-content/press/20040330.html.

IFPI (2004a) 'Mission.' Retrieved April 16, 2004, from http://www.ifpi.org/ site-content/about/mission.html.

IFPI (2004b) 'Copyright and Creativity.' Retrieved April 16, 2004, from http://www.ifpi.org/site-content/copyrightcreativity/what_is_copyright.html.

IFPI (2004c) 'What is Piracy?.' Retrieved April 16, 2004, from http://www.ifpi.org/site-content/antipiracy/what_is_piracy.html.

Literature

12

AGONISM AND LITERARY HISTORY

Stuart Sim

One of the most critical points to emerge from discourse theory is the need for agonism within cultures: that is, for sociopolitical relations based on radically different, clearly distinctive worldviews. What is being sought is something far more hard edged than the standard model of oppositional procedures and institutions to be found within the political systems of most Western societies these days. Laclau and Mouffe's *Hegemony and Socialist Strategy* is a wake-up call to the left to recognize the necessity of developing such relations, and agonism lies right at the heart of the post-Marxist ethos (and, for that matter, the postmodernist ethos as well).[1] Marxism no longer provides that agonism for Laclau and Mouffe, who argue that the left needs, as a matter of urgency, to cultivate the emerging new social protest movements if it wants to maintain its adversarial position against the dominant ideology:

> The "evident truths" of the past—the classical forms of analysis and political calculation, the nature of the forces in conflict, the very meaning of the Left's struggles and objectives—have been seriously chal-

lenged by an avalanche of historical mutations which have riven the
ground on which those truths were constituted. (Laclau & Mouffe,
1985: 1)

In effect, the left is being asked by discourse theory to bracket its traditional commitments and tactically seek new alignments among these various
mutations to ensure its continued influence on world affairs. It is a message
at least as relevant now as it was in the mid-1980s when Laclau and Mouffe
first proclaimed it—to the considerable displeasure of the Marxist establishment of the time, who saw this as amounting to a failure of nerve on the part
of these thinkers.[2] Agonism for this constituency meant the rejection of
Marxism and all its ideals, and even if these had been abused over the course
of the 20th century in both the Soviet and Maoist projects, this was still
regarded as undeserved and unacceptable treatment of the Marxist theoretical heritage. To be "post-" was to have moved over to the enemy camp; to
espouse agonism was at best to be naïve because it seemed to constitute an
admission that the left did not have all the answers to the world's political
problems—precisely what the left, both inside and outside the communist
bloc, confidently had been claiming for most of the 20th century. Discourse
theory has been a source of controversy since it was formulated: not Marxist
enough for the far left, yet still too Marxist for the center and the right.
Meanwhile, the mutations just keep mounting up, with the rise of Islamic
fundamentalism being the latest to leave the left confused as to how to
respond and who to support.[3]

Mouffe has, of late, developed the concept of agonism even further. Her
work in this area is echoing that of the American political scientist William
E. Connolly. Post-Marxism is more of a reactive than an active position
politically speaking, and agonism represents an attempt to overcome that
deficiency: In fact, it could be the concept that defines post-Marxism, its
core principle. The objective of this chapter is to consider the implications
of agonism for a discourse theory, post-Marxist aesthetics. Could this concept provide a focus for such an aesthetic? Perhaps even an updated, less
doctrinaire version of Georg Lukács' theory of critical realism? Aesthetics
has been one of the most successful areas of Marxist thought, arguably its
most enduring legacy now that it gives the impression of being in terminal
political decline (even if this does leave the aesthetic theory in the somewhat
invidious position of the grin left behind by Lewis Carroll's [1865/1971] dis-
appearing Cheshire cat in Alice's *Adventures in Wonderland*, with no body
of political practice to fall back on for validation). We can now consider
whether this success can be carried over into the realm of post-Marxism.

Here I briefly sketch out what Mouffe said on the topic of agonism,
then relate this to Lukács' theory of critical realism; finally, I give a brief
account of how agonism might function in literary history by applying it to

one of the seminal texts of the English novel tradition—John Bunyan's *The Pilgrim's Progress* (Part I, 1678; Part II, 1684/1960). Because that tradition in its earliest phase is often described as representative of an adversarial culture, with authors like Daniel Defoe and Samuel Richardson offering a robust challenge to dominant ideological values in their works of fiction, it will be instructive to see what Bunyan contributes to it right at its origins.[4]

MOUFFE AND AGONISM

In *The Democratic Paradox*, Mouffe made a strong case for the development of agonistic pluralism, a notion she took over from Connolly (Mouffe, 2000: 9).[5] Agonistic pluralism goes well beyond the Republican–Democrat division in U.S. politics, or the Labour–Conservative in British (and their various equivalents in other Western societies), to argue for a more subversive style of political practice. We find Mouffe (2000: 111) criticizing, for example, "*the typical liberal perspective that envisages democracy as a competition among elites, making adversary forces invisible and reducing politics to an exchange of arguments and the negotiation of compromises.*" Liberal democracy is seen to consist of two conflicting traditions: one concerned primarily with the notion of liberty (i.e., with human rights), the other with equality in the social and economic domains as well as in the political (socialism in its various forms, including Soviet Marxism in terms of its ideals, if not its, now discredited, actual practice). Liberalism is currently the dominant form in the West, and it tends to work toward the imposition of consensus and the elimination of dissent. The globalization movement represents the logical extension of this phenomenon, with its aim of bringing the whole world under a common code of economic policies, dictated by the World Bank and the International Monetary Fund, regardless of local circumstances and cultural differences.[6] The socialist tradition is in its turn just as committed to neutralizing its liberal opponents, if it is given the chance to do so, and is just as universally oriented in its aspirations—as the history of communism amply has proved. (One of the paradoxes left behind by agonistic pluralism is that it would seem not just to sanction, but positively to demand the encouragement of a viscerally anti-left far right political consciousness to counter such a possibility. Whether the left could ever cope with such a state of affairs is very much open to question.)

Mouffe's vision of democracy is very different from that promoted by the consensus model. What it should involve is, she argued, "*the recognition and the legitimation of conflict and the refusal to suppress it through the imposition of an authoritarian order*" (Mouffe, 2000: 113).[7] We must accept the paradox that the liberal and socialist outlooks will never be reconciled,

and that it is to society's benefit that they continue to exist in a state of agonistic tension with each other: that is the democratic paradox of the book's
title (for many on the left a paradox too far, one suspects; although one that
really needs to be thought through). Both Republican–Democrat and
Labour–Conservative would be classifiable as an authoritarian order, operating on the basis of the negotiation of compromises between the respective
parties, and the marginalization of real dissent (even within the parties themselves, where unity is traditionally a highly prized feature, especially among
the leadership). The assumption of such an order is that dissent could never
be brought within the sphere of compromise. For Mouffe this amounts to a
stifling of debate rather than the *"vibrant clash of democratic political positions"* she seeks in its stead as the norm (Mouffe, 2000: 104). Whether such
clashes really would be enough to keep right-wing populism at bay, as
Mouffe seems to believe, is a moot point: The stage at which agonism
becomes antagonism is difficult to pin down. How one would form a government in the midst of such permanently occurring clashes is another mystery, never mind a stable government that could carry out a coherent program of policies, but Mouffe's commitment to pluralism is well worth supporting none the less. When she asked for *"the never-ending interrogation
of the political by the ethical"* she distanced herself even further from a
Marxist past in which the ethical was all too frequently absorbed into the
political (the communist party claiming to embody both), leading to the
extreme authoritarianism exhibited by the Soviet regime for most of its existence when no effective opposition was tolerated (Mouffe, 2000: 140).[8] This
is a theory that is determined to arrest the slide into dogmatism—either
from the left or the right. Determined, as well, to prevent agonism from
turning into outright antagonism, where the elimination of dissent is often
engineered by extreme means—with both left and right being only too
skilled at the practice (Stalinism and fascism being pertinent examples).

   An aesthetic that took Mouffe's injunction to heart would seek out texts
that resisted the authoritarian order of their time, and/or deploy texts from
literary history to challenge such an order now. The politics of the text
would be approached through the imperatives of agonistic pluralism, and
would be particularly concerned with what each text could reveal to us
about the complex dialectic of agonism and antagonism in its historical period. I pay close attention to that dialectic in the discussion of Bunyan's work.

LUKÁCS AND CRITICAL REALISM

Something similar to this search for texts with which to resist the authoritarian order can be found in the work of Lukács, whose theory of critical

realism is the least doctrinaire aesthetic to emerge from the Soviet Marxist tradition. Critical realism enables Marxist critics to make assessments of works from pre-Soviet eras, or non-Soviet cultures, without imposing a communist worldview on the authors in question, or judging them according to a set party line. What authors are being judged on is not their politics as such, but whether they succeed in depicting the true character of the social relations in their society: which to a Marxist critic means the inequalities of that society, the class relations obtaining at the time of the text's production—all history being deemed to be the history of class struggle. The author must depict a *"world in whose shaping we play a part, and which in turn shapes us,"* such that this can be recognized unequivocally by the reader, who can then identify even more strongly with the plight of the oppressed as they struggle against exploitation (Lukács, 1963: 79). For Lukács, the work of Honoré de Balzac did show this, whereas that of Émile Zola did not (and from a later generation, Thomas Mann did and Franz Kafka did not). Balzac and Mann could thus be used to help build a socialist consciousness, regardless of their personal political beliefs. What counted was what they revealed about the wider social context their characters moved in, and the many pressures they had to cope with in their daily lives. As Lukács (1963: 78) noted approvingly of Mann, his fictional world *"is free from transcendental reference: place, time and detail are rooted firmly in a particular social and historical situation."* Mann, therefore, can be forgiven his bourgeois mentality; the notoriously unhistorical Kafka, however, cannot be. In the latter, the transcendental reference seems to imply that humankind has no control at all over its destiny, being instead at the mercy of mysterious forces—in the manner of the hapless protagonists of *The Trial* (1925) and *The Castle* (1926). This is a message of metaphysical pessimism that no Marxist can accept, because it denies the possibility of changing the course of history for the better.

As an aesthetic, critical realism is a considerable improvement on the doctrine of socialist realism, which *did* demand the reproduction of the communist party line (although to be fair, this was applied more to living authors than to the past). A.A. Zhdanov's (1977: 21) instruction to Soviet authors in 1934 that they must become *"engineers of human souls"* in the service of communism, has haunted Marxist aesthetics ever since. The artist as overt propagandist is not a popular idea within either the artistic or critical community. It certainly receives no support from Lukács, who, after Stalin's death particularly (for obvious reasons he was forced to be more circumspect beforehand), can be quite scathing about what fidelity to the socialist realist aesthetic could conjure up in literary terms:

> an otherwise interesting novel would be fatally marred by a scene in which a woman on a collective farm rejected the prize of a lamb she had herself brought up because communal is dearer to her heart than private

property. Or a group of young Komsomols set out to win a harvest competition; they succeed in this by giving up their lunch-hour—only the strict orders of the supervisor can make them take some food and have a proper rest. The supervisor regards their zeal as an indication of the imminence of communism. Yet we are told that this collective farm is situated in a backward part of the country. (Lukács, 1963: 129-30)

To Lukács (1963: 130) this is revolutionary romanticism rather than realism of any description, and it hinders rather than inspires the development of a socialist consciousness. Close reading of Balzac and Mann is far preferable to such wish fulfillment, which was more likely to induce an attitude of cynicism in the audience than ideological identification or reinforcement.

If considerably more sophisticated and generous in spirit than its counterpart, Lukács' theory of realism is not without its faults either. It is still fairly judgmental (although as he pointed out to a friend, "*I never pass judgment on a writer before I have studied him very thoroughly*" (Lukács, 1980: 184), and he had his blind spots as a critic, most notoriously over modernism. He refused to believe the latter could fulfill his criteria for literary value by means other than realism—which he defined on a broadly 19th-century model, with careful selection of detail by the author and a sense of "typicality" in the characterization (neither being the most precise of formulations for the sympathetic author to follow, unfortunately enough). Modernism, in Lukács' opinion, led to "*the destruction of literature as such*" (Lukács, 1963: 45): hence his denunciation of Kafka, Samuel Beckett, James Joyce, William Faulkner, and many other modernist icons.

Lukács' anti-modernist bias led to his well-documented clash with Bertolt Brecht in the 1930s, which made glaringly apparent the aesthetic fault line between Western and Soviet Marxism on this issue (ironically enough, given Lukács' key role in the development of Western Marxism).[9] Where Lukács saw realism, Brecht saw instead the tyranny of tradition: "*Were we to copy the style of these realists,*" Brecht noted of Lukács' championship of 19th-century authors like Sir Walter Scott, Stendhal, and Balzac, "*we would no longer be realists*" (Brecht, 1974: 51). Brecht's point was that literature was an enterprise in process, not a fixed set of procedures, which could not, or should not, be questioned by each new generation of authors. When cultural circumstances changed so should aesthetic theories, otherwise they would simply decline into dogma and lose any subversive force they may once have had: "*Methods become exhausted; stimuli no longer work,*" in Brecht's crisp summation (Brecht, 1974). Epic theater, with its deliberately un-lifelike quality and foregrounding of all the mechanisms of dramatic production (the "Alienation Effect"), was Brecht's riposte to the reactionaries, and it earned him the enmity of Lukács.

Ultimately, it would have to be said that critical realism is in the service of a monist rather than a pluralist worldview.[10] Lukács appreciates diversity only if it can be turned to account by the communist political project: Mann's bourgeois outlook, but not Kafka's. The goal is still the dictatorship of the proletariat, and there is that characteristic classical Marxist tendency to regard the proletariat as a homogeneous group for whom blanket prescriptions can be devised by theorists.

I would like to suggest that agonism could fill a similar role to Lukács' criteria for literary value, but this time around for a post-Marxist aesthetic, and, crucially, without the same judgmental tone that we find present even in Lukács. This is entirely appropriate for a movement that wants to retain the spirit of Marxism but without its doctrinaire qualities, particularly the methodological straitjacket classical Marxism tends to place on interpreters (even relatively independent-minded ones like Lukács). Post-Marxists would value texts most for their ability to articulate the agonistic relations of a society, but without necessarily seeing these as falling into some neat and tidy scheme where value judgments could be read off mechanically by the critic according to the prevailing party orthodoxy: dominant ideology and exploited masses confronting each other in monolithic fashion across the class divide. The politics of the text will not be so straightforward from a post-Marxist position; the discourse will be far less predictable (oriented toward pluralism rather than monism), and the dialectic of history will have to be considered open, and even wayward, rather than teleological. There *is* an agonistic dimension to Lukács, but it remains shackled to a very precise cultural schema that acts to restrict interpretive subtlety, even in as sensitive an interpreter as Lukács was capable of being. We know who is going to win, in other words—or at least, who is *supposed* to win.

AGONISM AND *THE PILGRIM'S PROGRESS*

We focus now on literary history, to see what we find when we look at a famous work of fiction like *The Pilgrim's Progress* from the perspective of discourse theory. Do agonistic relations feature there at the very origins of the English novel tradition?[11] Is an authoritarian order resisted? The answer in both cases is yes. Agonistic relations certainly play a very significant role in the narrative, which is at once an allegory of the Christian life (Protestant variety) and of the precarious situation of the nonconformist community under the Restoration settlement of the 1660s and 1670s. The basic setting of that narrative is a journey by a tormented individual, Christian, from the City of Destruction to the Celestial City, where he hopes to be received into the ranks of the spiritual elect. On the way, Christian is assailed by a large cast-list of characters, the majority of them hostile to his "progress," and he is continually forced to debate the rationale for his journey: in effect, to defend his ideological position, heavily based as this is in this turbulent historical period on his religious belief. Throughout the narrative, he is almost constantly in resist mode, as it were, refusing the various compromises and temptations he is regularly being offered by fellow travelers; as when the smooth-talking Worldly Wiseman puts the case for the quiet life:

> But why wilt thou seek for ease this way, seeing so many dangers attend it, especially, since (hadst thou but patience to hear me) I could direct thee to the obtaining of what thou desirest, without the dangers that thou in this way wilt run thy self into: yea, and the remedy is at hand. Besides, I will add, that instead of those dangers, thou shalt meet with much safety, friendship, and content. ... Why in yonder Village (the Village is named *Morality*) there dwells a Gentleman, whose name is *Legality*, a very judicious man (and a man of a very good name) that has skill to help men off with such burdens as thine are, from their shoulders: yea, to my knowledge he hath done a great deal of good this way. (Bunyan, 1678/1960: Part I, 19)

Although Christian is briefly swayed by Wiseman's line of argument, it is a recipe for self-indulgence and political disengagement that is incompatible with his belief system; as the figure of Evangelist, his mentor, is forced to make plain to him before Christian commits an unpardonable lapse from grace by giving up his journey:

> Mr. *Worldly Wiseman* is an alien, and Mr. *Legality* a cheat. ... Believe me, there is nothing in all this noise, that thou hast heard of this sottish man, but a design to beguile thee of thy Salvation, by turning thee from the way in which I had set thee. (Bunyan, 1678/1960: Part I, 23-4)

The narrative is largely structured around a series of set-piece debates, such as the one with Worldly Wiseman just presented, in which Christian comes to demonstrate considerable skill in making his opponents reveal themselves ideologically by pointed, not to say loaded, questions and extensive biblical reference that none of them can match. Thus the character of Ignorance, a rather innocuous soul who seems to bear no ill-will toward anyone, is shown through some deft rhetorical exchanges to be someone lacking any depth of religious conviction; someone happy enough to follow the conventional system of his day, whatever that might happen to be. Ignorance is unmistakably a conformist; a personality type who can only be despised by the nonconformist Christian:

> I know my Lords will, and I have been a good Liver, I pay every man his own; I Pray, Fast, pay Tithes, and give Alms, and have left my

> Countrey, for whither I am going. ... [B]e content to follow the Religion
> of your Countrey, and I will follow the Religion of mine. I hope all will
> be well. (Bunyan, 1678/1960: Part I, 123-4)

Harmless as he may seem, Ignorance is in fact part of the Restoration
authoritarian order, a walking representative of its hegemonic control over
contemporary English society where religious pluralism is being outlawed
in the name of national security. To be other than apathetic is to be a threat
to the system. Christian's verbal sparring with Ignorance evokes memories
of the Civil War of the 1640s, when religious division was rife throughout
the English nation, and Ignorance's irritation at Christian's relentless prob-
ing of his beliefs has a much wider political resonance: "*You go so fast, I cannot keep pace with you; do you go on before, I must stay a while behind*"
(Bunyan, 1678/1960: Part I, 149).

Occasionally, the confrontations spill over from the verbal to the physical, as in Christian's battle with the demon Apollyon, where the hero is
forced to fight for his very life against a creature who threatens him that, "*I
am void of fear in this matter, prepare thy self to dye, for I swear by my
Infernal Den, that thou shalt go no further, here will I spill thy soul*" (Bunyan,
1678/1960: Part I, 59). The authoritarian order declares itself uncompromis-
ingly at this point. To put it in Althusserian terms, having managed to deflect
the arguments put forward on behalf of the Ideological State Apparatus,
Christian must deal with the altogether cruder attentions of the Repressive
State Apparatus.[12] The latter does not take prisoners: it is plainly, and quite
unashamedly, antagonistic, the brute force underlying the surface civility of
the Restoration regime. If neither Worldly Wiseman nor Ignorance can do
the trick of turning nonconformists away from their mission, Apollyon is
always waiting in the wings to quash dissent by recourse to violence.

The Repressive State Apparatus is seen in action again when Christian
and his fellow pilgrim Faithful arrive in the town of Vanity-Fair. There, the
two nonconformists are met with overt hostility, their criticisms of the populace's sybaritic and irreligious lifestyle landing them in what is little better
than a show trial. Thus, we have Envy's deposition against Faithful in front
of the judge, Lord Hategood:

> My Lord, this man, notwithstanding his plausible name, is one of the
> vilest men in our Countrey; He neither regardeth Prince nor People,
> Law nor Custom; but doth all that he can to possess all men with cer-
> tain of his disloyal notions, which he in the general calls Principles of
> Faith and Holiness. And in particular, I heard him once my self affirm,
> That Christianity, and the Customs of our Town of Vanity, were
> Diametrically opposite, and could not be reconciled. By which saying,
> my Lord, he doth at once, not only condemn all our laudable doings,
> but us in the doing of them. (Bunyan, 1678/1960: Part I, 93)

It comes as no surprise when the judge is soon instructing the jury that, "*you see he disputeth against our Religion; and for the Treason he hath confessed, he deserveth to die the death*" (Bunyan, 1678/1960: Part I, 96). The jury proves only too ready to comply, and Faithful is promptly dispatched "*to the most cruel death that could be invented*" (Bunyan, 1678/1960: Part I, 97): an adversary force rendered totally invisible by a virulently anti-pluralist regime only too pleased to have an opportunity to demonstrate the extent of its power. Christian manages to escape from prison before a similar fate befalls him, but he is left in no doubt of the lengths to which the establishment will go to protect its position. It is all the more worrying to that establishment that Christian and Faithful have managed to make some converts to their cause while in Vanity-Fair, and indeed as we find out in Part II of the narrative when Christian's wife, Christiana, and her party arrive there on their pilgrimage, a change of consciousness subsequently does take place in the town ("*Persecution not so hot at Vanity Fair as formerly*," as the text's marginal note approvingly informs us [Bunyan, 1678/1960: Part II, 275]).

Bunyan's agonism is in the service of the nonconformist cause, which in his time is being persecuted by the Restoration regime of the Stuart monarchy and the establishment Anglican church.[13] Through the agency of a steady stream of characters that Christian meets on the road, this regime is shown to be advocating conformity, with its religious belief being prone to worldliness and compromise—what the period called "latitudinarianism."[14] We have what I have called elsewhere a "conflict of narratives," where competing factions within English society are locked in a struggle to determine the longer term future of the nation (Sim, 1998b: 67). The rights and wrongs of the various narrative positions are very much open to interpretation. One might be attracted to the unshakeable integrity of Christian's outlook, or to the pragmatism of his opponents (and the latter was the more successful, politically speaking, even if nonconformism did put down deep and lasting roots in English culture). What is important aesthetically, however, is that the agonistic relations of that society are laid bare. Critical realism would see this as a classic encounter between radicalism and the dominant ideology, and it is true that many Marxist critics have adopted Bunyan as an ally in the class struggle (the historian Christopher Hill being a notable example).[15] From a post-Marxist, discourse theory perspective, however, it is much more complicated than that. Yes, Christian is resisting an authoritarian order, but he is doing so in the name of yet another authoritarian order: Neither Christian nor his creator is a pluralist, and the default position on both sides of the debate is distinctly antagonistic in form. Co-existence is not what either has in mind; control over the other is the common objective. Worldly Wiseman and his associates want to rid English society of enthusiasts such as Christian; Christian wants a society ruled by the dictates of the Biblical "Word."

An analysis of the text reveals incommensurable narratives in open conflict with each other: a culture on the face of it inimical to adversarial politics. Resistance by nonconformists helps to keep the Restoration regime unsettled, but we must not glamorize it: in some respects nonconformism as practiced by Christian and his creator is close to being a form of fundamentalism[16] (note the obsession with the authority of the "Word," which is taken to resolve all disputes instantly: *"Except the word of God beareth witness in this matter, other Testimony is of no value"* [Bunyan, 1678/1960: Part I, 145]). The interrogation of the political by the ethical *does* have an end for this author, even if in real terms it is only realizable in fiction of conspicuously antagonistic intent.[17] Perhaps we have the makings here of the paradox that Mouffe wanted to preserve—uncomfortable though it may be. Not the least intriguing aspect of that paradox is the complex dialectic that is being played out between agonism and antagonism: a dialectic that is to be passed on to the new literary form of the novel, with its recognizably adversarial agenda. Maintaining that dialectic is what counts; as long as it is in operation then agonism is not being absorbed into the antagonistic ideological machine (Apollyon on the grand scale), and there is a "vibrant clash" of ideological positions to be recorded.

CONCLUSION: FOR AN AGONISTIC AESTHETICS

The critical question that discourse theory has to face is how to bring about the desired condition of agonistic pluralism. And it has to be admitted that Mouffe, along with the discourse theory community at large, is somewhat vague as to how we get there from where we are now. Vague as well about how we prevent agonism from hardening into an unproductive antagonism with the specter of authoritarianism lurking behind it. Steering between authoritarianism and consensus will make formidable demands on the left, not least in terms of the very different mind-set it will require from that of the past, when it was programmed for antagonism in the political arena against an easily defined, and just as easily reviled, enemy. That era, with its "evident truths," is now long gone and the task of rewriting the left's agenda, while still remaining true to the spirit of Marx's critique of unbridled *laissez-faire* capitalism and its impact on the vulnerable, overshadows all other theoretical concerns. As suggested earlier, Islamic fundamentalism may well present the most pressing problem on that score for the immediate future.

But none of this need deter us from using the concept of agonistic pluralism as an analytical tool in the aesthetic domain, and building up an

Заметьте

increasingly complex picture of the discursive formation in which the text is operating, as we saw with the case of Bunyan. When we move on to the novel proper in the early eighteenth century, a particularly rich site for discourse-theoretical analysis opens up. The novel is steeped in the sociopolitical concerns of the age, with individualism, the nature of the social bond, and the complexities of gender relations to the forefront (Defoe's work providing an excellent example of these in narrative play).[18] To some extent the critic becomes an adjudicator of intra-cultural conflict. Yes, there are implicit value judgments being made here (for agonism, against antagonism), but they are designed to open up rather than close off debate, and I take that to be the great selling point of the discourse theory approach to cultural analysis. The *"never-ending interrogation of the political by the ethical"* can only be beneficial for our culture in general, and the debate needs to be continued in as many areas of enquiry as possible.

NOTES

1. As in Jean-François Lyotard's concept of the "little narrative" (*petit récit*); see, for example, Lyotard (1984).
2. See Part I of Sim (1998a) for a selection of expressions of that displeasure. I deal with the issue at greater length in Sim (2000).
3. For a discussion of some of the difficulties involved, see Sim (2004).
4. See, for example, Karl (1975). Authors such as Defoe and Richardson are seen to champion, for the period, the culturally radical phenomenon of individualism, which has its roots in 17th-century religious nonconformity and the tradition of spiritual autobiography (see narratives such as *Robinson Crusoe* [1719/1972], *Moll Flanders* [1722/1981], and *Pamela* [1740/2001]).
5. For use of the term, see Connolly (1993). Dissensus fills a similar role in Lyotard (1984).
6. Just how much damage this process can do to vulnerable Third World nations is traced in detail in Stiglitz (2002), and Klein (2000).
7. Connolly (1991: x) similarly put the case for an "agonistic democracy" designed to *"disrupt consensual ideals of political engagement and aspiration."*
8. Although highly critical of that authoritarianism, Zygmunt Bauman (1992: 175) is nevertheless concerned at the political vacuum that has been created by the collapse of the Soviet bloc. His argument is that the resulting condition of *"living without an alternative"* has merely served to encourage the more extreme elements in Western capitalism. Of late, however, Islamic fundamentalism has begun to fill that vacuum and provide just such an alternative, resurrecting something like the Cold War mentality in the process (as in President George W. Bush's tactless call for a "crusade" against Islamic terrorism in the aftermath of 9/11).

9. Lukács' (1923) *History and Class Consciousness* spurred the Frankfurt School (Theodor W. Adorno and Max Horkheimer in particular) to develop the more philosophical approach to Marxist theory that is the hallmark of Western Marxism. Lukács, of course, spent much of his life distancing himself from a work that was so swiftly, and savagely, denounced by the Soviet authorities for the sins of "old Hegelianism," "revisionism," and "ultra-leftism." Given that he spent most of his life from the early 1930s onward living under Soviet regimes (first in Russia, then in Hungary), it seems reasonable to regard Lukács' later writings as part of the Eastern bloc tradition of thought.

10. I discuss Lukács' concept of critical realism in more detail in Sim (1994; see particularly chapters 3-5).

11. I explore Bunyan's importance for this tradition in more detail in Sim (1990) and Sim and Walker (2000).

12. See Althusser (1971).

13. Legislation was hastily drawn up after the Restoration of the Stuart monarchy in 1660 to curb the activities of the nonconformists. The Clarendon Code, a series of Acts of Parliament passed in the 1660s (e.g., the Conventicle Act, 1664), had the effect of criminalizing the substantial nonconformist minority in the country for its failure to attend Church of England services. As an indication of the authorities' determination to stamp out nonconformity, Bunyan was imprisoned in Bedford Jail from 1660-1672 for refusing to give up lay preaching to his Baptist congregation (an activity he promptly resumed on his release).

14. The character of latitudinarianism can be deduced from the remarks of the 17th-century Anglican clergyman (and one-time nonconformist), the Rev. Edward Fowler, that whatever actions "*are commanded by the custom of the place we live in, or commanded by superiors, or made by any circumstance convenient to be done, our Christian liberty consists in this, that we have leave to do them*" (quoted in Hill, 1988: 131). Bunyan angrily rejected such principles in works like *A Defence of the Doctrine of Justification by Faith* (1672/1989), arguing that he considered himself answerable to a higher, divine authority instead. The figure of Pliable in *The Pilgrim's Progress*, who abandons the pilgrimage he is undertaking with Christian when faced with the challenge set by the Slough of Despond, indicates that Bunyan equates latitudinarianism with a lack of moral fiber.

15. For Hill, Bunyan's "*deep roots in his own popular culture, and in the social realities from which that culture grew, together with his millenarian Puritanism, tenacious especially in defeat, combined to make* The Pilgrim's Progress *not only a foundation document of the English working-class movement but also a text which spoke to millions of this poor oppressed people whom Bunyan, like Winstanley, wished to address*" (Hill, 1988: 380).

16. A topic I followed up in more detail in an earlier work (Sim, 2004, chapter 3).

17. See also Bunyan's other major works of fiction: *The Life and Death of Mr Badman* (1680/1988), and *The Holy War* (1682/1980). The dialectic of agonism and antagonism is particularly strongly represented in the latter.

18. For more on this, see Sim (1990).

REFERENCES

Althusser, L. (1971) *Lenin and Philosophy and Other Essays* (B. Brewster, Trans.). London: Verso.

Bauman, Z. (1992) *Intimations of Postmodernity*. London: Routledge.

Brecht, B. (1974) 'Against Lukács' (S. Hood, Trans.), *New Left Review* (84): 33-53.

Bunyan, J. (1678-1684/1960) *The Pilgrim's Progress*, Parts I and II, J.B. Wharey and R. Sharrock (Eds). Oxford: Clarendon Press.

Bunyan, J. (1682/1980) *The Holy War*, R. Sharrock and J.F. Forrest (Eds). Oxford: Clarendon Press.

Bunyan, J. (1680/1988) *The Life and Death of Mr Badman*, J.F. Forrest and R. Sharrock (Eds). Oxford: Clarendon Press.

Bunyan, J. (1672/1989) 'A Defence of the Doctrine of Justification by Faith,' in *The Miscellaneous Works of John Bunyan*, vol. IV, T.L. Underwood (Ed.). Oxford: Clarendon Press.

Carroll, L. (1865/1971) *Alice's Adventures in Wonderland, and, Through the Looking-Glass and What Alice Found There*, R.L. Green (Ed). Oxford: Oxford University Press.

Connolly, W.E. (1991) *Identity/Difference: Democratic Negotiations of Political Paradox*. Ithaca, NY, London: Cornell University Press.

Connolly, W.E. (1993) *The Augustinian Imperative: A Reflection on the Politics of Morality*. Newbury Park, CA, London: Sage.

Defoe, D. (1719/1972) *The Life and Strange Surprizing Adventures of Robinson Crusoe*, J. Donald Crowley (Ed.). Oxford: Oxford University Press.

Defoe, D. (1722/1981) *The Fortunes and Misfortunes of the Famous Moll Flanders*, G.A. Starr (Ed.). Oxford: Oxford University Press.

Hill, C. (1988) *A Turbulent, Seditious and Factious People: John Bunyan and His Church*. Oxford: Clarendon Press.

Kafka, F. (1999) *The Castle* (W. and E. Muir, Trans.). London: Vintage.

Kafka, F. (1999) *The Trial* (W. and E. Muir, Trans.). London: Vintage.

Karl, F.R. (1975) *A Reader's Guide to the Development of the English Novel in the Eighteenth Century*. London: Thames and Hudson.

Klein, N. (2000) *No Logo*. London: HarperCollins.

Laclau, E., Mouffe, C. (1985) *Hegemony and Socialist Strategy: Towards a Radical Democratic Politics*. London: Verso.

Lukács, G. (1963) *The Meaning of Contemporary Realism* (J. and N. Mander, Trans.). London: Merlin Press.

Lukács, G. (1971) *History and Class Consciousness: Studies in Marxist Dialectics* (R. Livingstone, Trans.). London: Merlin Press.

Lukács, G. (1980) *Essays on Realism* (D. Fernbach, Trans.), R. Livingstone (Ed). London: Lawrence and Wishart.

Lyotard, J-F. (1984) *The Postmodern Condition: A Report on Knowledge* (G. Bennington and B. Massumi, Trans.). Manchester: Manchester University Press.

Mouffe, C. (2000) *The Democratic Paradox*. London: Verso.

Richardson, S. (1740/2001) *Pamela, or, Virtue Rewarded*, T. Keymer and A. Wakely (Eds). Oxford: Oxford University Press.

Sim, S. (1990) *Negotiations with Paradox: Narrative Practice and Narrative Form in Bunyan and Defoe*. Hemel Hempstead: Harvester Wheatsheaf.

Sim, S. (1994) *Modern Cultural Theorists: Georg Lukács*. Hemel Hempstead: Harvester Wheatsheaf.

Sim, S. (Ed) (1998a) *Post-Marxism: A Reader*. Edinburgh: Edinburgh University Press.

Sim, S. (1998b) 'Bunyan, Lyotard, and the Conflict of Narratives (or, Postmodernising Bunyan),' *Bunyan Studies* 8: 67-81.

Sim, S. (2000) *Post-Marxism: An Intellectual History*. London, New York: Routledge.

Sim, S. (2004) *Fundamentalist World: The New Dark Age of Dogma*. Cambridge: Icon Press.

Sim, S., Walker, D. (2000) *Bunyan and Authority: The Rhetoric of Dissent and the Legitimation Crisis in Seventeenth-Century England*. New York, Bern: Peter Lang.

Stiglitz, J.E. (2002) *Globalization and its Discontents*. Harmondsworth: Penguin.

Zhdanov, A.A. (1977) 'Soviet Literature—the Richest in Ideas, the Most Advanced Literature,' pp. 15-24 in M. Gorki et al., *Soviet Writers' Congress 1934: The Debate on Socialist Realism and Modernism in the Soviet Union*, H.G. Scott (Ed). London: Lawrence and Wishart.

13

LITERARY IMAGINARIES

On Experiencing (I)dterminacy
in German Modernism

Sascha Bru

In his essay *Effect of the Real*, Roland Barthes (1968) highlighted a dominant anthropological need to identify with a textual "reality effect." Limpid, familiarizing views on reality and history that give rise to such an effect, Barthes further stressed, are conventionalized constructs emanating from within and not from outside the realm of cultural representation. As much as his claims are commonplace in literary studies today,[1] it is curious to observe that few scholars have ventured to describe a "society effect" in the wake of his essay. What (if any) conditions fix a discourse leading to such an effect? How (if at all) can discourse be said to convey a sense of society? And what kind of subject or reader is required for identification with a representation of society to be successful? These are just some of the queries that appear to underlie Ernesto Laclau's (1994) *Minding the Gap: The Subject of Politics*. Laclau's essay (written in cooperation with Lilian Zac) explicitly mentions a society effect and much like Barthes' essay underscores a generally felt need to belong to society, because it is this sense of belonging that establishes our identity and allows for agency. In line with Barthes, Laclau also asserted that the finite materiality of discourse prevents us from coinciding with the full complexity of society as a whole. For one thing, no discourse can ever represent or include all identities present in society at large. Because of this, society, too, always shows itself as a discursive construct, not in the least in literary texts. By consequence, it must be possible to spell out some rules of society's design in literature as well.

The society effect, as I present it here, is a quasi-concept open to ongoing elaboration. I intend to provide no more than a sketch of it. My primal concern is to suggest an anthropological framework within which future inquiries can inscribe themselves, by showing how textual (in)determinacy can be related to the experience of the society effect in reading. Gerald Graff (1990: 165) noted that in the wake of poststructuralism indeterminacy has come to bespeak "*a limitation or failure of a text to fulfill its purpose. … The concept of indeterminacy proposes that a radical limitation is built into the activity of literary interpretation, whose very attempt to find a determinate meaning in literary works prevents it from succeeding in this enterprise.*" Graff then pointed out that before one can speak of indeterminacy, the need for determinacy and successful interpretation must be recognized and charted first. In this chapter, I put forward that the attempt to give a text a determinate meaning runs parallel with readers' attempts to position themselves within the representation(s) of society in it. Entering a text is entering a discursive hegemony that makes sense of the social. Laclau called such discursive hegemonies social imaginaries, comparing them with imaginative horizons against the background of which the social makes sense (Laclau, 1990: 64-65). Charles Taylor (2002), drawing on Benedict Anderson (1983), described a social imaginary "*not [as] a set of ideas; rather it is what enables, through making sense of, the practices of society.*" An imaginary is "*shared by large groups of people, if not the whole of society,*" and it presents "*the ways in which people imagine their social existence, how they fit together with others, how things go on between them and their fellows, the expectations that are normally met, and the deeper normative notions and images that underlie these expectations*" (Taylor, 2002: 91, 106). Social imaginaries in literary texts do not, of course, necessarily coincide with those of readers. This is why describing the process of identification with literary imaginaries is always as tentative and overdetermined as the study of hegemony itself. Meaning is never fixed or simply inherent to a text. It is always the result of a "circulation" between social formations, readers, and texts (Heath, 1977-78: 74). When we are dealing with historical literary texts, no doubt some knowledge of historical, extra-textual[2] discourses from the period that generated them is constitutive to our reading of them today. As Stanley Fish (1982) and scholars working in the wake of Pierre Bourdieu argued, the knowledge drawn on in reading much depends on the reader's educational background (or, more generally, his or her "habitus") and on the "interpretive communities" to which the reader belongs. As Derek Attridge

(2004) claimed, what is brought into play in reading further depends on what kind of instrumentality or purpose a reader attributes to a text. In brief, reading is a highly overdetermined practice or process. To claim, then, that readers tend to first look for determinacy, to create a sense of familiarity, would be careless, not in the least because it holds the risk of repeating Wolfgang Iser's reception-aesthetics, which quite consistently assumed a centered *"liberal humanist"* or *"implied"* reader to ground the necessity of determinacy (Belsey, 1980: 36). Laclau's positing of the Lacanian constitutive lack of the subject differs considerably from this "humanist" approach. For Laclau, it is precisely the subject's ongoing attempt to overcome its lack that replaces the need for determinacy. And in the end, this attempt helps to explain why and how the society effect proves so central to the act of reading.[3]

Turning to the complex literary representation of self and community in German "high" modernist and late realist writing, my focal point will be the work of Thomas Mann and Franz Kafka. As Georg Lukács once observed, sooner or later we are confronted with the question *Franz Kafka or Thomas Mann?* (Lukács, 1963).[4] Indeed, many scholars tend to oppose the former's "avant-gardist" to the latter's "realist" portrayal of self and society.[5] (See, among others, de Angelis, 1977; Hargraves, 2001; Heller, 1966; Pfeiffer, 1962). Claudia Liebrand and Franziska Schössler (2004: 15, author's translation) noted that *"Thomas Mann and Franz Kafka are traditionally understood in a relationship of mutual exclusion and opposition that also marks the contours of modernism."* Long after Lukács critics have tended to side with either Kafka or Mann, mainly because opinions differ on the counter-hegemonic potential of the strategies of representation employed by both writers (see, e.g., Adorno, 1970; Deleuze & Guattari, 1975; Fetzler, 1996). That the opposition between Mann and Kafka persists to this day suggests that Mann's "critical realism" and Kafka's "minor literature" provide more than just modernist documents or artifacts. Frequently, scholars characterize Kafka's writings as the apogee of indeterminacy, as the ultimate limit experience, whereas Mann is traditionally read as an author voicing determinacy. These features are most often explained by referring to Kafka's and Mann's different methods, styles and rhetoric, or to the way contextual elements infiltrated their work. Evidently, both formal elements, such as Kafka's style indirect libre or his frequent montage of characters' stories,[6] and contextual elements, as exemplified in Mann's encyclopedic grasp, contribute to the markedly different yet persistent society effects elicited by their respective works. In this chapter, I am not so much concerned with the ways the society effect is created, however, but with the way it affects the practice of reading. Drawing on Laclau, I would in particular like to illustrate how Mann and Kafka give rise to (in)determinacy not only through the use of formal or contextual elements, but above all by conveying a divergent view of society. This point is, of course, difficult to miss. Less obvious, however, is a rereading of Mann and Kafka in light of the society effect that shows them to be allies rather than adversaries.[7] Together, they give us a glimpse of the complex *act* of identification with representations of society. A glimpse, to be sure, is all we will ever get, since representations of self and society always occur through the staging of communities, which function both as *the basis of* and *in lieu of* society at large.[8] Hence, it is with an assessment of the depiction of community in literature that we will set out.

THE LOSS AND PERSISTENCE OF COMMUNITY: LUKÁCS' TWO MODERNISMS

Modernism's representation of self and community has been of interest to scholars at least since its neo-Marxist "con-text" (Lunn, 1982). In line with many Marxist enquiries, sociologically oriented scholars commonly articulate the modernist representation of self and community by referring to the dislocational and traumatic impact of modernity.[9] In response to the expansion of the mass market and the acceleration of the process of rationalization, new technologies and the fragmentation of intersubjective experience, modernism is traditionally said to convey a deeply felt alienation. Numerous modernists express anxiety, caused by a sense of constriction. Georg Kaiser's (1912) major expressionist drama *From Morn to Midnight*, for example, characterizes Weimar—once the town of Goethe, Schiller, and liberal ideals—as a site of imprisonment and vulgar materialism. Others voiced a feeling of being swept along by a brutal wave of raw energy. Georg Heym's poems *The Demons of the Cities* and *The God of the City*, for instance, evoke how a place of rational order is turned into a stage for irrational chaos. Similar apocalyptic scenes are encountered in Alfred Kubin's (1908) novel *The Other Side*. The desacralization of nature (as depicted in Kafka's [1922] *The Castle* and Robert Musil's chapter 40 in *The Mann without Qualities* [1924-42], traditional communal relationships ripped apart by strange forces such as demonic women (in Frank Wedekind's [1903] *Tragedies of the Sex*), disease (in Mann's [1913-14] *The Magic Mountain*), and the uncanny power of the unconscious (in Rainer Maria Rilke's [1922] *Duino Elegies*), all testify to a crisis in the representation of the social fabric and to the loss of a sense of belonging. That this loss should prove so central a theme in modernist texts highlights the fact that their narrators and characters experience difficulties in identifying with common "bourgeois" community forms such as the family or society life and the optimistic bourgeois outlooks on society. The same theme also accentuates, however, that a willingness or desire to belong to *a* community is very much prominent. As

Michael Levenson (1991: xii) observed: "*The dislocation of the self within society is recapitulated within modernist forms*" which nevertheless express "*the nostalgic longing for a whole self*." Lamented in these narratives is thus the eclipse of an "organic" *Gemeinschaft* in modern industrial society, which appears to suggest (as Ferdinand Tönnies foresaw) that even art has become incapable of expressing and creating a community (Tönnies, 1988).

In *The Handkerchief*, Walter Benjamin (1932) observed that "*if stories are to thrive, there must be work, order and subordination. ... Another reason no proper stories can be heard today is that things no longer last the way they should*" (Benjamin, 1999: 658). If one thing is to be observed about the narratives of Kafka and Mann, however, it is the fact that they last. Both authors' experience of and response to modernity is echoed to this day through their writings. In some way, their work still manages to convey a sense of modernism's angst. Lukács' uncompromising (1957) essay *Franz Kafka or Thomas Mann?* nevertheless radically opposed both works. His oppositional reading of both is, admittedly, very schematic and, in contrast with much of his earlier writings, framed by a rather narrow humanist-Marxist outlook. Pushing this narrow framework to the background, I nonetheless believe that his bifurcation provides an interesting starting point for a more in-depth analysis of Kafka and Mann. As seen earlier, Lukács' diametrical opposition between Kafka and Mann still stands with many critics. In my view, this remarkably persistent reader-response is related to the society effect in Mann and Kafka. On the one hand, Lukács noted, modernists like Kafka voiced their alienation and angst in *indeterminate* terms, that is, without making explicit the settings and possible social causes of their alienation. Through a far-reaching selection of detail, these writers also fail or refuse to arrive at the formulation of an alternative outlook on society. At first glance, many German modernists other than Kafka appear to illustrate Lukács' point. (To be sure, Lukács' own illustrations are drawn from non-German writers too; next to Gottfried Benn, Samuel Beckett, Albert Camus, André Gide, D.H. Lawrence, and many others are mentioned.) Numerous characters and narrators in modernism seem convinced of their own sanity in the face of a world that has gone mad. We need but think of Rilke's (1910) "hero" in *The Notebook of Malte Laurids Brigge*, who is "*so profoundly affected by the dislocated insanity of modern Paris that the shock uncovers the fragmentary nature and latent paranoia of his own personality: insane city and unhinged self are mirror images of one another*" (Sheppard, 2000: 15). Michael Fischer in Alfred Döblin's story *The Murder of a Buttercup* (c. 1905), Doctor Billig in Richard Huelsenbeck's (1922) *Doctor Billig am Ende*, the psychopath in Heym's short story *The Madman* (c. 1911) and Anton Gross in Franz Jung's *The Case of Anton Gross* (c. 1920) are other examples. Yet without doubt the best known example is found in Kafka's (1925) *The Trial*, to which I return further on. In all of these narratives, the main character discovers within himself an uncontrollable urge toward self-destruction caused by him losing touch with the social fabric. The latter, in turn, is quite consistently evoked in elliptic and "atmospheric" terms. In opposition to this avant-gardist branch in modernism, of which Kafka is seen as symptomatic, Lukács posited a second, *determinate* type of writing, which does arrive at a constructive analysis and the suggestion of a way forward. Calling Mann one of the last descendants of 19th-century realism, Lukács characterized his work as a "critical realism," which—contrary to the *"metaphysical Nothingness," "the vague, timeless world"* of the *"avant-gardist"* phantasms of Kafka and others— stages a world in which *"place, time and detail are rooted firmly in a particular social and historical situation"* (Lukács, 1963: 78). With Mann, we always find ourselves in a world anchored in a commonsensical society. Even when the author is tempted to explore the darker regions of modern experiences, as in *Doctor Faustus* (1947), with its move toward the demonic personified in the vanguard composer Adrian Leverkühn, the narrator always carefully traces the social causes of aberrant human behavior.[10]

In summary, to Lukács German literature from the first half of the 20th century bears witness to both the loss and persistence of the unity of self and community. In Mann's critical realism, community and self are posited in a relationship of determinacy made possible by references to other social discourses. In the vanguard phantasms of Kafka and others, self and community are portrayed in indeterminate terms. In the first instance, a way to overcome alienation is staged and the implied ("bourgeois") reader is offered the possibility to position himself within the representation of society. In the second, the subject is faced with the impossibility of overcoming alienation. As a consequence, Lukács implied, readers are not able to identify with Kafka's work, except in the negative, that is, by doubling the angst-ridden experience of his narratives that position readers outside society. As Laclau correctly asserted in his essay *The Time is Out of Joint*, however, Lukács tended to fix *"human emancipation ... in its contents by a full-fledged ideology"* (Laclau, 1996: 80). As is seen here, Lukács not only clearly misreads or overlooks certain passages in Kafka, he also suggests that nothing in Mann is indeterminate. As Peter Zima (1999: 90) observed, Lukács gave the impression that *"his interpretations of these authors are the only possible ones, [while] it is perfectly possible ... to interpret Thomas Mann as a modernist similar to ... Kafka"* by taking into account literary polysemy. The question is not, however, how Mann and Kafka could be read as kindred writers. It is rather how Lukács' response to Mann's writings as determinate and Kafka's as indeterminate can be accounted for. This question could be answered by referring to Lukács' own (shifting) theory of History and Totality, the Concrete and the Typical.[11] A much more subtle response to it, however, is obtained by turning to Laclau.

THOMAS MANN'S CRITICAL REALISM

Like Lukács, Laclau appears to favor the critical realist branch of high modernist literature, as is suggested by his essay *Minding the Gap*, which cites extensively from Mann's *Doctor Faustus* in order to bring out *"the very center of the problematic of the subject"* in modernity (Laclau & Zac, 1994: 12). The passage Laclau quoted is borrowed from a dialogue between Adrian Leverkühn and Serenus Zeitblom on the revolutionary and the archaic in music. It is worth reiterating here, because the conclusions Laclau draws from it with regard to the subject may well hold for the reader as well:

> "It would be tragic," I said, "if unfruitfulness should be ever the result of freedom. But there is always the hope of the release of the productive powers, for the sake of which freedom is achieved." "True," [Leverkühn] responded. "And she does for a while achieve what she promised. But freedom is of course another word for subjectivity, and some fine day she does not hold any longer, some time or other she despairs of the possibility of being creative out of herself and seeks shelter and security in the objective. Freedom always inclines to dialectical reversals. She realizes herself very soon in constraint, fulfils itself in the subordination to law, rule, coercion, system—but to fulfills herself therein does not mean that she therefore ceases to be freedom."
> "In your opinion," I laughed: "So far as she knows. But actually, she is no longer freedom as little as dictatorship born out of revolution is still freedom."
> "Are you sure of it?" he asked. "But anyhow that is talking politics. In art, at least, the subjective and the objective intertwine to the point of being indistinguishable, one proceeds from the other and takes the character of the other, the subjective precipitates as objective and by genius is again awakened to spontaneity, 'dynamized,' as we say; it speaks all at once the language of the subjective. The musical conventions today destroyed were not always so objective, so objectively imposed. They were crystallizations of living experiences and, as such, long performed an office of vital importance: the task of organization. Organization is everything. Without it, there is nothing, least of all, art. And it was aesthetic subjectivity that took on the task, it undertook to organize the work out of itself, in freedom."
> "You are thinking of Beethoven." (Mann, 1968: 184-5, quoted in Laclau & Zac, 1994: 11)

As Laclau noted, this dialogue attests to the (Lacanian) constitutive lack of the subject as well as to the crucial difference between subject and identity. Mann opens by suggesting that the subject can only be free and creative if it can express itself autonomously. But as soon as it expresses itself creatively, the content of what is said becomes objective (in a "dialectical reversal"), leaving the subject alienated from its identity in its own creation or discourse. The writing subject, who through writing finds itself positioned next to its readers, must therefore not be confused with its identity. The former is characterized by a lack of determinacy; the latter is its positive (determinate) and discursive shape. Identity, furthermore, is only possible by identifying with a pre-existing set of conventions and with a given community. As Mann put it, freedom (identity) can only realize *"herself in the subordination to law, rule, coercion, system."* And yet, *"to fulfill herself therein does not mean she therefore ceases to be freedom."* Put differently, identity is only possible within a determinate social setting that fills the lack of the subject and subsequently opens up the possibility of acting and effecting social change. It is in the slip from subject to identity that the pleasure (Lacan's *jouissance*) of reading emerges. This is not to say, of course, that a reader would be an empty shell when he or she picks up a text. It would be equally difficult, however, not to take into account Coleridge's famous "suspense of disbelief." Indeed, a reader certainly has an identity before reading, but we can assume the reader to be willing to temporarily bracket this identity in favor of the narrative (see Bordwell, 1985). If the subject does not identify with any community in such instances, if it does not take in a standpoint *in* the community represented (as Lukács would have it), then it can only experience its own constitutive lack, and in that case *"there is nothing, least of all, art."*

Interestingly, Mann's assessment appears to account for the dystopic undertone encountered in Kafka and others (and doubled by the reader Lukács). When the subject loses touch with all outlook on the social, it is thrown upon itself to experience its lack and lose sanity. Mann further appeared to illustrate Laclau's distinction between two types of narratives providing subjects with an identity and outlook on society—the distinction, that is, between social imaginaries and myths. As we saw, social imaginaries are hegemonic discourses shaping the social and defining the subject's place within society. Myths, by contrast, are not (yet) hegemonic, because not enough subjects identify with them for these discourses to gain general social relevance (Laclau, 1990: 61-65). Imaginaries could thus be said to produce a much more convincing society effect than myths, whereas the latter proffer (potentially alternate) ways to construct such an effect.

At one point, Mann's *Lotte in Weimar* stages the dominant social imaginary under the French and the Prussians at the end of the Napoleonic period. Although anti-Napoleonic myths are not uncommon at this time and even though the French and the Prussians clearly form an oppressive force, the public appears to accept their dominance:

We peered through the curtains at the tumult in the streets, we heard the crashing gunfire and the braying of horns. The fighting soon passed from the streets to the park and presently beyond the city limits. The enemy, alas, won his accustomed victory. And actually, against our wills, it seemed to us like a triumph of order over rebellion—a childish and foolish rebellion, as the event had proved. "Order and quiet are good— no matter what one owes them." We had to provide for the billeting of the French troops, and the town was straightaway burdened to the utmost limit of its capacity. Not only heavy but long was the burden laid upon it. Still, there was peace; the streets were open till sundown, and the citizen might go about his business under the oppressive protection of his victors. (Mann, 1968b: 130-31, quoted in Laclau & Zac, 1994: 15)

However, when the anti-Napoleonic coalition troops approach the city, bringing with them an alternative outlook on society, important shifts in the narrator's opinion begin to show:

The nearer they drew, the less were they called barbarians, the more the sympathies and hopes of society veered towards them and away from the French. That of course was partly because we began to see in them the victors one might hope to placate—even from a distance. But even more, it was because we human beings are by nature submissive. We need to live in harmony with outward events and situations. We need to come to terms with power—and now fate itself seemed to be giving the signal for change. In the space of a few days the barbarians, the rebels against civilization, turned into liberators. Their successful advance brought to a bursting point the general enthusiasm for folk and father-land. (Mann, 1968b: 138, quoted in Laclau & Zac, 1994: 16)

As this shift exemplifies, subjects choose to elevate myths to the level of imaginaries when they need to come to terms with *power*. In what is a typical Gramscian view on power, Mann's *Lotte in Weimar* illustrates that subjects tend to submit willingly to power as long as "order" and "civilization" are preserved and identity (regardless of its shape) remains in place. Paradoxically, not so much the *content* of the subject's identity and outlook on society, but the fact that such an outlook *functions* and "fills" the subject's lack proves central here. However, content gains importance when subjects are offered a choice between several potential hegemonies. *Lotte in Weimar* also shows that myths have to demonstrate their ability "*to become a realistic alternative for the organization and management of the community. ... The dislocation created by the war had autonomized the general need for a continuity of the communitarian order from the alternative political projects that attempted to guarantee such continuity*" (Laclau & Zac, 1994: 16).

When we briefly turn to Marcel Proust's *Remembrance of Things Past* (1913-27), we find similar shifts described in remarkably equivalent terms. Charles Swann's observations about Combray provide an interesting case:

> Middle-class people in those days took what was almost a Hindu view of society, which they held to consist of sharply defined castes, so that everyone at his birth found himself led to that station of life which his parents already occupied, and from which nothing, save the accident of an exceptional career or a "good" marriage, could extract you and translate you to a superior caste. (Proust, 1983: 16-17)

This strict worldview imposes itself on the "bourgeois" subject, and sets it apart from other "castes." Simultaneously, Proust sketched how the French Revolutionary idea of equality lives on within the very same middle-class milieu (Proust, 1987, vol II: 1097). This underlines that a discourse need not to be logical or consistent—that it in fact often carries within itself manifest contradictions. Myths thus generate (or perform) their own logic. They turn into imaginaries when they manage to convincingly articulate as many elements and identities as possible in chains of equivalence in order to subdue resistance. The frailty of the hegemony sketched in *Remembrance of Things Past* becomes very clear with the Dreyfus case, however. The affair makes "*the social kaleidoscope turn*" and quite suddenly pushes many Jews down on the social ladder (Proust 1987, vol. II: 194). Like Mann, Proust staged (a) dislocation(s) of a given hegemony only to describe how the communitarian order is subsequently restored, albeit at the cost of the Jews.[12]

In a markedly Lukácsian stance, Laclau stressed that discourses which manage to win subjects over and allow for identification always provide a "*realistic alternative.*" Following Barthes, "realistic" can be understood here as masking the materiality of discourse in favor of Reality. Not the lack of the subject must be underscored, but its "fullness" and unity with society. And it is this unity that gives rise to what Laclau called the *society effect*. This comes about when a discourse manages to convince subjects that it fully reflects, accounts for and coincides with the social. Or, as Laclau puts it: "*A fully achieved 'society effect' ... would have to be one in which the relationship between the effect and its cause would be entirely undisturbed, in which the fullness of the effect would entirely be derived from the fullness of the cause*" (Laclau & Zac, 1994: 17). The examples borrowed from Mann and Proust testify to an acute awareness within (critical realist) modernism of the subject's need to acquire an identity by identifying with a given outlook on society. Not only do these authors describe this need, they also show how it can and must be positively fulfilled. In doing so, they explicitly introduce various other discourses in their work, making the reader complicit in as well as aware of the acts of identification described. In this respect, Mann, Proust, but also Lukács can be read as scrutinizing an ongoing society effect of discourse, marked by moments of rupture but above all by a constant suturing of imaginaries. Yet at the same time it is this portrayal of consecutive myths and imaginaries that makes a text determinate, for Mann's modernism tends to foreclose openings through which a reader's imaginary can impede the text. This is not to say, of course, that such openings could not be (en)forced, but rather that the reader's attempt to construct a work's social imaginary is fulfilled. Even when discourses are dislocated a new myth is always introduced and elevated to the status of an imaginary. Determinacy thereby shows itself to be not only the result of method. Although it is clearly mirrored in Mann's method, from the level of his opulent sentence structure to the narrative scheme of the *Bildungsroman*, it also is related to the *continuity* of the society effect.[13]

KAFKA'S "MINOR LITERATURE"

It is stating the obvious that in Kafka we hardly ever find direct references to the concrete situation the author found himself in. Writing in mainstream German and not in Yiddish, witnessing the dissolution of the Habsburg Empire, the rise of anarchism, Czech nationalism and Zionism, Kafka's "minor literature" quite consistently downplays concrete historical events in favor of abstraction. Yet, as is revealed by his December 25, 1911 diary entry, entitled *A Character Sketch of the Literature of Small Peoples*, this does not cancel the political significance of literature. The text clearly defines culture as a site of activist intervention: *"A) Connection with Politics; B) Literary History; C) Faith in Literature, can make up their own Laws"* (translated in Suchoff, 1994: 140). As Russel Berman (1986: 262) noted, *"the same Kafka who has been represented as a prophet of alienation and hopelessness declares that 'literature is an affair of the people'."* This raises the question as to how Kafka, too, may prove instructive to our understanding of the society effect. Read against the backdrop of Laclau's essay, Kafka's phantasms could be said to bring out the society effect (or lack there of) in another way than Mann's work does.

For Laclau the success or failure of a discourse in eliciting a society effect is as dependent on its "realism" as it is on the way it conveys power. According to Laclau, *"power is [most often] located at some point within society, from where its effects would in some way spread over and around the social structure as a whole. ... Power is, in a sense, the source of the social"* (Laclau & Zac, 1994: 17). Through discourse, power appears to create a society effect. "Order," "organization," "the continuity of community"—all of these terms appear in some way synonymous with the society effect, because people accept the power invested in them. The value of Laclau's (often dense) argument in *Minding the Gap,* however, lies in linking the problematical relationship between the (realist) society effect and power to the issue of legitimacy. An imaginary presents itself as the only viable outlook on society. It produces a fullness of society in which everyone has a place and in which the question of power eventually even becomes redundant—for as we have seen, it is order and only in the second instance emancipation the (reading) subject strives for. As soon as there are several groups proposing myths *"that conflict with each other and that cannot be referred back to a single generating force,"* however, *"the reality of power constructs the irreality of society"* (Laclau & Zac, 1994: 19). In such situations of conflict, where the subject has to decide which myth to opt for, it is confronted with the contingency of its outlook on society as well as with a need to see power legitimated in one way or another. Laclau noted that *"power loses its legitimacy when it is unable to ensure the social order."* But power can only be legitimate *"when illegitimate outcomes are possible as well"* (Laclau & Zac, 1994: 22). Every outlook on society, in short, no matter how dominant and powerful, requires resistance and alternatives, which must be found illegitimate by the community that is addressed to keep the social order in place.

Willy Haas (1957: 62-68) recorded that Kafka once told him that Balzac was wrong to fully situate and integrate characters in their social surroundings. To Kafka, narratives such as Balzac's falsely privilege the power that dominant views exert on the subject. Put differently, they do not legitimate that power. By refusing to specify the location and other determinate markers in his narrative, Kafka could therefore be said to address the issue of power and legitimacy in identification. In this light, his phantasms often prove instructive in a way Mann's writings do not. Reminiscent of Proust's image of the social kaleidoscope referred to earlier, his diary, for example, stages an interesting counter-interpretation of what actually happens when the subject is forced to identify with a series of potential hegemonies. What happens is, in fact, nothing: *"They make for the purpose of reason or grounding [Gründlichkeit], fullness and completeness without gaps but only like a figure on the 'wheel of life': we have chased our little idea around in a circle"* (Kafka, 1951: 259, author's translation). Not only does Kafka claim here that identifying with and consenting to powerful narratives in the end prohibits fundamental change (see West, 1985). He also implies that such narratives are unable to ground and legitimate power. *The Castle* quite overtly thematizes this issue by first constructing and then deconstructing an imaginary with seemingly absolute power.

The Castle notoriously confronts us with a character, K., who lacks an identity and desires identification with a community. The site of power and surveillance in the narrative is a castle in which a seemingly lawless bureaucracy is located. The village community surrounding the castle fully adheres to its power: "*Nowhere had K. seen officialdom and life as interwoven as they were here, so interwoven that it sometimes even looked as if officialdom and life had changed places*" (Kafka, 1997: 53). Thus K., a land surveyor, is offered only the castle's power and opaque hegemony to identify with. As K. initially assesses the castle from "*the wooden bridge leading from the main road to the village,*" he finds himself "*gazing up into the seeming emptiness*" (Kafka, 1997: 3). Desperately seeking to fill this emptiness, K. sets out to define the limits of the castle's power, and in doing so also seeks legitimacy for the power the castle exerts. On various occasions we find K. looking at the castle thereafter, and the shifts in his perception are worth noting. Further in the narrative, we find him describing it as "*uncertainly, unevenly, britterly,*" strange, "*as if [he was] drawn by the timid or slapdash hand of a child,*" unable to overcome the feeling of being surveyed by someone in the castle (Kafka, 1997: 9). The further we move into the narrative, however, the more the indeterminacy of the castle begins to show determinate political effects:

> Looking at the castle, K. felt at times as if he was watching a person who was sitting there quietly, staring straight ahead, not so much lost in thought and hence cut off from everything as free and uncensored; as if the person had been alone, with no one watching him; he must be aware that he was being watched, but it did not affect his calm in the least and in fact—there was no telling whether this was cause or effect—the watcher's gaze found no purchase and kept sliding away. (Kafka, 1997: 89)

Here, the land surveyor K. so strongly identifies with the power exerted by the castle that he claims to be able to escape surveillance altogether. Taking the power of the castle to be absolute or at least overestimating it, K. becomes mesmerized by it: "*if an authority is good, why shouldn't people respect it?*" (Kafka, 1997: 164). On many other occasions, however, the illusion of the castle's benevolent power is shattered. This is the case, for instance, when K. witnesses Barnabas, a character allegedly working officially for the castle: "*K. had let himself be charmed by Barnabas's tight-fitting shiny silk jacket, which the latter now unbuttoned to reveal a coarse, dirty-grey, heavily mended shirt, covering the powerful square chest of a farmhand*" (Kafka, 1997: 28). In the face of absolute power, it is suggested here, there are but servants or hands. Freedom and absolute power simply cannot coincide.

It is at this point that the character of Amalia gains immense significance in *The Castle*. Ordered by one of the officials to go to the castle, to "*come immediately, otherwise—!*" (Kafka, 1997: 173), Amalia refuses to identify with the power structure dominating the village. The other villagers stigmatize her for this by gossiping about her. Amalia is even more indeterminate than K.: "*[w]ithout any special arrangements, without orders, or requests, almost entirely through silence"* (Kafka, 1997: 187). The villagers lose little time in connecting her silence with the power of the castle, interpreting it as critical of the castle's power and thereby immediately constructing her unconformity as an alternative doomed to remain unexpressed. Although Amalia may seem perfectly complicit with the castle's social imaginary, her silence and refusal to do an official's bidding can also be valued positively. Indeed, her story illustrates that "illegitimate" resistance is present within the very fabric of the village's subjecting and domesticating world. (As seen earlier, Lukács fully neglects such instances of resistance.) Amalia draws attention to the resistance latent in any power structure, and suggests that only when it is recognized, an alternative myth can be constructed. Literature can play an important role in voicing this resistance, as is suggested by the following passage: *"Often ... the writer can't hear at all sitting down, he has to keep jumping up to catch the words, sitting down again quickly to write, then jumping up, and so on"* (Kafka, 1997: 160).[14] Hence, in contrast with Mann, Kafka drew to the fore the moment of dislocation, sticking with it to suggest a moment of discontinuity and thus opening a gap, a paradigmatic rift as it were, for the reader to enter and to bring in other imaginaries or myths. Here, the reader is in a way invited to partake more actively in the community represented. As was the case with Mann, the stress on discontinuity is clearly mirrored on the level of style as well, especially by the brief and tendentially paratactic diction. Here too, however, indeterminacy appears to be more than just a matter of style. The *discontinuity* of the society effect seems to be at least as significant.

Occasionally in Kafka's work, as in *The Trial*, the reader is confronted with Kafka's own constitutive lack by the total absence of openings such as Amalia's story in *The Castle*. Narratives such as *The Trial* prove crucial to our understanding of the society effect in yet another way. *The Trial*'s famous apologue, the short history told in front of the door of the Law by a priest, is one of the novel's most tantalizing passages and one—it goes without saying—that has already been discussed by numerous others. In the apologue, a man learns that the priest guards a door of the Law intended for him only. In his essay, *Beyond Discourse Analysis* (1990), Slavoj Žižek labeled this apologue *"a myth"* that can only be understood in relation *"to a series of other myths and ... the rule of their transformation"* (Žižek, 1990: 255). He then contrasted the apologue with a scene in the second chapter, where a washerwoman guards another door of the Law, intended for K. only. The door is situated in the middle of workers' quarters and it is only by chance that K. enters the room where the door is guarded. The woman clearly possesses more knowledge about the Law than K., as is exemplified by the fact that she ignores K.'s excuse that he has actually come for a joiner names Lanz. The woman manifestly belongs to a community from which K. is excluded:

The The first thing he saw in the little room was a great pendulum clock, which already pointed to 10. "Does a joiner called Lanz live here?" he asked. "Please go through," said a young woman with sparkling black eyes, who was washing children's clothes in a tub, and she pointed her damp hand to the open door of the next room ... "I asked for a joiner, a man called Lanz." "I know," said the woman, "just go right in." K. might not have obeyed if she had not come up to him, grasped the handle of the door and said: "I must shut this door after you, nobody else must come in." (Kafka, 1985: 45-6, quoted in Žižek, 1990: 256)

Willingly submitting to a power the source of which remains unseen, K. decides to move from one room to the next because of an unuttered desire to identify with a community that appears *lawless*. As we read on, the woman resurfaces in the narrative, when she interrupts K.'s passionate address to the tribunal:

Here K. was interrupted by a shriek from the end of the hall; he peered from beneath his hand to see what was happening, for the reek of the room and the dim light together made a whitish dazzle of fog. It was the washerwoman, whom K. had recognized as a potential cause of disturbance from the moment of her entrance. Whether she was at fault now or not, one could not tell. All K. could see was that a man had drawn her into a corner by the door and was clasping her in his arms. Yet it was not she who had uttered the shriek but the man; his mouth was wide open and he was gazing up at the ceiling. (Kafka, 1985: 45-6, quoted in Žižek, 1990: 256)

This Munchian image is followed by an attempt on K.'s part to restore order. Convinced of his own sanity and of the madness of the whole situation, he attempts to get to the other side of the room to quiet down the couple, but is obstructed from doing so by the crowd surrounding him. Confused, he loses the thread of his exposé and finally runs off in rage. Overlooking *"the solidarity between this obscene perturbation and the court,"* K.'s fatal error is that he perceived the Law *"as a homogenous entity, attainable by means of consistent argument"* (Žižek, 1990: 257-58). Accused of an unspecified crime he did not commit, K. tries to come to terms with the Law and its community, only to be executed in the end. The vacancy of subject and society, it would seem, has never been exposed as dramatically as in this concise novel.[15]

Judith Ryan (1985: 260) said that *"the radicality of Kafka's methods becomes apparent when we accept indeterminacy as a functional part of the text."* I do not wish to contradict Ryan's claim. However, *The Trial* exemplifies that indeterminacy, when related to a society effect, corresponds to the scope or range of the power a narrative evokes. The novel shows how it is impossible to read it as containing an imaginary, for instance, because it presents the power of the Law as total, canceling the character's identity and agency. The community represented in *The Trial* thus appears to lose its society effect precisely because it forecloses resistance and disunion. Whereas Mann granted us the pleasure of continuity, Kafka shocked us into discontinuity. Maurice Blanchot (1995: 8) captured the limit experience that results from discontinuity quite succinctly by pointing out how the reader of Kafka often comes close to experiencing death: *"We do not die, it is true, but because of that we do not live either; we are dead while we are alive, we are essentially survivors."* When the shift from subject to identity is blocked, the reader's lack of community and belonging foreshadows his end, which was always-already his beginning. Lukács, however, was mistaken in labeling such an experience as *"metaphysical Nothingness."* In *The Trial*, it could be argued, the reader assumes the role of Amalia in *The Castle*, that is, he finds himself outside the novel's social order and yet partakes in it from within a space that the imaginary is *"essentially incapable of mastering"* (Laclau, 1990: 68-69). Not too long ago, Philippe Lacoue-Labarthe asked: *"why, after all, should the problem of identification not be, in general, the essential problem of politics?"* (Lacoue-Labarthe, 1989: 300). To literary scholars, the possibility of identification is as crucial as its impossibility or failure, it seems, if we want to get a glimpse of how literature elicits a society effect. Kafka and Mann, traditionally read as the two extreme poles of modernism, may well prove the poles of a more general experience in reading. Lukács' partial misreading of both authors remains significant, because it suggests that further inquiry into the society effect as well as discussions on the counter-hegemonic potential of literature will have to ascertain to what extent realistic strategies of representation give rise to determinacy and less conventional, vanguard modes of representation to indeterminacy.

NOTES

1. In the wake of Barthes' essay and in line with his *S/Z* (1970), narratologists such as Gérard Genette (1969), Philippe Hamon (1974), and Henri Mitterand (1980) further scrutinized the conventions of realist representation. The study of historiography, similarly, has largely taken the implications of Barthes's work to heart, as can be deduced from Hutcheon and Valdés (2002) and Fay, Pomper and Vann (1998).
2. Text is used here in a more narrow meaning than can be found in Barthes' work.
3. Perhaps the society effect will appear old news to literary scholars. After all, literature's ability to communicate a sense of society has been recognized at least since antiquity. From Plato's *eidetics* over Romanticist *eidaesthetics* to modernist

poetics (Chytry, 1989; Lacoue-Labarthe & Nancy, 1978) it would be rank folly not to underline the persuasiveness literary representations of society can have. Not surprisingly, therefore, the society effect is a theme in modern literary aesthetics from Lord Shaftesbury onward (see Kivy, 1976; Singer & Dunn, 2000: 13-78). It also frequently surfaces in 20th-century literary criticism, be it in sociologically oriented critics, from Neo-Marxists as Georg Lukács (1968) over Critical Theorists as Herbert Marcuse (1978) to Frederic Jameson (1981), or in reader-response critics, from the hermeneuticists Hans-Georg Gadamar (1977) and Hans Robert Jauss (1982) over the phenomenologists Iser (1978) and Fish (1982) to the many poststructuralists partly working in their tracks. However, I believe that literary theory so far has mainly managed to convey the pleasure of dovetailing with the effect. The radically constructivist discourse theory of Laclau may be complementary in setting out beacons for bringing out just how constitutive the society effect is to reading.

4. Lukács' reading of Kafka and Mann has been the subject of numerous studies. See, among others, Kruse (1988), Marcus (1988), and Sim (1994). See also Chapter 12, this volume.

5. Naturally, we can question the rigidity of Lukács' opposition, not in the least because Mann himself paid tribute to Kafka on several occasions (Mann, 1941, 1959). Various studies have also pointed at the role of determinacy in Kafka, which—as is seen further on—Lukács appears to downplay entirely (see, for instance, Dolezel, 1983; Garaudy, 1963; Philippi, 1966). Still, we need to recognize the substantial difference between both authors.

6. On the disorienting role of focalization in Kafka, see Heidsieck (1989).

7. I am, of course, not the first to read Mann and Kafka not as opposites but as complementary writers. For a recent example, see Hamacher (2004).

8. As David Aram Kaiser (1999: 3) notes, *"criticism has tended to follow Paul de Man in viewing [communities] in terms of the rhetorical figure of synecdoche (the identification of part and whole), while ignoring the political issues involved in a synechdocal account"* of society. Kaiser raises an important issue, which I can unfortunately not go into extensively within the scope of this chapter.

9. For a good overview of this tradition, see Sheppard (2000).

10. For more detailed and nuanced analyses of Leverkühn's role in *Doctor Faustus*, see Schmitz (1994) and Hilgers (1995).

11. Indeed, the concrete or "typical" and "totality" are concepts grounding his analyses. On Lukács' shifting and complex use of the second concept, see Jay (1984).

12. Naturally, by referring to Proust at this point I do not mean to equate his style and subject-representation with those of Mann. All I want to do here is to show how the society effect functions.

13. As is clear from his earlier readings of Balzac, Lukács was particularly interested in the way literature can describe macrological historical shifts (Lukács, [1951], 1965). As such he, too, recognized this continuity, but only through his understanding of history as a Hegelian continuity. Here, his views are in line with Barthes diagnosis of realism and historiography (see also note 1).

14. For an alternative interpretation of *The Castle's* political message, see Maria Wolf's (1987) article *Kritik der Hoffnung*.

15. It may be useful to remind ourselves here that the role of Law in Kafka has been
read in a similar fashion by others than Žižek. Various studies have drawn attention to the undecidability and aporia resulting from K.'s confrontation with an
indeterminate Law (see e.g., Beckmann, 1991; Derrida, 1992; Ernest, 1991;
Kirchberger, 1987; Stephens, 1978; Stern, 1976).

REFERENCES

Adorno, T.W. (1970) *Ästhetische Theorie*. Frankfurt: Suhrkamp.
Anderson, B. (1983) *Imagined Communities: Reflections on the Origin and Spread of Nationalism*. London: Verso.
Attridge, D. (2004) *The Singularity of Literature*. London, New York: Routledge.
Barthes, R. (1968) 'L'effet de Réel,' *Communications* (11): 84-89.
Barthes, R. (1970) *S/Z*. Paris: Seuil.
Beckmann, M. (1991) 'Franz Kafkas Romanfragment 'Der Prozess': Verzweiflung als 'Selbst'-Gericht,' *Colloquia Germanica* 24(3): 203-36.
Belsey, C. (1980) *Critical Practice*. London, New York: Methuen.
Benjamin, W. (1999) *Selected Writings*, Vol. 2. Cambridge, Mass.: Harvard University Press.
Bermann, R. (1986) *The Rise of the German Novel: Crisis and Charisma*. Cambridge: Harvard University Press.
Blanchot, M. (1995) *The Work of Fire* (C. Mandel, Trans.). Stanford, California: Stanford University Press.
Bordwell, D. (1985) *Narration in Fiction Film*. Madison: University of Wisconsin Press.
Chytry, J. (1989) *The Aesthetic State*. Berkeley: University of California Press.
de Angelis, E. (1977) *Arte e Idiología de la Alta Burguesía: Mann, Musil, Kafka, Brecht*. Madrid: Akal.
Deleuze, G., Guattari, F. (1975) *Kafka: Pour une Littérature Mineure*. Paris: Minuit.
Derrida, J. (1992) 'Before the Law,' pp. 181-220 in J. Derrida, D. Attridge (Eds) *Acts of Literature*. New York: Routledge.
Dolezel, L. (1983) 'Proper Names, Definite Descriptions and the Intentional Structure of Kafka's The Trial,' *Poetics* 12(6): 511-26.
Ernest, W.B. Hess-Lutich (1991) 'The Rhetoric of Misunderstanding in Kafka's The Trial,' *Journal of the Kafka Society of America* 15(1-2): 37-52.
Fay, B., Pomper, P., Vann, R. (Eds) (1998) *History and Theory: Contemporary Readings*. London: Blackwell.
Fetzler, J.F. (1996) *Changing Perceptions of Thomas Mann's 'Doctor Faustus': Criticism, 1947-1992*. Columbia: Camden House.
Fish, S. (1982) *Is There a Text in This Class? The Authority of Interpretive Communities*. Cambridge, Mass.: Harvard University Press.
Gadamer, H.-G. (1977) *Die Aktualität des Schönen*. Stuttgart: Philipp Reclam.
Garaudy, R. (1963) *D'un Réalisme sans Rivages*. Paris: Plon.
Genette, G. (1969) *Figures II*. Paris: Seuil.

Graff, G. (1990) 'Determinacy/Indeterminacy,' pp. 163-176 in F. Lentricchia and T. McLaughlin (Eds) *Critical Terms for Literary Study*. Chicago, London: University of Chicago Press.

Haas, W. (1957) *Die literarische Welt: Erinnerungen*. München: List.

Hamacher, B. (2004) 'Wieviel Brüderlichkeit bedeutet Zeitgenossenschaft ohne weiteres! Franz Kafka und Thomas Mann–Versuch eines 'Kulturtransfers',' pp. 361-384 in C. Liebrand and F. Schössler (Eds) *Textverkehr: Kafka und die Tradition*. Würzburg: Königshausen und Neumann.

Hamon, Ph. (1974) 'Qu'est-ce qu'une Description?,' *Poétique* 18: 215-235.

Hargraves, J.A. (2001) *Music in the Works of Broch, Mann, and Kafka*. Rochester: Camden House.

Heath, S. (1977-78) 'Notes on Suture,' *Screen* 18(4): 48-76.

Heidsieck, A. (1989) 'Kafkas fiktionale Ontologie und Erzählperspektive: Ihre . Beziehungen zur österreichischen Philosophie der Jahrhundertwende,' *Poetica* 21(3-4): 389-402.

Heller, P. (1966) *Dialectics and Nihilism: Essays on Lessing, Nietzsche, Mann and Kafka*. Amherst: University of Massachusetts Press.

Hilgers, H. (1995) *Serenus Zeitblom: Der Erzähler als Romanfigur in Thomas Manns 'Doktor Faustus.'* Bern: Lang.

Hutcheon, L., Valdés, M. (Eds) (2002) *Rethinking Literary History: A Dialogue on Theory*. Oxford: Oxford University Press.

Iser, W. (1978) *The Act of Reading*. London: Routledge and Kegan Paul.

Jameson, F. (1981) *The Political Unconscious*. Ithaca, NY: Cornell University Press.

Jauss, H.R. (1982) *Ästhetische Erfahrung und literarische Hermeneutik*. Frankfurt: Suhrkamp.

Jay, M. (1984) *Marxism and Totality: The Adventures of a Concept from Lukács to Habermas*. Cambridge: Polity Press.

Kafka, F. (1951) *Tagebücher 1910-1923*. Frankfurt: Fischer.

Kafka, F. (1985) *The Trial*. Harmondsworth: Penguin.

Kafka, F. (1997) *The Castle*. London: Penguin.

Kaiser, D.A. (1999) *Romanticism, Aesthetics, and Nationalism*. Cambridge: Cambridge University Press.

Kirchberger, L. (1987) *Franz Kafka's Use of Law in Fiction: A New Interpretation of In der Strafkolonie, Der Prozess, and Das Schloss*. Ottendorfter Series, Neue Folge, 22. New York: New York University.

Kivy, P. (1976) *The Seventh Sense*. New York: Burt Franklin.

Kruse, J. (1988) 'Lukács' Theorie des Romans und Kafkas In der Strafkolonie: Eine Konstellation im Jahre 1914,' *German Studies Review* 10(2): 237-253.

Laclau, E. (Ed.) (1990) *New Reflections on the Revolution of Our Time*. London: Verso.

Laclau, E. (1996) *Emancipation(s)*. London: Verso.

Laclau, E., Zac, L. (1994) 'Minding the Gap: The Subject of Politics,' pp. 11-39 in E. Laclau (Ed.) *The Making of Political Identities*. London: Verso.

Lacoue-Labarthe, Ph. (1989) *Typography: Mimesis, Philosophy, Politics*. Cambridge, Mass.: Harvard University Press.

Lacoue-Labarthe, Ph., Nancy, J.-L. (1978) *L'Absolu Littéraire*. Paris: Seuil.

Levenson, M. (1991) *Modernism and the Fate of Individuality: Character and Novelistic Form from Conrad to Woolf.* New York: Cambridge University Press.

Liebrand, C., Schössler, F. (Eds.) (2004) *Textverkehr: Kafka und die Tradition.* Würzburg: Königshausen und Neumann.

Lukács, G. (1963) *The Meaning of Contemporary Realism.* London: Merlin Press.

Lukács, G. (1965) 'Balzac und der Französische Realismus,' pp. 431-520 in *Georg Lukács Werke.* Band 6. Berlin: Luchterhand.

Lukács, G. (1968) *Theorie des Romans.* Berlin: Luchterhand.

Lunn, E. (1982) *Marxism and Modernism.* Berkeley: University of California Press.

Mann, T. (1941) 'Foreword,' in F. Kafka. *The Castle.* New York: Knopf.

Mann, T. (1959) 'Homage,' in F. Kafka. *The Castle* (W. and E. Muir, E. Wilkins and E. Kaiser, Trans.). New York: Knopf.

Mann, T. (1968a) *Doctor Faustus.* London: Penguin.

Mann, T. (1968b) *Lotte in Weimar.* London: Penguin.

Marcus, J. (1988) *Georg Lukács and Thomas Mann: A Study in the Sociology of Literature.* Amherst: University of Massachusetts Press.

Marcuse, H. (1978) *The Aesthetic Dimension.* Boston: Beacon Press.

Mitterand, H. (1980) *Le Discours du Roman.* Paris: Presses Universitaires de France.

Pfeiffer, J. (1962) *Die dichterische Wirklichkeit: Versuche über Wesen und Wahrheit der Dichtung.* Hamburg: R. Meiner Verlag.

Philippi, J.-P. (1966) *'Das Schloss': Reflexion und Wirklichkeit.* Tübingen: Niemeyer.

Proust, M. (1983) *Remembrance of Things Past* (C. K. S. Moncrieff, T. Kilmartin, and A. Mayor, Trans.). Harmondsworth: Penguin.

Proust, M. (1987) *À la recherche du temps perdu.* 4 vols. New Pléiade edition. Paris: Gallimard.

Ryan, J. (1985) 'Our trial: Kafka's challenge to literary theory,' *Novel* 18(3): 257-266.

Schmitz, H.-G. (1994) 'Leverkühns Welt: Überlegungen zur Theorie der literarischen Fiktion,' *Orbis Litterarum* 49(1): 1-18.

Sheppard, R. (2000) *Modernism–Dada–Postmodernism.* Evanston, Illinois: Northwestern University Press.

Sim, S. (1994) *Georg Lukács.* New York: Harvester Wheatsheaf.

Singer, A., Dunn, A. (Eds) (2000) *Literary Aesthetics.* London: Blackwell.

Stephens, A. (1978) "Es ist aber Zweigeteilt': Gericht und Ich-Struktur bei Kafka,' *Text & Kontext* 6(1-2): 215-238.

Stern, J.P. (1976) 'The Law of the Trial,' pp. 22-41 in F. Kuna (Ed) *The Kafka Debate: New Perspectives For Our Time.* New York: Gordian Press.

Suchoff, D. (1994) *Critical Theory and the Novel: Mass Society and Cultural Criticism in Dickens, Melville, and Kafka.* Madison, Wisconsin: The University of Wisconsin Press.

Taylor, C. (2002) 'Modern Social Imaginaries,' *Public Culture* 14(1): 91-124.

Tönnies, F. (1988) *Gemeinschaft und Gesellschaft.* Darmstadt: Wissenschaftliche Buchgesellschaft.

West, R. (1985) 'Authority, Autonomy, and Choice: The Role of Consent in the Moral and Political Visions of Franz Kafka and Richard Posner,' *Harvard Law Review* 99(4): 384–427.

Wolf, M. (1987) 'Kritik der Hoffnung,' pp. 51-87 in F. Schirrmacher (Ed) *Verteidigung der Schrift: Kafkas Prozess.* Frankfurt: Suhrkamp.

Zima, P. (1999) *The Philosophy of Modern literary Theory*. London: Athlone.
Žižek, S. (1990) 'Beyond Discourse Analysis,' pp. 249-260 in E. Laclau (Ed.) *New Reflections on the Revolution of Our Time*. London: Verso.

14

"THESE REALLY COMPREHENSIBLE POEMS THAT REALLY TOUCH YOU"

The New Realist Discourse in Flemish Poetry

Erik Spinoy

A VERY SHORT HISTORY OF (WESTERN) LITERARY HISTORIOGRAPHY

This chapter reflects on the way Laclau and Mouffe's discourse theory can contribute to the study of literary history. I begin this chapter with a brief (and necessarily extremely simplifying) retrospective of the development of scientific literary historiography in the West.

It goes without saying that Western literary historiography as it is currently being practiced has come a (very) long way since the first attempts were undertaken to transform what was initially a practice that served other purposes (e.g., the glorification of the national cultural heritage) into a discipline worthy of the name science. These first attempts were made by positivism and *Geistesgeschichte*. In the first case, the origin of literary phenomena was sought in objective causes such as the author's hereditary predisposition, the author's biographical and social antecedents and/or the author's nationality (race), which were supposed to lead, in an entirely deterministic fashion, to the phenomenon as it presented itself to the literary scientist. In the second case, literature was seen as the emanation of the *Geist* that was characteristic of a certain era.

Starting in the early 20th century, the criticism of especially the positivist approach to literature by formalist and early structuralist tendencies led to a disparaging of literary history altogether, to the benefit of the autonomous study of literary texts.[1] Where in these traditions literary history was studied, the main inspiration was usually the literary practice of the avant-garde, which of course stressed innovation and transgression. This induced authors such as the Russian Formalists Viktor Shklovsky (Chklovski, 1973) and Jury Tynjanow (1982) and the Czech structuralists Jan Mukařovský (1974) and Felix Vodička (1976) to advocate a form of literary history in which a central role was given to those texts, oeuvres, and currents that successfully transgressed prevalent literary norms and codes.[2] The formalist-structuralist way of conceiving literary history represented an important step forward, because it contributed to de-essentializing literary phenomena and to developing a model of literary dynamics gradually ridding itself from positivist determinism. At the same time, it continued to show traces of essentialism, because it departed from the assumption that genuine and/or important literary works would per definition be associated with features such as complexity, singularity, and nonconformism. Notwithstanding this, its reflection did heighten the awareness that the status and meaning of a (body of) literary work(s) in literary history are not inherent and unchanging properties, but are instead conferred on it (them) by means of what we will further call discursive practices. And although the formalist-structuralist reworking of the study of literary history was motivated by the search for a principle governing (determining) literary evolution (alienation, innovation, etc.), the models it came up with all allowed for a considerable degree of openness and contingency, as they—implicitly or explicitly—presented literary evolution as driven by a competition between various alternatives for the established literary order at a given time and place—a competition of which the outcome could not be predicted.

In the meantime, this unmistakable steering away from determinism and essentialism remained absent in Marxist literary studies proper, which—even in its more sophisticated forms—continued to claim it was able to determine the objective meaning and value of literary phenomena by situating them, one way or another, in a version of Marxism's teleological narrative.

The final blow[3] to determinism and essentialism in Western literary studies was dealt by the "linguistic turn" in the humanities. In the theory and practice of literary studies, poststructuralism and deconstruction radicalized the tendencies already present in the formalist-structuralist tradition.

This allowed literary phenomena to be redefined as being devoid of any pre-given essence: They are simply phenomena that, in a given discursive context, will be defined as literary. This definition is formulated by the discourse that, at a given time and place, has acquired dominance—a position that does not result from a necessary deployment of History but from a struggle for dominance, which could very well have had another outcome. This amounts to saying that the meaning and value of literary phenomena are fixed (or unfixed and reinscribed) in a context of political struggle. If this is so, the question literary historiography has to answer is not: What are the great works (the canon) of (a national) literature? And neither is it "Which are the laws governing literary history?" Instead it should be, "What are the political processes in which meaning and value are attributed to literary phenomena?" Here, the possible link between literary historiography and Laclau and Mouffe's discourse theory becomes obvious. Indeed, as discourse theory is a postessentialist theory designed to study political processes, it may prove rewarding to investigate if and how it can contribute to the study of literary development. In the following, I demonstrate that the specific concepts and tools forged by Laclau and Mouffe, which were originally developed within the context of political science, can also find application in the field of Literary Studies.

The case I use to make my point is that of new realist poetry in Flemish literature. As one may know, Flemish literature is now generally considered to be a part of Dutch literature, with which it shares the language.[4] At the same time, however, Flemish literature has to a large extent developed autonomously. This can be explained in the first place by the fact that, as one of Belgium's national literatures, it has since its creation in the 1830s—the years following Belgium's independence—been embedded in a profoundly different historical and socio-political context.[5] It is also due to the fact that Flemish literary life depended to a large extent on local literary institutions (publishers, literary magazines, literary prizes, etc.) and—not to forget—local informal literary-artistic networks (literary friendships, local literary scenes, etc.). In recent decades, the contacts between Dutch literature in the Netherlands and in Flanders have certainly intensified. Notwithstanding this, even a relatively recent phenomenon such as the rise of new realism in Flemish poetry remained almost entirely an internal affair, in which Netherlandic-Dutch poets, critics and readers were almost entirely absent and which therefore went by almost unnoticed in the Netherlands. It should be noted in this context that power relations between the Netherlandic and Flemish segments of Dutch literature are unequal, and in this sense somewhat comparable with the power relations between motherland and colony. From a Flemish perspective, Netherlandic literature often functions as a model to be emulated and/or as an oppressive imperialistic force to be fought. From a Netherlandic perspective, Flemish literature is generally viewed either as a quaint and (with a few exceptions) negligible appendix of

Netherlandic literature or as a rich source of otherness and exotism. In the case of Flemish new realism, the Flemish writers and critics involved in the movement generally rejected the Netherlandic model and especially the brand of new realism that had developed in the Netherlands in the early 1960s. On the Netherlandic side, the Flemish new realist movement was ignored and hardly any of the Flemish new realists succeeded in establishing a reputation for themselves in the Netherlands.[6]

As it happens, Flemish neorealism has already been studied extensively in the early 1990s (Brems & De Geest, 1991; Evenepoel & De Geest, 1992). In these studies, the theoretical framework used for the description of neorealism was made explicit to a limited extent only, but it is clear that the researchers involved did try to reconstruct the literary-political process that led to the rise, dominance and rapid dislocation of new realist discourse.[7] As a consequence, these studies are particularly suited as a basis for demonstrating the specific contribution the tools and concepts used in discourse-theoretical analysis can make to literary history.

PREVIOUSLY IN FLEMISH POETRY: THE DISLOCATION OF THE EXPERIMENTALIST DISCOURSE

The situation in Flemish poetry in the second half of the 1960s was one in which the hegemonic discourse found itself in a state of dislocation. In the early 1950s, an "experimentalist" avant-gardist discourse had become hegemonic in Flemish poetry, relieving and marginalizing an outspokenly traditionalistic discourse. What was initially the poetical discourse and creative practice of a small group of writers and literary critics soon came to be perceived as *the* valid articulation of contemporary poetry and profoundly reshaped Flemish poetry. However, as is pointed out by discourse theory, discourses are permanently in a state of reconstruction. Contexts change and force discourses to rearticulate themselves, new speakers arrive and "warp" the discourse by investing it with their particular aspirations. The experimentalist discourse, too, was permanently rephrased and reorganized, eventually leading to a drastic displacement. The young experimentalists coming to the fore in the early 1960s had, for the greater part, become increasingly radicalized and intolerant (Brems & De Geest, 1991: 13-14). As is observed by Laclau, this makes a discourse vulnerable to attack from competing discourses. For a discourse to become or remain hegemonic, the particular group (in this case, the latest generation of experimentalist writers and critics) advocating it has, among others, "*to demonstrate its rights to identify its own particular aims with the universal emancipatory aims of the communi-*

ty" (Laclau et al., 2000: 46). The problem with radicalism is that this demonstration risks to founder. In more traditional terms, one could say that the radical experimentalists that had come to the fore in the early 1960s had increasingly estranged themselves from the Flemish "poetic community."

Another factor that needs to be given attention has to do with the fact that a hegemonic discourse has to credibly present itself as a response to an oppressive force. In the case of experimentalism, this enemy[8] was traditional humanism, which was accused of suppressing crucial aspects of human existence (vital instincts, the subconscious). However, following the rapid marginalization of traditional humanism and the concomitant traditionalist art and literature, it became hard to convincingly represent them as still posing a serious threat and to uphold the image of experimentalism as a liberating discourse. Both factors contributed to creating conditions favorable to the rise of a new discourse aspiring towards hegemony. This new discourse could be expected to frame the old discourse as having itself become the oppressive force and to formulate the promise that it would rid the poetic community from its tyrannical reign.

A final factor that contributed to the eventual delegitimation of the youngest mark of the 'experimentalist' discourse was, I believe, the disarticulation of the experimentalist chain of equivalence.[9] In the early years, this chain of equivalence had helped enhance experimentalism's credibility by associating experimentalist poetry with ascending or at any rate recent hegemonies in other domains. One of these domains was the visual arts. Experimentalism presented itself as the literary equivalent of a late strand of surrealist painting known as the Cobra group, which was made up of Dutch, Belgian, and Danish painters. Cobra was quick to rise to international prominence, and this canonization of course enhanced the authority and prestige of experimentalism in poetry. Another link in the experimentalist chain was existentialism, which dominated the European philosophical scene after World War II. In the 1960s, however, these links in the experimentalist chain of equivalence were challenged—in the visual arts by variants of new realism and pop art, in philosophy and the humanities by the onslaught of structuralism and Marxism. As a consequence, the chain of equivalence that had at first served to strengthen the position of experimentalism increasingly became a liability.

As a result, the experimentalist discourse had by the second half of the 1960s clearly lost its mobilizing force in Flemish poetry. After a few years in which the future direction of Flemish poetry remained unclear, an alternative discourse gradually began to take shape. In 1970, this discourse was for the first time clearly articulated under the name of new realism. The rapidity with which it subsequently succeeded in hegemonizing the field of Flemish poetry showed that "the time was ripe" for it (i.e., that experimentalist discourse had weakened to the extent that it was in no way able to resist new realist competition).

In the following, attention is turned to the way in which the new discourse was articulated, how it succeeded in mobilizing the support of the
"poetic community" and especially in uniting the group of poets who were
to exemplify new realist poetic practices. Furthermore, I demonstrate that,
inevitably, within the "universal" discourse of new realism particular differences continued to exist. Finally, the discussion of the case of Flemish new
realist poetry also illustrates that discursive revolutions are never total: they
always have to take into account a range of pre-existing and "naturalized"
views (i.e., in the case here views of what poetic practices "essentially" are).
A failure to sufficiently do so can contribute to deligitimating the discourse
and the practices motivated by it.

KREATIEF ON "NEW REALIST POETRY": RELUCTANT COLLABORATORS

One of the specificities of Laclau and Mouffe's discourse theory is that it
takes into account the agency of historical actors/groups. As seen earlier, the
conditions were given for the articulation of a poetical discourse that would
take over from the experimentalist hegemony. However, the dislocation of
the old poetical discourse cleared the way for several possible alternatives.
Which discourse would eventually prevail was co-dependent on the agility
and energy with which the individual actors in the field constructed and
defended their specific alternative. In the case at hand, the actor who saw his
efforts crowned with success was Lionel Deflo, the editor of the literary
magazine *Kreatief*, who in 1970 took the initiative of publishing a special
issue of his magazine under the title *New Realist Poetry in Flanders: A
Documentation*. The issue consisted of a programmatic introduction by
Deflo himself, a list of questions he submitted to nine young poets,[10] the
poets' replies to his questions and samples of their poetic practice, and
reproductions of images produced by contemporary Flemish artists.

The challenge confronting Deflo was that he had to succeed in uniting
the poets he had invited to collaborate to his special *Kreatief* issue. The realization of this goal was far from self-evident. There was no pregiven solidarity among the nine poets, who had very different antecedents and collabo-
rated in different literary magazines, each of which had more or less its own
poetical and artistic agenda. As a matter of fact, when reading the answers
the invited poets supplied to the questions Deflo had submitted to them, one
is struck by their diversity. They show unambiguously that the writers
assembled here are "limited historical actors," with their own particular
interests and aspirations. When interrogated by Deflo on their attitude
toward "new realism," many adopted a waiting attitude or even unambigu-

ously resisted identification with the new discourse. A salient example of this is provided by De Coninck, who would soon go on to become the most prominent and influential poet and critic emerging from the new realist generation. De Coninck's reply to Deflo's questions is highly ambivalent to say the least. While claiming to appreciate new realism, he at the same time implicitly but forcefully dissociated himself from it, invoking different arguments and observations. The first of these is a theoretical rejection of literary movements as such because, in his view, they are generally too extreme and one-sided. According to De Coninck, truly important poets always operate outside or, at the most, in the margin of literary movements. In line with this view, he rejected the radical poetry produced by the earlier new realism in the Netherlands. As for Flanders, his rejection was even more outspoken: *"Flemish new realism? Tell me who you mean, I hardly see anybody"* (Deflo, 1970: 140).

The same distancing can, in a more implicit way, be found in Het parlandisme,[11] an article De Coninck published at the end of 1970 (i.e., at the exact time Deflo tried to mobilize him and other young Flemish poets for the new realist cause). De Coninck blatantly ignored Deflo's efforts—and his prospective fellow new realists—by choosing as the subject of his essay only a number of poets from the Netherlands, whom he presents as typifying a recent trend (not a current or movement) in Dutch poetry he calls not new realism but *parlandism*, which is a broader term in the sense that, although all new realists are parlandists, certainly not all parlandists are new realists. Both instances, De Coninck's reply to Deflo's questions and the 1970 article, allow us to reconstruct his position as one that betrays an unwillingness to compromise his own (particular) views and preferences for the benefit of the discourse Deflo would have liked him to identify with. Undoubtedly, this unwillingness was reinforced by the fact that in Netherlandic-Dutch poetry the meaning of the signifier new realism had already been fixed, generating a subject position that he could not approve of. Next to the 'ideological' determination not to compromise the poetical views De Coninck had identified with, considerations of a political-strategic nature also may have played a role. Wholeheartedly and unambiguously embracing a new discourse that aspires towards hegemony is of course a risky business. If the discourse fails to become hegemonic, the actors that have embraced it without reservations are likely to go down with it. On the other hand, if it *is* successful, those who have refused any association with it risk having no part in its success. Therefore, the safest bet would be to march along while at the same time sufficiently keeping one's distance. In Žižekian idiom this reaction to the interpellation by the discourse could be rendered as: "Yes, I do speak the discourse, but the discourse is not really me. I am not actually in it."[12]

The case of De Coninck is instructive, and helps explain the prudence and ambivalence with which most of the selected poets reacted to Deflo's initiative. However, hesitant as they were, they did collaborate, thereby providing Deflo with the necessary backing and legitimacy for elaborating a new hegemonic discourse, that is, a discourse that aims to forge a new "collective will"—among the poets concerned, but also and especially within the wider "poetic community." As can be expected, this discourse is first and foremost articulated in Deflo's programmatic introduction to the New Realist Poetry issue of *Kreatief*. How did Deflo operate in order to merge what Laclau and Mouffe (1985: 128) called *"the differential and, hence, positive positions"* taken by the poets? How did he try to universalize his discourse?

THE BUILDING BLOCKS OF THE NEW REALIST DISCOURSE: COMMON ENEMY, EMPTY SIGNIFIER AND CHAIN OF EQUIVALENCE

As Laclau indicated, the first condition that is to be fulfilled for bringing this about is the designation of a *"common enemy"* (Laclau, 1996: 41) or *"oppressive sector"* (Laclau et al., 2000: 46). In this case, an elite that supposedly oppresses (blocks the identity of) most other groups in the poetic community. In Deflo's text, it does not take long for the enemy to be identified: The tyrants, as he depicted them, are a small group of authors, critics, and readers who cultivate a hermetic poetry and a view of the poet as a Chosen One. This condemned elite supposedly believes the poet to be elevated above the crowd and writes cryptic poetry that can only be grasped by a privileged, initiated audience and thus deliberately excludes most other readers. In painting this picture of the enemy, Deflo conflates elements from the romanticist-aestheticist and the experimentalist traditions, as is evidenced by the following passage from his introduction, which calls for a struggle against the exclusion of the majority of actors in the poetic domain:

> The poem, born from the experience of everyday lived reality, is to be given back to the everyday reader. Was this possible in the hypersubjective, metaphorical, hermetic language of the postexperimental poet? Did not the Language Acrobats, the Deep Professors, the Armchair Aesthetes and the Great Moguls of the Word condemn the poem to an isolated eternal existence, separated from Life [?] Did the Poet remain a God in the Depth of his Thought, exalted high above the worm-eaten mortal? (Deflo, 1970: 79)

As one can see, in the first of his rhetorical questions Deflo referred to the experimentalist tradition, postexperimentalism being the name given to the youngest generation of experimentalists.[13] The phrase *"a God in the Depth of his Thought"* alludes to a famous programmatic verse line by Willem Kloos, the poet who contributed most energetically and successfully to forging the literary discourse of the Eighties Movement, which became hegemonic in Netherlandic-Dutch poetry at the end of the 19th century. The romantic individualist-aestheticist ideology of this movement was immensely influential in the whole of Dutch poetry and continues to be a point of reference even today.

The enemy being identified, the discursive scenario that promises to defeat him and in doing so liberate ("unblock") the manifold oppressed identities in the poetic community can be outlined. As seen in the quoted passage, Deflo considered the enemy's *"notorious crime"* (Laclau et al., 2000: 45) to be that he exalts poetry, thereby withholding it from *"the everyday reader"/"the worm-eaten mortal"* and separating it from *"the experience of everyday lived reality"* or *"Life."* This situation is to be reversed: *"The poem ... is to be given back to the everyday reader,"* and poetry is to closely remain in touch with (everyday) reality. Even this short passage reveals which are the key words in Deflo's discourse: reality, life, everyday experience. Unsurprisingly, the master signifier in this text pleading the cause of new realism is *reality*. This is not as trivial a conclusion as it may seem. In Deflo's discourse, reality functions as what Laclau and Mouffe called an empty signifier. It is not so much the meaning of the word reality that is important here—one could even say: on the contrary. What matters is that it refers to a situation of fullness that is projected to arise once the enemy will have been defeated and the "good" (realist) poets have given back poetry to the everyday reader.[14] At the end of his text, Deflo gives a taste of what is in store for poetry and its readership once new realist poets will hold sway. He does this by—provokingly[15]—recounting a personal anecdote. On the occasion of a modest birthday party for his 3-year-old son, Deflo decides to treat the invited family members to a recital of new realist poetry:

> nobody is obliged to believe it: breathless, the entire family clan, which normally loathes poetry, savored the poems together with the whipped cream. And what's more: they wanted more! No whipped cream, that is, but more of these "really comprehensible poems that really touch you!" My sweet heart, what more can you want?!

This tableau is of course highly ideologically charged: Ordinary people, who have so far always felt excluded from the realm of poetry, are suddenly given access to it. Their identity as readers/listeners of poetry, which up until then had been blocked following the exclusionary behavior of the poetic elites, is now allowed to unfold. The exclamation at the end is significant: as the phrase explicitly states, there is nothing left to be desired, a situation of fullness has been reached—the implication being that new realist discourse will spread this fullness throughout the poetic community, which will itself expand to include "real," "ordinary" people. This horizon is in fact what the signifier "reality" refers to in Deflo's new realist discourse.

The emptiness of the signifier "reality" is also functional in another way. Not only does it announce the happy outcome of the struggle against the elitist/hermeticist enemy, it also—by its very emptiness—serves as a surface of inscription for a plurality of *particular* aspirations and thereby helps *universalize* the new realist discourse. The various actors (groups, individual) that are interpellated by the new realist discourse can, so to speak, read their respective particular programs into it as long as the signifier in question remains empty (enough). Rereading Deflo's text from this perspective, one will be struck by the care he takes to avoid precisely defining "reality" and therefore also "new realism." In the first line of his text, he does promise *"a clear focus"* (*een scherpstelling*) with regard to new realism, and in the second paragraph he announces that his text will try to answer the questions: *"what exactly is new realism in poetry? And what is, more specifically, Flemish new realism?"* (Deflo, 1970: 79). The initial impression is that Deflo will, as a matter of fact, try to give a precise definition of "new realism," as he immediately excludes one possible interpretation of it: *"the term new realism has nothing in common with Nouveau Réalisme in the visual arts, which was launched by French Pop propagandist Pierre Restany"* (Deflo, 1970: 79). When one reads on, however, it soon becomes clear that this seemingly firm exclusion is nothing but a rhetorical trick Deflo uses to convince the reader that he will be given the *"clear focus"* he was promised. In the following sentences, the promised clarification does not materialize, on the contrary: *"What is it, then? Revalorization of 'reality'? A new vision? A reaction? A shift of mentality?"* The initial questions are only answered with new questions, which themselves do not get definitive answers in the rest of the text. Moreover, one will have noticed that, in the quoted passage, Deflo puts "reality" between quotation marks, thereby indicating that the term can be defined in multiple ways. This inference is confirmed by the endnote that accompanies the word "reality" and presents itself as a further elucidation: *"The notion 'reality' here includes all domains of reality, such as social reality, economic reality, cultural reality, religious reality, etc."* (Deflo, 1970: 83). In other words, reality can mean just about everything. Deflo consistently takes care not to fill in the emptiness of the signifier. On closer scrutiny, "reality" in Deflo's text refers first and foremost to the resistance against the common enemy and the fullness his defeat is supposed to bring about, and thereby opens itself to identification by various groups and individuals with, in the last instance, incompatible demands.

Deflo's strategic reluctance to give a precise definition of "reality" and "new realism" is consistent with the fact that he himself adopts a low profile. The New Realist Poetry issue of *Kreatief* is not announced as a manifest or a program, but far more modestly as a *documentation*. The pragmatic implications of this choice are important: The term documentation suggests that Deflo does not intend to dictatorially impose his own personal views. Instead, and in line with the anti-elitist views he claims to hold, he underlines his intention to humbly serve the (everyday) reader of poetry: this is "*a documentation for the poetry consumer*" (Deflo, 1970: 79). In the same vein, he refrains from any attempt at telling the invited poets what they should do or believe. He simply puts a small number of questions to them in order "*to obtain first-hand, truthful information, from the horse's mouth*" (Deflo, 1970: 79). In short, Deflo minimizes his own role and input by presenting himself as merely an impartial observer, a reporter or field worker trying to objectively describe a pregiven situation—the "*situation of an innovative trend in poetry that has of late been at a premium in the Southern Netherlands.*"[16] Of course, such a stance must be met with the greatest suspicion. In fact, and as we have seen, Deflo does not simply describe what "Flemish new realism" is, he makes a substantial contribution to constructing and articulating it. However, in order to do so, he must first of all uphold that there *is* an essential, pregiven reality that corresponds to the name "new realism."[17] Second, Deflo's pragmatic positioning is strategically useful: It serves to present him as a moderate and tolerant figure, catering to the needs of the wider audience and trying to faithfully capture the characteristics of the "*mental climatic zone*" (Deflo, 1970: 79) the selected poets dwell in without aiming to discipline them into programmatic concord. Deflo even allows for a considerable degree of pluralism within the new realist ranks, since in submitting his questions to the nine selected poets he does not want "*one bell*" to sound but "*nine bells with nine voices*" (Deflo, 1970: 79). As noted earlier, this low profile and the deft use of the empty signifier "reality" serve the same purpose: universalizing the discourse and thereby raising its chances to become hegemonic. The more the discourse is felt to defend "universal"[18] values and interests, the more it can find acceptance with poets, critics and audiences. Within the discourse, however, the particularities are allowed to subsist.

Another effective way of articulating the particular efforts of groups and individuals into a common struggle consists in the creation of an associative series of ideological views and struggles, which are often incarnated and summarized by symbolically charged names, events, images, and so on. As mentioned earlier, the technical term Laclau and Mouffe (1985: 128) used to refer to such a series is chain of equivalence. Discourses (and therefore also ideologies) are not logically constructed ensembles, in which convictions and beliefs are cogently derived from each other or are necessarily interdependent. The set of views they defend is more of an aggregate, a provisional (partially fixed) coalition of positions and ideas in which historical actors can "recognize" themselves. This general rule also holds for Flemish new realist discourse. The chain of equivalence proper to it clearly threads itself through (is co-articulated by) the whole setup of the New Realist Poetry issue of *Kreatief* (i.e., through the introduction, Deflo's questions, the poets' replies and sample poems, the mottoes and the visual material interspersed among the texts).

In his introduction, Deflo distances himself not only from the afore-mentioned aesthetic-romantic and experimentalist traditions, but also part-ly from new realist poetry in the Netherlands: The group around the liter-ary magazine *Gard-Sivik* and its successor *De Nieuwe Stijl* is criticized, whereas poets and critics from *Barbarber*, another literary magazine, are referred to as authorities and examples of good poetic practice. This results in a whole series of names appearing in connection with a positive or nega-tive appreciation: As a Flemish new realist poet, you like J. Bernlef and dis-like C.B. Vaandrager. As far as references to the international poetic scene are concerned, Deflo only mentions positive examples: the American poets William Carlos Williams and Marianne Moore, and the "Liverpool poets." Furthermore, Deflo establishes a link between Flemish new realist poetry and recent developments on the international visual art scene. As we have seen, *"Nouveau Réalisme"* is rejected. Most other recent/contemporary trends and currents, however, are embraced, albeit in an extremely vague and unobliging way, as Deflo does no more than approvingly mention *"Pop Art and other international art currents"* (Deflo, 1970: 79-80). Another link in the chain is the contemporary social and political context, which is—certain-ly for those belonging to the younger generation—of course still dominated by the progressive discourse aiming at democratization and emancipation. Once again, Deflo makes the link in a very cautious way. On the one hand, he does claim: *"NRP [New Realist Poetry] corresponds to a general trend towards democratization"* (Deflo, 1970: 82). On the other hand, he not only leaves room for different strands of social and political commitment in Flemish new realist poetry but also makes clear that even those who do not—directly and vehemently or more indirectly and subtly—try to change society are therefore not to be excluded from the NRP circles. Further links in Deflo's introduction are for the greater part produced by the negation of the ideas and practices of the older poetic discourses he repudiates: he advo-cates a poetry thematizing everyday reality and personal anecdotes (vs. ivory tower/autonomy), aiming to be communicative and accessible (vs. elit-ism/the cult of marginality), and characterized by a plain style inspired by spoken language (vs. "poetic language"/hermeticism) and by humor and understatement (vs. seriousness/self-importance).

Deflo's introduction thus draws the outlines of Flemish new realist identity in the following way:

- romanticism / experimentalism
+ negation of romanticism / experimentalism (accessible, plain style, humor, subject matter taken from everyday life)
+ reality (social and political reality, everyday reality, etc.)
+/− new realist poetry in the Netherlands
  + *Barbarber*
  - *Gard-Sivik / De Nieuwe Stijl*
+ new trends in international poetry
+ (most) new trends in the visual arts
− *'Nouveau Réalisme'*
+ democratization in the social and political domain

The + axis is in all cases implicitly linked to positions taken by the younger generations, locally and abroad. This allows us to further extend the chain of equivalence with a binary opposition present in most ascending hegemonic discourses: new/young (innovative[19]) versus old (old-fashioned, obsolete). Deflo himself and the poets he has invited are all associated with the privileged pole of this pair (they are all young,[20] and the poets are labeled [by Deflo] as innovative). As it seems, the individual poets collaborating in this issue are not necessarily linked to all elements in the chain of equivalence: The presence of one or two of them seems to suffice for a poet to be identified as a new realist. This explains why a chain of equivalence is, next to (an) empty signifier(s) signifying the fullness that will follow the defeat of the common enemy, a powerful tool in creating and advancing a hegemonic discourse: It allows the union of various groups and individuals under a common flag without abolishing their particularity. In this case: it allows poets heavily influenced by contemporary visual arts (e.g., Jooris) to march along with poets primarily interested in ending the reign of literary experimentalism and old-hat romanticism (e.g., De Coninck) and poets aiming to contribute to social and political change (e.g., Abicht, Van den Bremt[21]). In line with his strategic choice for a low profile, Deflo has taken care to construct his chain of equivalence on the basis of what he knows about the poets and their concerns and of the information the poets' answers to his questions have provided him.

THE LINK WITH THE VISUAL ARTS:
NEW REALIST POETRY // MODERN ART

Elements of the chain of equivalence that was described previously are scattered throughout the *Kreatief* issue. In the space allotted to me in this chapter, it is impossible to demonstrate this for each of the features enumerated earlier. Therefore, I will limit myself to one example: the link NRP—visual arts. As we saw, Deflo's introduction had only vaguely referred to *"Pop Art and other international art currents,"* which had *"fecundated"* the changed mentality of the 1960s underlying NRP. In the issue itself, however, this link is elaborated. To begin with, it is illustrated with reproductions of paintings by various artists. Some of these belong to a group of mainly Flemish painters called the New Vision, with whom especially Roland Jooris had privileged relations. Other contributing artists were NRP Jan Vanriet himself, who would go on to become a painter of some renown, especially in Flanders, and Flemish painter Pol Mara, who represented a slick and not uncontroversial version of pop art and was energetically promoted by Luc Wenseleers, another contributing poet. It should be noted that the *"international art currents"* Deflo spoke about are represented here by local artists, a choice that was no doubt dictated by practical considerations (remuneration, copyright) but probably also by the (Deflo's) wish to highlight the fact that most of the invited poets did have networks linking them with local innovative contemporary artists. This intention can also be inferred from the fact that the third of Deflo's five questions specifically aims to elicit answers concerning the poets' relations with contemporary art. The formulation of the question deserves some comment. Already the introductory sentence is revelatory: *"The experimental poetry of the Fifties Movement stood in a close relationship with contemporary abstract art"* (Deflo, 1970: 84). It is obvious what Deflo is trying to do here: As was said earlier, the experimentalist discourse in poetry had derived much of its legitimacy from the link it had established between its own poetic practice and contemporary painting, more notably the Cobra movement, which had rapidly harvested international success. By 1970, however, Cobra art had itself become "old" and part of the hegemony to be beaten. Following the example of the experimentalists, a competing discourse on the rise can raise its level of credibility by allying itself with an ascending discourse in the visual arts. This seems to be exactly what Deflo has set out to achieve.

The actual questions following the introductory sentence show that Deflo believes he already knows what that cognate discourse in the visual arts will be: *"Do you also see parallels in Flanders between the so-called 'New Vision' in the visual arts … and new realist poetry? In what way?"* The question begs the answer: yes, there are parallels between NRP and a new artistic movement, and that movement is the group of painters gathered in the "New Vision." It is interesting to note the differences between the assumptions implied in these questions, which were of course formulated before Deflo had received the poets' answers, and the position taken in the introduction, which was written afterward. The questions presuppose a rather close relationship between NRP and the New Vision painters; the introduction only vaguely mentions an affinity with recent tendencies in international art. In between, something has happened which has dislocated this aspect of Deflo's discourse and obliged him to reformulate his representation of the link with the visual arts. That event—this (in Lacanian-Žižekian jargon) irruption of the "Real"—is that the poets did not answer as could be hoped and expected: Out of the nine interrogated poets, only two (Jooris and Van Ryssel; see Deflo, 1970: 85-86 and 96) wholeheartedly affirm that the New Vision has been important for their NRP. Poet-painter Vanriet acknowledges the influence of the New Vision, but is quick to point out that also a number of Flemish/Belgian and international painters, mainly pop artists, have been of vital importance to Flemish NRP.[22] Wenseleers does not separately answer Deflo's third question, and he does not extensively refer to the contemporary visual arts. The New Vision group is not mentioned at all. He defines his own poetry as "pop poetry," and claims that it is modeled after international pop art as he had come to know it since the early 1960s. As can be expected, Wenseleers also stresses the importance of the work of his favorite Flemish artist Pol Mara for his own poetry. Lasoen is an even more discordant voice, as she seems to downplay the importance of the New Vision— which she seems to equate with *"new realist painting, Pop Art, etc."* (Lasoen cited in Deflo, 1970: 105-106)—for Flemish NRP. Lasoen does see obvious similarities between the two, but believes that these are to be ascribed primarily to shared ideas and intentions. This view is more or less shared by Segers (cited in Deflo, 1970: 124), who does admit however that at least in the case of Jooris the influence of *"painting depicting the new vision"* has been a direct source of inspiration, and by De Coninck (cited in Deflo, 1970: 139), who—in a rather short reply, symptomatic of his limited interest in the visual arts—concurs with Lasoen in stressing the shared ideas of Flemish NRP and contemporary art, which he, however, identifies not as the New Vision but as pop art.[23] Van den Bremt (cited in Deflo, 1970: 150) equates new realism not with the New Vision group but with pop art, which he sternly rejects because he considers it to be too uncritical of *"neo-capitalist reality."* Finally, in his reply, Abicht does not even respond to Deflo's third question. This can partly be explained by the fact that he characterizes his contribution as no more than *"the beginning of an answer"* (Abicht cited in Deflo, 1970: 144). However, even the short text he does submit shows that for him the equation NRP—progressive (in Abicht's case: Marxist) action for social and political change is far more essential than the link with contemporary art.

In short, the answers to Deflo's third question show a great variety in points of view with regard to the influence of recent tendencies in the visual arts in general and of the New Vision group in particular. As we saw, this forces Deflo to rearticulate his discourse for it to be able to universalize the particular aspirations that are to be found in the poets' replies. Still, despite the poets' diverging views of the matter and Deflo's uneasy maneuvering, the final impression the *Kreatief* issue leaves behind is that, in one way or another, recent art is an essential link in the Flemish new realist chain of equivalence and therefore also an integral part of its identity. The relation between both as it is articulated here can be represented formulaically as:

Flemish new realist poetry

//

modern art

    =

       the New Vision (or individual artists belonging to it,
           such as Raveel, Willaert, etc.)

       AND/OR

       Pol Mara (and other Belgian artists working in the same
           vein, such as Jean Bilquin)

       AND/OR

       international pop art (e.g. Peter Blake)

in which the // is taken to mean:

       is influenced by

       AND/OR

       departs from cognate ideas and intentions.

The same observation holds for the other aspects of new realist identity as it is articulated by Deflo: the interpretations given to the empty signifier "reality," the revalorization of everyday life, the mixed response to NRP in the Netherlands, the international literary examples, new realist style, the link with progressive emancipatory and democratic discourses, and so on. Here, too, the positions taken by the individual poets are far from uniform—they are even on many occasions contradictory, as in the case of the poets' views of the importance of contemporary art and especially of the New Vision group for their own poetry and for Flemish new realist poetry in general. The same holds for the (generally implicit) hierarchies constructed between the various elements of the new realist chain of equivalence: some feel the rendition of everyday life is primordial, for others poetry's commitment to social and political change is all-important, whereas a third fraction primarily explores the links with the visual arts. Nevertheless, the all over impression the *Kreatief* issue conveys is that of a relatively coherent discourse on poetry. The ingredients identified by Laclau and Mouffe (common enemy, empty signifier[s], chain of equivalence) seem to suffice in order to create this effect.

The success of a discourse that strives for hegemony is never guaranteed. In other words, if such a discourse does become hegemonic, this is the contingent result of what is basically a political process. The word contingent, however, is not to be interpreted as a synonym of arbitrary. As we have seen, the conditions for the rise of the new discourse were favorable—the old discourse was in a state of dislocation—and the historical actor who tried to hegemonize his discourse—Deflo—did all the right things: He conjured up the image of a common enemy, he advanced an empty signifier, and subverted the internal differences by incorporating them into an anti-experimentalist/romanticist chain of equivalence. All of these moves were instrumental in universalizing the new realist discourse. Deflo's efforts bore fruit: As is shown in the study on Flemish NRP by Brems and De Geest (1991) and the more comprehensive account by Evenepoel and De Geest (1992), Deflo's action on behalf of new realism succeeded in making the young literary movement into a runaway success. Critics in literary magazines but also in the mainstream Flemish media felt obliged to take notice of the young current and tried to answer the question: *"What is Flemish new realist poetry?"* The *Kreatief* issue was immediately sold out and would be, with a modified introduction, reprinted as a book three times (Deflo, 1972).

THE DECLINE OF THE NEW REALIST DISCOURSE

However, the new realist hegemony was relatively short-lived. Already in 1974, new realist poet Jan Vanriet edited, under the title *"Omtrent de werkelijkheid"* (*About reality*), another special *Kreatief* issue, which was, among other things, a sort of photo album of the new realist movement. Looking back on what new realism was, it symbolically concluded the mini-era of the hegemony of new realist discourse. A thorough investigation into what brought about this rapid decline falls outside the scope of this chapter, but if I were to conduct this investigation my research hypothesis would probably go along the following lines.

First of all, hegemonies in the cultural sphere have in recent times become exceedingly volatile and ephemeral.[24] There is no reason why the discourse of Flemish new realist poetry would constitute an exception to that rule. Another possible explanation for the relative ephemerality of the new realist discourse is that, when a discourse becomes hegemonic, its oppression-by-a-common-enemy story tends to lose at least part of its credibility, which in its turn is likely to result in a weakening of the mobilizing and solidarizing force exerted by the discourse. This seems to hold in the case of Flemish new realism, too: The rapid success of the new discourse revealed how weak the opponent had become in reality. Just as anti-communism became pointless after the collapse of communism, anti-experimentalism became superfluous once the consensus was established that the experimentalists that had come to the fore in the 1960s had *"nothing to say,"*[25] which led to their swift and effective marginalization.[26] Paradoxically, rapid and total victory tends to undermine the victorious discourse.[27] As soon as the common enemy has vanished, particularistic tendencies within the discourse tend to grow stronger—a process that can lead either to the rearticulation of the discourse by one of these tendencies or to the breakup of the discourse altogether.[28] A final explanation I see for the fading away of the new realist discourse is the continued resistance to it by poets, critics and "ordinary" readers. New realism did not succeed in stabilizing its hegemony because its poetic and discursive practice was at odds not so much with older discourses on poetry as a whole but with the "discursive debris" left by these discourses (i.e., with a number of "received ideas" inherited from these older discourses and believed to capture the essence of what poetry is and what poets do). After the first infatuation with new realist practice was over, the new poetic discourse was increasingly criticized for its heresy with regard to this imputed essence. This is a typical effect of what Torfing (1999: 70), in his introduction to Laclau and Mouffe's discourse theory, called *sedimentation*. For its practice to have been experienced as entirely legitimate, Flemish new realism would have had to attune its practices more to the ideas that were sedimented within the Flemish poetic community—or else it would have had to fight its discursive struggle against these sedimented ideas with greater talent, vigor, and perseverance by producing and circulating a discourse on poetry capable of rebutting them and by steadily publishing poems that by their sheer continued presence helped remold this so-called essence of poetry.[29] When it came to bringing this about, however, new realism in Flemish poetry proved unable to deliver.[30]

As can be inferred from the preceding, the end of new realism's hegemony did not signal the end of everything it stood for: just as the discourses preceding it, it made an impact that outlasted the period of its hegemony. After new realism, it had for instance become well nigh impossible to depict the poet as a lofty, sacrosanct figure. The use of a markedly "poetic" language or a hermetic oracular language did not become highly exceptional or entirely excluded in Flemish poetry after new realism, but they both ceased to be the norm they used to be at given times in the history of Flemish poetry. This evolution would have been unthinkable without new realism's clear preference for a plain style and an immediately accessible language. In short, some of new realism's central tenets have themselves become sedimented into the poetic consensus and therefore also in the identities of most readers, critics, and poets.

The new realist movement also and especially changed the identities of the poets who participated in it. As we saw earlier, the reactions of some of those invited to contribute to the New Realist Poetry issue of *Kreatief* bore witness to their great reluctance. In the discourse-theoretical jargon, one could say that they initially refused to identify with Deflo's new realist discourse. Earlier, I suggested two possible reasons for this, the first being fear that the discursive order Deflo's new realist discourse intended to establish would not leave sufficient room for or would even run counter to the pursuit of their particular aspirations, the second one that a clear and unambiguous, "high-profile" identification with a discourse striving for hegemony is risky: If the discourse fails to hegemonize the discursive field, agents who have identified themselves with it too closely may find themselves permanently marginalized.

Still, all of them contributed to the *Kreatief* issue, as they would generally participate in the movement's subsequent manifestations. As said earlier, one could suspect that at least some of them did so for opportunistic reasons. Indeed, why refrain from taking part in a movement that seemed to hold the promise of being able to conquer the center of poetic activity—a promise that would, as a matter of fact, turn into reality quite soon?[31] Seen in this light, the individual poets could be presented as calculating and manipulative poet-politicians, exploiting the new realist movement as a vehicle for furthering their personal interests. However, I believe this way of presenting things would capture only one—albeit important—aspect of what went on in the new realist movement. Another aspect is that, as shown earlier, Deflo did his utmost to universalize the discourse (i.e., to turn it into a surface of inscription suited to the needs of the different particular parties involved and allowing them the necessary room for maneuvering). In this way, he created the necessary conditions for the poets to "recognize" themselves in the discourse he submitted to them—and it would seem that they did at least partially and/or for some time.

A good example of the ambivalent way in which the poets involved identified with the new realist discourse advanced in *Kreatief* is again De Coninck who, in his reply to Deflo's questions (i.e., before the new realist discourse had been articulated by the New Realist Poetry issue), had bluntly expressed his profound skepticism with regard to the existence of a new realist movement in Flemish poetry and had initially rejected the label "new realism" for referring to the new tendencies in Flemish poetry and certainly to define his own poetic practice. Soon afterward, however, De Coninck started to use the label himself and even—although in a highly ambivalent way—identified with it. In an interview given in 1977 De Coninck said:

> The funny thing is that hardly any of the new realists accepts that he is
> a new realist. I am not bothered by it, if I have to attribute myself to a
> current, I prefer the new realists over the new experimentalists. I have
> nothing against currents, I can swim, haha. And I have nothing against
> the common-or-garden poetry some of the new realists write. (161)

This is a highly interesting passage. It first of all confirms the essential solidarizing role of the common enemy (in this case, (post)experimentalism).
The importance of this supposed enemy is underlined again further on in the
interview, where De Coninck considers "*the great merit*" (De Coninck
1977: 161) of new realism to be its revolt against the excesses of experimentalism. In other words, in as far as new realism presents itself as a common
struggle against the negation of a whole range of poetic identities, De
Coninck can identify with it. When it comes to positively defining his individual position, however, he makes sure to keep his distance from the other
Flemish new realists. His claim that he "has nothing against" the poetic
practice of some of his fellow new realists sounds condescending and stresses that he himself has always held an unmistakably particular position within (or in the margin of) new realism. This ambiguity offers the advantage
that it sufficiently dissociates him from new realism, which by the time he
gave the interview had become an outdated and delegitimated discourse. By
not overidentifying with it, De Coninck remained from the very beginning
on the safe side, all the more so because the particular features that distinguished him from other new realists were in fact proven, sedimented views
of poetry. As suggested previously, I believe that the decline of new realism
was caused among others by the resistance to its production, which was
based on exactly such sedimented views. It is quite normal, then, that De
Coninck would readily—and especially so after the new realist hegemony
had eclipsed—be perceived as (one of) the (only) new realist(s) who was
aware what the essence of poetry was and who therefore wrote good poetry. De Coninck's position in the late 1970s was even further strengthened by
the fact that the "neo-romantic" discourse, which came to relieve neo-real-
ism, was based on a number of the sedimented ideas that De Coninck had
propagated from the very beginning of his career as a poet. In striking contrast to Deflo, who would become marginalized as soon as the discourse he
had advanced lost its hegemonic position, De Coninck went on to become
one of the most influential figures in recent Flemish poetry and poetry criticism. Again, by no means do I want to suggest here that this is the result of
a *necessary* process.[32] However, it is not something that came to happen
purely by chance either: It is the *contingent* outcome of political struggles in
the literary domain—which is to say, in layman's terms, it is the result of (in
this case De Coninck's) energetic agency and deft discursive maneuvering[33]
on the one hand, and pure and simple good luck[34] on the other.

CONCLUSION

This chapter should not be read as an attempt to supplement or even supplant the existing studies on Flemish NRP. These not only cover the entire history of new realism but have also been conducted in much greater detail. Rather, I have built on the information on the subject gathered by them to reflect on the question of how the analytic tools supplied by Laclau and Mouffe's discourse theory can be used in (re)writing literary history and especially the history of literary movements.

In my view, the new realist movement in Flemish poetry has to be conceived of not as a pregiven essence—a prelinguistic "reality"—that was subsequently articulated, but as a discourse (i.e., as a product of articulation from the very outset). If this assumption is correct, it can be expected that discourse-theoretical analysis is apt to enhance insight into the way literary movements originate, rise to prominence and subsequently fade way.

Especially Laclau and Mouffe's views of how discourses succeed in obtaining and occupying a hegemonic position—the empty place of the universal—and the concepts they use in developing these views (radical exclusion of a common enemy/oppressor, empty signifier[s], chain of equivalence) can be helpful for literary historiography. In fact, and as we indicated earlier, the use of the discourse-theoretical framework in the study of literature can be viewed as the logical radicalization and elaboration of tendencies already present within literary theory to conceive of literary development as the product of contingent political processes. So far, these theoretical insights have all too rarely been translated into concrete analyses. Discourse theory may point the way to amending this situation.

NOTES

1. Not untypically, Culler's well-known introduction to "structuralist poetics" contains hardly any reference to what was then fashionably called the diachronic aspect of literature (see Culler, 1975).
2. Further, and influential, elaborations of earlier formalist and structuralist theories of literary history can be found in the work of Soviet semioticians (Lotman) and French structuralists (Barthes, Kristeva).
3. To be taken, of course, *cum grano salis*. To begin with, the daily practice in dealing with literature and literary theory proves that essentialism is far from being rooted out and probably never will be. Also, the brevity of my exposé forces me to tell a story of teleological necessity, which runs counter to my intentions. Still,

I do believe that the criticism of essentialism represents an important theoretical advance within the development of literary history.

4. In the current state of affairs, differences with Dutch as it is spoken in the Netherlands subsist and even seem to become more extensive. Nevertheless, Flemish Dutch is generally considered to form an integral part of the Dutch language. It is nowadays the only official language in the northern part of Belgium and of the majority of the Belgian population. This is, however, a relatively recent situation. In the 19th and part of the 20th centuries, Flanders was characterized by a "social bilingualism": The ruling classes generally spoke French, the lower classes some form of Dutch. As a consequence, the term Flemish literature was for a long time ambiguous, because it could refer to either literature written in Flemish Dutch or literature written by Flemings (in either French or Dutch). Some of the most important Flemish authors, such as Émile Verhaeren and 1911 Nobel Prize winner Maurice Maeterlinck, wrote their entire work in French.

5. One of the most important differences being the social position and valuation of Dutch itself (see endnote 4): while in the Netherlands, Dutch was the official language and the language of the ruling class, in Belgium it initially enjoyed hardly any cultural prestige as it was only spoken by the lower classes. The creation of Flemish literature in the 19th century was intimately linked to the rise of a romantic nationalism that would soon clash with official Belgian nationalism, while comparable nationalistic tensions were absent in the north. Other historical differences are, for example, the fact that Flanders, as opposed to the Netherlands, where Protestantism was the predominant religion, was for a long time dominated by Catholicism, which had a profound impact on cultural life, or the fact that Belgium was drawn into World War I, whereas the Netherlands were able to maintain their neutrality.

6. The notable exception would be Herman de Coninck, but even this poet, who made his debut in 1969, had to wait at least until the 1980s before he was taken seriously in the Netherlands. Even then, he was appreciated there more as a critic than as a poet, while in Flanders De Coninck's poetry was (and is) immensely popular. The only other Flemish new realist poet to publish in the Netherlands was Roland Jooris. This, however, did not happen before 2001 (i.e., more than 30 years after the Flemish new realist movement got underway). Jooris was 65 at the time of his first book publication in the Netherlands.

7. In their introduction, Evenepoel and De Geest (1992: 4) called their study "*an attempt to reconstruct the discursive situation of new realism in Flanders,*" and explicitly stated their intention to refrain from value judgments. Instead, they wanted to investigate how value is attributed.

8. I borrow the term enemy from Laclau (1996: 41). Following Schmitt, Mouffe (1993) distinguished between enemies (who are to be destroyed) and adversaries (whose ideas are to be fought but whose existence is to be tolerated). In Mouffe's view, it is typical of pluralistic democratic orders that the different parties involved in the political process construct their opponents not as enemies but as adversaries. However, even within pluralistic democratic orders the cultural sphere is not necessarily pluralistic and democratic. Moreover, the term enemy offers the advantage of not occulting the fact that in cultural battles the losing parties are often entirely and permanently annihilated as "legitimate" actors (artists, critics, etc.).

9. As Laclau and Mouffe see it, identities are not only discursively constructed by means of a logic of difference, but also through a logic of equivalence, which allows a particular group to identify its own struggle with the struggle of other groups. This serves to universalize these particular struggles, and helps simplify the social and political space groups and individuals find themselves in. The combined operation of the logics of difference and of equivalence makes this space appear meaningful and understandable. I return later to the use of chains of equivalence in the discussion of new realist discourse.

10. These poets were Roland Jooris, Daniël van Ryssel, Patricia Lasoen, Jan Vanriet, Gerd Segers, Luk Wenseleers, Herman de Coninck, Ludo Abicht, and Stefaan van den Bremt.

11. The title of this essay is hard to translate. It refers to the *hausse* of "parlando" poetry in Dutch (i.e., poetry written in a style resembling spoken language).

12. Žižek (1997: 21) even claimed that this is the standard form of identification with a discourse: "*an ideological identification exerts a true hold on us precisely when we maintain an awareness that we are not fully identical to it.*" In other words, and paradoxically, resistance to identification is essential to its success.

13. The name is strategically useful for Deflo because it allows him to draw a neat dividing line between these late, "extremist" experimentalists and the earlier experimentalists, some of whom had become canonized to the extent that a depreciation of all experimentalists would harm the credibility of Deflo's discourse. In addition to this, the "post"-prefix easily evokes pejorative connotations.

14. Laclau (1996: 15) defined an empty signifier as a "*signifier of fullness as such, of the very idea of fullness.*"

15. The modernist-experimentalist tradition forcefully rejects references to the poet's individuality and aims to create an "impersonal" poetry. Relating a personal anecdote in this context is therefore an ostentatious transgression of this doxa. It would become one of the most characteristic practices of new realism.

16. For some time, the Dutch-speaking part of Belgium was often referred to as the Southern Netherlands. This term has presently gone out of use and been replaced by Flanders.

17. In the first paragraph of his text, Deflo (1970: 79) refers to this so-called "given" as "*the present situation.*" In studying literary movements, it should be kept in mind that they are, first and foremost, the "*retroactive effects of naming,*" although the promoters (or detractors) of the movements in question will usually do their utmost to suppress this insight.

18. The quotation marks serve to underline that all universality bears, as Laclau (e.g., 1996: 57) reminds us, the traces of the particular circumstances in which it arose.

19. In the very first sentence of his introduction, Deflo announces that he will discuss "*an* innovative *tendency in poetry*" (Deflo, 1970: 79; emphasis added)

20. The oldest being Roland Jooris and Ludo Abicht, who were born in 1936 and were therefore 34 at the time the *Kreatief* issue was published. Most others, however, had not yet turned 30. Jan Vanriet and Patricia Lasoen were only 22.

21. Abicht's poems in this issue have telling titles such as "the long voyage to the land of peace," "the third world" and "the last of the algonquins." The last poem denounces the injustice done to the Native Americans. And Abicht's poem "eve" is dedicated "to rosa Luxemburg" (Abicht cited in Deflo, 1970: 144-149). Van

den Bremt's poems are less politically explicit. Still, his rejection of poetic narcissism in the poem "present-day Flemish poetry" leads him to praise Revolutionary Man in "cuba": "*man makes the world with his hands/makes the world with the very hands/he uses to burn his past behind him*" (Van den Bremt cited in Deflo, 1970: 153-154). At the time, the proper name Cuba was of course highly ideologically overdetermined, also and in particular in the Netherlands and Flanders. Major authors such as Hugo Claus and Harry Mulisch overtly and ardently sympathized with the Cuban revolution.

22. What's more, Vanriet (cited in Deflo, 1970: 114) approvingly referred to a.o. Martial Raysse, an artist belonging to the *Nouveau Réalisme* categorically rejected by Deflo in his introduction. It is not clear whether Deflo was aware of this dissonance and if so, why he would have chosen to maintain it.

23. In doing so, De Coninck follows Wenseleers. This is hardly surprising: De Coninck and Wenseleers were both editors of the literary magazine *Ruimten*. Both refuse to accept Deflo's suggestion that the New Vision group is the all-important influence on Flemish new realism. Once again, particularity subsists under the cover of the universalizing discourse Deflo tries to propagate.

24. To the extent even that one could say that the positive valuation of change and innovation has become *the* sedimented rule of cultural practice in the broad sense of the term, including, among others, lifestyles and consuming patterns. In this context, I stress that, in my view, the decline of new realism in Flemish poetry was probably not to be ascribed to "intraliterary" change alone, but also to changes in all or most of the domains that made up the "*Flemish new realist discourse chain of equivalence*" — or, more concretely: to pop art and New Vision painting becoming "something of the 1960s," the international literary examples going out of fashion, the radical democratic-emancipatory discourse running out of steam, and so forth.

25. The expression is De Coninck's (1978: 487).

26. This fate is exemplified by third-generation experimentalist Van Maele, who in the course of the 1960s seemed to be well underway to becoming a central figure in Flemish literature, but was brushed aside and widely depreciated following the new realist onslaught (see Spinoy, 2003a: 103-104). Other names that can be mentioned here are those of Hedwig Speliers and Leopold M. van den Brande. It is worthwhile stressing in this context that in the literary domain, too, hegemonic discourses form an integral part of praxis and that their dominance has very *real* consequences, including steering decisions on who will be denied access to institutions, resources, and so on.

27. The best example of this in Dutch literature I can think of in this context is the previously discussed Eighties Movement in the Netherlands, which in the beginning of the 1880s vigorously swept aside the popular "Preachers' Poetry" (*Domineespoëzie*) — only to dissolve a few years later.

28. New realism would be followed in Flemish poetry by neoromanticism. In fact, this development can be seen as a reinforcement and radicalization of the "De Coninck tendency" in new realism. From the very beginning, De Coninck had advocated a "realist romanticism." In 1978, he published an essay with the significant title: "*About New Realism and Old Romanticism.*" Neo-romanticism can therefore be seen as something between the articulation of a genuinely new discourse and the rearticulation of parts of the old new realist discourse. This

explains why the transition between the two discourses was a particularly peaceful one, with older new realist and younger neoromantic poets sometimes working side by side, as was the case in the originally new realist literary magazine *Yang*. In 1983, also Deflo's *Kreatief* published an issue on neo-romanticism.

29. As Torfing (1999: 70-71) explained, sedimented views are institutionalized views, the political origins of which are suppressed—which is itself of course a political process. This implies that challenging them may prove difficult but also that it is not impossible. Such challenging would require bringing to light and reactivating these origins.

30. Most of the new realist poets quickly "faded away": They stopped publishing poems or their production remained limited at best. Those who continued to publish usually did so in a fairly marginal way. Deflo himself did not succeed in acquiring the stature of an authoritative critic. It is perhaps no coincidence that the only new realist poet who quickly became successful as a poet and later on also become an influential voice in poetic criticism was De Coninck, whose ideas can be described as a compromise between new realism and sedimented romantic views of poetry. At any rate, because of the "moderate" character of his ideas, De Coninck's practice only partially contributed to subvert received ideas.

31. This is in fact the reverse side of the strategy described in the previous paragraph: An all too close identification with a discourse aspiring toward hegemony holds the risk of utter marginalization, no identification with it at all would imply forfeiting the chance of reaping the profits of hegemony. The ambiguous position of most poets as I see it is at least partially the result of compromise and negotiation.

32. That literary events and developments were bound to happen is what literary histories implicitly often suggest, thereby naturalizing what are in fact the results of political processes.

33. In the case of a poet, this term can be taken to include the poetry itself—in which case the writing and publishing of poems and poetry collections are considered as moves in the "poetry game"—and the (poetical) discourse on poetry.

34. The "good luck" factor is of course beyond the control of the agents involved in the struggle. This does not mean, however, that it is beyond explanation. The strengthening of the position of the "romantic new realist" De Coninck in the late 1970s can be explained by the rise of the neo-romantic discourse, even though this was no necessary development and De Coninck could in no way have foreseen and/or controlled it.

REFERENCES

Brems, H., Geest, D. de (1989) *Barbaar in mijn Mond: Poëzie in Vlaanderen 1955-1965*. Leuven: Acco.

Brems. H., Geest, D. de (1991) *Opener dan Dicht is Toe: Poëzie in Vlaanderen 1965-1990*. Leuven: Acco.

Chklovski, V. (1973) *Sur la Théorie de la Prose*. Trans. G. Verret. Lausanne: Éds. L'Age d'Homme.

Coninck, H. de (1970) 'Het Parlandisme,' *Dietsche Warande en Belfort* 115(10): 738-748.

Coninck, H. de (1977) ['Interview taken by W.M. Roggeman'], pp. 157-178 in W.M. Roggeman (Ed) *Beroepsgeheim 2: Gesprekken met Schrijvers*. Rotterdam: Nijgh & Van Ditmar.

Coninck, H. de (1978) 'Over Nieuw Realisme en Ouwe Romantiek,' *Ons Erfdeel* 21(4): 485-491.

Culler, J. (1975) *Structuralist Poetics: Structuralism, Linguistics and the Study of Literature*. London: Routledge and Kegan Paul.

Deflo, L. (Ed) (1970) 'Nieuw-realistische Poëzie in Vlaanderen: Een Dokumentatie,' *Kreatief* 4(3): 1-156.

Deflo, L. (Ed) (1972) *Nieuw-Realistische Poëzie in Vlaanderen. Een Dokumentaire Bloemlezing*. Brugge, De Bladen voor de Poëzie. [Printed twice in 1972, third edition in 1976]

Evenepoel, S., Geest, D. de (1992) 'Nieuw-realistische Poëzie in Vlaanderen. Ontstaan, Doorbraak en Profilering van een Literaire Beweging,' *Spiegel der Letteren* 34(1): 1-88.

Laclau, E. (1996) *Emancipation(s)*. London, New York: Verso.

Laclau, E. et al. (2000) *Contingency, Hegemony, Universality: Contemporary Dialogues on the Left*. London, New York: Verso.

Laclau, E., Mouffe, C. (1985) *Hegemony and Socialist Strategy: Towards a Radical Democratic Politics*. London: Verso.

Mouffe, C. (Ed) (1993) *The Return of the Political*. London: Verso.

Mukařovský, J. (1974) *Kapitel aus der Ästhetik*. Frankfurt a.M.: Suhrkamp.

Spinoy, E. (2003a) 'De Kanker van een Diepgewortelde Droom: Over Marcel van Maele,' pp. 99-115 in *M. van Maele, Scherpschuttersfeest*. Antwerp: Houtekiet.

Spinoy, E. (2003b) 'Extase en Ontnuchtering: Guido Gezelle en Herman de Coninck Beyond Discourse,' *Gezelliana: Kroniek van de Gezellestudie* (1): 45-71.

Torfing, J. (1999) *New Theories of Discourse: Laclau, Mouffe and Žižek*. Oxford: Blackwell.

Tynjanow, J. (1982) *Poetik*. Leipzig, Weimar: Gustav Kiepenheuer Verlag.

Vodička, F. et al. (1976) *Die Struktur der literarischen Entwicklung*. München: Fink.

Žižek, S. (1997) *The Plague of Fantasies*. London, New York: Verso.

15

BOTH SELF AND OTHER

The Construction of "Flanders" in National Socialist Literary Discourse

Ine Van linthout

Flanders, the Dutch-speaking part of Belgium, was occupied by Nazi Germany from May 1940 to September 1944. Because the National Socialist regime perceived the Flemish as culturally and racially cognate to the German people, efforts to point out similarities between both peoples can be found in German National Socialist writings from the very beginning of the Nazi reign.[1] Yet, the question of how Flanders was depicted by the regime between 1933 and 1945 is more complex than it might seem at first sight. Although the Nazi propaganda machine could be expected to construct Flanders as a part of its self, a number of factors made such an easy assimilation impossible. From a National Socialist point of view, the Flemish were certainly closer to Germany than the French, and even closer than the Dutch with their long tradition of free-thinking and liberalism. However, they could not be put on a par with, for instance, the German-speaking regions that belonged to Germany before the Versailles treaty and that were therefore, from an ideological perspective, an easy prey for assimilation. The national borders that separated Flanders from Germany politically and made the Flemish people part of the Belgian state created an additional obstacle. Although the Nazi regime rejected Belgium ideologically, politically, ethnically, and culturally, it could not ignore its existence as a diplomatic, military, and economic entity and had therefore, at least for a number of years, to accept the status quo. In addition to this, the Flemish were perceived in Germany as an idyllic, epicurean, and self-sufficient people of *bon vivants*. This image, which was mainly based on the novels by Felix Timmermans and the paintings by Pieter Brueghel, pictured a Flanders that did not ask for any kind of interference from abroad, let alone from the Germans. Considering this series of complicating factors,[2] attempts to answer the question how Flanders was portrayed by the Nazi regime have to start by evaluating the implications of these factors for the process of image construction. How did they interfere with the regime's original intentions? To what extent did they influence the actual image?

A second preliminary point concerns the fact that cases such as that of the image of Flanders in Nazi Germany systematically find themselves outside the theoretical scope of research on image formation. This may have to do with the manifold challenges the topic confronts its researchers with. First of all, the historical period in question is, even today, framed by simplified narratives that do not only interfere with, but sometimes even discredit attempts at scientific nuancing and unbiased analysis. Second, the literature in question is ideologically invested to such a degree that mainstream literary studies often consider it too close to propaganda for it to be a valid object of research. Third, what is involved here is a relationship between nations or peoples that does not fit in with the prevailing (postcolonial) research interest in the discourse of the oppressed (colonized, marginalized) and the focus on the other as inherently different from the self. With respect to this last point, the topic at hand requires a theoretical and methodological rethinking of the complex relation between the self and the other.

Starting from these observations, the analysis of the construction of "Flanders" in Nazi Germany (1933-1945) in this chapter will successively discuss the complex relationships between the self and the other and those between intended and actual images. Both issues are analyzed from the angle of literary studies. This perspective appears from the composition of the research corpus: a selection of literary and cultural journals that functioned as the mouthpieces of the regime's controlling literary institutions, and a number of novels on Flanders that were published in German(y) between 1933 and 1945. Thanks to this combination of text materials, two different levels of the literary system can be addressed: the level of programmatic reflection on literature by the regime's politico-literary apparatus, and the level of the actual book production during its 12-year reign. The differentiation and comparison between the two corpora will prove to be of crucial importance for the analysis of the image of Flanders created by German National Socialism. Second, the choice for a literary studies perspective underlies the study's explicit aim to investigate the specific role of literary discourse and literary strategies in an unambiguously political image-formation process.

Although the primary focus is firmly situated in the domain of literature, the complex and interdisciplinary character of the topic requires a theoretical and methodological openness to neighboring research areas. The choice to enter into a dialogue with discourse theory is based on several considerations. One of these is that, with its focus on *"issues of identity formation, the production of novel ideologies ... and the structuring of societies by a plurality of social imaginaries"* (Howarth & Stavrakakis, 2000: 2), discourse theory promises to supply tools enabling us to understand and analyze the complexities of political identity and image construction. A second and more important consideration is that discourse theory emphasizes the limitations of totalizing discourses, showing that identities and images cannot be reduced to the original interests and intentions of their producers. The main impact of discourse-theoretical ideas on this study will therefore lie in their potential to sharpen the focus on the inevitable negotiations that hampered a smooth realization of the Nazi regime's intended image of Flanders.

For each of the two chosen issues, the chapter first discusses how they are dealt with in current research and subsequently reflects on how discourse theory can enrich and refine the analysis.

THE COMPLEX RELATION
BETWEEN SELF AND OTHER

In research on identity formation, identities are generally understood in terms of a self–other dialectic (i.e., a simultaneous process in which both the self and the other are constructed). This conceptualization is not without its ambivalences, however. On the one hand, a wide range of analyses within literary image and postcolonial studies acknowledge the relationship between the self and the other to be *"infinitely more complex than any dichotomous distinction allows"* (Norval, 2000: 224). They explore the ways in which *"the outside infects the inside and vice versa, making any simplistic dualism and either/or thought suspect"* (Norval, 2000: 224). They demonstrate, for instance, how self- and other-representations are interrelated by exploring the *"mutual interaction and interdependence of the English image of 'Ireland,' of the Irish image of 'England' and of the English and Irish auto-images of themselves as related to both these hetero-images"* (Leerssen, 1986: 10; see also Hoenselaars, 1992). Similarly, they show how colonial discourse, although it is generated within the colonizing societies and cultures, can become a discourse with which the colonized identify, subverting the colonizers' representation by turning it into an assertion of their distinctiveness (Ashcroft & Ahluwalia, 2001: 63). They also point out the complexity of self–other relationships that follows from the fact that the adjective "national" in "national image" refers to the viewer-nation as well as to the nation viewed (Boerner, 1975: 375), which means that the image of the other has often less to do with the represented other than with the representing self (Said, 1978: 12). Prominent French comparatists Jean-Marc Moura and Henri Pageaux translated this view methodologically by shifting the focus of attention from the relationship between the image and the object it represents to the relationship between the image and the social imaginary of the society that produces it:

> On l'a vu, les mises en scène de l'étranger se jouent toutes sur le fond
> d'une stratégie se rapportant à l'imaginaire social. Qu'elles le représen-
> tent à des fins d'adhésion ou de contestation de l'identité du groupe,
> images idéologiques et utopiques font d'abord de cet étranger l'élément
> central d'une problématique "autochtone." (Moura, 1992: 282)

Mention should also be made here of Homi Bhabha's exploration of the space "in between" the self and the other. Bhabha conceptualized the possibility of "new," hybrid identities, neither belonging to the pole of the self nor to the pole of the other, but situated in a "third space." He defined this space as an irreducible excess of meaning emerging from the dialogue between the self and the other (Leitch, 2001: 2377). A final variant can be found in the psychoanalytical approach initiated by Sigmund Freud and Julia Kristeva, which internalizes the other as part of the self — as "*something which is known and familiar, but repressed, made strange and thereby displaced onto an alien other*" (Van Alphen, 1991: 11).

So, on the one hand, there are multifarious efforts to capture the complexity of self–other relations and the impurity of relational identities (see Norval, 2000: 225). On the other hand, however, these efforts continue to conceive of and investigate the self and the other as clearly separated entities. Even Bhabha's third space and Kristeva's "other within" require the reference to a mutually exclusive self and other, in Bhabha's case because he located the hybrid identity between strictly separated entities, in Kristeva's because she defined the other as "*Étranger à nous-mêmes*" (Kristeva, 1988), that is, as a foreign, repressed, and therefore externalized part of the self. The encounter between the self and the other is systematically missed, which has considerable theoretical consequences for the analysis of self–other relations.

The first consequence of this mutual delimitation — which can be partly attributed to the philosophical and ethical stance that others should be respected as irreducibly and inherently different from the self — manifests itself in the privileging of corpus materials and the elaboration of theoretical frameworks that reflect and express this ideal. Although the resulting studies[3] are very valuable, they are based on a highly selective corpus of materials, and leave the need to critically describe, analyze, attempt to understand and raise consciousness about deviating models unanswered. It is therefore important that the levels of *what should be* and *what actually is*, the ethical-philosophical and the empirical levels so to speak, are not (con)fused. A second consequence of conceiving the self and the other as two separate entities is the widespread confusion in literature on the subject between the terms other (or hetero) and foreign. As a result, representations of the other are turned into constructions of contrast and antagonism. To cite just a few examples, *Metzler Lexikon* (1998: 232-234) described comparative image studies as:

> eine literaturwissenschaftliche Forschungsrichtung innerhalb der vergleichenden Literaturwissenschaft, die nationenbezogene *Fremd-* und Selbstbilder in der Literatur selbst sowie in allen Bereichen der Literaturwissenschaft und -kritik zum Gegenstand hat.[4]

What is first characterized as *images of the foreign and the self*, is in the following sentence denoted as *hetero- and auto-images*:

> Sie beschäftigt sich dabei mit der Genese, Entwicklung und Wirkung dieser "Hetero- und Auto-Images" im literarischen und außerliterarischen Kontext.[5]

Brunel and Chevrel's (1989: 25, author's emphasis) introduction to their *Précis de littérature comparée* defines literary image studies as "*l'étude des représentations de l'étranger dans la littérature.*" And Joep Leerssen paraphrases self- and other-images as "*images of the* foreign *and of the familiar*" (Leerssen, 1986: 9, author's emphasis). Through the frequent substitution of "foreign" for "other," the relation of mutual delimitation between the self and the other is—consciously or not—turned into a relationship of binary opposition.[6] Consequently, representations that do not construct the other as inherently different or foreign remain unaccounted for. Third and finally, the delineation between the self and the other seems to favor an *a priori* research focus on constructions of sameness *or* of otherness. Most studies on image formation opt for the latter, along the lines of Said's study on orientalism as "*a political vision of reality whose structure promoted the* difference *between the familiar (Europe, the West, 'us') and the strange (the Orient, the East, 'them')*" (Said, 1978: 43, author's emphasis), "*a form of thought for dealing with the* foreign" (Said, 1978: 46, author's emphasis) that is "*based upon an ontological and epistemological* distinction *made between 'the*

Orient' and ... '*the Occident*'" (Said, 1978: 2, author's emphasis). Less frequent is the focus on the discursive construction of sameness, as Ruth
Wodak noticed in 1999. *If* it is examined, it invariably concerns examples in
which the other is eventually absorbed by the self (e.g., the National
Socialist image of Austria) or integrated into it (e.g., the construction of
minorities as part of the nation state). In both cases, the result of the process
is one single identity (respectively, Nazi Germany and the multicultural
nation state).

On the basis of this critical overview, the question can be raised: What
if the delineation is not so clear? What if corpus materials bear witness to a
failure or impossibility to construct the other as either foreign from or identical with the self and display a complex mixture of the two? What to do, for
instance, with the German National Socialist image of Flanders, which can
neither be characterized as an image of the self, nor as an image of the foreign, nor as a new, third identity in Bhabha's sense of the word? The concepts image of the foreign or *Fremdbild* are hardly applicable to Flanders
since, in the corpus under consideration, indications of foreignness are
explicitly neutralized by terms like *vertraut* (familiar), *heimisch* (homelike),
gleich (similar), and *eigen* (own). As a result, Flanders does not qualify for
the categories of the threatening enemy, the exotic or the merely tolerated
other. The concepts image of the self and *Selbstbild* do not apply either,
because the Nazi German self could not absorb Flanders as easily as the
German-speaking regions mentioned earlier. Whereas the Nazi regime
could justify the annexation of the latter as a homecoming, the insurmountable differences between Flanders and Germany in the fields of language, literature, culture, history, religion, politics, and so on, could not but lead to
an acknowledgment of Flanders' singularity, of the "typically Flemish," of
the "beyond the German borders." As a result, Flanders and Germany
remained two different entities and identities.[7] Finally, Bhabha's conception
of a hybrid, "in-between" identity does not accurately describe the Nazi
image of Flanders either: any "excessive" meaning that would have made
Flanders inherently different from Nazi Germany was systematically submitted to attempts of domestication by the totalitarian state.

Consequently, the study of the Nazi image of Flanders that is produced
by the selected corpus materials requires another theoretical and methodological framework. This framework should first of all recognize the need
for a terminological and semantic differentiation between *the image of the
other* and *the image of the foreign*, between *the representation of the other*
and *the construction of otherness*. Second, it should not depart from a clear
separation between the self and the other, but rather think in terms of gra-
dations, and position its research object on a gliding scale between the self
and the other. As a result, the focus on the interaction *between* images of the
self and the other will be complemented with a focus on the interaction of
the self and the other *within* a certain image and the following questions will

become prevalent: How much sameness and how much difference is allowed within a particular image? How much difference subsists into a construction of sameness or a construction of the self? How much sameness is granted to the other? What are the tensions that exist between the two? Which negotiations and compromises does the image construction require? To what extent do these negotiations result in a complex mixture of sameness and difference, of self and other?

Discourse theory does not provide a ready-made framework for answering these complex questions, but it opens up a whole terrain of investigation in which they can be explored. In the analysis presented here, the tools supplied by Laclau and Mouffe are not used in the exact same way they were originally put to work,[8] but their use is inspired by the frame of thought in which they originated. This displacement is made possible and even encouraged by discourse theory's explicitly interdisciplinary character: On the one hand, the theory itself selects, adopts, and adapts concepts and insights from different disciplines, functionalizes them for the study of political identity formation and integrates them into its own critical and theoretical framework. On the other hand, it presents itself as "*sufficiently open and flexible enough to be adapted, deformed and transformed in the process of application*" (Howarth & Stavrakakis, 2000: 5), and thus encourages researchers to not merely subsume their empirical cases under the theoretical concepts and logics it offers, but to use them in novel ways. This openness is proof to the consistency between discourse theory's ideas and its methods, both of which reject essentialist approaches that predetermine the outcome of research and thus preclude the possibility of innovative approaches.

The discourse-theoretical concepts singled out for the study of the complex image of Flanders in German National Socialist literary discourse are equivalence, chain of equivalence, logic of equivalence, and equivalential pole. According to discourse theory, the logic of equivalence "*constructs a chain of equivalential identities among different elements that are seen as expressing a certain sameness*" (Torfing, 1999: 301). If this logic is accepted to be predominant in Nazi German identity and image formation, the concept contributes to the analysis in two different ways. First, it accounts for the well-known fact that National Socialist ideology constructs its vision of the world in terms of a polarity between us and them, good and bad, legitimate and illegitimate:

> The more predominant the logic of equivalence is, the more important becomes the particular social antagonism for the structuration of the social. Thus, the infinite expansion of a chain of equivalence tends to establish a clear-cut political frontier, which divides the discursive space into two camps: friends and enemies. (Torfing, 1999: 126)

Discourse theory defines these two camps as chains of elements that have nothing but their affirmation or negation of a certain signifier in common—a signifier that can be identified here as the ideal of a "pure Germanic race." The more elements are caught up in this chain, the more the meaning of the elements is emptied out, up to the point where they are constructed as nothing more than an affirmation or a negation of the common signifier—as, in this case, either "a part of" or "a threat to" the Germanic race.[9]

In this context, it is also important to remember that the logic of equivalence does not entail the annihilation of the other's differences but, on the contrary, even presupposes difference: "*[I]dentities become inscribed in chains of equivalence that construct them in terms of a certain 'sameness,'*" yet "*to be equivalent ... they have to differ, ... otherwise there would exist a simple identity between them*" (Torfing, 1999: 124-125). Whereas in a democratic context positive chains of equivalence make[10] the differences between their elements temporarily irrelevant (e.g., when different political parties or governments unite in the face of a common enemy and stress their commitment to common values; see Torfing, 1999: 125), in the totalitarian context of the Nazi regime positive chains of equivalence function as a means to strategically acknowledge, yet simultaneously domesticate possible differences. With respect to Flanders, for instance, this strategy helps the Nazi regime incorporate Flanders' obvious differences into its construction of German-Flemish sameness. In the following, I will clarify what I mean by this.

The National Socialist regime had two main reasons to acknowledge the "typically Flemish." Because it had to win the consent of the German and the Flemish people, it had to take into account the factors that could possibly threaten the credibility of its propositions. These factors were first of all the obvious differences between Flanders and Germany, and second the fact that the Flemish people were not ready to give up their distinctiveness. This meant that the regime had to somehow integrate these differences in its image of Flanders and convey the impression that Flanders' singularity remained intact. However, if it would admit that the Flemish were inherently different from the Germans, this would jeopardize the legitimacy of the— at first only first cultural, then also political—annexation of Flanders. Hence, in the construction of a Flemish identity, it highlighted Flanders' supposedly close relations and similarities with (Nazi) Germany, stressing among others "*the increasing feeling of affinity and solidarity between the Flemish and the German people*" (see Peuckert, *Nationalsozialistische Monatshefte*[11] 1941: 105), "*the particularly close bond between German and Flemish literature*" (see Payr, NSM 1941: 632) and "*the cultural friendship between Germany and Flanders*" (see *Nationalsozialistische Bibliographie*[12] 1939: 9/41). It also constructed the war as an event that brought the two peoples together. The war could be one in which Flemish and German soldiers fought side by side or a *"tragischer Bruderkampf"*[13] (Peuckert, *Bücherkunde*[14] 1943: 171) in which *"sich deutsche und flämische Blutsbruder zerfleischen mußten"*[15] (Peuckert, NSM 1936: 594). As a matter of fact, the latter case was even judged the more interesting one, because it could be used to stage a spontaneous, unexpected, and therefore all the more credible discovery of the profound solidarity and familiarity between Flanders and Germany. Accordingly, the controlling National Socialist literary institutions explicitly promoted novels dealing with the two world wars and used blurbs, prefaces, and reviews to systematically steer the reception of these novels in the direction of a sudden insight into Germany's and Flanders' common roots. The following excerpt, taken from the blurb of Jozef Simons' *Flandern stirbt nicht*, is a representative case in point:[16]

> Durch den deutschen Einmarsch aufgebracht und durch eine unklare Vergangenheit an Belgien gebunden, kämpften [die Flamen] im belgischen Heere gegen uns, um mit der Zeit einzusehen — schon nach wenigen Monaten — daß sie auf der verkehrten Seite stritten und litten. ... Ihre Lebensnotwendigkeit als Volk weist sie eigentlich auf die deutsche Seite, ... Sollen sie nicht ... zu den Deutschen übergehen, nach der Seite, wo ihr gegebener Platz ist, von der Natur und Politik für sie bestimmt?[17] (Fromme, 1937)

In this way, the supposedly close relations and similarities between Flanders and Germany were highlighted in order to lay the foundations for the construction of Flemish-German sameness. Still, the introduction of a common signifier was needed for this sameness to take concrete shape. To achieve this, both peoples were inscribed in a positive chain of equivalence by lumping them together as "Germanic." The following excerpt from the German war novel *Dörfer in Flandern* by Ulf Uweson is exemplary in this respect. In line with many other German war novels dealing with Flanders, this novel is not set in the battlefields, but in one of the Flemish homes where German soldiers found quarter. The fragment demonstrates in a more than obvious way how the "spontaneous" discovery of similarities between the Flemish families and the German soldiers raises their awareness of a common Germanic essence:

> Der junge Deutsche hatte sich am ersten Abend mit dem Hausvater und seiner Frau und der Großmutter und den zwei Töchtern mit um den Herd gesetzt, und es war ihm dabei, als gehöre er zu der Familie, wohl, weil das Blut gesprochen: Germanen dort wie hier. Und als ... Matthijs Moens ... eifrig und immer eifriger von dem Kampf germanischer Menschen gegen Andersrassige erzählt hatte, und die glühenden Gesichter der Seinen und deren leuchtende Augen das Gesprochene als Heiliges bewiesen, ... da wußte sich der siebzehnjährige Deutsche nicht

mehr im Feindesland. Germanischen Boden galt es ihm hinfort zu verteidigen.[18] (Uweson, 1942: 7)[19]

The subsumption of these similarities under the common denominator Germanic still did not allow the Nazi image makers to guarantee the "typically Flemish" and parry the reproach of imperialism. At this point, the logic of equivalence casts light on the totalitarian practice of both acknowledging and domesticating the typically other. One can observe the regime dividing the Flemish characteristics into two categories. First, there are the qualities it admits are "typically Flemish," for instance Flanders' borderland position:

> So kam es, daß Flandern ein halbes Jahrtausend unter volksfremden aus-ländischen Herrschern sein gefahrenumdrohtes Dasein bewahren mußte—eine geschichtliche Tatsache, die den sozialen und politischen Charakter des flämischen Volkes bis in unsere Tage in verhängnisvoller Weise mitbestimmen sollte.[20] (Peuckert, NSM 1941: 100)

After the selected differential aspects have been constructed as "typically Flemish," the logic of equivalence is put to work, transforming them into symbols of a unifying Germanicness. Thus, Flanders' border position—first constructed as constitutive of Flanders' specificity—is given a specific function within the Germanic Reich:

> heute wie je germanischer Vorposten gegen den Westen, wo aus dem Süden die sogenannte culture latine mit allen kulturpolitischen Kampfmitteln germanisch-flämisches Volkstum und germanischen Kulturraum zurückdrängen möchte.[21] (Peuckert, NSM 1942: 315)

On the level of the concrete text, this construction leads to a constant inter-twining of "Flemish" and "Germanic." The fact that *"Flandern blieb in Volkstum, Sprache und Kunst immerdar flämisch"* is called *"ein Wunder ger-manischer Rassen- und Volkstreue"*[22] (Peuckert, BK 1943: 170). Flanders' specificity is attributed to its *"ungebrochenem völkisch-germanischem Instinkt und Verantwortungsgefühl"*[23] (Peuckert, NSM 1943: 435) and its *"germanischem Kern"*[24] (Peuckert, BK 1943: 174). All this results in the acknowledgment of *"die germanische Dominante der flämischen Stammesart und Kunst"*[25] (Peuckert, BK 1943: 173) and of *"das gemeinsame Reich, zu dem das Flamentum blutsmäßig-schicksalhaft mit allen seinen Eigenarten gehört"*[26] (NSB 1943: 1/3 39).

As opposed to this selection of "specific" characteristics, the second cat-egory contains features the regime considers to be incompatible with its ide-ological views and political ambitions. They include Flanders' strong Catholic roots, its francophone bourgeoisie and the fact that it is part of the

Belgian state.[27] Instead of being inscribed in the positive equivalential chain of "Germanicness," these features are ascribed to the negative pole and reinterpreted as a threat to the Flemish(-Germanic) identity. The logic of equivalence that is at work here exposes how distinctive features feared to elude the regime's grasp are not just neutralized but quite literally excluded from the image of Flanders created by German National Socialism.

As clear-cut and transparent as this enterprise may appear in theory, on the concrete empirical level of the text this process of inscription results in multifarious tensions or even contradictions between the strategic necessity to acknowledge the "typically Flemish" on the one hand and the ideological and political construction of a Nazi Germanic unity on the other. The delicate balancing act between the two is constitutive of the Nazi image of Flanders, but simultaneously carries the seeds of its subversion. A significant illustration of this is the above-mentioned concept *"Grenzland"* (borderland, frontier area). "Grenzland" is in itself a versatile word, since it does not establish to which side of the border its signified belongs. Thus, the notion could either be given a strategically neutral appearance or an explicit ideological orientation, for instance by turning—as was frequently done in national socialist literary discourse—the Germanic-Latin borderland Flanders into *"a Germanic bulwark against the Latin enemy."* However, the "Grenzland" label could also be used to represent Flanders as hostile toward the regime, for instance by constructing it as a dangerous *"frankobritische[s] sprungfeld"*[28] against Nazism (Jurda, NSM 1940: 433). A second implication of the "Grenzland" notion was that it made Flanders prone to lose its Germanic purity and go to waste for the Germanic world once and for all. The regime was very well aware of this danger and emphasized over and over again that Flanders, in spite of it being a borderland, had been able *"to safeguard its Germanic essence"* (see Peuckert, NSM 1941: 99) and *"resist Latin pressure as the Western pillar of the Germanic world"* (see Tränckner, *Europäische Literatur*[29] 1944: 4/24).

A final feature on the textual level that mirrors the tension between the self and the other *within* the construction of Flemish-German sameness is the closely knit network of metaphors that are used. National Socialist literary discourse on Flanders shows a clear juxtaposition of, on the one hand, metaphors articulating Flanders and Germany as two strictly different entities and, on the other, metaphors that emphasize both peoples' inextricable and unquestionable bond. The preference for one of these two metaphoric clusters depended on the intended audience, the topic of the text and the medium in which it was published. The journal *Europäische Literatur*, for instance, which addressed an international audience and presented itself as neutral, tended to speak of "neighbors" and "building bridges," whereas the journals *Nationalsozialistische Monatshefte*, *Bücherkunde*, and *Nationalsozialistische Bibliographie* as well as most German novels on Flanders generally referred to Flanders as a "brother people" or a "blood relative."

Wherever possible, both strands were combined, as in the recommendation that Flemish literature should seize the opportunity *"zur gründlichen und gerechten Auseinandersetzung mit dem Wesen des deutschen Nachbarn, der ja auch ein germanischer Blutsverwandter ist"*[30] (Peuckert, NSM 1939: 864).

THE COMPLEX RELATION BETWEEN INTENDED AND ACTUAL IMAGE

Many, if not all, recent studies on image construction start from the premise that there is no simple correspondence between image and reality. With regard to the field of national image studies, Joep Leerssen (1997) stated:

> What is "typical" of a given nation is no longer considered to emanate from a characteristic, hereditary essence inherent within that nation, but rather from a specific way of perceiving that nation. Nationality now counts ... as a modality of perception and reputation [rather] than ... a matter of essence or substance. (285)

However, most studies still seem to depart from the assumption that there is a transparent, one-to-one-relationship between the image as it is intended by the producer and the image as it results from the image-making process. This assumption becomes manifest in two recurrent practices. The first of these is to take programmatic utterances for granted and to piece together the image that is supposed to result from them using matching examples. With respect to the research object under investigation, this would result in presenting the *actual* image of Flanders as a direct reflection of national socialist ideology's *intentions*. I illustrate the fallacy of this approach with a concrete example.

In National Socialist thinking, language was seen as a crucial criterion, second only to race, for determining the essence of a people. In line with this general position, the regime propagated and promised the realization of an exclusively Dutch-speaking Flanders in the near future. This prospect was presented as realistic since Flanders had supposedly remained "Germanic" in essence thanks to its unbroken biological and racial vitality (see Peuckert, NSM 1941: 100). When going through the corpus materials, a great number of examples can be found in which the image of Flanders produced by National Socialism fits the regime's general ideological stance. One such example is that the increasing influence of the French language in Brussels is already rhetorically reversed in anticipation of its real undoing. In addition to this, it is promised that the Northern part of France, *"dieses weite*

Gebiet … vornehmlich oder teilweise von flämischen Menschen bewohnt und bearbeitet"[31] (Peuckert, NSM 1942: 316), will be reclaimed for its Dutch mother tongue. Last but not least, there is the polemic against the so-called *"Franskiljons,"*[32] *"die verwelschten Auch-Flamen"*[33] (Peuckert, NSM 1936: 594), who are

> zwar flämisch geboren, … aber auch äußerlich erkennbar wurzellos geworden und verstädtert … , indem sie ihre Muttersprache einer *civilisation* (= Verbürgerlichung) *de Paris où [sic] de Bruxelles* aufgeopfert haben, damit ihre Erstgeburt um ein Linsengericht verkaufend.[34] (Peuckert, NSM 1936: 588)

Within the literary field, this polemic results in frequent attacks against Flemish authors writing in French, as is shown by the warnings that Germans should not base their image of Flanders on the literature of

> den zwei volksfremden Französlingen Maeterlinck und Verhaeren. Beide haben ihr flämisches Blut und damit ihr Germanentum an das romanische Parisertum verraten. Diese Tatsache sollte für jeden Deutschen genügen, daß er die Bücher Verhaerens und Maeterlincks mit demselben Abscheu aus der Hand legt wie die Machwerke eines Heinrich Mann und Genossen.[35] (Peuckert, NSM 1936: 590)

German readers are advised to gather their information on Flanders from "real" Flemish authors, who have not succumbed to the French domination and have thus remained loyal to their Flemish blood (see Zimmerman, BK 1942: 161).

If one would exclusively focus on these examples, it would be easy to conjure up a perfect match between general ideology and actual image—as image studies do more often than they generally admit. However, besides the many matching quotes there are a considerable number of quotes that do *not* fit the general ideological stance but demonstrate an opportunistic logic of their own. The fate of French-speaking Flemish author Charles De Coster, for instance, was completely different from that of his francophone Flemish colleagues. Although De Coster was the child of a Walloon mother, Nazi literary criticism decided to overlook his French roots and language, and even claimed:

> Dieses Werk konnte nur ein Flame geschrieben haben, und zwar ein Flame, der nicht allein seine heiß geliebte Heimat bis in die letzte Faser kannte, sondern auch selbst das niederdeutsche Wesen in seiner ganzen Vielfalt und Tiefe verkörpert hat.[36] (Hartmann, NSM 1940: 475)

The fierceness with which Charles De Coster was protected against skepticism appears from the fact that the controlling literary institutions severely reprimanded literary scholars who did not show the required appreciation. Martha Hechtle, who in 1942 published a book on Flemish literature from 1830 until the present, was sanctioned with a publication ban for describing Charles De Coster as a "*Ganz- oder Halbwallone*"[37] (Hechtle, 1942: 22) and his novel *Tyll Ulenspiegel* as "*gekennzeichnet durch eine strenge intellektuelle Schärfe, wie sie den Flamen [. . .] fremd ist*"[38] (Hechtle, 1942: 23). According to Nazi criticism, Hechtle had distorted the true character of Germanic Flanders in criticizing De Coster and therefore forfeited the right to write about Flemish literature (Peuckert, NSM 1943: 436f).

The frequency of "counter-examples" such as De Coster proves that his case can be taken as indicative of the fact that general ideological positions—here toward French-speaking Flemings—are subordinated to other considerations as soon as the latter are judged to be more important or strategically convenient. In De Coster's case, it was undoubtedly his novel *Tyll Ulenspiegel* that constituted the dislocating factor for the Nazi propaganda machine.[39] For reviewers and other literary mediators, this ideological inconsistency meant they had to keep themselves informed as to which authors and novels they were to reject as "impure" and which ones they were to depict as "genuinely Flemish." The Nazi regime conveniently covered up its opportunism by ascribing sound literary judgment to racial intuition and instinct.

The second, opposite practice consists in identifying the image that appears from the text corpus with its producer's intentions.[40] With respect to the present case study, the National Socialist emphasis on Flemish devoutness could be taken to mean that the regime wanted to present Flemish piety as an intrinsic characteristic of the Flemish. In reality, however, the idea of a religious Flanders was at odds with the regime's original intentions. This appears for instance from the directive given to literary authors, translators, reviewers, and publishers that they should not depict a pious Flanders but rather contribute to freeing the Flemish from their "*geistigen Fesseln*"[41] (Peuckert, NSM 1943: 438). Novels should not have priests as protagonists nor people that "*immer wieder zu weich und traumverloren wirken*"[42] because these were not held responsible for their actions "*sondern Gott, der je nach der Stärke des jeweiligen Gebetes hilft*"[43] (anonymous, BK 1939: 311). Instead, readers should be made familiar with the "real Flemish" the Nazi regime wanted its ideal Flanders to be populated with (see Peuckert, BK 1943: 174).

This tension between approval and rejection of Flanders' religiosity can be explained as a consequence of negotiation, the need for which arose because of the strong Catholic roots of the Flemish people. These were a thorn in the flesh of the Nazi propaganda makers, as they constituted an obstacle to the spread of National Socialist ideology. That is why the regime

decided to domesticate and reinterpret Flemish Catholicism as a devoutness
of a less-threatening kind, for instance as a piety *"aus angeborenem Hang
zur Mystik und aus Naturverbundenheit feindlich und fremd aller
Dogmatik"*[44] (Peuckert, NSM 1941: 103). However, within the literary field,
this enterprise proved anything but simple. Because an important part of
Flemish literature was religiously inspired, the regime had to recur to a range
of rhetorical maneuvers in order to distinguish the novels they needed from
those they wanted to reject. The easiest task was definitely the denigration
of the latter. The rejected novels were associated with concepts like
Catholicism, clericalism and confessionalism, which within National
Socialist semantics had become largely synonymous with Catholic oppression, clerical dogmatism and confessionalist propaganda. As a result, they
were dismissed for displaying a *"streng kirchlich katholische Melodie, die
manchmal ... geradezu in eine Propaganda Fidei ausartet"*[45] (Peuckert,
NSM 1939: 863) and for being *"keineswegs wertvolle Stücke einer konfes-
sionellen Winkelliteratur"*[46] (863), a *"pedantische Aufzählung sämtlicher
Wallfahrtsorte und Wunderwirkungen"*[47] (Peuckert, BK 1938: 689) or

> eine banale und kunstlose Aneinanderreihung farbloser
> Pastorenanekdötchen, in denen betenderweise vor nahezu jedem
> katholischen Ortsheiligen auf den Knieen gelegen und um die Erfüllung
> der seltsamsten und kleinlichsten Wünsche der Himmel bemüht wird—
> kurzum: schönster blühender Kitsch und Musterbeispiel konfes-
> sioneller Winkelliteratur statt echter religiöser Dichtung.[48] (Peuckert,
> NSM 1941: 880)[49]

The religious novels that needed to be saved despite their religious character were dissociated from their Catholic character and reassociated with a
more palatable Flemish religiosity. They were praised for expressing a
"besonders eigene starke Katholizität"[50] (Peuckert, BK 1942: 5) and
*"keinen Katholizismus römischer Prägung, sondern eigener niederländisch-
er Art"*[51] (Peuckert, NSM 1936: 593); for depicting Flemish religiosity as
the *"höchste Ausdruck der geheimen Lebensgesetze des flämischen
Volkes"*[52] (593); or for describing the Flemish as pious but at the same time
"von fremder Art und klerikalen Einflüssen noch so unverstellt"[53]
(Peuckert, NSM 1944: 251). This delicate exercise results in a permanent
give and take, which is confusing not only for the reader, but also for the
image-makers themselves, who were frequently confronted with elements
resisting rearticulation. Where a reformulation of Flemish Catholicism as a
Germanic variant of devoutness did not suffice, they were compelled to
acknowledge Catholic influences in Flanders, immediately attributing them
to an outside cause (the Belgian state) and presenting them as an additional threat to the Flemish identity.

The examples of francophone imperialism and Flemish piety both show that the Nazi regime could not and did not simply transfer its ideological intentions to the images it produced. This observation should warn against the fallacy of equating ideological intentions with actual images and urge to take into account the negotiations and discursive maneuvers that complicate the relationship between intention and realization. With its process-oriented focus on the creation, disruption, and transformation of identities, discourse theory offers a wide array of tools to examine the regime's need to constantly renegotiate the images it intends to produce. Its framework turns on the fact that any straightforward realization of the Nazi regime's intended image of Flanders will necessarily fail into a research premise rather than a research goal. It exposes the constitutive unfixity of images, which is what makes all image formation possible (condition of possibility) and what at the same time explains why all attempts to ground images are necessarily provisional and precarious ways of naturalizing or objectivizing what are in fact political constructions (condition of impossibility; see Torfing, 1999: 62). Against this background, the image of Flanders that was projected by German National Socialism can be conceptualized as the product of a hegemonic project. The main objective of this image building process was to fix the meaning of the signifier "Flanders" in the desired fashion. Choosing from a variety of different options and strategies (structural undecidability),[54] it aimed to create a consensus for the option selected by the regime and to radically exclude all others. At the same time, it attempted to cover up the contingency of its choices by presenting them as natural and founded in a historical essence.

As Jacob Torfing remarked, and as can be observed in the large majority of image studies, this structural unfixity or undecidability generally remains unnoticed. Not only in totalitarian but also in democratic societies, the contingency of decisions is covered up by first privileging unity over dispersion, necessity over contingency, presence over absence, and so on, and then naturalizing the first halves of these pairs as self-evident essences. The study *Metaphors We Live By* by cognitive linguists George Lakoff and Mark Johnson (1980) demonstrates to what extent such hierarchical pairs are anchored in the metaphorical framework Western societies use to interpret the world. Image studies should run counter to this "usual" perception and reach down to the undecidable infrastructure of images (that is: reveal the operations performed during the hegemonic image formation process and present images as the product of negotiation and (re)construction in an undecidable discursive terrain [see Laclau, 1988]). This means that, on the concrete methodological level, the focus should shift from the results of image formation to the processes that make the contingency of discursive structures visible and to the traces contingency has left on the surface level of the text.

DETECTING CONCRETE PROCESSES
OF NEGOTIATION

Before concluding, I take a look at two typical processes of negotiating and re-articulating (in casu the Nazi regime's) original interests and their actualization. The way these processes are studied may serve as a methodological guideline for other empirical research on image construction processes.

The Mutual Conditioning of the General and the Particular

A first factor that disturbed the straightforward realization of the intended image of Flanders was the attuning of the general to the particular and vice versa that the Nazi image-makers were bound to perform. As they applied the regime's ideological positions to the Flemish context, inconsistencies and contradictions inevitably arose, as the particularity of the context did not allow for a simple application of an ideology that was formulated in a different context. Consequently, the regime's general ideological positions became, in Laclau's words, "*sooner or later entangled in their own contextual particularism and ... incapable of fulfilling their [general] function*" (Laclau 1995: 156; see Torfing, 1999: 181f).

As for the attuning of the particular to the general, it was shown earlier how the constituents of Flanders' particularity were modified and weakened by their insertion into the Germanic and anti-Germanic chains of equivalence. An interesting example of the opposite negotiation process, the attuning of the general to the particular, is provided by the negotiations that occurred when the regime addressed different audiences. A comparison of the internationally oriented literary journal *Europäische Literatur* with the journals addressing a German audience shows that the former brings a different selection of authors and uses different metaphors and attributions in order to successfully interpellate its intended readers. Another example of this kind of negotiation is the modification of Nazi Germany's hierarchy of enemies when dealing with the Flemish context. Because the regime apparently did not perceive the Jews as a sufficiently powerful threat for Flemish identity, it substituted them with an enemy that worked for both Flanders and Germany. The obvious choice was Germany's centuries-old rival France, which could be used to rearticulate the tensions between the francophone bourgeoisie and the Francophile Belgian state apparatus on the one hand and the Flemish people on the other as an opposition between the Germanic and the Latin world. Thus, for the Flemish context, the opposition "Germanic" versus "Jewish" was subordinated to the opposition "Germanic" versus "Latin." A third and final example is the inversion of the general hierarchy between written language and dialect when dealing with the Flemish situation. Whereas in Germany written language was privileged over dialects (the former unifying, the latter dividing the German people), with respect to Flanders this hierarchy was opportunistically reversed, as Flemish dialects—in contrast to the written languages Dutch and German, which neatly confirmed the historically grown separation between Flanders and Germany—crossed the national borders. In each of these cases, "the general" was weakened in order to win over "the particular."

The Constant Threat of Dislocation

A second point of attention are the so-called dislocations—disruptions of the symbolic order (the general ideology, the intended image)—by events (facts, situations, existing images) that cannot be represented or domesticated by that order. On the empirical-methodological level, dislocating factors can be detected at different levels of the literary system. A comparison of the actual book production during the Nazi reign with the meta-level of the book reviews published in National Socialist cultural and literary magazines between 1933 and 1945 shows that the former is a constant factor of dislocation for the image the regime intends to produce. Symptomatic examples are the reactions of the controlling literary-political institutions to Martha Hechtle's portrait of De Coster as the French-speaking "half-Walloon" he actually was; to Carl Hanns Erkelenz's compilation of Flemish stories that profile Flanders as a profoundly Catholic country; and, more importantly, to the persisting popularity of the Flemish author Felix Timmermans, whose novels presented the German audience with the image of an idyllic, rural Flanders of *bon vivants* and self-sufficient peasants. If image research fails to include and compare different levels of the literary system, its conclusions will inevitably be one-sided. If it would for instance focus on the actual book production alone, it would be compelled to conclude that Felix Timmermans was *the* Flemish author the regime wanted to put forward. If only reviews were taken into account, on the contrary, the conclusion would be that the appreciation for Timmermans was rather limited, because the regime encouraged literature that presented Flanders as a struggling and oppressed people who had not succeeded in throwing off the yoke of its many oppressors by itself and Timmermans's novels did not fit this profile: they presented the German reader with a self-enclosed Flanders that did not ask for any outside interference. The logical conclusion would therefore be that Timmermans had only a few publications to his name in the Nazi era. Only when both levels are distinguished and compared, the complexity of the actual situation comes to light. On account of Timmermans's popularity and the profound influence of his novels on the Germans' image of Flanders, the regime could not simply dispense with the Flemish author for fear of causing a "credibility gap" between the prevailing image of Flanders and the image it wanted to produce. In order to construct a credible image, it had to hybridize its original interests, fusing the image of an idyllic with that of an oppressed Flanders (see Van linthout, 2003: 345-348). The researcher's task, then, is to capture the double role of dislocations as both destabilizing and constitutive—creating a lack at the level of meaning and simultaneously calling for new discursive constructions to suture the lack.[55]

CONCLUSION

In guise of conclusion, it can be said that discourse theory helps researchers recognize and concretize the need for a process-oriented focus in image studies. With respect to the empirical-methodological level, the discourse-theoretical framework shows the importance of not reducing tensions and contradictions surfacing in the actual image to accidental inconsistencies. Instead, they should be analyzed as visible traces of a complex image formation process. With respect to the ideological level, discourse theory helps recognize the fact that the identification of intended image (or general ideology) and actual image is based on the illusion that totalitarian hegemonic practices can actually and fully reach their goal. Of course, it remains important to analyze and expose to what extent the Nazi rulers effectively managed to hegemonize the discursive space. However, it is just as important, if not more so, to point out the ways in which their hegemonic practices were, at least on the discursive level, bound to fail.

NOTES

1. Although the question of continuity is not dealt with in this chapter, it is obvious that the Nazi regime could build on previous—mostly unofficial, cultural—relations between Flanders and Germany. On the political level, especially the so-called *Flamenpolitik* during World War I should be mentioned. With this policy, the German occupier tried to detach the Dutch-speaking population in Belgium from the Belgian state, for instance by realizing some of the pre-war Flemish demands like the dutchification of the University of Ghent, the introduction and implementation of laws imposing the use of Dutch in public life (administration, justice, education, etc.) in Flanders as well as the administrative division of Belgium into a Flemish and a Walloon region. Germany could rely on

the support and help of the "activist" wing of the Flemish Movement (see *Nieuwe Encyclopedie van de Vlaamse Beweging*, 1998).

2. Other obstacles, such as the fact that the Nazi regime was anything but mono-lithic or the changes taking place between 1933 and 1945 (due, among others, to the regime's growing imperialistic ambitions) go beyond the limits of this chap-ter and, therefore, are not treated here.

3. For instance, analyses of postmodernist novels that subvert illusionary certain-ties, of immigrant literature that explores the third space, of postcolonial litera-ture that exposes power relations, and so on.

4. "a research area within comparative literary studies that investigates national images of the foreign and the self in literature and all fields of literary studies and literary criticism."

5. "It deals with the origins, development and impact of these 'hetero- und auto-images' in the literary and extra-literary context."

6. At least Leerssen (1986: 9) explicitly admitted that the concept of foreignness in itself presupposes a polar relationship with its supplement, the "native" or "familiar," against which it takes shape.

7. Here, the difference between *identity formation* and *image formation* is method-ologically important.

8. The main difference lies in the fact that discourse theory—which was designed to further a "should-be" democracy—is in this chapter used to critically analyze and describe an empirical totalitarian context.

9. Discourse theory is used on two different levels here: to trace the construction of the "essential" in National Socialist totalitarian discourse and to deconstruct this enterprise from a democratic point of view.

10. Or rather: "are supposed to make," since this might well be an illustration of a "should-be" supposition that is in contrast with reality.

11. The *Nationalsozialistische Monatshefte* (NSM) characterized itself as the "only central political and cultural mouthpiece of the NSDAP." It was founded in 1930 and changed hands from Adolf Hitler to Alfred Rosenberg in November 1933.

12. The *Nationalsozialistische Bibliographie* was first published in 1936 as the mouthpiece of the *Parteiamtliche Prüfungskommission zum Schutze des NS.-Schrifttums*, a literary controlling institution that was led by Philipp Bouhler. It only contained bibliographical references and annotations of the publications the institution recommended.

13. "tragic fratricidal battle."

14. The *Bücherkunde* (BK) was established in 1934 as the mouthpiece of the "*Amt Schrifttumspflege bei dem Beauftragten des Führers für die Überwachung der gesamten geistigen und weltanschaulichen Schulung und Erziehung der NSDAP*" (i.e., the literary controlling institution headed by Alfred Rosenberg). The jour-nal addressed all mediators of German literature and intended to be, according to its publisher Hans Hagemeyer, the "*most reliable critical medium ... that Germany has had since Lessing*" (BK 1934: preface).

15. "Flemish and German blood brothers were forced to slaughter each other."

16. *Flandern stirbt nicht. Das flämische Fronterlebnis* (*Flanders Will Not Perish. The Flemish Front Experience*) is the German translation of the Flemish novel *Eer Vlaanderen vergaat* by Jozef Simons, which was first published in Flanders in 1927. The blurb is written by the German reviewer Franz Fromme.

17. "Provoked by the German invasion and attached to Belgium by a hazy past, [the Flemish] fought against us in the Belgian army, only to realize after some time— already after a few months—they were fighting and suffering on the wrong side. ... As a matter of fact, their vital necessity as a people directs them to the German side, ... Should they not ... go to the Germans, to the side where they belong, that is destined for them by nature and politics?"

18. "The first night, the young German joined the father and his wife as well as the grandmother and the two daughters at the open fireplace, and he felt as if he belonged to the family, most likely because the blood had spoken: Germans here and there. And after ... Matthijs Moens ... had told with increasing ardor about the battle between Germanic people and people of other races, and the glowing faces of his family and their shining eyes proved the words to be sacred, then, the seventeen-year-old German realized he was no longer in enemy country. He would from now on defend German soil."

19. The *Nationalsozialistische Bibliographie* (1939 vol. 10, p. 18) significantly comments the first publication of this book in the following way: "*Eindrucksvolle Darstellung der Weltkriegskämpfe in Flandern. Besonders hervorzuheben ist die Schilderung des Verhältnisses der deutschen Soldaten zu den Flamen, das auf Grund der gemeinsamen rassischen Herkunft ein außerordentlich freundschaftliches war.*" ("Impressive representation of the World War battles in Flanders. Especially recommended for its portrayal of the relationship between German soldiers and the Flemish, which by reason of their common racial descent was an exceptionally friendly one.")

20. "That is why Flanders had to lead a perilous existence under foreign rulers for half a millennium—a historical fact that would determine the social and political character of the Flemish people in a fateful way."

21. "today as much as in former times a Germanic outpost against the West, where—coming up from the South—the so-called culture latine would like to push back the Germanic-Flemish nature and Germanic culture area with all cultural-political weapons."

22. "Flanders always remained Flemish in its national character, language and art," "a miracle of Germanic loyalty to race and people."

23. "undiminished racial-Germanic instinct and sense of responsibility."

24. "Germanic essence."

25. "the dominant Germanic quality of the Flemish nature and art."

26. "the common Reich, to which the Flemish with all their peculiarities belong by blood and fate."

27. These examples are elaborated in the second part of the chapter.

28. "Franco-British spring board."

29. The journal *Europäische Literatur* was published from May 1942 to September 1944. Although it claims to be the initiative of a number of renowned European authors, it was founded, financially supported and ideologically supervised by the Nazi Ministry for Propaganda, which was of course headed by Joseph Goebbels.

30. "a grounded and just analysis of the essence of the German neighbor, who is, after all, a German blood relative as well."

31. "this vast area which is mainly or partly inhabited and cultivated by Flemish people."

32. This term was also used by Flemish nationalists as a pejorative denotation for the francophone Flemish upper class.
33. "gallicized Also-Flemish."
34. "although born Flemish, these *Franskiljons* have, even visibly, lost their roots and become urbanized by sacrificing their native language for a Parisian or Brussels civilization (= becoming bourgeois), thus selling their birthright for a mess of potage."
35. "of the Francophile defectors Maeterlinck and Verhaeren. Both have betrayed their Flemish blood and with it their Germanic nature to the Latin-Parisian civilization. This fact should be sufficient reason for every German to lay aside the books of Verhaeren and Maeterlinck with the same disgust he feels for the botches of Heinrich Mann and the likes of him."
36. "This work could only be written by a Fleming—a Fleming to be sure who did not just know his dearly beloved homeland through and through, but himself incarnated the Low German character in its entire diversity and depth." Occasionally, the author was even characterized as "*ein Germane vom reinsten Blut*" ("a German of the purest blood") (Peuckert, NSM 1936: 590).
37. "entirely or half Walloon."
38. "marked by an intellectual sharpness that is untypical of the Flemish."
39. De Coster's *Tyll Ulenspiegel* was instrumentalized as the "*Bible of the Flemish*" ("*Flamenbibel*") by Flemish nationalists and the national socialist regime alike, because its protagonist symbolizes Flanders' ongoing struggle against the foreign occupier. Moreover, just like the left wing of the Flemish Movement (e.g., the *Vlaamse Kommunistische Partij*), the Nazi regime emphasized the book's outspoken anti-clericalism and presented it as proof of the negative influence of Catholicism on the Flemish people.
40. For instance, by basing one's conclusions on a journal's paratext, programmatic utterances or general ideological propositions.
41. "spiritual chains."
42. "forever appear all too soft and faraway."
43. "but God who helps according to the power of their respective prayer."
44. "pious, but inspired by an innate urge for mysticism and a proximity to nature hostile and foreign to all dogmatics."
45. "strong ecclesiastical Catholic tone, that sometimes ... nearly culminates in Propaganda Fidei."
46. "in no way valuable pieces of confessional thesis literature."
47. "a pedantic list of places of pilgrimage and miracles."
48. In English, it is not possible to differentiate between *Dichtung* und *Literatur*. It is important to note that in Nazi vocabulary, especially when both are used in the same text or fragment, *Literatur* is negatively and *Dichtung* clearly positively connoted.
49. "a banal and artless run-down of colorless little anecdotes about priests, in which—kneeling before local Catholic saints—people pray for the fulfillment of the most peculiar and trivial heavenly wishes—in short: *utter kitsch* and a typical example of confessional thesis 'literature' instead of real religious literature."
50. "very own kind of strong Catholicism."
51. "a Catholicism that is not of a Latin, but of an own Dutch kind."
52. "the highest expression of the secret vital laws of the Flemish people."

53. "still undistorted by alien and clerical influences."
54. It may be useful to recall that "undecidable" does not mean "unlimited." As Derrida specifies, undecidability is always an oscillation between possibilities (possible meanings, but also possible acts). These possibilities are themselves highly determined and embedded in strictly defined (discursive—syntactical or rhetorical—but also political, ethical) contexts. They are in other words pragmatically determined (see Torfing, 1999: 64). In the case under investigation, the limits of the "undecidable" are imposed by both the represented object ("Flanders") and the representing subject (Nazi regime).
55. Within the frame of this chapter, only one type of dislocation can be discussed. Another important type of dislocation that deserves attention in process-oriented image studies has to do with the fact that—in order to be efficient—images have to (at least minimally) keep up with reality. Especially in the totalitarian, imperialistic, and turbulent context of the National Socialist era, it is illuminating to examine how the frequent discrepancies between intention and reality are dealt with, which tensions they create, whether they are domesticated or result in a complete reworking of the image of Flanders.

REFERENCES

Source references

Nationalsozialistische Monatshefte. Zentrale politische und kulturelle Zeitschrift der NSDAP (1933[1930]-1944), Alfred Rosenberg (Ed), München: Zentralverlag der NSDAP, Franz Eher Nachf.
Bücherkunde der Reichsstelle zur Förderung des Deutschen Schrifttums [Later: Monatshefte für das deutsche Schrifttum]. Organ des Amtes Schrifttumspflege bei dem Beauftragten des Führers für die Überwachung der gesamten geistigen und weltanschaulichen Schulung und Erziehung der NSDAP (1934-1944), Hans Hagemeyer [Later: Bernhard Payr] (Ed), Bayreuth: Gauverlag Bayerische Ostmark.
Europäische Literatur (1942-1944), Berlin: Deutscher Verlag.
Nationalsozialistische Bibliographie. Monatshefte der Parteiamtlichen Prüfungs kommission zum Schutze des NS. Schrifttums (1936-1944), Reichsleiter Philipp Bouhler (Ed), Berlin: Zentralverlag der NSDAP, Franz Eher Nachf.

Erkelenz, C.H. (1939) *Unsere Liebe Frau aus Flandern.* Salzburg, Leipzig: Anton Pustet.
Fromme, F. (1937) [blurb of] J. Simons: *Flandern stirbt nicht. Das flämische Fronterlebnis.* Wolfshagen–Scharbeutz: Franz Westphal.
Hartmann, W. (1940) 'Tyll Ulenspieghel im Bilde: Erich Klahns künstlerische Neuschöpfung von Charles de Costers flämischem Volksbuch,' *Nationalsozialistische Monatshefte* (125): 475-480.
Hechtle, M. (1942) *Die flämische Dichtung von 1830 bis zur Gegenwart.* Jena: Eugen Diederichs.

Jurda, K.F. (1940) 'Die Niederlande und Belgien,' *Nationalsozialistische Monatshefte* (124): 433-434.

'Küppers, Heinz: Deutschland und Flandern. Grundzüge einer Kulturfreundschaft' (1939) *Nationalsozialistische Bibliographie* (9): 41.

'Maurice van de Walle: Germanischer Aufbruch. Flanderns Stirb und Werde' (1943). *Nationalsozialistische Bibliographie* 1(3): 39.

Payr, B. (1941). 'Kritik der Zeit,' *Nationalsozialistische Monatshefte* (136): 632.

Peuckert, F. (1936) 'Flanderns Dichtung im deutschen Raum,' *Nationalsozialistische Monatshefte* (7): 586-595.

Peuckert, F. (1936) 'Gute und wesentliche Übersetzungen ausländischer Literatur: Das junge Flandern und seine Dichter,' *Bücherkunde* (11): 345-348.

Peuckert, F. (1938) 'Von jenseits der Grenze: Unsere Liebe Frau aus Flandern von Carl Hanns Erkelenz,' *Bücherkunde* (12): 689-691.

Peuckert, F. (1939) 'Zweierlei Flandern? Neue flämische Erzählungen und Romane in deutschen Verlagen,' *Nationalsozialistische Monatshefte* (114): 861-864.

Peuckert, F. (1941) 'Flanderns Volkstum in Vergangenheit und Gegenwart,' *Nationalsozialistische Monatshefte* (131): 99-111.

Peuckert, F. (1941) "Und Flandern?' Neue Bücher aus Flandern in deutschen Verlagen,' *Nationalsozialistische Monatshefte* (139): 877-880.

Peuckert, F. (1942) 'Germanische Besinnung und Aufbruch in flämischen und holländischen Zeitschriften,' *Nationalsozialistische Monatshefte* (146): 314-317.

Peuckert, F. (1942) 'Flandern in Vergangenheit und Gegenwart: Neue flämische Bücher in deutschen Verlagen,' *Bücherkunde* (1): 3-6.

Peuckert, F. (1943) 'Flandern gestern und heute: Neue Bücher aus und über Flandern,' *Nationalsozialistische Monatshefte* (158): 434-439.

Peuckert, F. (1943) 'Germanische Züge im Antlitz des jüngeren flämischen Schrifttums,' *Bücherkunde* (5): 169-175.

Peuckert, F. (1944) 'Brückenschlag von Flandern zum Reich: Geschichte, Werk und Aufgabe eines flämischen Verlages,' *Nationalsozialistische Monatshefte* (163): 247-253.

Simons, J. (1937) *Flandern stirbt nicht: Das flämische Fronterlebnis.* Wolfshagen-Scharbeutz: Franz Westphal.

Tränckner, C. (1944) 'Berichte über Bücher: Begegnung mit Flandern,' *Europäische Literatur* (4): 23f.

'Übersetzungen: Stijn Streuvels: Die große Brücke' (1939) *Bücherkunde* (6): 309-311.

Uweson, U. (1942) *Dörfer in Flandern.* Wolfshagen-Scharbeutz: Franz Westphal.

'Uweson, Ulf: Wir fochten in Flandern' (1938) *Nationalsozialistische Bibliographie* (10): 18.

Zimmermann, G. (1942) 'Der deutsche Mensch in seinem Lebensraum: Bildwerke von Erna Lendvai-Dircksen,' *Bücherkunde* (9): 159-162.

Secondary References

Ashcroft, B., Ahluwalia, P. (2001) *Edward Said.* London: Routledge.

Boerner, P. (1975) 'National Images and their Place in Literary Research: Germany as Seen by Eighteenth-century French and English Reading Audiences,' *Monatshefte für deutschen Unterricht, deutsche Sprache und Literatur* (4): 358-370.

Brunel, P., Chevrel, Y. (Eds) (1989) *Précis de littérature comparée*. Paris: Presses Universitaires de France.

Hoenselaars, A.J. (1992) *Images of Englishmen and Foreigners in the Drama of Shakespeare and his Contemporaries: A Study of Stage Characters and National Identity in English Renaissance Drama, 1558-1642*. Rutherford: Fairleigh Dickinson UP.

Howarth, D., Norval, A.J., Stavrakakis, Y. (Eds) (2000) *Discourse Theory and Political Analysis: Identities, Hegemonies and Social Change*. Manchester: Manchester University Press.

Howarth, D., Stavrakakis, Y. (2000) 'Introducing Discourse Theory and Political Analysis,' pp. 1-23 in D. Howarth, A.J. Norval and Y. Stavrakakis (Eds) *Discourse Theory and Political Analysis: Identities, Hegemonies and Social Change*. Manchester: Manchester University Press.

Kristeva, J. (1988) *Étrangers à nous-mêmes*. Paris: Fayard.

Laclau, E. (1995) 'Subject of Politics, Politics of the Subject,' *Differences* 7(1): 145-164.

Laclau, E. (1998) 'Metaphor and Social Antagonisms,' pp. 249-257 in C. Neson and L. Grossberg (Eds) *Marxism and the Interpretation of Culture*. Basingstoke: Macmillan Education.

Lakoff, G., Johnson, M. (1980) *Metaphors We Live by*. Chicago: University of Chicago Press.

Leerssen, J.Th. (1986) *Mere Irish and Fíor-Ghael: Studies in the Idea of Irish Nationality, its Development and Literary Expression Prior to the Nineteenth Century*. Amsterdam, Philadelphia: John Benjamins.

Leerssen, J.Th. (1997) 'The Allochronic Periphery: Towards a Grammar of Cross-cultural Representation,' pp. 285-294 in C.C. Barfoot (Ed.) *Beyond Pug's Tour: National and Ethnic Stereotyping in Theory and Literary Practice*. Amsterdam, Atlanta: Rodopi.

Leitch, V.B. (Ed.) (2001) *The Norton Anthology of Theory and Criticism*. New York, London: W.W. Norton and Company.

'Metzler Lexikon Literatur- und Kulturtheorie: Anstze, Personen, Grundbegriffe' (1998) Stuttgart and Weimar: J.B. Metzler.

Moura, J.-M. (1992) *L'Image du Tiers Monde dans le Roman Français Contemporain*. Paris: Presses Universitaires de France.

'Nieuwe Encyclopedie van de Vlaamse beweging' (1998) Tielt: Uitgeverij Lannoo.

Norval, A.J. (2000) 'Trajectories of Future Research in Discourse Theory,' pp. 219-236 in D. Howarth, A.J. Norval and Y. Stavrakakis (Eds) *Discourse Theory and Political Analysis: Identities, Hegemonies and Social Change*. Manchester: Manchester University Press.

Said, E. (1978) *Orientalism*. New York: Pantheon Books.

Van Alphen, E. (1991) 'The Other Within,' pp. 1-16 in R. Corbey and J.Th. Leerssen (Eds) *Alterity, Identity, Image: Selves and Others in Society and Scholarship*. Amsterdam, Atlanta: Rodopi.

Van linthout, I. (2003) "Flandern, halte dich bereit, als Westmark in dieser Welt deinen Platz einzunehmen.' Westforschung, Literatur(-wissenschaft) und Flandern im Nationalsozialismus,' pp. 325-350 in B. Dietz e.a. (Eds) *Griff nach dem Westen: Die 'Westforschung' der völkisch-nationalen Wissenschaften zum nordwesteuropäischen Raum (1919-1960)*. Münster: Waxmann.

Wodak, R. (1999) 'The Discursive Construction of National Identities,' *Discourse &*
    Society 2: 149-173.

ABOUT THE AUTHORS

David M. Boje is the Arthur Owens Professor in Business Administration in the Management Department at New Mexico State University. His latest passion is Rabelaisian analyses of McDonaldland (peaceaware.com/McD), a follow-up to his work in Disney-Tamara-land, and Nike-land. He has published numerous articles in top management journals. He is past chair of the Research Methods Division of the Academy of Management and founding president of the Standing Conference for Management & Organization Inquiry. He serves on 13 editorial boards, is regional editor of the *Journal of Organizational Change Management*, associate editor for *Qualitative Research in Management & Organization*, and founding editor of *Tamara Journal*.

Sascha Bru is assistant professor of Literary Theory at Ghent University (Belgium). He has published on various modernist and avant-garde authors, and has edited a number of special journal issues on avant-garde literature. He has recently finished *The Invention of Politics in the European Avant-Garde, 1906-1940* (2006); and is currently preparing a book on modernist avant-garde writing in the state of exception. He is also editor of the vanguard literary magazine *Yang*.

Yue Cai is lecturer in the Management Department at Central Missouri State University. Her teaching and research interests include global strategic competence, storytelling/narrative strategy, business consulting, and organizational behavior. She has published a number of journal articles. She is a member of the Academy of Management, as well as an active board member of Sc'MOI. Her current research involves the reconciliation of the predominant Western strategy paradigm with the ancient traditions of the east.

Anabela Carvalho is assistant professor in the Department of Communication Sciences of the University of Minho, Portugal, and currently Director of Undergraduate Studies in Communications. She received her PhD from University College London (Department of Geography) and has been conducting research on media representations of social and political issues and on various forms of environmental communication. She has published on topics such as discourses on climate change, the present challenges for science communication, and depictions of the Iraq war in the media in *Comunicação e Sociedade, Critical Discourse Studies, Public Understanding of Science, Risk Analysis* and other journals and edited books.

Nico Carpentier is an assistant professor working at the Communication Studies Department of the Vrije Universiteit Brussel (VUB - Free University of Brussels). He is co-director of the VUB research center CEMESO and a board member of the European Communication Research and Education Association (ECREA—formerly ECCR). His theoretical focus is on discourse theory, his research interests are situated in the relationship between media and journalism, and especially toward social domains such as war and conflict, ideology, participation and democracy.

Hernán Cuevas Valenzuela is a Chilean associate lecturer in the Institute of Political Science of the Pontifical Catholic University of Chile. He has been awarded an M.Phil. in Cultural Studies from the University of Birmingham (UK) and is currently finishing his PhD in the Government Department of the University of Essex (UK).

Benjamin De Cleen obtained his master's degree in Communication Studies from the Free University of Brussels (VUB). He graduated in 2004 with a thesis analyzing the discourse of the International Federation of the Phonographic Industry (IFPI) on music downloading. He is currently working as research assistant at the VUB, preparing a PhD thesis on "political correctness" in the debate on the multicultural society in North Belgium.

Evangelos Intzidis is a graduate of the Pedagogical Academy of Thessaloniki (1982) and Department of Linguistics (Aristotle University of Thessaloniki) (1991). He has participated as a scholar in the National Endowment for the Humanities Seminars at Columbia University (1993) and holds a master's in Educational Leadership and Management from the RMIT-University of Melbourne (Department of Industry-Professional and Adult Education) (2003). He is currently associated with the University of the Aegean for LLL policies (University of the Aegean, Rector's Council) and is a lecturer in the Postgraduate Program of the University of the Aegean on Gender and New Forms of Education and Training in the Information Society.

Germán Martínez Martínez, from Mexico, completed his PhD in the Ideology and Discourse Analysis Program at the University of Essex. He has been a visiting-lecturer in Latin American studies at the University of London (Royal Holloway, Queen Mary, and King's College). His research interests include: Mexican national identity discourses and ethnicity; representations of Latin-American cities in film and literature; Latin-American novels about dictators of the region; the Spanish-American bildungsroman; Catholicism in Latin America; contemporary Mexican politics and Latin-American political culture.

Lut Lams is a lecturer in the Sinology Department of the Catholic University of Louvain (KUL) and the Department of Languages and Literature of the Catholic University of Brussels (KUB). She studied Germanic Philology at the Catholic University of Louvain, got a master's degree in Literary Theory at Carnegie Mellon University (CMU, Pittsburgh), and completed her PhD at the University of Antwerp (UA). Her areas of scholarly interest include linguistic pragmatics, political communication, media discourse analysis, ideology critique, and language and politics in China. She has published various articles on identity politics and nationalism in China/Taiwan/Hong Kong, Chinese official discourse, and cross-Strait relations as represented in Chinese/Taiwanese media discourses.

N.Y. Potamitis is an honorary research fellow at the University of Birmingham, where he received his PhD in Modern Greek Studies in 2004. He publishes on Balkan cinema, and on Greek film in particular.

George Prevedourakis holds a BA degree in International Relations (University of Sussex) and a master's in International Conflict Analysis from the London Center of International Relations (University of Kent). He is currently a PhD candidate at the University of Exeter.

Henrieta Anşoara Şerban finalized in 2006 her Romanian Academy PhD on "Paradigms of Difference in the Philosophy of Communication," supervised by Dr. Angela Botez. She is a (communication) researcher at the Institute of Political Science and International Relations of the Romanian Academy and graduated from the Faculty of Chemistry (1993) and the Faculty of Political Science and Public Administration, English section (2000), both at Bucharest University and Faculty of Mass Communication at the National School of Political Studies and Public Administration, graduate studies (1996). She has published more than 50 articles and studies.

Stuart Sim is professor of critical theory in the Department of English Studies, University of Sunderland. His research specialties are contemporary critical and cultural theory (particularly postmodernism, poststructuralism, and post-Marxism), and 17th- and 18th-century English prose fiction (particularly John Bunyan, Daniel Defoe, and Laurence Sterne). He is the author or editor of 23 books, his work has been translated into 14 languages, and he is a fellow of the English Association.

Eric Spinoy is a Senior Lecturer Dutch literature at the Department of Modern Languages and Literatures of the University of Liège (Belgium). His research interests include modern and contemporary Dutch poetry, problems and methods of literary history writing, and contemporary discourse theories. He is also an established poet and has published extensively in this area.

Ine Van linthout received her PhD in Literary Studies from the University of Antwerp and the Humboldt University of Berlin. She studied Germanic Philology at the universities of Namur (FUNDP), Leuven (KUL), and Cologne. Her main area of research is the interaction between literature, politics and image construction, especially with respect tot the image of Flanders in Nazi Germany. Previous articles on this topic include *Eine Nation in der Nation. Das Nationskonzept im deutschen Flandernbild zwischen 1933 und 1945* (1999), *L'impossibilité d'une littérature belge. La Belgique vue par l'Allemagne nazie* (2003) and a contribution to *Griff nach dem Westen. Die 'Westforschung' der völkisch-nationalen Wissenschaften zum nordwesteuropäischen Raum (1919-1960)* (2003). Her PhD project was awarded a prize by the Belgian Federation of University Graduate Women in 2005.

Yow-Jiun Wang holds a PhD degree from Stirling Media Research Institute at the University of Stirling and is working as an assistant professor in the Department of Taiwanese Literature at National Cheng Kung University in Taiwan. Her research interests concern new media and social change, discourse theories and Cultural Studies.

AUTHOR INDEX

SUBJECT INDEX

Printed in the United States
204660BV00002B/1-30/P

9 781572 738102